ICSE Exams 2026

All in One®

ENGLISH LANGUAGE

PAPER 1

Class 9 & 10

Author
Neha Singh

arihant
SUCCESS AND NOTHING LESS

arihant
SUCCESS AND NOTHING LESS

ARIHANT PRAKASHAN
(School Division Series)

卐 *ADMINISTRATIVE & PRODUCTION OFFICES*

Regd. Office
'Ramchhaya' 4577/15, Agarwal Road, Darya Ganj, New Delhi -110002
Tele: 011- 47630600, 43518550; Fax: 011- 23280316

卐 *Head Office*
Kalindi, TP Nagar, Meerut (UP) - 250002, Tel: 0121-7156203, 7156204

卐 *SALES & SUPPORT OFFICES*
Agra, Ahmedabad, Bengaluru, Bareilly, Chennai, Delhi, Guwahati, Hyderabad, Jaipur, Jhansi, Kolkata, Lucknow, Nagpur & Pune.

PO No : TXT-XX-XXXXXXX-X-XX

Published By Arihant Publications (India) Ltd.

For further information about the books published by Arihant, log on to www.arihantbooks.com or e-mail at info@arihantbooks.com
Follow us on

卐 *PRICE* ₹385.00

PRODUCTION TEAM

Publishing Managers	*Cover Designer*	*Inner Designer*
Mahendra Singh Rawat & Keshav Mohan	Salman Shaikh	Ankit Tyagi
Project Head	*Page Layouting*	*Proof Reader*
Manju	Lalit Chaprana	Harsh Agarwal

Index *cum* Study Planner

One Book- Endless Features

to Help you Succeed

Composition Writing

In this section, Topics such as Description, Short Story, Debate, Picture Composition, Narrative are covered. Steps to write a composition and Points to be kept in mind while writing a composition are also covered. Sample of each composition is given in simple and easy to understand language.

CHAPTER 1

Composition Writing

Descriptive Composition

A description is a piece of writing that elaborates a person, place, thing, feeling or state of mind. It outlines the understanding of a person about the thing to be described. It encompasses the factual details in a vivid manner. The person who is describing must know all the concerned facts about the thing to be described. The language should be kept simple so that the message can be conveyed in an easy way. In the examination, word limit for the descriptive composition is 300-350 and its weightage is 20 marks.

EXAM PRACTICE

1. You are a regular visitor to your school library. Describe your library. Give details of the familiar sights. What do you see and feel as different students come in and check out the books? Why is this place so important? [2023]
2. Which do you prefer-morning, afternoon, evening or night?

   Describe your favourite time of the day. What are the sights, sounds, smells and feelings that you associate with your favourite time of the day? Why do you like this part of the day better than the others? [2020]
3. Summers are becoming hotter with each passing year. Write a description of one such very hot day. What did you see and hear as you walked outside. How were birds and animals affected? [2019]

8. You were on a school trip and were on your way back to the hotel late night when your school bus, full of children, broke down in a deserted place. Describe what you saw and experienced as you looked around. How was the problem solved? [2013]
9. People play a very important role in our lives. Describe in vivid detail any one person and show how he/she has been a very special influence in your life. [2012]
10. Think of a time when you achieved a personal goal. Say why the goal was important to you and how you achieved it. Describe how you felt on achieving it. [2010]
11. A school carnival or fete is a great occasion for fun with friends. Describe one such event in

Exam Practice

In Exam Practice, Board Questions and Practice Questions are given with their answers.

Self Assessment

At the end of the chapter, there are unsolved questions for practice and assessment of students. By practising these questions, students can assess their preparation level for the chapter.

SELF ASSESSMENT

1. Describe why you believe in friendship between a man and a woman based on your own experience.
2. Provide details on the house you're living in. Would you like to change something about it, move away to another location, or stay without fixing anything? Why?
3. Describe the hosted rooms. Share ideas how the college/ university/community could unite to make this place better.
4. Help your readers picture the best day of your life using vivid descriptions, different examples and original comparisons.
5. Describe the introductory day in any of the existing educational institution - school, college, or university - using the entire spectrum of emotions.
6. While on a picnic, you and your friends decide to go sailing. Unfortunately, your boat collapses in a violent storm. However, all of you manage to swim safely. Give a vivid account of the incident.
7. Describe an object which you believe has once saved your life or prevented adverse consequences for you or for any person close to you.
8. Find appropriate words to describe something you wanted so bad that you were ready to steal it due to the fact you did not have enough money to buy it.
9. Pick one of the recent technological innovations. Write a description explaining why this particular thing plays an important role in the development of modern society.
10. You have lived in your ancestral house since birth. The house is to be sold so that flats may be built. Mention the circumstances that led to this decision and describe your feelings about moving out of this house.

One Book- Endless Features

to Help you Succeed

Formats of Formal Letter

The ICSE Board had published two formats of writing a formal letter.

Format 1

Write a letter to the Police Commissioner of your city drawing his/her attention to the menace of hawkers outside your school. Tell him/her what dangers they pose and offer solutions for their rehabilitations.

Flat 236, Block C,
Hill Crest View Apartments,
Salem Street,
Coonoor-26 — Sender's Address

23rd February, 2018 — Date

The Police Commissioner,
Police Commissioner's Office,
6 Cavalry Road,
Coonoor-3 — Receiver's Address

Dear Sir/Ma'am, — Salutation

I write to draw your attention to the menace of hawkers outside St. Paul's school in Nehru Nagar of our town. I am the Secretary, Swach Bharat Club, St. Paul's School. — Introduction

The hawkers sell open food and cheap toys. A number of our school students cluster around them and the lane in front of our school is blocked, dirty and congested.
I would request you to look into this problem and have the hawkers move into the field behind our school. This would ensure that they are not deprived of their livelihood and the area in front of our school is kept clean and congestion fee.
The hawkers must also be warned about the importance of necessary hygiene and the sale of clean food. This will ensure that students do not fall sick after eating food sold by the hawkers. — Informative Paragraph

I trust that you will consider my suggestion and take the necessary steps as outlined in my letter to you to deal with the menace of hawkers outside the school. — Conclusion

Thanking you,
Yours truly,/Yours faithfully
Santosh Haldar — Complimentary Closure

Specimen of Formal Letter, ICSE 2019

Standard Formats

In Letter Writing, Notice & E-mail Writing Standard formats prescribed by ICSE are given. This will help students to learn proper format of each writing tasks.

CHAPTER 1

Functional Grammar

Tenses

(Verb Forms)

Tenses are the forms of verb that tell about the time and state of an action.
According to this, there are three kinds of tenses, which are
1. **Present** (the time that is running)
2. **Past** (the time that is gone)
3. **Future** (the time that is to come)

These tenses indicate the time at which an action is taking place. Each tense has four sub-types. They are
(i) Simple Tense
(ii) Continuous Tense
(iii) Perfect Tense
(iv) Perfect Continuous Tense

Sample Papers

To make students practice of examination in real sense, there are 3 Sample Question Papers at the end. All these Sample Question Papers are exactly prepared on the latest syllabus & pattern of examination.

Functional Grammar

In this section, all the topics are covered which will help students to answer the questions. Proper definition, rules, exception, structures are given to help students to understand the topic.

ICSE
SAMPLE PAPER 1
Fully Solved

English Language-X (Paper-1)

Time : 2 hrs — Max Marks : 80

1. Answers to this paper must be written on the paper provided separately.
2. You will not be allowed to write during the first 15 minutes. This time is to be spent in reading the question paper.
3. The time given at the head of this paper is the time allowed for writing the answers.
4. Attempt all five questions.
5. The intended marks for questions or parts of questions are given in brackets [ ].

(Do not spend more than 30 minutes on this question)

1. Write a composition (300 - 350 words) on *any one* of the following: [20]
(a) You had to attend an important event which you could not miss. You had to use public transport but there was a sudden transport strike. Narrate your experience in detail.
(b) *'Examinations are not a way of assessing a person's ability.'* Express your views either for or against this statement.
(c) Your class visited a Biodiversity Park. Describe in detail what you saw there.
(d) Write a short story beginning with the line: 'I just wish I had ....'.
(e) Study the picture given below. Write a story or a description or an account of what the picture suggests to you. Your composition may be about the subject of the picture or you may take suggestions to from it; but there must be a clear connection between the picture and your composition.

Latest Course *Structure*

Aims:

1. To develop and integrate the use of the four language skills i.e. listening, speaking, reading and writing for the purpose of effective communication.
2. To develop a functional understanding of the grammar, structure and idiom of the language.
3. To develop the capacity to read efficiently and access information effectively.
4. To develop an appreciation of good literature.
5. To experience, through literature, the thoughts and feelings of the peoples of the world.

There will be two papers:
Paper 1: English Language; Paper 2: Literature in Eng lish.
Each of these papers will be of two hours duration.

PAPER 1	English Language	(80 Marks)	**PAPER 2**	Literature in English	(80 Marks)
	Internal Assessment	(20 Marks)		Internal Assessment	(80 Marks)

PAPER 1 - ENGLISH LANGUAGE

(Two Hours) 80 Marks

Five questions will be set, all of which will be compulsory.

Question 1: Candidates will be required to write a composition of about **300-350** words from a choice of subjects which will test their ability to: organise, describe, narrate, report, explain, persuade or argue, present ideas coherently with accuracy and precision, compare and contrast ideas and arrive at conclusions, present relevant arguments and use correct style and format.

The subjects will be varied and may be suggested by language or by other stimuli such as pictures. The subjects will be so chosen so as to allow the candidates to draw on first-hand experience or to stimulate their imagination.

With one subject, a number of suggestions about the content of the composition will be given, but the use of the suggestions will be optional and a candidate will be free to treat the subject in any way that he/she chooses.

The organisation of subject matter, syntax, punctuation, correctness of grammatical constructions and spelling will be expected to be appropriate to the mode of treatment required by the subject.

Question 2: Candidates will have to write a letter from a choice of two subjects requiring either a formal or an informal mode of treatment. Suggestions regarding the content of the letter may be given. The layout of the letter with address, introduction, conclusion, etc., will form part of the assessment. Special attention must be paid to the format of the letter with emphasis on vocabulary appropriate to the context.

Question 3: Candidates will be given a specific situation and will be required to:

(a) Write the text for a notice based on given directions.

(b) Write an e-mail on the same content as the notice.

Question 4: An unseen prose passage of about 450 words will be given. Uncommon items of vocabulary, or structure will be avoided. One question will be set to test vocabulary. Candidates will be required to show an understanding of the words/phrases in the context in which they have been used.

A number of questions requiring short answers will also be asked on the passage. These questions will test the candidates' ability to comprehend the explicit content and organisation of the passage and to infer information, intention and attitude from it.

The last question will consist of a summary that will test the candidates' ability to distinguish main ideas from supporting details and to extract salient points to re-write them in the form of a summary. Candidates will be given clear indications of what they are to summarise and of the length of the summary.

Question 5: There will be a number of short answer questions to test the candidates' knowledge of functional grammar, structure and use of the language.

All the items in this question will be compulsory. They will consist of correct use of prepositions, verbs and transformation of sentences.

Some Excerpts from

'Analysis of Pupils' Performance'

ICSE English Language Class 09 & 10 (2020)

The document 'Analysis of Pupils' Performance, in ICSE Class 10 & ISC Class 12 Examination, is prepared by Research Development and Consultancy Division (RDCD) of the Council for the Indian School Certificate Examination (CISCE).

The purpose of this document is to provide feedback to schools in terms of strengths and weaknesses of the candidates in handling the examination.

TOPICS FOUND DIFFICULT / CONFUSING BY STUDENTS

Essay writing:

To compose a creative composition in 300-350 words was beyond the powers of many candidates. Consequently, the weaker candidates resorted to either copying parts of the comprehension passage in the middle of the essay or copied the passage in its entirety. Many candidates found it difficult to express their thoughts in English and therefore, used words in mother tongue to express their views.

Letter writing:

In the formal letter, the consequences of wastage of water, was not understood by many candidates. The idea/concept of waste of water was misconstrued by many. Candidates took it for wastage of water in homes.

Notice and Email:

(i) The connection between the two was not understood by some. In some centres, incorrect format was used.

(ii) The event/purpose behind hosting the carnival and who the host was/ who the letter was addressed to was not understood by some candidates.

Comprehension:

- Most of the candidates got confused with the meanings of the words. They could not bring out the sense given in the passage.
- All questions based on analysis/ understanding were not understood by many candidates. Many of the answers in part (b) seemed to centre around the idea of independent study - it was as if the candidates could not move past that one main idea.
- The Summary was disappointing - candidates seemed not to have been able to grasp which portion of the text was required to be referred to for the answer.

Grammar:

The rules of grammar were not clear to many candidates.

SUGGESTIONS FOR STUDENTS

- Refer to the syllabus while going through each topic.
- Take up reading as a regular habit.
- Make it a practice to read newspapers, periodicals and story books. Read journals and magazines on a variety of topics.
- Listen to famous personalities' oration to enhance your vocabulary. Involve yourself in debate sessions to develop your speaking skill.
- Converse in English at school and at home.
- Read the question paper well before start answering it.
- Consult encyclopaedias and the internet if this resource is available to you. Be careful to do so under adult supervision and to only consult authenticated resources.

Composition Writing

CHAPTER 1

Composition Writing

Descriptive Composition

A description is a piece of writing that elaborates a person, place, thing, feeling or state of mind. It outlines the understanding of a person about the thing to be described. It encompasses the factual details in a vivid manner. The person who is describing must know all the concerned facts about the thing to be described. The language should be kept simple so that the message can be conveyed in an easy way. In the examination, word limit for the descriptive composition is 300-350 and its weightage is 20 marks.

Points to be Kept in Mind While Writing a Description

- Make sure that you note down some ideas before you begin describing it.
- Use clear and concise language.
- While describing something, appeal to the senses of the reader. Explain how the thing smelled, felt, sounded, tasted or looked.
- Use simple language and avoid writing very long sentences.
- Leave the reader with a clear impression. It should evoke a strong sense of familiarity and appreciation in the reader.
- Always present an organised, objective and logical description.

Sample Description 1

There has been heavy rain in your city/town. You went to school but found that it was closed because of the rain. Describe the sights and sounds near the school and narrate how you finally reached home and spent the rest of the day. *[2017]*

Ans. It had been raining very heavily since last night with lightening and sound of thunder terrifying us. In the morning, the streets and roads were flooded but still I got ready for school. I took a raincoat and left.

While walking, I saw that there was water everywhere. At some places, it was knee deep. Fewer people could be seen on the roads. The roads had disappeared under the water and one could cross it only by walking through it. I saw no student of my school on the way except Mr. Sharma . He teaches Maths at our school and rarely takes leave. Though the rain had stopped, water drops were falling from the tree leaves as if it were raining. The sky had again become dark with heavy clouds suggesting that it could rain anytime again, so I was walking at an escalated speed.

When I reached the school, I found a big notice announcing that the school was closed for the day as water had entered the ground and some classrooms. There were some other students who had ventured to the school inspite of all odds.

Some of them left after reading the notice while others stayed back, talking and playing with their friends. I decided to go back home since the weather looked uncertain. As I was leaving, I saw Rishi, a friend of mine, enter the school campus. I greeted him and shared the news with him.We live nearby so we decided to go together. He told me that the road he took wasn't submerged in water, so we took that path.

On the way, I saw a few huts which were in a very bad condition. The tin sheets on top of a few had fallen down. They were being put back in place by people. Nearby, a couple of trees were struck by lightning and had fallen on the footpath. The road, however, was cleaner than the one I took and thus, I reached home in little time.

My mother was waiting for me. She told me to change into clean clothes as soon as she saw my wet trousers. I was given a hot cup of milk and told to study at home. Soon, it started drizzling again. Looking out the window, I wondered how the rain had troubled people and prayed it would stop soon.

Sample Description 2

Describe your visit to a slum area and express your concern on how poverty has affected our society.

Ans. In order to survive, a person needs proper food, clothing, shelter, healthcare and education. When a person cannot meet these requirements properly then he/she is said to be poor. Thus, poverty refers to the state where a person fails to acquire these minimum levels of subsistence and in turn suffers from malnutrition or starvation. Poverty as such, is one of the major problems in India. It is the rootcause of many socio-economic problems including population explosion, low level of education, unemployment, child labour, etc.

Once I visited to a slum near my college. There I saw that 90 per cent of the residents of the slum could barely manage the meal for one time. They had just a pairs of clothes and they wore them every day. Areas around the slum were very dirty and unhygienic. Poverty has been plaguing our country for a long time. From late 19th century to early 20th century, it intensified, peaking in 1920s. Over this period, the colonial government, banned the production of garments and other finished products manufactured by artisans.

Additionally, the conversion of more land into farms was encouraged for increased agricultural exports from India. Eastern regions of India along the Ganges river plains were dedicated to producing poppy and opium for export. This moved unemployed artisans into farming and transformed India into a region increasingly abundant in land, unskilled labour and low productivity. Consequently, India became scarce in skilled labour, capital and knowledge, and the intensity of poverty became severe.

The problem of poverty persists because of a number of loopholes in the system. The encouragement of non-governmental organisations and private sector individuals in tackling poverty is imperative, along with measures taken by the government to eradicate poverty. In achieving this goal, poor welfare programmes introduced by the government play a major role.

The Government of India has launched some schemes namely MGNREGA, Gramin Awas Yojana, Atal Pension Yojana, Garib Kalyan Yojana, etc. aiming at uplifting the life of the poor, which are seen as a sure shot method to counter the problem of poverty.

EXAM PRACTICE

1. You are a regular visitor to your school library. Describe your library. Give details of the familiar sights. What do you see and feel as different students come in and check out the books? Why is this place so important? *[2023]*
2. Which do you prefer-morning, afternoon, evening or night?

   Describe your favourite time of the day. What are the sights, sounds, smells and feelings that you associate with your favourite time of the day? Why do you like this part of the day better than the others? *[2020]*
3. Summers are becoming hotter with each passing year. Write a description of one such very hot day. What did you see and hear as you walked outside. How were birds and animals affected? *[2019]*
4. You had been waiting outside the examination hall. Describe what you saw and the sounds you heard when you arrived at the place. What were your feelings? Describe how the scene changed once you entered the hall and the examination started. *[2018]*
5. You walk home from school one afternoon to find the door unlocked and on entering you are shocked to see the house in total disarray. You call out but get no answer. Describe in detail what you saw, the reason behind your house being in total disarray and how you found your family. Mention also how the experience ended and what impact it had on your life. *[2016]*
6. Describe in detail the view from your bedroom window. Does your room overlook a park? A busy street? What are the sights, sounds and smells that you would typically see, hear and experience at different times of the day? *[2015]*
7. Describe an early morning walk through your city or town in winter. Give details of the smells, sights, sounds and feelings you experienced. *[2014]*
8. You were on a school trip and were on your way back to the hotel late night when your school bus, full of children, broke down in a deserted place. Describe what you saw and experienced as you looked around. How was the problem solved? *[2013]*
9. People play a very important role in our lives. Describe in vivid detail any one person and show how he/she has been a very special influence in your life. *[2012]*
10. Think of a time when you achieved a personal goal. Say why the goal was important to you and how you achieved it. Describe how you felt on achieving it. *[2010]*
11. A school carnival or fete is a great occasion for fun with friends. Describe one such event in your school. *[2010]*
12. You went to Egypt for a trip and visited the Great Pyramid of Giza. Describe the Great Pyramid of Giza.
13. Recently, you visited the 'Bandhavgarh National Park'. Describe your visit.
14. The waiting room at a railway station presents a wonderful opportunity to observe human behaviour.

    Describe an experience when you reached early to catch a train and had to spend some time in the waiting room with different kinds of people.
15. A village fair is very different from a city one. It is usually held annually and is connected with a religious festival or harvest. The purpose of such fairs is usually trade and to exhibit and sell village handicrafts. Describe one such fair.
16. You are a spectator at a cricket match. Trouble erupts suddenly in the stadium and you witness a riot. Give a vivid description of the scene.

Answers

1. Books are called man's best friends and best place to find them is a library. I as a bibliophile look books and you would often find me sitting in the library reading on of the detective mysteries there. Thus, it is safe to say that library is my favourite place to go to in the entire school and I relish my time there. The shelves are stacked with thousands of books that the school has accumulated over many decades. There are many kinds of fiction, non-fiction books and academic available for students and teachers to choose from. I am personally fond of the fiction section, with books ranging from classics, horror, crime and fantasy books. The library also has some interesting non-fiction categories, such as biographies. The familiar Mrs. Chawla, the librarian, can often be seen sitting behind her desk, waiting for students to return or issue books.

   I often feel amazed by the whole idea of a library where students can come and take the books without worrying about having to buy them. Whenever I see the students selecting the books they want to read or take home with them, I find they have a sense of excitement and anticipation just like me. I often feel that none of this would have been possible had the library not existed. It feels as if the knowledge of the entire world, everything that each of us would need to know to be successful in our lives awaits us in the library. I often think of how the books that people check out would help them in their future and if they would look back and think of how this present moment changed their perception or sparked their interest in a particular thing. It all starts with one book.

   The place is incredibly important for all the students as it gives them the freedom to read what they wish, a freedom that course books don't often provide. It also gives them the opportunity to learn and grow their knowledge of things outside the curriculum and get inspired by the lives of others through selected biographies. Moreover, Mrs. Chawla is incredibly kind and helps the students with finding books and often ignores the fines when the students tell them why they couldn't return the books on time.

2. **Morning**

   The best time of the day for me is morning. Usually, I get up at 5 o' clock in the morning. Getting up early makes me feel pleased as I can offer prayer to God which enhances my energy and I can start my day with a refreshed mind. It is still dark at this time in the early morning and the birds are just starting to wake up. Its pretty calm and quiet all around. I breathe fresh air and take my tea while standing in my balcony. The sky looks like a canvas where God paints a streak simply dividing the dark from the light. Gradually, more colours come out, red being the first.

   The clouds float like cotton balls circling the nucleus of sky, the Sun. The Sun rises by spreading golden yellow colour all over the sky and soon the birds start chirping. After I finish my tea, my mother asks me to freshen up and get ready for school. Then, I have my breakfast. While taking breakfast, I usually plan my schedule. I can easily do it with a fresh mind. At 7:20 am, my school bus come. I usually take a window seat. It is a pleasure for me to see the activities in early morning. Generally, there are students and parents on the footpath waiting for their school buses. Sweepers are busy in cleaning the roads. Owners of grocery shops are just opening their shutters. Newspaper boys are busy in distributing papers and there are few vehicles in roads. Within 10 minutes, I reach my school gates. I enjoy the charm of morning and prepare myself for the whole day.

   Afternoon

   The best time of my day is the afternoon.The afternoon is the time of day that starts in mid-day and ends in evening. It is the time of the day when I can relax after a hectic schedule. Afternoon is the time when the Sun is descending from its daytime peak position. During this time, the Sun moves roughly from the centre to the Western part of the sky. Sunlight becomes bright and glaring. Everybody is busy with their work, there are lots of vehicles on the road; sometime it creates traffic jam. This is the time when I come back from school and relax. Usually, I return home by 2:30 p.m. However, many times I get late in reaching home. At home, first I change my clothes as it gives me feeling of freshness.

   Then, I read the newspaper as I do not have time to read it in the morning. Sometimes, I watch television and play with my pet dog. It gives me pure joy. There after, I chat with my mother and tell her about the activities in school. She advices me about my study. While we take our lunch. It is really a fun time for me. My mother always makes my favourite dishes and my pet dog sits before us expecting food. I give him some food inspite of my mother's disapproval. In the afternoon, I usually take a nap to refresh my body muscles and mind. Scientific research proves that the ability to remain alert is associated with proper resting time.

So, taking rest in afternoon rejuvenates me to do my studies properly in the evening. As it is considered as relaxing time, it can be fully utilised for our extra-curricular activities. In the afternoon, I attend guitar class twice a week. It gives me immense pleasure and enhances my mind.

Evening

For me, the best part of the day is between five to seven in the evening. It is truly a relaxed and peaceful time for our family after a hectic morning at school or at the office. My mother whose day started at 5:00 am would be relaxing in our balcony with a cup of coffee and some snacks and I would be sitting by her chatting about the whole day activities in schools and tuition centre. It is the best time when we can share our views about everything. My father would be in his favourite chair reading the newspaper or watching news on the television.

After a while, I play with my dog who loves to run around with me. Sometime, I go to the nearby park to play with my friends. We have great fun on the swings, often screaming or singing which reduces our tiredness and rejuvenates us.

Later, as I sit on the grass to rest, I admire the scenery around me. There are lots of flowers blooming in our park. Now, it is time for sunset. The Sun, a golden ball of fire, is sinking behind the buildings. Gold, pink, orange and yellow colours are displaying in the sky, making it a huge painting of our artist. Birds are seen flying back to their nests. All the plants and trees are looking beautiful in the twilight.

The stillness and quietness of the evening make me feel at peace with everything. It is the time when the crickets start to chirp and the surrounding becames quiet. Now, it is the time to return back home. Coming back home, I take some light snacks and prepare myself for doing homework.

Thus, evening is my favourite time of the day, a time of beauty and quietness when we can relax after a hectic day schedule.

Night

My favourite part of the day is night. After taking my dinner, it is the time which I can spend according to my wish. In the night time, my surrounding is most peaceful, noise-free and distraction free. In this time, I can study attentively. I can learn a topic in just one attempt and that retains longer in my memory.

I prefer night time as it signifies that I can just relax and study. There is no stress. I feel comfortable and do my work. It is time for which I wait all through the day. It is my favourite time to watch TV and eat too. It is my comfort zone when I can do anything I wish to do.

After spending the whole day in school, in coaching centre and then in hobby centre, my full body requires rest. It is only possible during the night. Lying on my own bed, makes my body muscles relaxed. This helps me to boost my energy.

Scientific studies suggest that the brain works actively at night, thus it is more effective to study before I go to bed. Studies also suggest that a good amount of sleep at night also helps good memory retention. So, I take atleast 7 hours sleep every night. This proper resting time helps me to start my next day with energy.

3. I was spending the summer holidays in my small native village. It was the beginning of June when I had to go out to the post office in the nearby village for some work. The morning was very stuffy. There was not a single cloud in the sky or any breeze to dry my sweat as I walked the three-kilometre distance on the cart track. As the Sun rose higher and higher, it shone more strongly. Although I was wearing a cap, I felt the Sun's heat. However, I walked on the ground that seemed as hot as a furnace.

Then, hot winds began to blow and the dust started swirling around me. I saw that the condition of birds and animals was as bad as mine. The birds were trying to seek shelter in the trunk of leafless trees. I saw some black buffaloes which had lain down in a pond which still had some water, although the water was very dirty. The trees and bushes looked withered. The grass was yellowed and totally dry. The cart track was deserted, as all people were indoors. I did not meet anyone during the 30 minutes I walked to the post office.

By the time, I finished the work at the post office, it was 2 p.m. I was dreading the trek back home. However, I was lucky to find a small dhaba in this village where I could eat lunch and relax till the evening in the shade. As I had nothing to do back at home, I decided to do back just that. After eating a delicious lunch, I dozed off while sitting under the fan in the dhaba.

The heat continued till evening. When I woke up, I found that the Sun was about to set. After having tea at the dhaba, I started the walk back home. People had begun to move about. The silence of the village was broken by the shouts of some hawkers. The village was coming to life. I hastened my steps and was soon back at home. The first thing I did was to have a bath and change into fresh clothes. I was feeling comfortable again.

4. Examinations sap the examinees of energy and make them sleepless for nights. But then, it has not so far been possible to devise a better way of judging their ability. So, they are a necessary evil which all students have to face.

Students have to work hard for months. As the crucial day arrives, they reach the examination hall in tension.

I had a similar experience during my Board examination. A few minutes before the start of the first paper, I saw a strange scene outside the examination hall. An eerie silence prevailed there. The examinees were carrying their books and notes in their hands which they had already mugged up and were now trying to revise. Most of the examinees were not inclined to talk to anybody. But a few, sitting or standing in groups of two or three, were seen discussing some points. I did not form a group, rather stood alone to wait for the Supervisor to turn up.

Even the dullest students appeared to be great scholars outside the examination hall. They were reading their books most attentively. Some of them may have been thinking of devising some means of copying or how to behave if they were caught copying.

Most of the students reached the examination hall well before time. They looked at the notice-board to find out their room and even tried to locate their seats. As soon as the bell rang, all the students entered the hall. A few examinees reached the hall late and entered in a state of great excitement. The supervisor was lenient and accommodated them. Soon, everyone was seated in silence. The only sound was that of the supervisor who was getting ready to distribute the papers and announcing the rules of the exam. No one talked or tried to recall anything, rather everyone prayed and prepared to do their best.

5. I returned home from school in the afternoon. When I reached home, I found the door unlocked. I went inside and was shocked to see the house in total disorder. I called my mother, who would usually be home at that time, but nobody answered. When I entered the drawing room, the whole furniture was turned up side down. Every bag and almirah was emptied, throwing everything on the floor. It seemed that the whole house was searched for something. What was more disturbing and strange was that nothing was stolen; even the i-phones and i-pods were on the desks, along with my mother's wallet.

As I was worried about my mother and younger brother, I enquired all my mother's friends and our relatives. She was at one of her friends' house. Hearing about the incident, my mother arrived home in ten minutes and was equally horrified to see the house in such a condition.

My mother informed me that she had gone to meet her friend who had got a lottery of one crore. She might have not locked the house properly in a hurry. Later, after much investigation, it was found that some small children, who were playing outside, were chased by some monkeys. In panic, the children, seeing the door unlocked, entered the house to hide but the monkeys followed them. A long hide and seek game ensued between the children and the monkeys. The monkeys were responsible for throwing everything out of the closets and the furniture was turned upside down by the children.

Somehow, the children managed to hide themselves in the store adjacent to our bedroom. Monkeys left and went outside the house. We all breathed a sigh of relief that there was no theft or robbery. It took at least two hours to set the house again in order.

It was really an unforgettable day in my life as I got really scared looking at the condition of my house and not one member of my family member present. But, I thanked God that my mother's mistake resulted in saving small children from being bitten by monkeys.

6. My bedroom is the zone of maximum comfort for me. The mere sight of my bed, study table, almirahs, etc. dispels all my fatigue and freshens me up. The view from the window is very beautiful. My window overlooks a park. The park has tall and wide trees which attract a variety of birds like parrots and white pigeons. The grass and bushes are neatly trimmed and the little plants bear flowers in many colours. There is a jogging track too built inside it. Indeed, just one look outside the window has such a soothing effect on me, which is beyond description.

In the morning after waking up, I see people running and jogging on the track. I also hear the sounds and hoots of birds. Besides, the breeze of dawn coupled with the aroma of trees, prepares me to kickstart my day on a positive note. I, however, enjoy the evening view the most.

When I return home in the evening, the sweet smell of the trees and the sight of little kids playing in the park rejuvenate my soul. The rays of the setting Sun are scattered all over the sky giving it the most radiant look. The birds are seen returning to their homes and there is a pleasant and calm aura all around.

I gaze at all the trivialities and activities that are visible from my window while taking my evening snacks and tea. Sometimes, my sister joins me and we chat and discuss the various things and people we see in the park. We also miss the regular visitors of the park if they do not turn up. The comfort that one draws at one's home is unmatched by all the luxuries of expensive hotels and buildings. Even more comforting is that little corner which one calls one's bedroom.

Therefore, the window of my room and the view of the park are seemingly little things but together they make up an integral part of my daily routine.

7. A morning walk is very rewarding. It is only at this time in the cities that the roads are not crowded. There is hardly any traffic. One can enjoy a walk in the lap of nature. As one walks, one's worries and anxieties vanish away. The sheer delight of the movement is enough to make the day.

I go for morning walk with my friends to a nearby park where we take two or more rounds. As we set out from our home, we see the street deserted except for a few walkers like us. There are couples in track suits walking briskly along. There are also groups of elderly men gossiping and laughing among themselves. Youngsters are seen wearing ear phones and jogging to their favourite songs.

In the quietness of the morning, I can hear the chirping of the birds, parrots and pigeons. They are seen flying from one branch of a tree to another. Amidst the sheet of thin white fog, the colourful flowers in the park give solace to the heart and a feast to the eyes. The fragrance of the sweet smelling flowers fills my mind with freshness.

The pure fresh air of the morning, devoid of the poisonous gases exhaled by the innumerable vehicles running to and fro in the city streets, gives a boost to the body to battle the day's hectic schedule. Gradually, penetrating through the dense fog, the first rays of the sun gleamer and shine across the park. Now, the body begins to respond well to the movements of the limbs and the flow of fresh, cool air one breathes. The momentum now sets in and the legs appear to walk effortlessly. One feet glides over the other as if trying to be the first to land ahead.

An hour later, it is time to stop as the empty stomach demands attention. By the time we return from our walk, many tea-stalls and sweet shops open up to make tea, fresh sweets and snacks. We stop at our favourite shop where we indulge in hot tea and *samosas*. Words are insufficient to describe the feelings one undergoes during winter morning walks and the experience of indulging in hot and tempting snacks after that.

8. We had been looking forward to our school trip from the very first day in Class X. Every year, our school plans tours for every class and it is always a special affair. This year, we went to Nainital for three nights and four days. We left for Nainital late in the night. We reached our hotel in the morning and after breakfast, our teachers advised us to take some rest. After some rest, we got ready and gathered for lunch. After lunch, we left for local sight seeing. We also did some shopping from the local markets. It was evening then and our teachers took us for dinner. We dined at a local restaurant which was famous for its food.

It was dark when we left for our hotel where we were staying. Singing songs, we had hardly reached half way when suddenly the bus broke down. It was around 11 pm and we were in a deserted place.

The driver left the bus to find a garage so that he could get it fixed. The hills and trees outstretched on both the sides. It was quite frightening.

Our teachers were also worried but they kept themselves calm and instructed us to remain quiet and not to make any noise, as it may draw attention of anti-social elements. At a distance of 200 metres, we saw some light, for there were lamps burning. We all moved towards it with some hope. On reaching there, we saw a group of friends who were camping there. They were singing, dancing and enjoying themselves around the bonfire. When we approached them and explained our unpleasant state, they were ready to help us.

They offered the students their tents for use. We all had such a nice time dancing, singing and sharing some of our school experiences with them. It soon became the most memorable trip ever.

Then, noodles were prepared and everyone enjoyed their late night noodles around the bonfire. We were awake until the first rays of the sun indicated that it was morning. The bus was redeemed and so we all bade our goodbyes to the lovely people who helped us and made our trip an exciting adventure to be cherished life-long.

9. When reflecting on personal influences in my life, no one has had a greater impact than my father. He is a role model for me. He always stands by my side. Whenever I fall down, he encourages me to stand up by myself and on my own feet. I have always admired his open mind, compassion and sense of understanding. He is a very reserved man, but has a great sense of humour and always knows how to put a smile on my face. One good lesson my dad has taught me is that you most likely won't have the answer to everything but that is what life is for, to learn from your mistakes and find those answers you are looking

for. From him, I also learned that I should always speak my mind with confidence and honesty.

My father has always taught me right behaviour. I still remember the day when my father sat next to me and said, "Hey son, the most important thing to help you to become a successful person is your honesty. Never lie to anyone and never lie to yourself." After saying that, he slowly explained the value of honesty. He told me that every bad situation in the world began with a lie. When a person steals something, he lies to the law; when a husband cheats on his wife, he lies to his life. I always think back on these words whenever I am in trouble.

In every aspect of my life, my father continuously pushes me to excel. Whenever I feel like giving up, or have a question or a concern, I know I can always call on him for advice. His teachings are a cure for my selfishness. He taught me to consider everyone as a part of my family and to love people by sharing and giving. From him, I have learned that sometimes you have to put other's needs ahead of your own but not to the point that they start taking advantage of you. His strength seems to be unbreakable during hard times and he is extremely determined to accomplish anything he sets his mind on.

I hold great esteem for how he stands up for what he believes in and never backs down. I am what I am because of him and whatever I will achieve in my life will be credited to him.

10. All members of my family were extremely ecstatic when I showed them my appointment letter mentioning my selection for the post of aeronautical engineer in HAL, Mumbai. I was proud to be among the elite ten who had been selected from thousands of applicants from across the country. It was indeed a matter of great pride and a dream come true for me.

Ever since I was a child, I had nurtured this goal of becoming an aeronautical engineer. As a child, I had a special fascination for planes and what made them fly, their mechanisms and everything related to them. I would sit for hours drawing figures of planes and pondering over their dimensions and the laws governing propulsion. Planes and helicopters became an obsession of mine, so much so that I would often dream of flying one. I knew that the path I had chosen for myself was beset with difficulties and many hurdles, which required great perseverance.

I silently let this great dream grow within me. At times, I realised that it was futile to chase a goal which was beyond my grasp. But, my principal's speech on the occasion of the farewell of my batch changed all that and filled me with such inspiration that I instantly knew that I had to achieve my dream of becoming an aeronautical engineer. I wanted to prove to myself, my family and to the world that I could do it.

After years of hardwork and sweat, today, I proudly stand with my appointment letter in hand and thank God for a fabulous mentor, who initiated the entire process of achieving this goal and always stood by me and for my wonderful parents who supported me in whatever I did and believed in me. I also realised that there is no shortcut to success.

11. The word 'carnival' itself brings forth tremendous excitement in the hearts of kids and adults alike. The word spells enjoyment and an occasion of fun with friends and family. Every alternate year, our school organises a carnival for students, their families and friends.This year, our school organised the carnival in the month of December and aptly called it the 'Christmas Carnival'. A lot of preparations and hard labour went into making this carnival a successful event.

This year, we had fifteen game stalls and seventeen food stalls. The junior and senior students were divided into groups and deployed at each stall in such an organised manner that they not only got an opportunity to shoulder the responsibility of the stall but also got time to visit other stalls and enjoy the carnival along with their friends.

Amongst the game stalls, the most popular ones were Nine Pins, Ring the Duck, Shoot the Basket, Test of Strength, etc. However, the greatest attraction was The Golden Goal stall, where one had to kick a football into a three-foot ring suspended in the air, grossed the highest amount of money.

A large variety of fast food items was served at the various food stalls. There was a persistent rush at the *Chaat* stall, the *Pakoras* stall and the *Dosa* stall. The coffee stall also turned out to be a huge favourite. As the evening progressed and the chill increased, everybody wanted to grab a cup of coffee. The people also enjoyed many rounds of 'Housie' while many of the senior students interacted with the crowds in the guise of clowns and other cartoon figures and held the interest of little kids.

The carnival came to an end late in the evening with the prizes for the 'Lucky Draw' being announced. The first prize was a LCD Television and was won by a student of Class VI. The second prize was a 230 litre refrigerator and the third prize was a Samsung Washing Machine. There were also ten consolation prizes which consisted of ten Titan wrist watches.

This year, the carnival was a grand success with a record breaking fifteen thousand people attending the event, hats off to our dedicated team of teachers and the able guidance of our Principal.

12. The biggest of Egypt's many ancient pyramids, the Great Pyramid of Giza, is situated 16 kilometres East of Cairo in the Giza plains. The apex is missing and there is no historical record of one having ever existed.

There is no surviving record as to when, how or by whom the Great Pyramid was constructed. It has usually been accepted that it was built sometime in the third millennium BC but many modern scholars mention that at that time the engineering skills of the Egyptians were inadequate for such a gigantic undertaking. Moreover, the design of the pyramid incorporated certain mathematical formulae that were unknown at that time.

Apart from the mystery of its origins, the Great Pyramid possesses mysterious properties. Modern visitors have noticed the mummified remains of small animals which had evidently wandered into it. Despite the strangely humid atmosphere of the king's chamber, the body had not decayed but had been preserved through dehydration. This observation gave rise to the idea that the pyramid shape itself has played a part in the marvellous preservation of the mummified bodies.

Recently, much research has been done on the physical properties of the shape of a pyramid and great many experiments have been carried out with pyramids of various sizes and materials, ranging from proper models, a few centimetres high to outdoor constructions of wood and plastic, large enough for a person to sleep in. Most amazing results have been recorded, like food is preserved, milk turns to yoghurt, plants grow more quickly, blunt razors are sharpened, toothache is cured and those who meditate attain an exalted state of consciousness when living in a pyramid. It seems that a special energy field is created by the pyramid shape and this accumulates towards the apex.

13. During autumn break, my family planned to visit Bandhavgarh National Park, which is situated in the Umaria district of Madhya Pradesh. My father planned everything and had booked two rooms in a resort situated near the park. We went by our own car as it is more convenient for family outings. We started our journey early morning around 5 am and stopped only for breakfast and lunch. At around 6:15 pm, we reached the resort. We decided to rest for the night and go around the park the next day. Bandhavgarh has one of the highest density of Bengal Tigers known in the world and is a famous natural hub for white tigers. Our very first three-hour drive in Bandhavgarh Tiger Reserve had converted us into total tiger devotees.

The next day, we saw a large male tiger, named Charger, the undisputed hero of Bandhavgarh. This chance sighting of the tiger became the highlight of our entire trip. We realised that our guide, Dewan, was a terrific tiger tracker. His mind worked very sharply, like that of a tiger.

It was he who helped us spot Charger. It was a massive creature, royal in stature, assured of itself, walking with a relaxed attitude and a full stomach. Charger demonstrated his masculinity as he marked his territory at regular intervals. Over the next two days, we happened to see Charger twice again.

On the last day, on an elephant's back, we were taken very close to yet another tigress and her two full grown cubs.

Four days, ten individual tigers, sixteen sightings, we could not ask for more. Bandhavgarh had more to it than just tigers. During the safari drive, we got opportunities to watch three species of vultures, lesser adjutant and woolly-necked storks, the resident brown fish owl, green pigeons, peacocks and peahens of all shapes and sizes and the famous malabar pied hornbills. The total number of bird species recorded in the area is nearly 25. It was an experience of a life-time and worth the effort. I will cherish those memories for a long time to come.

14. The waiting room of a railway station is one of the best places to observe human behaviour closely. I was enroute Delhi to Kolkata but due to an unfortunate misunderstanding was forced to switch trains at Lucknow. The time gap was two hours between both trains; hence, I had no other option, but to take refuge at the waiting room of the railway station.

As I entered the waiting room, a foul smell tickled my nostrils which soon I became accustomed to. The announcement of the arrival of a train caused some seats to get vacant and I quickly occupied one to make myself comfortable. Opposite to me, a family of five was busy haggling over some petty issue. Apparently, the wife had forgotten to complete some household chores before leaving and the husband was scolding her for the same. Their three children, the eldest being not more than eight years old, were chasing each other around the waiting room and the mother was screaming her head off trying to control them.

On another bench, sat an elderly couple who were hardly talking to each other. They seemed to be too lost in a world of their own, probably weighed down by the worries of this relentless world. Suddenly, the old lady said something which brought a smile to the otherwise serious face of the gentleman and he keenly began to observe the three little ones playing with each other. Another newly married young couple sat in the farthermost corner of the room talking in hushed voices to each other. Fortunately, the next announcement was for their train and they were replaced by a contingent of women hockey players who were returning from a match.

By their upbeat mood and excitement, one could easily guage that they had won their match and were now eager to get back home. It was indeed a very interesting two-hour wait. Isn't it strange that when a person sits idle, he/she notices a variety of human behaviour which normally a troubled mind would have overlooked? Such was the case with me and believe me, I enjoyed every moment of it till the arrival of my train was announced.

15. A village fair is very different from one in a city. The village folk seek entertainment in fairs and festivals. It is usually held annually and connected with a religious festival or harvest time. The purpose of such fairs is usually trade and to exhibit and sell village handicrafts. The shopkeepers open temporary stalls in such fairs. The magicians and jugglers also entertain people and make money.

Punjab is a land of vibrant people who celebrate festivals and other occasions with great zeal and zest. Baisakhi is one such occasion as it marks the beginning of the harvesting of crops, signifying reaping the fruit of their labour. Last year, I went to visit my maternal uncle in Punjab. I was overjoyed to see the fair which was spread over a large tract of open land. The stalls were tastefully decorated with ribbons and buntings. Young girls in beautiful bright dresses were being irresistibly drawn towards the stalls where bangles of all colours were displayed.

The greatest attraction of the fair was the wrestling bouts being held in a big open ground surrounded by the spectators. Big prizes had been announced for the wrestlers winning over their respective rivals.

There was a vast variety of sights that attracted the attention of the visitors. A motor cyclist was running his vehicle on the walls of a pucca pit. A magician was showing his tricks. There was also a snake charmer, a monkey show and a bear dance. Children were especially interested in buying balloons and toys. The shopkeepers who had put up their stalls of eatables were having a hay day. *Pakoras* and *jalebis* could not be missed by anybody as they are the favourite with the Punjabis. However, the greatest attraction of the fair was 'Bhangra', the folk dance of Punjab, which was being performed enthusiastically by a few young boys. The cattle fair was a sight not to be missed since the best breeds of cattle-the cows, bulls, horses, buffaloes, etc. were brought for sale. In this way, fairs show the rich cultural heritage of a state to the people in the stands.

16. "Dhoni Dhoni," shouted the crowd as Mahendra Singh Dhoni, the Indian cricket captain, faced the fast bowler of Pakistan. There was dead silence as the ball failed to strike the bat and hit Dhoni's pad. The bowler and the entire Pakistani I team jumped with joy, appealing to the umpire for an LBW.

Not convinced he signalled to the third umpire. A tense silence followed as the crowd waited for the decision. As the board flashed NOT OUT, the entire stadium reverberated with joy. The situation seemed hopeless for India was trailing by 33 runs with only two overs to spare, in the World Cup's final match at the Feroz Shah Kotla ground in New Delhi.

The tension in the crowd increased as the run rate per over mounted. Unhappy with the slow scoring, a section of the crowd started raising slogans and hurling bottles into the field. This was objected to by others, and soon a melee ensued.

In the free for all that followed, people ran helter skelter for cover, causing a stampede. Women and children caught in the stampede cried out for help. Utter confusion prevailed in the stadium for well over fifteen minutes. The match was halted and the organisers appealed to the audience to remain calm and maintain order, for the match to continue.

In the meantime the local administration immediately swung into action, the police used mild force to quell the rioters. They rounded up some mischief mongers and herded them out of the stadium. The injured were provided first aid by the paramedics, while the seriously injured were carried away on stretchers to the ambulance. Some semblance of order being restored, the umpires decided to continue the match.

Not losing hope I and my friends started waving the Indian tricolour and shouting, "We want four, We want four." Soon the entire stadium reverberated with this slogan. Taking a cue from the crowd, Dhoni in the very first ball of the over struck for a four. This was followed by two consecutive fours and a six. This proved to be the turning point of the match. Now with victory in sight, the crowd became ecstatic, bursting crackers and beating drums.

There was pin drop silence as the over progressed, with just ten runs coming of the first five balls. The tension became palpable as the last ball was bowled. He valiantly lifted the ball over the long on boundary, with bated breath we watched as a fielder ran after it, and to our dismay, took a brilliant catch just as his outstretched leg crossed the boundary rope. The third umpire's decision was called for and with the light blinking green, bedlam broke loose in the stadium. The crowd went berserk with joy and happiness. I embraced my friends, jubilant at India's victory.

SELF ASSESSMENT

1. Describe why you believe in friendship between a man and a woman based on your own experience.
2. Provide details on the house you're living in. Would you like to change something about it, move away to another location, or stay without fixing anything? Why?
3. Describe the hosted rooms. Share ideas how the college/ university/community could unite to make this place better.
4. Help your readers picture the best day of your life using vivid descriptions, different examples and original comparisons.
5. Describe the introductory day in any of the existing educational institution - school, college, or university - using the entire spectrum of emotions.
6. While on a picnic, you and your friends decide to go sailing. Unfortunately, your boat collapses in a violent storm. However, all of you manage to swim safely. Give a vivid account of the incident.
7. Describe an object which you believe has once saved your life or prevented adverse consequences for you or for any person close to you.
8. Find appropriate words to describe something you wanted so bad that you were ready to steal it due to the fact you did not have enough money to buy it.
9. Pick one of the recent technological innovations. Write a description explaining why this particular thing plays an important role in the development of modern society.
10. You have lived in your ancestral house since birth. The house is to be sold so that flats may be built. Mention the circumstances that led to this decision and describe your feelings about moving out of this house.

CHAPTER 2

Narrative Composition

A narrative composition is an oral and written description of an event or a series of events that takes place in one's life, which is presented to its readers and listeners in the form of a story or an essay, providing them with the necessary details in proper order so that the message is conveyed thoroughly.

A narration is similar to storytelling, with a simple difference in context-of fact and fiction. A story can be based on imagination while a narration is based purely on the real life experience or incident.

In the examination, word-limit for the narrative composition is 300-350 and its weightage is 20 marks.

Purpose of Writing a Narrative

Narrative writing is very important in our day-to-day life. It helps in sharing our stories of personal experiences with others and allows us to gain empathy. It also helps the most shattering incidences to reach out to the world.

Points to be Kept in Mind While Writing a Narrative

- Create an outline of the basic parts of your narrative.
- Use past tense to describe a past incident.
- Use contrast and comparison to add variety and interest.
- Describe your narrative using vivid details, recreating the experience for your readers or listeners.
- Narrate your experiences keeping in mind the small details that are important for your readers or listeners to know.
- Identify and remove any information that seems to distract from the focus and main thread of the narrative.

Sample Narrative 1

Narrate an incident from your own experience when you helped a friend who was in trouble. Explain what happened. What did you do to make the situation better? *[2017]*

Ans. **The Joy of Being One's Own**

I still remember what happened when we had gone for a picnic. Everything was going fine when suddenly, my friend Kaushal got a call from his sister that his parents had met with an accident. Kaushal was devastated and did not know what to do. As he belonged to a lower middle class family, he did not have enough money to hire a taxi and reach home fast. I assured Kaushal not to worry and left the picnic in the middle. I took out whatever money I had in my savings account, called a taxi and left for the spot where his parents had met with accident. Kaushal is the eldest in his family; he has two younger sisters.

He was unable to take any decision as the unexpected tragedy had left him too shocked to react. Kaushal had a very few relatives and most of them were unwilling to render any help. I called up all my friends and requested them for help. Kaushal's parents were admitted in a hospital and the surgery could take place only after the required amount had been deposited. I called my father and explained him the situation. As he himself was a doctor, he reached the hospital and talked to other doctors about Kaushal's parents. Meanwhile all my friends gave away not only their pocket money but also reserved money and an amount of ₹ 25000/- was arranged. I bought some snacks and juice for Kaushal and for his sisters who were crying miserably. The next two days were very crucial. Kaushal's father needed some blood which was voluntarily donated by my parents and the parents of my friends who had come there at the hospital. I didn't leave Kaushal alone even for a minute. My mother took his sisters to our home as there was nobody to look after them. After the surgery was done, Kaushal's parents survived and Kaushal relaxed a little.

In those days of need I spent most of my time with Kaushal, reassuring him that everything was going to be alright. Kaushal, till today, remembers this help. He had returned the money but he says he can never pay back the cooperation and help given by me, my family and our friends. Kaushal's whole family treats me like their own son and loves me dearly. I feel very proud of myself.

Sample Narrative 2

You are of forgetful nature. Once you bought a lottery ticket and kept it safely. Later you were informed that you have won the first prize on your lottery ticket. But where was the lottery ticket? Narrate how you managed to find out the lottery ticket.

Ans. **The Search of Forgotten Lottery Ticket**

The agent, Mithun, who had given me or had rather persuaded me to buy a lottery ticket came running to me one day. "Sir", he exclaimed, "take out your lottery ticket, your number has won first prize worth ₹ 5 crore." I scrabbled around, "Lottery, what lottery ticket?" He was shocked. He reminded me that fifteen days ago he had persuaded me to buy a lottery ticket of Maharashtra State Lotteries. He had also asked me to keep it safely. Alas! I did not remember anything about the lottery ticket. He asked me to go home and search for the ticket. He was concerned about his 5 lakh which he was going to get when I would claim my prize money of ₹ 5 crore. I closed my shop and went home along with him. I tried to recall where I had kept the lottery ticket but just could not. I reached home and rang up my wife to come home from office immediately as there was some urgent matter to attend to. Meanwhile, I tried to search the lottery ticket in my cupboard. I took out all my diaries, as sometimes I would keep important papers in those diaries. But, the ticket could not be traced. I searched all the possible places—my study table, drawer, folders, between the files but there was no trace of the lottery ticket. My wife came, alarmed at why she was called so urgently from office. When I told her about the lottery ticket, she too could not recall where the ticket was kept. For three hours, we searched all the possible places, looking nervous and dejected at the thought whether we had thrown away the lottery ticket.

Suddenly, a smile came on my wife's face as she remembered that she had given the lottery ticket to our son to keep it safely. We immediately rang up our son who was in the office. He confirmed to our delight that the ticket was with him. He rushed home immediately with the ticket. What a relief it was to have found it finally! I had lost all hopes of claiming the money as the ticket was not traceable at all, but finally we all celebrated that we were millionaires.

EXAM PRACTICE

1. Imagine a situation where you get an opportunity to change one thing in your school. What would it be? Why do you want to change it? How would you bring about the change? *[2023]*

2. Describe a time when all the lights in your locality went off. What were the sounds you heard as you sat in the darkness? How did you feel when the lights came on? *[Sem II 2022]*

3. Have you ever said or done something that changed the life of another person? Give an account of your words or actions that led to this change and describe how the experience made you feel. *[2020]*

4. Your class had to conduct a morning assembly. Write an account of how you prepared for it, what your role was and what you gained from the experience. *[2019]*

5. Narrate an incident from your own experience when you helped in preparing a meal. Explain what you did and what you gained from the experience. *[2018]*

6. Narrate an incident from your own experience when you expected to do very well, but for some reason were unable to do so. Explain what happened and why it happened. What lesson did you learn from it? *[2016]*

7. You had booked a ticket on an early morning train. However, you woke up late and missed it. You then decided to run to catch a bus to the next station where you hoped to catch up with the train. Narrate the entire event, how you felt, the effort you made and how you finally caught the train. What did you learn from this stressful experience? *[2015]*

8. Think of a time when you found yourself in an embarrassing situation. Narrate how you got into that situation, how you dealt with it and the lesson you learnt from it. *[2014]*

9. Teaching someone else how to do something can be a rewarding experience. Think of a skill that you have helped someone to develop. Perhaps you taught someone how to swim or to bake a cake or helped someone learn how to study more effectively.

   Narrate the events that made up the process of teaching the skill and say what made the experience important and memorable for you. *[2013]*

10. Relate a special incident or experience in your life which you still recall with happiness. *[2011]*

11. Narrate a story of a boy, who had to struggle a lot for education.

12. Write about your most weird dream and mention the unusual things that happened in your dreams.

13. Narrate a murder incident which took place in front of you.

14. You are Jatin. Once you had a nerve-wrecking experience when you were locked in a room with a big cobra. Narrate the incident and how you came out of that situation.

15. Write a narrative comparing life to riding a roller coaster.

16. Recall a remarkable event of social importance in your city or locality. Give a little of its background, the event as it occurred and its impact on the lives of people.

Answers

1. Modifications and updations has become the norm of the era. We can always find things for improvement and change. Hence, if I get the opportunity to change one thing about my school, I would change the way of communication which leads to the wastage of paper. There are times where I feel that my school is too reliant on using paper even for small things. For instance, the school library still puts up the issue slips on the books to keep record of issuing history and find out when a book is due to be returned. They also use the issuance register book for recordkeeping. The teachers also use attendance register books for marking attendance in the classroom. Further, any message to be passed within the school premises is written on a paper and then passed.

I personally feel that in the modern day and age where certain alternatives are available, we should try and minimise our usage of paper. Global warming is a serious issue and trees are helpful in protecting our environment from the climate change. The environmental effects of paper production include deforestation, the use of enormous amounts of energy and water as well as air pollution and waste problems. Given the situation, it is important to consider methods that are more environment-friendly.

I would like to digitise all the recordkeeping in the school, including the library and class attendance. This could be easily done with the help of any smart-device, such as a tablet or laptop. I would also like to encourage the school to switch to recycling the used paper and using recycled notebook for work. Students should also be given the option to email their assignments and homework. If my school can reduce the unnecessary use of paper, it can contribute in fighting climate change too.

2. **The Night When the Lights Went Off**

It was a dark rainy night; the rain came down hard, with no intent of stopping anytime soon. I lay relaxed on the couch watching TV when suddenly there was a loud crack of thunder. Perhaps, there was a power disruption due to the thunderstorm brewing outside. I could barely see anything and resorted to waving my arms in front of me to avoid bumping into any furniture. The bright moon was high in the clear sky. I went to the kitchen where my mother was cooking food for us. I searched the kitchen cabinet where I could find some candles when I found them, I lit them up with the help of gas stove.

Then, we set the dining table and all three of us, i.e. my father, mother and I had candle-lit dinner. Since, it was raining heavily, we could hear sounds of lightning and thunder along with the constant patter of rain. The winds were gushing loudly and trees were swaying. Because of this, breeze was blowing all through the house making us feel cool. After dinner, we sat in the balcony and started playing *Antakshari* and sang songs. Hearing us, our neighbours also joined us and we had a great time. We did not even realise that we had been playing for at least two hours. At that time, the rain stopped but the wind was still blowing. It was past midnight and we were still sitting in the balcony waiting for power to restore.

After about thirty more minutes, we were going to our bed to sleep when the power got restored. Seeing this, we took a breath of relief and went to bed to have a good night's sleep. I was happy that we could sleep till late next morning as it was a holiday.

3. Most things that change a person's perception happens to be an experience that they have gone through and learned from. And of all these experiences, there are some rare instances when an individual becomes the agent or the cause of bringing change in someone's life.

Recently, I had the opportunity to become a medium of bringing such a change in somebody's life. It so happened that I accidentally bumped into a very old friend of mine. It look us some moments to recognise each other as both of us had changed a lot but when we did, we exclaimed with joy.

She had left the city because of her father's transfer and had come back to attend a family function. We decided to sit in a coffee shop and spend some time with each other while discussing our lives. She was very happy because her father had been recently promoted and they were prospering financially. I was so happy to see her enjoying life.

We had been sitting there for an hour, when we realised that it was getting dark. When the bill came, she insisted upon paying my share as a treat for her father's promotion. I hesitated at first but then gave in. She paid the bill and gave the remaining amount as a tip to the waiter. I was a little surprised but didn't say anything. Just as we stepped out of the coffee shop, it started raining. Since both of us had to go in the same direction, we decided to take a rickshaw.

However, because of the rain, we couldn't find any.

Suddenly, a rickshaw pulled in front of us. We asked if he would take us to Pandav Nagar.

He agreed and said that he would charge fifty rupees. I was about to get on the rickshaw when my friend told the old man that she only give him thirty rupees. I was surprised to hear this. It had been three years since she left the city and the prices had increased. What the old man was charging was fair enough.

But my friend kept on arguing. And it was at that moment that I said, 'Isn't it strange that we tend to spend extravagantly in places where we have to show off our prosperity, but when it comes to pay a fair price to a hardworking man, we start negotiating?" My friend immediately realised that I was referring to her gracious tip in the coffee house. She felt ashamed and quietly got on the rickshaw. The old man safely dropped us home and happily took the money.

I saw that my friend had understood the real meaning of happiness when she saw the gleam in the eye of the old man as he held the fifty rupees note in his hand. This episode made my friend a little more humble and compassionate.

4. I am the Class Monitor for Class X in our school. One week before Teachers' Day, our school Principal informed me that my class will conduct the Morning Assembly on Teachers' Day and we should start preparing for it.

That day, I asked my classmates to wait in the classroom during the short morning break and announced this decision of the Principal. I also informed two classmates that they would look after the public address system and lighting arrangements. The remaining students of our class (35 in number) would ensure that all the school students were seated in their respective places well before the 'Principal' arrives. I was to act as the Principal.

The programme decided was that after I made the announcements for the day, one student would speak on a topic of interest for five minutes. We chose a highly vocal girl, Rashmi, to speak on the importance of Teachers' Day. For the next two days, we rehearsed our roles in the auditorium. I made some improvements in what Rashmi had prepared by using simple words. I also asked her to speak slower than her normal speed. The two boys in charge of the sound and light arrangements also checked that all the equipment was in working condition one day before the day.

Teachers' Day finally arrived. My classmates came 15 minutes earlier than usual and ensured that all students were seated. When the bell rang for the start of the assembly, I came out from behind the curtain and walked up to the podium. Simultaneously, all the students stood up. After we had greeted each other, we sang Vande Mataram. Then, I told the students to sit down and made two announcements. After that, Rashmi spoke very enthusiastically on her topic. The rehearsals had paid off handsomely in her case. After singing the National Anthem, I announced the end of the assembly.

From the experience of conducting the morning assembly, I have gained the knowledge that conducting any important event successfully requires proper and detailed planning. I also learnt that it is very important to conduct rehearsals to iron out any flaws before the actual event.

5. **When I Help to Prepare a Meal**

When I was in Class 10 and it was the summer holidays, I thought I would help prepare a meal. It was early morning. Mother had gone for grocery shopping and my sister was asleep. I decided to help in preparing breakfast by making an omelette. I had seen mother making it many times, so how difficult could it be?

I took two eggs, two tomatoes and a large onion. I chopped the onion on the work surface just as I had seen chefs do it. Then, came the tomatoes. I washed them and started chopping them. Suddenly, I cut my finger in hurry. There was no bleeding but it was just as painful.

It took me two or three attempts to crack open the eggs and drop them into the whipping bowl. The spices were next. Mother always kept the spices on the top shelf in the kitchen. I couldn't reach them, so I got a stool and, climbing on it, got the chilli powder and salt. I put all the ingredients in the bowl with the eggs and whisked them. I lit the stove, put the big frying pan on it and poured some oil in it. However, some oil spilled on the floor too.

Till the pouring of the batter into the pan, everything was going perfect. Then, I wondered what was used for turning the egg upside down in the pan. Soon, I was running all over the kitchen, searching all the shelves and drawers to find the cooking spoon; all the while the omelette was sizzling in the pan. Finally, I found the spoon and made a rush to turn over the omelette. I managed to do that without breaking or spilling it out of the pan, only to see a very nicely browned, or rather burnt, side up.

While I was busy taking it out in a plate, someone came up behind me. It was Mother. I was dumbstruck. She was angry at seeing the kitchen in a mess; the drawers all open, and some salt and chilli powder on the stove and countertop. She found a fit punishment for me: I had to eat the burnt omelette. Sitting on the table and eating the omelette, I realised it didn't taste as bad as it looked. My first cooking experience had turned out to be a minor disaster.

6. Life Lessons Learnt

Very recently, I learnt a lesson for life which I am never going to forget. I live in a locality with independent houses. Recently, a man shifted to a house close to my house. He became quite friendly with my children and often used to give them sweets and toys. He became friendly with my parents also. Suddenly, he stopped coming in the park. He did not meet anyone for many days. One day, my sister Kavya and I were playing with the bat and ball and the ball went into this neighbour's house. We were very sure that our neighbour would allow us to pick up the ball. We rang the bell which was answered after a long time. We asked him, if he could give us our ball but that man very sternly said "No" and closed the door. We were really surprised at his behaviour. He was so friendly but his sudden change of behaviour perplexed me.

Suddenly, one idea struck me when I saw the water tank behind his house. We wanted to get our ball so we climbed the water tank and jumped inside our neighbour's house. The door was open. Nobody was there. We went inside and tried to look for the ball under the bed.

I saw the ball. Hurriedly, I took the ball and along with it came a gold bar. We took out both the ball and the gold bar and climbed up the water tank again. Reaching my house, I found my father watching a news on TV.

I couldn't believe my ears when the news reader read that 20 gold bars were stolen from a jewellery shop. They showed a picture of the gold bars and it was exactly like the one we had found. I quickly told the whole story to my father who immediately called the police. The police came and searched this neighbour's house and gold bars were recovered and he was arrested.

The police informed my parents that the man was a thief, a smuggler and under his pleasantness wanted to carry on illegal activities.

I realised that this person should not have been trusted and I should have thought over the reason that he was trying to be so friendly with his neighbours. I learnt the lesson that we should never trust a stranger.

7. A Lesson of Punctuality

The alarm bell buzzed at 3:00 am to wake me up from my sleep so that I could catch my train which was to leave for Udaipur at 5:00 am. However, I put the alarm off and went back to sleep.

Around 3:45 am, my phone rang. I reluctantly answered, half asleep. On the other end of the call was my cousin who enquired whether I had got ready to leave the house for the station. Her question "What time will you reach the station?" made me wake up at once. I looked at the watch and rebuked myself for sleeping extra, when ideally I should have been getting ready. I told her that I would reach the station at 4:30 am and hurriedly put the phone down. I got up from my bed and rushed to the bathroom.

By 4:10 am, I reached the cab stand. However, there was no cab to be found.

In a state of panic, I called up my friend who stayed nearby. Thankfully, he answered my call and rushed to help me. He drove as fast as he could and we reached the station exactly five minutes before the scheduled time. However, to my utter shock, I was on the wrong platform. I hurried to the platform where my train was waiting. Unfortunately, by the time I reached the platform, the train was rolling on its wheels. My cousin was shouting at me from inside the train and asked me to run. I ran as fast as I could but missed it. I couldn't believe what had happened. I did not know what to do. Other passengers were looking at me and some were mocking at my carelessness. However, an old couple came and suggested me to catch a bus to the next station where I might catch up with the train.

I hurried to the bus stand which was nearby. Thankfully, the bus was about to leave. I found myself a seat and prayed to reach in time. To my relief, the bus dropped me an hour prior to the scheduled timing of the train. I bought water, drank some and splashed the rest on my face.

This stressful experience taught a very important lesson to me of punctuality. Time and tide wait for none. It's better to be early than late.

8. An Embarrassing Day in My Life

The proverb "Pride comes before a fall" became very apt for me. I was also good in academics and managed to come in the first three ranks in the class with the minimum of effort. The result was that I became egotistic and started making fun of my classmates especially because some of my class fellows laughed at my witticism. This encouraged me on and I started misbehaving when some lenient teachers were present.

One day, when the Hindi period started, our teacher walked into the class just as the bell rang. I had just sat down when the previous teacher had left and I did not notice our Hindi teacher coming in. All the children around me stood up and wished her. I was still sitting and before I could get up, she saw me seated and thought that I was trying to insult her. As a punishment she made me stand the whole period on the chair. The whole class kept looking at me, whispering and laughing. Instead of stopping the children, she asked me how I felt to be at the receiving end for once. I had never felt so humiliated in my life. On the top of it, she pointed out at my hairstyle and compared it to the one we see in the promotional advertisement for the candy 'Centre Shock'.

Everyone burst into peals of laughter. I felt ashamed and realised how other children felt when I ridiculed them. Thankfully, I was made to sit down in the next period. No one was in a mood to study as it was the last period of the day. One of my friends imitated the way our Sanskrit teacher spoke but in a very exaggerated manner. I could not help and burst out laughing.

My teacher got so furious at me that she lost her temper and took me to the Principal's office. There, I stood outside the office for almost twenty minutes. To add to my embarrassment, there was a football tournament in our school that day.

Children from other schools were also participating. One of them happened to be my neighbour with whom I never got along. When he passed by me and snickered, I wished the Earth to crack and swallow me up.

What an embarrassing day! I shall never forget it. I resolved that I would never behave like that ever again.

9. Baking Cupcakes

It really does seem that children are becoming interested in cooking again. I don't know if it's due to the success of cooking shows on television, such as Masterchef and Junior Masterchef. My brother's kids are definitely more interested in how a particular dish is made and even ask, "Can I cook tonight?"

Cupcakes, in particular, give reasonably quick results and the children enjoy frosting and decorating them. So, I decided to teach them how to make cupcakes. Cupcakes are so easy to make that they are ideal for children to bake. I always think the best cupcakes for kids to make are those where all the ingredients are put in the bowl together.

While teaching them how to bake a cupcake, I asked them to follow these steps.

First, I listed all the ingredients that were needed—butter, caster sugar, plain flour, baking powder, salt, eggs and vanilla extract. I also told them the exact quantities that were required. Once all the ingredients were in place, I instructed them to preheat the oven to 180°C/350 F. Then, I told them to line the muffin tin with paper cases. I explained to them how the batter or mixture is made and all the tricks involved in making it, the consistency needed and how to correctly mix all ingredients without over mixing the batter or incorrectly whipping the eggs. After the mixture was ready, the next step was to teach them how to grease the paper cases and put the mixture into them. After that, the cupcakes were kept in the oven for 18 to 20 minutes until risen, golden and firm to touch.

Once the cupcakes were out of the oven and ready, I told them to let them cool completely. It was time for the decoration of the cupcakes. The kids were overjoyed at it. They decorated the cupcakes with colourful frosting and sprinkles. The kids made very creative cupcakes. It was a memorable experience for them and for me. Their tiny little hands served me each of their cupcakes and we relished eating them together while cracking jokes.

10. Marvellous Result

It was the last week of May. My Class X examination result was to be declared that day. I had been waiting for this day with anxiety and curiosity. I got up at six o'clock in the morning, took bath and prayed to God to grant me success. I was somewhat uneasy and restless. My mind was swinging between hope and fear. It was a strange mix of anxiety and expectation. I was not sure what was in store for me. My parents had high expectations from me.

At one moment, I was sure that I would score good marks while at the next, I feared what would happen if I performed badly or failed. At ten o'clock, I went to the school with my mother to get my result. Other children also came with their parents. My hands were shaking and heart was throbbing.

My class teacher handed over my result to my mother. Immediately, a wide smile spread across her face. She hugged me tightly and told me that I had stood first in the class with 98.9% marks. Soon, I met the Principal and other teachers. They all congratulated me. In the evening, when I returned home, I saw many of my relatives and friends had come to congratulate me. My father welcomed them cordially.

He seemed to be very proud of me. We spent the whole day cheerfully.

The whole atmosphere of the house was at once changed. Friends and relatives kept pouring in to congratulate me. Tea and sweets were served to all who came. Many of my relatives brought sweet boxes for me. All were in a jolly and happy mood. My mother prepared nice dishes for dinner. I also invited two of my friends for dinner.

Never before had I been so happy. Even today, when I recall this incident, it brings immense joy and happiness to me. It was indeed one of the happiest days of my life which I shall remember for many years to come.

11. A Struggle for Education

One day, while working in the coal mine, a young boy named Booker T Washington overheard a conversation between two miners. They were talking about a good school for coloured people in Virginia. The boy had never heard of any such school, apart from the one in his town and decided to study in that school. But, he had no idea where it was. His only ambition was to reach Hampton.

In the fall of 1872, he decided to leave. Finally, as decided, he started for Hampton. Not being far from home, he realised that he did not have enough money to pay his fare to Hampton.

By walking, begging for rides in wagons and cars, somehow he managed to reach Richmond, Virginia, which is about 82 miles from Hampton. He was tired and hungry on reaching the city. It was late in the night. He was completely out of money and without any acquaintances in a big city. Being extremely exhausted, he crept under a sidewalk and rested the whole night, using his satchel as a pillow. The next morning, he saw himself near a large ship. He went and asked the captain if he would permit him to unload the ship in order to get money for food. The captain consented and the boy worked hard for long to earn money for his breakfast. The captain was pleased with his work and asked him if he desired to work for a small amount of money per day. The boy readily accepted the offer.

One day, he thanked the captain of the vessel and reached Hampton with 50 cents in his pocket. He presented himself to the head teacher of the school who asked him to sweep the recitation room properly. The boy did it just perfectly without even a speck of dirt. When the head teacher was unable to find dirt even in the corners, she remarked, "I guess you will do to enter this institution."

The boy felt that this was the best examination he had ever passed.

12. People from Space

The night was cold, a thick fog hung outside my window. I was trying to catch some sleep which was eluding me. My mother had just put me to bed wishing me sweet dreams but it seemed that sleep was miles away from me.

I paced up and down, clutching the shawl to myself and switched on the television to see if there was any interesting programme on it. The movie 'Mars Attacks' was being aired of which I had read good reviews. It was an exciting movie about strange unpredictable creatures from Mars landing on Earth. The movie kept me spellbound. After it was over, I stretched myself on the bed and fell fast asleep. After some time, I got disturbed by a knock at my door. I woke up to see, before me, a strange looking boy with two antenna like objects sticking out of his head over a hairy body. His owl like eyes resembled the characters I had just seen in the movie. I screamed in fright but he said something in a strange language. He turned on a small device which helped me to understand what he was saying and *vice-versa*. I learnt that he indeed had come from Mars. He extended his thin wing hand for friendship but I was scared of him and chose to do *namaste* instead.

He talked about life on Mars, telling me that it is much bigger than our planet Earth. They do not eat, rather they survive on noble gases that are in abundance there. However, unable to take it any longer, I politely requested him to let me sleep, for I had to wake up early to attend school. He reacted with haste. Snatching the translator from my hand, he pointed his gun at me and in a flash I was in flames. I screamed with all my might "Help, Help, this boy from Mars has killed me."

I suddenly felt a splash of cold water on my face. Opening my eyes, I saw my mother looking down at me. How relieved I was to realise that it was all but a dream.

13. The Murder

I was returning from my office very late at night that day. A thick blanket of fog covered the area and hence there was zero visibility. I didn't take my car that day, so I was walking towards my apartment complex from the bus stand. As I was nearing my home, I heard a very strange noise. I stopped to look at where that noise was coming from, but there was no one around. So, I ignored and continued walking in the same direction.

After walking a few steps, I heard the same sort of noise from behind the bushes. I thought that some wild animal must be hiding there and just then, a car entered the gate of my apartment. As the car approached me, I saw two men, with guns in their hands, come out of the bush and open fire and quickly drive away. The man who was driving the car, lay dead. I was too horrified to move and a sudden chill ran down my spine. I had not, in my weirdest imagination, dared to think about this. The whole incident took place at an arm's distance from me and I could do nothing to save the person. I didn't even know who the man was and what was he doing there, as I had never seen him in our area before.

Later on, the guard and the police came running and soon the media crowded that place. The police took me for interrogation and recorded my statement and the next day this news was in the paper. Later, we got to know that the man who got killed was a smuggler and the boys who killed him, accused him of taking their money and ditching them. The boys were soon arrested and put in jail.

The incident is still fresh in my memory and everytime I remember it, I get goose bumps. This is something that I will never forget all my life.

14. My Encounter with A Cobra

I was posted at a small place called Hoshiarpur in Punjab. Electricity used to be very irregular during the monsoon months of July and August. I can still remember it was 20th August, 20XX. For the last two days, it had rained non-stop, paralysing everything. But, being a doctor I could not stay indoors. I had to attend the patients in the hospital.

It was 7:30 in the evening when I returned home tired. There was no electricity so we had to use lanterns or torch. I entered my bedroom as I wanted to change and relax for some time. As I entered and closed the room, I heard a thud. To my shock and fear, a cobra, black in colour, appeared near the door. I had a very small torch with me using which I could see the enormous serpent sitting coiled. As there was only one door, I could not rush out of the room. I just sat on my bed and tried to call the servant. I called my servant to the bathroom door and told him of my predicament and instructed him to fetch a lantern and a ladder. After another long wait, I heard continuous voices, followed by the scraping of the ladder against the outer wall of the house. When the lantern was passed inside the room, I turned my head realising that the cobra was behind me. I saw it lying near the bedroom door two feet away. Leaning forward very slowly, I picked up the heavy bath-mat, raised it high and let it fall as the cobra was sliding over the floor towards me. Fortunately, I judged my aim accurately and the bath-mat crashed down on the cobra's neck six inches from its head. I took a hasty stride to the veranda door and in a moment was outside among the crowd of men armed with sticks and carrying lanterns.

All of them entered the bedroom and caught hold of cobra on a stick as it was hurt and almost paralysed by my hit. It was taken out to the fields. I thanked God for saving me from a life-and-death struggle with a big snake in the locked room.

15. Life is Like a Roller Coaster

I have never really liked roller coasters. The first and only time when I rode a roller coaster, I was fifteen and naively excited. I lacked the foresight to remove my glasses before boarding, a silly mistake. Stupidly, my friends did not warn me about it either. However, like a lamb brought to slaughter, I was calm, innocently curious about what would come next.

Soon, I was at the very top with the entire amusement park spread below my feet. As I was confronted with the vertical descent below, all spidery dark metal curving sharply down and away, my stomach started twisting uncomfortably. The realisation that this was definitely not where I wanted to be became a solid block of panic tearing at my chest as the coaster paused for a moment and then sliced downward and curved into a corkscrew, straining to throw us off. I wanted to scream, I really did, but the whole of my mental capacity was focused on somehow preventing my glasses from slipping off my face using sheer willpower.

Somehow, the ride was over and I made it off and onto the nearest bench, sanity without my glasses my glasses fell off on the downward descent. I breathed a sigh of relief that I survived.

The experience taught me that like any well-designed coaster, life has its twists and turns and steep drops but it also has ups. Agony is inevitable but it does not last forever and we are stronger and wiser having lived through it, even if only by a little bit.

16. Protest for Justice

In December 2012, the brutal rape and subsequent death of a 23-year-old female student in Delhi quickly gained attention in India and abroad.

The woman was beaten and raped in a moving bus. Medical reports later said that the woman suffered serious injuries to her abdomen, intestines and genitals due to the assault. In the days immediately following the inhumane incident, protestors staged large demonstrations at Delhi's India Gate and outside government buildings including Rashtrapati Bhavan, the official residence of the President of India.

People no longer wanted to sit back and wait for the government's action. They knew very well that 'Justice delayed is justice denied'. Thus, thousands of protestors clashed with police and Rapid Action Force units.

Demonstrators were *lathi* charged, shot with water cannons and tear gas shells and arrested. Similar protests occurred throughout the country. Thousands of people silently marched while others started a hunger strike. Protests also occurred online on social networking sites like Facebook and WhatsApp, with users replacing their profile images with a black dot symbol. Tens of thousands of people signed petitions protesting the incident and demanding justice.

Many of the mourners carried candles and wore black outfits and some pasted black cloth across their mouths. Some of the protestors drew slogans on papers spread on the road, condemning the incident and demanding stricter laws and speedy judgement. The incident made breaking news all across the globe. It sparked protests across South Asia, including marches and rallies in Nepal, Sri Lanka, Pakistan and Bangladesh.

The demand for severe punishment for the perpetrators led to the death sentence for four of the accused while one died in the police custody and one was a juvenile who was given the maximum sentence of 3-year imprisonment in a reform facility. The incident left a deep scar on the minds of everyone. This was a remarkable event of social importance where the entire world stood together and demanded justice.

SELF ASSESSMENT

1. School life is full of ups and downs. Describe some of the happy and sad moments of your ten years of school life.
2. 'All's well that ends well'. Narrate an incident that reveals the truth of this statement.
3. Write about a time when you were late for an important function. What lesson did you learn?
4. Express your views regarding if you could go back in time and make some pleasant changes thereupon. What would they be?
5. Narrate an experience that was most frightening to you and elaborate how you overcame the fear.
6. Mention that one thing that you are afraid to lose in life and state why you loved that thing so much.
7. Suppose you got a billion dollar. State how you would spend this sum in the welfare of humanity.
8. Everyone has a mix of good and bad days in their life. Express the most disastrous day of your life.
9. 'All that glitters is not gold'. State the experience that taught you how appearance can be deceiving.
10. You are what you risk. In the light of this statement, state the biggest risk you have ever taken.

CHAPTER

3

Debate/Argumentative Composition

A debate is a formal discussion or an argument on a subject on which people have different opinions. It is used as a means of putting your points forward to convince the audience about the point of view. In this type of composition, the person is free to express his/her views by writing either in favour of or against the topic. In the examination, word-limit for the debate/argumentative composition is 300-350 and its weightage is 20 marks.

Points to be Kept in Mind While Writing a Debate

- Prepare the debate properly by considering both the positive and negative aspects of the topic. (for and against)
- Make it clear in the beginning whether you are speaking for or against the motion.
- Debate should always have a good introduction to grab the audience's attention and garner their interest in the topic.
- Bridge the gap from opinion to reason.
- Give some examples in support of your view.
- In the end, sum up your opinion.

The following expressions can be included to enhance your debate and to make it more emphatic

- I support the motion whole heartedly
- I strongly oppose the motion
- In my opinion
- I'd like to present my views
- I totally disagree with the view
- I reject/submit/sympathise agree

Sample Debate 1

It is better to be in a group. At times, isolation gives solace. Considering this, write a debate on the topic 'Joint family set up is better to live In'.

Ans.

For the Motion

Respected Principal, staff members and my worthy opponents. Today, I am going to speak in the favour of the motion 'Joint family set up is better to live in'.

In India, joint family system has been in existence since ancient times. The father is considered the head of the family and undertakes all the responsibilities of his family. Everyone in the joint family is delegated a responsibility, and mutual understanding and cooperation are the key words to its efficient working. If we live in a joint family setup, we learn to be tolerant of others. Sharing is another quality which can be very well imbibed while living in a joint family. The greatest blessing of such a family is that there are many people who support you in time of distress or crisis.

Happiness and sorrow are equally shared by all members of the family. The grandparents are able to spend time with their grandchildren and take proper care of them if their parents are out for work. Security of children does not become the cause of stress for parents in a joint family as one or other family member is always there to help. Contrary to this, in nuclear families, children are left either in the creche or at the mercy of maids who are not a proper substitute for family members. At the time of any festival, it is fun to be together and celebrate the festival with enthusiasm. Financially, you may be better off in a joint family as financial burdens are shared by all the earners equally and the spare money can be utilised by the younger lot in an appropriate manner. So, in my point of view, a joint family setup is certainly better than living alone in a nuclear family.

Thank you

Against the Motion

Respected Principal, staff members and my worthy opponents. Today, I am going to speak against the motion 'Joint family set up is better to live in'.

While a joint family setup is a traditional family unit of India, it is full of issues that may affect an individual negatively. The main problem that one faces in a joint family is lack of privacy and interference of others in one's personal matters. The grandparents pamper their grandchildren and often turn children into spoiled brats. The lack of discipline among such children may cause problems at a later stage. In a nuclear family, the mother is able to look after the needs of her children well, whereas in a joint family she hardly finds time to spend with her children. Moreover, there is financial advantage in nuclear family. The family earns, spends and saves money for themselves. Parents can invest money for the education of their children and pay individual attention to their children and think about their careers.

In a joint family setup, decision-making becomes very difficult as everyone tries to advise the other as per his/her perception and understanding of the situation. This can result in continuous nuisance if there is disharmony among family members, specially the ladies of the house. The discord between them disturbs peace of mind of elders as well as that of young children. In comparison, there is more harmony and cooperation in a nuclear family as all the members are responsible and understand one another's needs.

Women in a nuclear family are free and may pursue the career of their choice whereas this becomes very difficult in joint family. People in a nuclear family are able to spend more time in their social circle. Hence, joint family set up doesn't seem appropriate in the modern world.

Thank you

Sample Debate 2

'School days are the happiest days of our lives.' Express your views either for or against this statement. *[2017]*

Ans.

For the Motion

Respected Principal, staff members and my worthy opponents. Today, I am going to speak in favour of the motion 'School days are the happiest days of our lives'.

We are surrounded by our own group of friends and enjoy every moment of school time. Be it Sports or Yoga, Maths or English period, there is giggle and laughter over matters which may not be humourous for others. We are free from worries which adults face, and enjoy life as it comes. These are happy carefree days.

Moreover, pretending to be hurt, playing pranks on the teachers and not doing homework are some of the naughtiest things we remember of our school days. In our school days, we have no tension of earning money as whatever we need is provided by our parents or we are given money to buy that thing. A healthy competition makes school life a fun. No matter what kind of competition it is, whether of studying, playing or speaking in debate, all inculcate in us the spirit of determination and self-confidence without gorging the feelings of enmity for anyone.

School days are happy not only in the context of fun, but also in the context of learning. We learn very important lessons of life, like respecting our elders, sharing our things with friends, helping one another and so on.

During school days, holidays are best realised. For us, they are like a gift from God himself as we do not have to get early. We can have the fun of playing cricket or football in the morning or watch our favourite programme on TV. The school trips cannot be forgotten because the company of our best school buddies and teachers adds to the happiness.

So, the time spent in school is the golden period of one's life as one does not need to pay heed to the worldly problems rather one needs to realise the happiness that each moment provides one during one's school days.

Thank you

Against the Motion

Respected Principal, staff members and my worthy opponents. Today, I am going to speak against the motion 'School days are the happiest days of our lives'.

The first reason to say this is the unnecessary competition that we have to face during school days. We have to compete for everything from occupying a seat in our school bus to securing the top position in the class. We are supposed to give our best performance and get the best regardless of our own choice. This makes our life stressful and full of tension and worries. The second reason is the less time we are given to play and for recreation. If we do not score or perform as expected by our parents and teachers, we are made to feel guilty and like we are nothing.

The third reason is toward the discrimination on the ground of performance in the exams. When it comes to scoring marks in exams, everybody pressurises us to get the highest marks in exams. People's behaviour towards us changes according to the marks we score.

The behaviour of some of the classmates is also very disturbing as they trouble all the class and fight with the weak students. They create such an atmosphere in the class that one starts feeling insecure. Even the teachers do not pay heed to their mischief. The tension of homework is always looming as all the teachers give a lot of homework which has to be completed on the same day and if it is incomplete, the students have to face punishment. Even the holidays are not free. The students are given homework that consumes all their time. Some of the teachers are of the habit of using abusive language and beatings. They make their students' life hell if they are not followed. Besides all these we are left with no choice but to curse ourselves, an experience that no one wants to go through. So, each day we pass at our school is full of stress that does not let a child live free, rather he/she feels confined. Thus, I do not agree with the statement.

Thank you

EXAM PRACTICE

1. 'School examinations do not test intelligence' Express your views either for or against this statement. *[2023]*
2. 'More learning happens outside the classroom than inside it.' Express your views either for or against this statement. *[Sem II 2022]*
3. 'A family without pets is an incomplete family.' Express your views either for or against this statement. *[2020]*
4. 'Closed Circuit Television (CCTV) must be installed in every class room.' Give your views either for or against this statement. *[2019]*
5. 'Money is important for happiness.' Express your views either for or against this statement. *[2018]*
6. 'The use of mobile phones must be allowed in schools.' Express your views either for or against the statement. *[2016]*
7. 'All girls or all boys schools provide a better learning environment than co-educational schools'. Express your views either for or against the statement. *[2015]*
8. 'Boarding schools are far better than day schools for the all-round education of a child.' Express your views either for or against this statement. *[2013]*
9. A working woman is a dynamic personality. She knows the intricacies of lives. She can instil the values better. Summing all these, draft a debate on 'Working Women are Better Mother'.
10. Money is pleasure and pain like the faces of a coin. It is more of pain and less of pleasure. 'Money causes more harm than good.' Express your views either for or against this statement. *[2012]*
11. Assistance is necessary for the growing buds. But, this assistance should not be purely commercial in nature. In the light of this statement, justify 'private tuitions being necessary evil'. *[2011]*
12. 'More lessons are learnt on the sports field than in the classroom.' Express your views either for or against this statement. *[2010]*
13. 'The use of mobile phones has lowered active social life and has become an addiction.' Express your views either for or against this statement.
14. 'No other subject taught in school is as important as Moral Science'. Express your views either for or against this statement.
15. 'The computer will soon replace the book.' Express your views either for or against this statement.
16. A concern for environment is a concern for everyone. In the light of this statement, write a debate on the topic 'Using your own transport is better than using public transport'.

Answers

1. **For the Motion**

Evaluation is the key to testing one's academic knowledge and not intelligence.

Good morning to one and all present here. We all know that evaluations or pen-paper examinations have been accepted by everyone as one of the best ways to test a student's knowledge, understanding and learning. But does it test the practical skills that are required in the world? Does it test a student's presence of mind or precisely state the positive of one's personality?

The answer is no. Hence, I stand in favour of the motion that School examinations do not test intelligence. While success in school examinations may reflect the knowledge and hard-work of a student, it may not necessarily reflect their intelligence levels or their potential. It only tests, the factual knowledge that the student learn from books and in classes.

We all agree that each individual is unique in their own way and there is not one particular pattern of defining intelligence. The school examinations, however, do have a particular pattern and those who fit the mould tend to succeed in it. History is full of examples of such individuals who didn't particularly fit in the pattern of school or examinations but went on to become great individuals in their fields. The great Mathematician, Ramanujan, was so fond of Mathematics that he failed most other subjects. Albert Einstein generally didn't like lectures or tests. It would not have been possible for either of them to be considered as intelligent had they been judged based on their examination results only. The complexity and intelligence of their minds is reflected in their groundbreaking theories and research work. It was only when they were allowed to think freely instead of being restricted by the education system that they could achieve their true potential.

It is also important to understand that academic success isn't the only form of human intelligence. Some students are great at other activities like sports or art. These activities involve just as much effort and intelligence as conventional academics and examinations. For example, the strategies involved in playing sports, the detailing required to complete a painting or the imagination required to write a novel are all different forms of intelligence. Hence, the human intelligence cannot be limited to just school examination.

Against the Motion

Evaluation is an essential criteria that tells us the level of learning possessed by a child.

Good morning to one and all present here. We all learn a variety of subjects in our school. But do we check if the child has understood and learnt the basic ideas or concepts that are crucial to life. The answer is examinations. Therefore I stand against the motion that 'school examinations do not test intelligence.'

While I agree that examination does not completely test a student's intelligence, it cannot state that intelligence and examination have no relation. We know that some students work really hard and do not often get the best results, while some can get top results by working less than others. This kind of a situation shows us that intelligence does have a role in examination.

It is also important to take into consideration that many universities and schools provide scholarship on the basis of the examination results. Some universities also consider the examination scores of a student before accepting them. This helps us understand that examinations can be extremely helpful for teachers to assess the students. Especially because there are generally many students at the same level, it may not be possible for a teacher to individually assess each student. Examinations can help them to find out the students that are able to understand the subject and those who need more help to improve.

It is generally believed that school is helpful to lay the foundation for the things that we do in our future lives. Examinations are important in this regard as they help the students to test how much they learnt from what was taught to them. This can reflect the knowledge, dedication and work put in by a student to their studies and acts as a crucial indicator of their general level of intelligence. Thus, good examination result is a reward that a student receives in return for their effort and speaks volumes about their intelligence.

2. For the Motion

Respected Principal, honourable teachers and my dear friends. Today, I am here to express my views in favour of the motion. 'More learning happens outside the classroom than inside it'.

Learning cannot be simply equated to marks, grades, degree or job. It is a life-long process. Getting a good education is just a key to enter the society, but it does not ensure success in our lives. To be successful, we must experience the world outside the classroom, as schooling days are just a small chapter in our lives. We learn the realities of life only when we enter the society.

Learning is one of the most important things we do in life. It starts pretty much when we're born. In fact, many say learning begins earlier. We listen to the sounds of the world. Our ears get used to the different patterns of intonation. This is when we first start learning a language. We spend our childhood years doing nothing but learning. We learn more from our family and the society than what we learn from school books.

Education in a classroom is like feul to a car, whereas education outside is like the engine which propels the car forward through the journey of life. Education outside the classroom is often just as valuable if not more as the lessons children learn from textbooks. Hands-on learning and community involvement often allow young minds to expand their horizons and explore topics that are not offered in school. Learning outside the classroom can help raise achievement, improve classroom behaviour and improve the engagement of students, including those who are hard to engage in the classroom environment. In a classroom scenario, the routine is fixed and predictable which spare the students from changes needed to adapt oneself into the world. A student can read about a culture or watch a video about the ocean, but it does not have the same impact as seeing the sculptures and paintings live or enjoying the marvels at an aquarium. This can hold especially true when it comes to learning and experiencing science.

So, in my opinion, learning outside the school helps us a lot in our learning style. Although people learn in different ways, I'm sure that they will learn much faster when they experience the outside world. Schools are just the microcosm of the real world, as the real world is bigger and more diverse.

Thank you

Against the Motion

Respected Principal, honourable teachers and my dear friends. Today, I am here to express my views against the motion. 'More learning happens outside the classroom than inside it'.

Learning is arguably the most important activities that human beings engage in. It is through learning that we are able to acquire new knowledge and skills. It can therefore be said that learning is integral for the development of the society. Due to the importance of learning, many societies have come up with formal institutes where learning takes place. These institutes include schools where students attend and gain information on a wide variety of subjects.

Students can interact with one another when they learn in a classroom setting. All students are learning and teaching others at the same time. All of the experience outside starts with the classroom. Students can build on each other's ideas and produce better final results. In addition to this, students are more motivated to learn when other individuals who are also engage in the same learning surround them. But when children learn outside the classroom, they may remain deprived from this experience and end up learning alone. Learning outside the classroom can surely give them new experiences but those experiences can be both positive and negative for which students may not be prepared to handle.

Contact with the teacher in classroom learning leads to better learning outcomes for the student. Teachers are a very important part of the learning process since they act as informative guides and make children disciplined. Interaction with the teacher also increases the concentration level of the individual. Students have to learn on their own outside the classroom. No one is there to guide them and make them learn the importance of discipline in life to become successful.

Learning requires a significant amount of time to be dedicated to the activity. Classroom learning is well-structured and the teacher has a program of what the students should learn. This is not the case with leaning outside the classroom. There are no prepared schedules and life teaches lessons in its way. Although we gain a lot of knowledge outside the classroom, it is because we can implement the knowledge that we learnt inside the classroom. Therefore, classroom learning can provide in-depth knowledge how to be prepared for life.

Thank you

3. For the Motion

Respected Principal, honourable teachers and my dear friends. Today, I am here to express my views in favour of the motion 'A family without pets is an incomplete family'. Pets are really a part of our everyday lives and part of our families. They provide companionship and help to reduce our loneliness. Sometimes playing with pet reduces our stress. It may help in lowering the blood pressure of elderly members in the family.

Having a pet delivers a great sense of responsibility to the child. Feeding and caring for pet encourages childhood responsibility. Children with pets display improved impulse control, social skill and self-esteem. Kids with pet go outside more frequently to go for walks, run and play in the park. All these enjoyments with pets give them associated health benefits. Children who grow up in homes with pets have less risk of developing common allergies and asthama. Thus, pet owners require fewer doctor's visit.

Research shows children who live in homes with a dog can have fewer ear infections, respiratory tract infections and require fewer antibiotics. The exposure to animals at a young age stimulates their immune system. Pets teach kindness and compassion. Pets are perfect for teaching children about empathy and responsible as kids feel proud of themselves for taking care of another living being.

Children can learn trust from their pet. A pet offers unconditional support when a child or anyone in the family is sad, angry or upset. We can always trust our pets. They never betray us. Pets like dog give safety to our family and lots of entertainment to family members. Pets teach adults as well as children valuable life lessons which have great significance in our life.

Thank you

Against the Motion

Respected Principal, honourable teachers and my dear friends. Today, I am here to express my views against the motion 'A family without pets is an incomplete family'. First of all, maintaining a pet is an expensive affair. You have to maintain their health which includes expensive food items, immunisation or visit to the Veterinarians.

Today, we are leading very busy schedule in our life. Who has enough time to look after the pet? Most of the parents are professional and the children are busy with their schools and other activities. Nobody has time to play with the pets or look after them. Pets have to spend long hours in home without any companion. It makes them anxious and irritated. To solve this problem, some family appoint servants to look after pets. But these paid persons are not rarely kind to the pets.

Sometimes pets like cats, dogs carry infectious diseases. It is not good for a child below 10 years of age. Thus, the parents should be cautious while selecting pets for their family. A pet might prove harmful if you do not get the right kind of pet for your family's need. For instance, if someone buys a dog like, German Shepherd or Saint Bernard for his small flat, it is harmful both for them and the pet. These large dogs need atleast 2 hours of exercise, i.e. need enough space for run and play. If you cannot provide this, it will ruin the health of the dog.

The family with young children should be very careful while getting a pet. Until the children are of a responsible and trainable age, parents should properly choose the pet. If the child is too young, sometimes they may be hurt by the animal accidentally. Finally, we should remember that bringing a pet home means we also have to adjust with them. Pets like cat, dog, bird can make noise in the middle of the night. So we have to prepare ourselves to take these challenges positively, when we decide it's time for a pet, otherwise being a pet owner only creates problem.

Thank you

4. For the Motion

We have all heard or read stories of children being ill-treated by unsympathetic teachers at schools around the world. These incidents happen, as they are reported regularly in the media. Accordingly, everyone has their own opinion on whether a school should have CCTV cameras installed.

Respected Principal, honourable teachers and my dear friends. Today, I am here to express my views in favour of the motion 'Closed Circuit Televison (CCTV) must be installed in every class room'.

There are many advantages of installing CCTV cameras in every classroom which the Principal can monitor. The first is that this move will deter bad behaviour, both by the students among themselves as well as by the teacher towards the students. If the students know they are being watched, they might be better behaved. This might prevent bullying and intimidation.

Further, teachers and students can be protected from false accusations later on. If there was an incident regarding safety (for instance, a fight, bullying, etc.), CCTV cameras will be able to capture the incident and what is happening for the police (if required), and the recording can be used as evidence. A lot of times incidents like these happen and there is no evidence against the perpetrator, but closed circuit cameras would be able to capture what is happening.

The teachers can also use past recordings for improving classroom management and also work on their problem areas. Even the Principal can evaluate a teacher's effectiveness by analysing the video footage.

However, the most important advantage is the trust generated in parents' minds when they come to know that the Principal is monitoring every classroom. Parents will feel more secure for their children if they know that the classrooms are being constantly monitored. Parents of new students being admitted to the school will be put at ease when they discover that the classrooms have cameras. So, it will encourage them to send their children to one school over another.

For all these reasons, I believe CCTV in the classrooms at our school can be a good thing. Parents can come in, see the footage and any problematic situation can be settled faster than it could have been previously, without the cameras.

Thank you

Against the Motion

Respected Principal, honourable teachers and my dear friends. Today, I am here to express my views against the motion 'Closed Circuit Televison (CCTV) must be installed in every class room'.

The biggest problem with installing CCTV cameras in classrooms is that teachers and students would feel that the school principal does not trust them. Teachers will be afraid of using innovative methods of teaching due to the fear of being misunderstood by the Principal. They would be afraid to take up any classroom activity other than the 'done' thing, as they may fear that it may be used against them. This could lead to a 'guilty until proven innocent' attitude. It can create an authoritarian atmosphere and students may come to school with a sense of apprehension. Another important issue which goes against installing CCTV cameras is that of intrusion of privacy of the students and teachers. This is a legal issue. Teachers and students would be worried whether there are any hidden cameras installed in places other than classrooms also which they are not aware of and which would invade their personal privacy.

A further issue is regarding the cost to the school of such systems compared to the benefit they will give. The whole system will need not only the cameras. The associated equipment includes a digital video recorder (DVR) to record information from the cameras, a switcher to view scenes from different cameras, power supply for the system and the extensive cabling involved. With such a large expenditure, the school Principal and management will definitely want a commensurate return in improved learning, better security and, ultimately, better results from the students. It means that the Principal will be overworked unless he hires an assistant to help him with the monitoring. This will again bring up the matter of intrusion of privacy, as the assistant will not be of the same stature as the Principal.

Thus, if we do a cost-benefit analysis of installing CCTV cameras in classrooms, it is doubtful whether the benefits will outweigh the costs.

Thank you

5. **For the Motion**

Respected Principal, teachers and my worthy opponents. Today, I stand before you to present my views in favour of the motion 'Money is important for happiness'.

Everybody in the world needs money for not only their basic needs but also for other needs. Hence, there is no harm in earning money as per capacity and need. Swami Vivekananda once said that earning money is a duty for the family men. But need is a relative term. There is no limit to need. 'Give me more' has become the philosophy of this age. This never-ending demand makes many people money-earning machines and forever unhappy. Happiness comes from fulfilment of physical, emotional, and mental needs. These are fulfilled by the three equal and independent parts of wealth: economic, social, intellectual. Money is the main component of the economic part of wealth. So, money is one of the important resources that is needed for happiness.

Indian philosophy always teaches us how to be satisfied with limited resources. A man needs a minimum amount of wealth for survival and to lead a dignified life. So, we should be satisfied with whatever money, amenities, power and resources which are available to us as per our highest capacity. There is no trouble in trying our best for all out success and upliftment. But when the final outcome is decided, we should accept it with satisfaction that we have done our best. This will also make us happy.

We should also remember that many people have less money or resources than us. They have less food, clothes and other basic needs for survival and for leading a dignified life. But they are still happy. You may wonder why. It is obvious that they are happy with the money they have. They thank God and are always obliged to Him for what wealth they possess. They never blame anybody or compare themselves with anybody. They are contended and satisfied with what they have. However, if they did not even have this much of wealth, they may have faced various issues in life which could bring unhappiness. They may lose the opportunity to fulfil their aspirations and always regret this matter later on in life. An example is a typical rural farmer who cannot progress in life due to his inability to get loans from financial institutions, as he cannot furnish collateral to guarantee the loan. Thus, lack of such wealth will cause permanent unhappiness.

Thank you

Against the Motion

Respected Principal, honourable teachers and my worthy opponents. Today, I am here to express my views against the motion 'Money is important for happiness'.

Most individuals are of the view that a good amount of wealth results in happiness, while some believe that being very rich has its own problems. I agree that a lot of money always brings with it many unforeseen problems as well.

Money and its vicious power to attract humans to fulfil their various wishes, at any cost, has always been debated. Earning sufficient money for one's basic needs and amenities, as well as to fulfil their family obligations and provide them with suitable comforts of a modern life, are very much justifiable. However, the problem is that more wealth leads to a feeling of greed and a sense of invincibility amongst family and peers. As a result, a sense of suspicion, envy and jealousy creeps in within social relationships and takes a heavy toll on family matters as well. For instance, the recent war of words in public between two wealthy brothers, due to difference of opinion, for sharing and taking control of the vast business empire left over by their father. Such instances, due to fear of personal financial loss, lead to a permanent damage in relationships and split among members of a family.

Secondly, gaining more financial clout, and enjoying the material luxuries the world has to offer, comes with its own set of sacrifices. Many high-earning corporate CEOs and senior level management at most large companies struggle with their daily hectic work schedules and get overburdened by the responsibilities, with the only aim of maximising the profit at any cost. This results into them not being able to devote enough time to their family and friends, as well as a deterioration of their physical and mental well-being, and later lead to life-threatening diseases. A recent survey showed that more than 40 per cent of top executives in India are suffering from high-blood pressure and stress related issues.

In conclusion, I believe that having too much money not only leads to issues in personal and family relationships, but also deprives one of a healthy and peaceful way of life that can be enjoyed with just sufficient money.

Thank you

6. **For the Motion**

Respected Principal, honourable teachers and my dear friends. Today, I am here to express my views in favour of the motion 'The use of mobile phones must be allowed in schools'.

Students enjoy learning with technology, so our educational environment has to be tailored based on the technologies. Cellphones can be of great use in schools if they are well integrated. The integration of technology in classroom is a good idea as cellphones can be used for educational purposes. Today, we have smart phones which can perform task as performed by a normal computer. Students can use cellphones to access library content, download and read e-books, engage in classroom polls, etc.

The teachers should give students more educational assignments or activities which require using cellphones. This can shift a student's interest from using cellphones to text each other to use it gain more knowledge.

The people who say using cellphone is bad must realise that it is very hard for the schools to enforce that cellphones are not allowed and students will bring them any ways.

So, it is better to make the students use the cellphones constructively. Cellphones can make the children organise, can improve their safety as they will be able to contact people in medical and safety related incidents. If we trust our children with computers, we must trust them with cellphones too. Many students share photos and videos with friends using social platform. So, a student can record all lectures using a cellphone and share them with friends who were not able to attend school. Teachers can assign homework tasks to their students using cellphone which can be time saving both for teachers and students.

Thank you

Against the Motion

Respected Principal, honourable teachers and my dear friends. Today, I am here to express my views against the motion "The use of mobile phones must be allowed in schools."

Allowing cellphones to school would be equivalent to giving an open invitation to distractions. This is because mobile phone can be a big distraction for youngsters as instead of paying attention to teachers, they would be busy playing with their cellphones. Not only this, with a cellphone in every child's hands, there would be an unhealthy competition to see who has got the latest model and the hottest brand.

In school, children use mobile phones to send text messages. They spend time playing games. Some of the students put on their earphones and listen to songs while the teacher is explaining the subject related to matter. In the past, there have been instances of children making inappropriate videos of other children.

At this age, the mind is tender and gets influenced easily. Cellphones can be seen as a means used by students for cheating during examinations. They can simply text anyone and ask for assistance. Moreover, mobile phones spoil the healthy and learning school decorum. Schools are meant for imparting education, knowledge and life skills. Thus, the cellphones should not be allowed inside the school premises.

If teachers have to make a call, they can use school landline or if a kid needs to call their parents, they would be allowed to use the landline. The children must be guided and counselled by the teachers and parents about how to use cellphones judiciously. School authorities must monitor children. Discussions can be done to make the children aware of the advantages and disadvantages of using mobile phones in schools.

Thank you

7. **For the Motion**

Respected Principal, honourable teachers and my dear friends. Today, I am here to express my views in favour of the motion 'All girls or all boys schools provide a better learning environment than co-educational schools'.

It has been noted that an all-girls or all-boys school can provide a more structured learning environment for both boys and girls. Boys and girls differ in the way they act, how they learn and their interests and abilities. They need an educational environment tailored to meet their unique needs. In general, boys are more physically active, assertive and comfortable learning in a more chaotic environment than girls. Girls are able to sit still and prefer a quiet, focused and orderly classroom. In all-girls or all-boys schools, the curriculum and course offerings provide advanced work in areas of the children's greatest interests and natural abilities. Moreover, single-sex schools encourage children to take risks in expressing themselves as they learn without the fear of embarrassing themselves in front of the opposite sex.

Without boys in their classes, girls are more likely to be leaders and reach higher levels of achievement which leads to greater self-confidence and higher professional aspirations. In the secondary and senior secondary classes, single-sex schools remove the distraction of the opposite sex allowing students to focus more seriously on their schoolwork.

A study conducted states that single-sex schools develop greater self-confidence and broader interests especially among adolescents. Girls report that they feel more comfortable, they can interact more with teachers and develop a more favourable attitude towards subjects such as Math and Science.

In addition, schools for boys allow adequate time for male maturation and benefit them by giving them more structure and discipline due to their tendencies of restlessness and aggression.

Furthermore, separating girls and boys fosters an environment of non-stereotyping and encourages learning. It also promotes interest for boys in humanities course and they feel more at ease. It benefits girls as co-educational schools foster obsession over hair and clothes and tend to make them distracted. The students in all girls or boys schools also feel the freedom to attend classes usually associated with the opposite sex, such as in subject Biology.

Thus, in my opinion, all girls and all boys schools provide a better learning environment than co-educational schools.

Thank you

Against the Motion

Respected Principal, honourable teachers and my dear friends. Today, I am here to express my views against the motion 'All girls or all boys schools provide a better learning environment than co-educational schools'.

Co-education for long has been debated in our country.

Education in general sense is a form of learning in which the knowledge, skills, values, beliefs are transferred from the teacher to his disciples. The modes of education do not vary as per the sex of the students. Thus, education cannot be divided on the lines of sex.

When it comes to schools, there are many more important issues than having same sex schools. In fact, the age-old belief of same sex schools being better than co-educational schools has been long dismissed by the impressive results of the latter. Not only have the students of co-educational schools done academically well, but also it has been seen that they are more confident beings than the students of same sex schools. When girls sit along with boys in the same classroom, it helps develop a cordial relation among students and instils in them a spirit of sports, mutual harmony and brotherhood. Moreover, co-ed schools offer a diverse curriculum that is available to all students, de-emphasising gender-linked stereotypes related to course work. Co-ed schools encourage all children to explore a broad range of banning opportunities. Today is an age where men and women work together and compete with each other in offices, homes, etc. thus co-education teaches or prepares them to interact with the opposite sex in the future. Boys and girls learn to respect one another and cooperate as equals. As such, this system of study helps both the boys and girls to improve their confidence and also provides for an excellent foundation in developing realistic and meaningful relationships.

Thank you

8. For the Motion

Respected Principal, honourable teachers and my dear friends. Today I am here to express my views in favour of the motion. 'Boarding schools are far better than day schools for the all-round education of a child'.

Students in a boarding school show better progress and are supposed to be more disciplined. Furthermore, there are many special help programmes available there such as mentor-mentee programme in a boarding school. The purpose of this mentor-mentee system is to provide guidance to students about academic matters and to foster a close and constructive professional relationship between students and the staff of the faculty.

While all lecturers in the faculty are potentially academic advisors to all students who seek their advice, each teacher who is a mentor, is assigned particular responsibility to a small group of students which are the mentees. In day schools, programmes like this are not present.

Moreover, by staying in a boarding school, children will learn to be independent and deal with difficult and tough situations on their own. This is because students, who are in boarding schools, are mostly far apart from their parents. They usually have to make their own decisions, unlike day school students who always depend on their parents. This will help them grow as an individual and bring out the best in them.

Boarding school can also produce individuals who are very creative. This is because they can make students do things that day school students cannot do such as dorm decoration. They need to decorate the dorm with some challenging themes. Moreover, small class size, diverse curricula and individual attention from faculty and advisors give boarding students many distinct advantages so that students can focus on their education well.

At the same time, the teachers can give more attention to individuals who do not understand a topic as the number of students in the class is less. Boarding school reduces compartmentalisation, because academic studies are blended with other activities, such as sports. This natural juxtaposition increases the appeal of both pursuits.

In conclusion, I want to emphasise that boarding schools are better than the normal day schools because it produces individuals who can tackle the real world where their attitude and discipline, determine their success.

Thank you

Against the Motion

Respected Principal, honourable teachers and my dear friends. Today, I am here to express my views against the motion 'Boarding schools are far better than day schools for the all-round education of a child'.

In my opinion, day schools are better than boarding schools. Many day schools offer co-educational facilities and this is an important requirement in terms of today's world. Interacting with the opposite sex in the early years, will enable children to be comfortable in the presence of the opposite sex when they reach a stage where they might have to work alongside them in an official environment.

Although, there may be a few boarding schools that offer co-education, day schools clearly outnumber the boarding schools doing this and co-education in day schools is a much more accepted and existent structure, especially in India.

Day schools are a preferred option as they are much less expensive than a boarding school. Tuition fee in day schools is cheaper. Most of the good quality day schools are relatively cheaper than boarding schools and this is another reason why parents opt for day schools over boarding schools.

Day schools allow parents to admit students in private tuition of their choice as well, in case their children need extra coaching. Most boarding schools in India have fees that is a bit exorbitant and unless parents are willing to fund a new experience and style of education for their children, most average Indian parents prefer day schools. Day schools are a better option for those parents who wish to have close supervision over their children.

Day schools also enable constant parent-teacher contact and this helps the parents monitor the progress of their children in terms of both academic and extracurricular activities. This is also an important aspect of a day school. Parents can provide moral guidance if they are in constant contact with their children and this is possible only if the children are admitted in a day school.

Moreover, if children are used to the comforts of home, they might find it difficult to survive in a boarding school. Day schools enable the children to relax a bit more than boarding schools. In a boarding school, students are required to take part in many events and many students find it difficult to deal with this schedule.

Furthermore, in case of any sickness or injury, parents can be with their children immediately if they are admitted in a day school.

Thank you

9. For the Motion

"The hand that rocks the cradle is the hand that rules the world." It is very true that mothers play an important role in the growth and development of the future generation. These days, there is a fight between two kinds of mother, working and non-working. Mothers are constantly fighting and debating to figure out who is the better parent. In my opinion, an educated and a working woman will have a more positive impact on the child and hence, is more capable of moulding the destiny of the future generation.

Respected Principal, honourable teachers and my dear friends. Today, I am here to express my views in favour of the motion 'Working woman are better mothers'.

Now, when the women are moving shoulder to shoulder with men and moving ahead in life, debating if they are better mothers is like emotionally blackmailing and making them weak.

It is also like accusing them that they are neglecting their responsibility of bringing up their children well. They should not be made to feel small for wanting and working to move forward in their professional life. In the age of equality, women are increasingly encouraged to 'have it all' by balancing their career, children and marriage in order to be seen successful. And still, they are accused.

It's like maintaining a double face. On one hand, people talk about the necessity of a woman to actively participate in the country's economic growth and then when she steps out, they shout that she is not balancing her home and office with the result that her children are running astray.

It is also not necessary that the women who stay at home prove to be perfect or better mothers. The children of mothers who stay at home are more pampered whereas a working mother's children are more disciplined. Also, working mothers are able to guide their children better by providing them with the right amount and kind of exposure.

I think it is not right to constrain and limit women to house-keeping and child-rearing and waste the abundant potential which is within them. We should not, thus, be stuck in tedious arguments about whether women, especially mothers, should or should not work. What is noteworthy is that it is the happiness of a woman we should really be talking about.

Thank you

Against the Motion

Respected Principal, honourable teachers and my dear friends. Today, I am here to express my views against the motion 'Working woman are better mothers'.

If a woman is working outside the home, she can only feed her baby once or twice a day and that is not enough for the well-being of the child.

A child learns by example and so the first school of the child is the home and his first teacher is the mother. If a woman works outside the home, how would she have the energy to tell bed-time stories and moral lessons to the child?

She may not be there at meal-times and the child would have to be kept in the care of a maid. Such a mother won't be able to ensure that her child gets proper nourishment in his all important formative years.

When a woman is at home, she has enough time to spend with her children not because she has less work to do but because, being at home, she is there for the child whenever needed. The children get time to share their problems, happiness, fun and curiosity with their mother. She teaches them manners, traditions and customs. A child's best friend is its mother but if she is too busy taking care of both the home and her job, how would she have the time and energy to be there for the child?

A working woman has to leave her child when it is barely a month old. She remains constantly worried about her child. A child cannot be looked after properly in her absence. As a result, baby-sitters are hired, who often turn out to be a fraud. Moreover, a woman who works outside, suffers from the guilt of not being able to spend enough time with her child. This affects her relationship with the child. She either over-indulges with the child to compensate of the lost time or becomes very strict because she does not want the child to get spoilt.

Hence, I would like to conclude that non-working women make better mothers than working women. If a woman stays at home and looks after children, it is definitely more beneficial for both to her own well-being and that of her children.

Thank you

10. For the Motion

Respected Principal, honourable teachers and my dear friends. Today, I am here to express my views in favour of the motion 'Money cause more harm than good'.

It is a common saying that "Money is the root of all evils". Idealists wonder why we cannot live in a world where everyone is equal and where there is no greed or jealousy resulting from status differences. Unfortunately, they overlook the fact that our desire to have higher status than others is part of human nature and nothing can change it.

Money comes and goes but what stays are memories with our family and friends. Man kills man for money. Abundance rarely brings anything other than increased sorrows, wars, crimes and robbery which is happening because of money. More and more people are finally realising that money cannot bring them the happiness they crave for. A person is not willing to sacrifice his happiness and freedom to obtain economic status. We want certain things and money is necessary to enjoy them happily.

Moreover, money is only needed to provide us with a

safe and comfortable home, food to eat and the ability to visit friends and family other than that one doesn't need more money at all.

There are things that are far more important than having money, things like spending time with family and loved ones, and enjoying what you like to do. Time is more valuable than money, you can get more money but you cannot get more time. If one has to work fifteen hours a day and never gets time to spend with family, friends and spend that money, then what good does it do? You have not lived a perfect day, even though you have earned your money. While money can't buy happiness, it certainly let you choose your own form of misery.

Once our basic needs are met, we find richness in being together and enjoying the simple things. We certainly have to be careful to set our priorities correctly to avoid regrets later in life. Money can help fill a loss of material needs, but learning to be content is far more important. Though money can buy status, friendship or even save you out from a sticky situation but all these evaporate, once your money vanishes. However, time invested in love and quality friendship lasts eternally.

Thank you

Against the Motion

Respected Principal, honourable teachers and my dear friends. Today, I am here to express my views against the motion 'Money causes more harm than good.'

In my opinion, money is an essential commodity that helps us run our life. Without money, people will stop working with eagerness.

When there is equality everywhere, the determination to work will decrease. A person, who works hard, will get the same benefit as a person who is lazy. Hence, it will be wrong. Ultimately, everyone will stop working and there will be no progress, no development and everything will come to a stand still.

I would like to state that though money is not everything but money is something very important. Beyond the basic needs, money helps us achieve our life's goals and support the things we care about the most—family, education, healthcare, charity, adventure and fun. It helps us get some of life's intangibles—freedom or independence, the opportunity to make the most of our skills and talents, the ability to choose our own course in life, financial security and much more. With money, much good can be done and much unnecessary suffering can be avoided or eliminated.

However, with money people choose these positions because they are not motivated or qualified enough to do anything else. Money is simply a representation of the value of work. Certainly, work doesn't cause more harm than good! People do misjudge the value of some work compared to others but this is a fault of our values and assessment of how to value work–it's not the fault of money.

Moreover, it is money that creates respect and honour for someone. It is money that tames the most shrewed people. Money can give us the power to make a difference in the lives of others. It gives us the time to develop and nurture our relationships.

Thus, I would like to conclude by saying that it is a requirement of life in a society to be able to exchange goods, ideally through a universal token such as money, just like it is a requirement of life as an individual to be surrounded by air to breathe.

Thank you

11. For the Motion

Respected Principal, honourable teachers and my dear friends. Today, I am here to express my views in favour of the motion 'Private tuitions are a necessary evil'.

Private tuition is a part of the learning process that has become a backbone and a big part of our system of education. Private tuition has existed for decades and will always exist because we have a system of education which is coupled with competition.

Without that additional coaching, it is not easy for a student to compete with their classmates. Very often what they get in class is highly inadequate for them to clear the competitive exams. To be successful, they are compelled to seek extra coaching outside school hours to stay in the race to pass the finishing line.

Today, the syllabus taught in class is not sufficient for those who are in quest for knowledge or who are on the competitive track. Very often, the teacher finds themselves in front of an uncooperative class who deliberately puts a spoke in their wheel and makes their work a real ordeal. A teacher, in spite of all the skills and competence, if does not get the cooperation of the class, is utterly unable to make progress and is never able to deliver good.

Therefore, those who are in search of knowledge, are compelled to have recourse to private tuition.

Moreover, private tuition helps in improving the performance of the child. It can be complementary when the lessons done in the class have not been fully understood by the student.

Generally, a classroom is not conductive to individual teaching. The teacher-pupil interaction highly spoken of is not possible in the class due to large class-size. A teacher normally tries to avoid a dull student. So, such a student may fail to catch the eye of the teacher. In such cases, private tuition may be helpful. The pupil may not only be taught, but also made to work at exercises which they would normally avoid in class.

If the tuition teacher is earnest, the pupils can progress and improve gradually.

Some of the topics that are not covered in the class or which require supplementary reading could very well be done in the tuition hour. Additional exercises could be done, better reading is possible which may lead to better understanding. Thus, private tuitions are necessary as they provide the needful things to the students.

Thank you

Against the Motion

Respected Principal, honourable teachers and my dear friends. Today, I am here to express my views against the motion 'Private tuitions are a necessary evil'.

In earlier days, tuition was not necessary as education was not so emphasised. But, now-a-days, many students prefer to go to tuition because they believe that it helps achieve success in examination. They may sign up for tuition either because they are forced by their parents or just out of their own willingness. Some students decide on studying by themselves. However, deciding on taking tuition has great pros and cons on student's achievement and life.

Private tuition makes a child depend more on the teachers and the notes they give rather than on himself. Children, who take tuitions, give stereotype answers because they don't use their own mind to produce answers rather they become machines of learning answers.

Private tuition can be a financial burden to parents who are poor. Taking tuitions is very expensive as well and not everyone can afford to send their children for extra private tuition.

According to research, those children, who take tuitions, don't study seriously in the class because they feel that they can learn and grasp the topics while taking tuitions. This way they disturb the whole class and also waste the time of serious minded students. Now a days, we can see that lots of teachers are more inclined in giving private tuitions as it has become a source of extra income for them but this is completely against the noble profession of teaching. Teacher should make a target to set the maximum output in the class/school so that the tuition trend fades away and every child can get an equal opportunity to learn from his teachers.

Moreover, tutors provide additional homework on top of those given by the teachers in school. Sometimes, tutors do arrive at the wrong timing. For instance, students are not in the mood to learn or have gone through a hard day work in school and are, therefore, mentally tired. Despite such a bad timing, the tuition sessions may still have to carry on, which make it unfruitful.

Some students treat their tutors as a walking dictionary, expecting them to furnish answers to the homework given by school without thinking through the solutions by themselves over time. This can make them mentally lazy.

Thus, in my opinion private tuitions are not mandatory.

Thank you

12. For the Motion

Respected Principal, honourable teachers and my dear friends. Today, I am here to express my views in favour of the motion 'More lessons are learnt on the sports field than in the classroom'.

In a student's life, extracurricular activities empower them to make their own active decisions and also help them gain an accurate experience, skills and confidence to lead them on the path of their future. It is considered true that through participation in sports and different games, students learn cooperation, teamwork, leadership skills and time management. If you consider deeply, the sports field is a minifield of life.

Whatever we experience or learn here serves to be an invaluable experience to us for life. Sports foster friendship and cooperation. Sportsmen forget caste and religious differences and become friendly with one another.

Often sportsmen have to live together while undergoing training and participating in competitions. They understand one another and learn to make the adjustments in life. In other words, they learn the virtue of tolerance. Moreover, when they go to other countries to participate in international competitions, they are not merely competitors but the messengers of goodwill. This way, they spread goodwill and love throughout the world.

Furthermore, young people have surplus energy and if this is fruitfully utilised, the foundations are laid for a healthy society, where people are fully aware of the need for discipline, cooperative effort, team spirit, etc.

They also learn to cultivate the vital quality of learning how to work as a team, to become not only good winners, but also good losers. The statement "The battle of Waterloo was won on the play fields of Eton" implies that playing games and the spirit of sportsmanship helps inculcate lasting values, which make us good citizens, apart from promoting 100 per cent physical fitness.

Sports also teach us that failure does not mean absolute doom. It simply gives us the courage to rise and fight again. Perhaps failure makes us tougher for the next round of fight. Moreover, sports naturally instructs people to play the game of life with its right spirit, which is what matters most, not victory or defeat.

Thus, in many ways, the education we receive and the lessons we learn from sports outweigh what we learn in our classrooms.

Thank you

Against the Motion

Respected Principal, honourable teachers and my dear friends. Today, I am here to express my views against the motion 'More lessons are learnt on the sports field than in classroom'.

As more time is spent on sports field, no time is left to pay attention to the academics. The student gets stressed due to non-performance in the academic field and many times their frustration can be noticed in their playing strategy.

Due to tough competition, every team wants to win. Instead of learning tolerance, the players develop a habit of recoursing to unprofessional tricks so that their team could win.

So, many times, instead of being tolerant and full of competition spirit, the player adheres to unethical practises, which in longer run, harms them.

Sports does teach lessons to the children but not always good ones. Many children are not naturally talented and only come across failure and embarrassment on the sports field. This may hurt their confidence and may put them off any sort of exercise for life. Many other activities can teach team work and other life skills, e.g. hiking and camping, playing in a land or raising money for charity, etc.

Sports make people too competitive and encourage the worst side of human nature. Apart from this, sports encourage cheating, disrespecting opposite team members and referee and drug abuse. These problems are worse in professional sports where the need to make money adds further pressure to win by any means. Too much competition can lead to stress and depression and thus affects a person mentally and physically.

Thank you

13. Good morning to one and all present here.

Mobile phones undoubtedly, are one of the most spectacular developments, ever to have taken place in the field of telecommunication. They offer the easiest and simplest way to stay connected, with our near and dear ones, thus augmenting and invigorating our social life. However on the contrary, they have actually lowered active social life and have become an addiction for the youth of today.

The young generation is enamoured by this latest gadgetry. Smart phones undisputedly offer many conveniences, like access to the Internet, entertainment, social networking and the ability to use idle time, (time spent in travelling or in leisure) to best use. It is however some of these conveniences that have actually eroded social life.

The urge to stay connected with our own circle of friends and relatives, has made us a social outcast in the society in which we live. It is quite common to find a group of youngsters sitting together in a place talking on phone to people far away, unmindful of the presence of others around. They are thus more concerned and connected to people far away, than to those around them. Such behaviour dissuades them in cultivating new friendship, in the mistaken belief that they are more secure by staying connected to their known circle of friends. This virtual networking, actually weakens their active social life.

The convenience of utilising the idle time also affects us socially. Business executives and professionals are the worst sufferers. They have no time for leisure as they can be called for work whenever the need arises. This not only affects their social life, but also their family life. The ringing of a mobile is a real nuisance on occasions like an important meeting, praying or participating in a funeral.

Nevertheless it is now becoming indispensable and an addiction because of many value added features that provide social networking and entertainment. These features have caught the imagination of the youth who spend hours on their smart phones. According to psychiatrists, this causes compulsive disorders and is one of the biggest non-drug addiction in the 21st century. Spending excessive time with mobiles isolates the person from the society.

Mobile addicts tend to neglect obligations towards family, work or study and drift away from friends. Being victims of low self-esteem, they have problems of developing social relations and are more comfortable in the virtual world. They feel insecure without their phones. In its absence they suffer from anxiety, irritability and sleeplessness. Besides the addictive influence of mobiles, medical research has proved that it can cause serious health hazard for the frequent user.

Undoubtedly mobile phones have made our lives more safe and comfortable. However, like all good things their excessive use has adversely impacted our social life and has now become an addiction.

Against the Motion

Respected Principal, honourable teachers and my dear friends. Today, I am here to express my views against the motion. 'The use of mobile phone has lowered active social life and has become an addiction'.

In my opinion, mobile phones keep one in constant contact with people one considers important. Active social life in the hectic pace of life today has been lowered by our busy schedules not by our mobile phones. On the contrary, mobile phones help us stay connected with our family and friends, regardless of which part of the world they may be living in. In the past, letters and telegrams were the major means of communication. A letter sent from India to a person in the US took a minimum of three weeks to reach and an equal amount of time was taken for its reply to reach India. Even if one tried to call from the land-line, one had to use ISD and STD facilities which may or may not be working and which were prohibitively expensive. Now, the rates are so low and the connectivity so good that we can talk everyday through our mobiles, as we wish.

Moreover, it is easier to visit our loved ones today because all we have to do is call and find out if they are at home and then visit them. Coordinating a party is much easier with the use of mobile phones. Whether, it is reserving a ticket for the railways or for the aeroplane, one need not to stand in a long queue or call an agent as it can be done easily using the internet on the mobile phones. Our life is becoming more and more convenient and the mobile phone has become an indispensable device in our lives. Nothing more than a cell phone comes to great help in an emergency.

Mobiles have also made shopping, navigation and staying up to date possible at the click of a button. Moreover, by using mobiles, parents can be less worried about their kids and stay in constant touch with them. Using mobile phones have made communication easier than before. Thus, mobile phone has become a crucial part of our life. It has made communication easier and quicker. It is not an addiction but a necessity.

Thank you

14. For the Motion

Respected Principal, honourable teachers and my dear friends. Today, I am here to express my views in favour of the motion 'No other subject taught in school is as important as Moral Science'.

In today's rat race, values are eroding fast. Children go to schools daily thinking how to scale heights they will reach, how rich education can make them. In today's cut throat competition, even the parents instruct their wards that they should top in the class. Childhood is a very impressionable age. The mind is like soft wax, so whatever one is taught at a tender age leaves a deep impression.

Therefore, Moral Science must be made a compulsory subject in school curriculum. It is also a science of human soul and a mirror of one's inward mind and one's ethics. Moral science inculcates values in mankind and value education is very vital from childhood. Schools should shoulder the responsibility of imparting moral values to them. In order to make them self-reliant, confident and responsible citizens, they need to be imparted with value based education, which only Moral Science can do. After all, today's child is tomorrow's citizen.

Moral Science is not a religion based subject. Rather it eliminates fanaticism, superstition and violence. It preaches 'Love All, Serve All'. This value is lacking in today's generation. It helps a child to pay heed to their conscience and not to be led away by worldly show. However, theoretical knowledge is not enough. Teachers should make their life exemplary to their students. The lives of great patriots or spiritual leaders must be brought to the forefront. Only moral science can stem the tide of rapid value erosion and motivate the students towards a healthier life. A child is then trained emotionally, mentally and physically how to be a responsible citizen or a good son or daughter. They can resist wrong peer pressure, intolerance, and through right conduct lead forward their nation.

One becomes more understanding, patient, pious, decent and wise. One learns to do things without any selfish motives. Pleasure is derived in doing things for others as one feels that one is doing it for welfare.

Therefore, there can be no doubt about the fact that no other subject taught in school is as important as Moral Science. Let the light of spirituality shine through the eyes of the little ones.

Thank you

Against the Motion

Respected Principal, honourable teachers and my dear friends. Today, I am here to express my views against the motion 'No other subject taught in school is as important as Moral Science'.

I would rather emphasise the point that knowledge is power and this power comes through learning not merely Moral Science but all other subjects prescribed in schools. The study of all the subjects will unravel the vast potentialities that can enrich our life and resolve many mysteries about the universe. Whereas not much effort is required to learn ethics and morality, much mental labour is involved in learning subjects dealing with different branches of learning. Moral Science teaches us about what is morally good or bad which can be learnt spontaneously and instinctively by watching the behaviour of the elders we come across daily.

The great advancement in technology in conquering time and space has been possible because much more emphasis is being laid on the study of science. Now, environmental study is being given more importance and it is made a compulsory subject at all levels of school education.

The harmonious development of a student's personality can only be possible with equal emphasis on the study of all subjects and not becoming isolated by simply meditating on God, Life and Death. Let such things be special subjects of religion and metaphysics to be taken up only by those exclusively interested in this particular branch. The more we learn about other subjects, the richer will be our knowledge.

Thank you

15. ### For the Motion

Respected Principal, honourable teachers and my dear friends. Today, I am here to express my views in favour of the motion 'The computer will soon replace the book'.

Computers have already taken a major role as an information resource today. Computer technologies such as hypertext and the internet remove the geographical constrains of print media and allow for a new method of distributing and reading documents. Books will always be affordable and concrete sources of information but the next ten years will bring computers that are faster to access, convenient to use and hold more information than books. With the internet, one piece of information is accessible from millions of computers around the world. A researcher may need to travel no further than his/her computer to find a document in a virtual library 3000 miles away. In the next 20 years, print media may not be able to keep up with the exponential growth of information because the density of information on a computer is far greater than that of a book, the internet already holds more data than any physical library. A typical computer hard drive can hold around 2000 novels. In addition to their seemingly unlimited storage capacity, computers also provide much faster access to information, e.g. looking upwards in a dictionary might take a few minutes while computers can give the definition for any word and pronounce it for you immediately. The computer's speed and space will make it a necessary technology as we move into a new millennium.

The future will bring even greater advantages to the computer over the book. Soon, computers will have screens that are crisper and more comfortable to view than a printed book. With new technology, computer screens will no longer strain the eyes and it will become feasible.

Technology will soon produce a computer that is as compact, durable and comfortable to read as a book but that could contain thousands of books in electronic form. Although computers will never completely supplement books, we may soon rely on them more than books. Computers will meet our needs of information storage and distribution and will be a convenient way to hold more information in less space than today's book.

Thank you

Against the Motion

Respected Principal, honourable teachers and my dear friends. Today, I am here to express my views against the motion 'The computer will soon replace the book'.

Computer, any day, is far more expensive than books. Unlike books, it needs power through batteries and mains to work. One cannot lie in bed and read them leisurely and if milk or syrup spills on them, the damage could be much more. Computers can get infected by viruses and are not completely dependable but a book in a shelf is very dependable. It does not make you strain your eyes as computers do.

Moreover, with the help of computers, students simply copy-paste and the matter is complete. The pride of a library and collecting the first edition as well as autographed books of an author will have no relevance. A book reveals the nature of a person but with a computer no one can know who is an avid reader and who is not.

A book somehow has a sense of belongingness. The printed book can easily be read and stored. Students can write their notes and refer to them at any time. The computer troubles its users, while a book is perfect for relaxation. The joy of placing your hands on a book and reading through its pages is ecstatic and can never be for replaced by computer. One can even sleep with a book on one's bedside and wake up in the morning to continue reading.

No one is going to put computers into the hands of kindergarten students and moreover not everyone can afford to have a computer. So, let's forget about such an idea and live realistically. Books may have their limitation but they can never be superseded by computers. No one wants to lose the joy of reading a book and at the end pronouncing to himself that, 'It is finished'.

Thank you

16. For the Motion

Respected Principal Sir, staff members and dear students. Today, I am going to speak in the favour 'Using your own transport is better than using public transport'.

'Why not use it, when one has it?'

Everywhere, it has been suggested that the public transports should be used or rather it should be the first choice of the passanger. I feel that if the whole city starts using the public transport, how is it going to work?

Let's take the metro for an example. A metro has six to eight coaches to accommodate the crowd, but what will happen if the whole city gets stuffed in those eight coaches. It will become very suffocating for the passangers which can easily lead to dizziness. There are full chances of the people falling sick in the long run. Moreover, there are huge jams because of these public transport, as the rickshawalas and autowalas park their vehicles anywhere and that is the root cause of all the jams, as half of the roads are covered by them.

Similarly, the public buses move in a very haphazard manner stuffing people. The crowd is a mix of people from all backgrounds and there is a huge possibility of the pick pockets robbing people, stealing their money or valuables.

If one doesn't have a vehicle or cannot afford one, one is left with the only option of using public transport but when one can afford a vehicle, one should always use it for convenience.

Using own vehicle saves a lot of time and is safer than travelling in public transport.

If one owns a vehicle, one doesn't have to think much about going to a place all of a sudden, whereas using the public transport in times of urgency involves a lot of time and physical activity like changing from one platform to another.

So, for the sake of convenience and comfort, one should always use and prefer one's own transport over the public transports.

Thank you

For the Motion

Respected Principal Sir, staff members and Dear student. Today, I am going to speak in the against motion 'Using your own transport is better than using public transport'.

Today, we, the people of 21st century, roam as freely as the birds do. We reach wherever we want to go in no time and without giving much thought to it. This is possible because of our efficient public transport system.

Earlier, travelling used to be such a big matter of concern because of inefficient public transport system and non-availability of metro and low floor buses. As a result, people had to use their own transport and this not only increased the number of vehicles on road but also the pollution levels. With the exponential increase in the number of private vehicles, the traffic jams on the roads became common and this led to the wastage of one's time and money.

Now, with the evolution of the public transport, everyone finds it convenient to travel by metro and low floor buses. This is also cheaper and more time saving than using one's own vehicle. As more and more people use the public transport, the traffic on the road is reduced to a great extent and so is the pollution.

Travelling in the public transport also helps one in remaining physically fit as it involves a lot of physical activity. In order to catch a bus or a metro, a person needs to walk quite a lot and this adds to their physical activity.

Whereas, on the other hand, the usage of one's vehicle makes one lazy as one gets used to the comfort of it and hence detests any kind of physical activity. Public transport is cheaper than using one's own vehicles for commuting. It also saves one from the unnecessary stress and exertion that happens while driving one's vehicle.

Thus, in my opinion, public transport is a blessing in disguise and we must make full use of it.

Thank you

SELF ASSESSMENT

1. Schools and businesses should give more incentives for people to do volunteer work'; Express your views for or against the motion.
2. "Teenagers today are more worldly-wise than their parents." Explain your views for or against the motion.
3. "Advertisements for alcohol and tobacco products should be allowed". Express your views for or against the motion.
4. "The commercialisation of festivals has eroded their real significance." Express your views either for or against the statement.
5. "High schools should provide daycare services for teachers who have children." Express your views for or against the motion.
6. "All the schools should make it a requirement to teach arts and music to their students." Express your views for or against the motion.
7. "Posting student's grades on bulletin boards publicly motivates them to perform better." Express your views for or against the motion.
8. "Schools should conduct mandatory drug testing on their students." Express your views for or against the motion.
9. "All the parents should be required to attend parenting classes before having a child." Express your views for or against the motion.
10. "Admission to tep institutes guarantees a successful career." Express your views for or against the motion.

CHAPTER

4

Short Story

Story writing is a creative but difficult art of composition. It requires a lot of creative thinking, planning and mastery of narrative skills and language. A short story is a narrative of moderate length that revolves around a single incident involving one or more characters. It must have a proper beginning, middle and an end. A story needs to be well-planned and written in an interesting manner. In the examination, word-limit for the short story is 300-350 and its weightage is 20 marks.

Steps to Write a Short Story

There are no specific rules for writing a story, but there are countless ways to create an interesting one.

- To write an interesting story, the writer must think like the central character to get or catch his/her emotions and qualities.
- As a story is a short description of any scene or incident, the details should be mentioned creatively to develop a reader's interest.
- While building the plot of the story, the writer should make sure that the sequence of events is proper, to avoid confusion and complexity.
- A very important part of the story is an apt ending to add significance to it. A justified climax is an unsaid expectation of the readers.

Points to be Kept in Mind While Writing a Story

- Before writing, concentrate on the topic and story outline.
- Story should be written in an easy and comprehensible language.
- The style of writing should be lucid and logical.
- Events should be chronologically organised in the story.
- Write a story in past tense. However, as per the requirement present or future tense can also be used.
- Focus should be only on the central incident.
- Add twist to your story to keep the readers intact.
- Consequences/climax of the story should be clear and satisfying.

Sample Story 1

Write an original short story entitled 'The Gift'. *[2018]*

Ans. **The Gift**

The story begins about two months ago when I had just given the final exams of my BCA degree. I would become a graduate in about two months' time, when the results would be declared. After this, my father wanted me to take over running of our family's computer sales and service showroom, as he was keeping in bad health. My birthday was falling two days after the last paper of my exam was scheduled. For a few weeks, I had been admiring a new model of a Royal Enfield Bullet bike in a dealer's showroom. I had told my father that it was all I wanted for my 21st birthday. On the morning of my birthday, my father called me into his office in the computer showroom.

He first wished me a happy birthday and then told me how much he loved me. He opened his desk drawer, brought out a gift wrapped rectangular box and presented it to me. Curious, but somewhat disappointed, I opened the box and found a leather-bound Bhagwad Gita in it. I got very angry at him, so I blurted out, "With all your money, you gave me a book?" Then, I decided to leave my home (my mother had passed away two years ago and I had no siblings) and stormed out of the house, leaving the gift on his desk.

I went to live with one of my close friends who was working and staying in an independent flat. I started looking for a job while awaiting my result. However, after a month, I got the information that my father had suffered a heart attack and was hospitalised. I rushed to the hospital, but it was too late. He had passed away.

Soon, our family lawyer phoned and told me that in his will, my father had left me all his possessions including the ownership of our computer business. With a heavy heart, I went through his papers and soon found the Bhagwad Gita he had given me. It was still gift-wrapped. In tears, I opened the packing and began to turn the pages. Suddenly, a key taped to a small envelope dropped from the book. It had a tag with the dealer's name, the same dealer in whose showroom I had seen the bike I wanted. On the tag was the date of my birthday and the words 'Paid in full'.

Sample Story 2

Write an original short story that begins with the words "It was raining hard that night. In my hurry to get into the house, I didn't notice the black car parked across the road, I realised something was wrong when....." *[2017]*

Ans. **A Pleasant Surprise**

It was raining hard that night. In my hurry to get into the house, I didn't notice the black car parked across the road I realised something was wrong when I heard strange muffled voices coming from inside the car. Was I being followed? Were there some robbers sitting inside that car ready to undertake robbery in any one of the houses or what was it?

I was really terrified when suddenly I saw a man all dressed in black or should I say a dark hidden figure getting out of the car. He didn't even look like a human being. He turned his head and I quickened my pace. "He must've noticed me", I thought while I was shivering from the coldness and fear. As soon as I tried to ring the bell of the house, that man called out, "Excuse me". I was terrified at that man's call and wanted to run away but could not. The man asked me if I knew a mechanic nearby as he was a stranger to this city and was heading towards Delhi, where his mother was admitted in a hospital. I was still not sure whether I should trust that man but, at the same time, my father opened the door.

I just decided to go inside the house when my father happened to have a glance at that stranger. Suddenly, my father screamed with excitement, "Oh Shreekant! How come you are here? You had disappeared so suddenly." That man looked at my father and came running towards him and screamed, "Oh Pulkit, is this your house? Are you settled in this city?" My father replied him in affirmation and further asked him to come inside as the weather was really bad. I was totally confused as I didn't know the stranger and my father was asking him to come inside. My father introduced me to that man, who was his class fellow some 22 years back. After finishing college, they had not been in touch with each other. My father was really excited meeting his old class fellow. He called a mechanic to get his car repaired and invited him to stay and rest till the rain got over. So, initially what was scary for me, turned out to be a pleasant surprise for my father.

EXAM PRACTICE

1. Write an orginal short story in which two children and their school teacher are the main characters. *[2023]*
2. Write a short story in which the main characters are an old woman, a small child and a little puppy. *[Sem II 2022]*
3. Write an original short story entitled 'The Secret'. *[2020]*
4. Write an original short story in which two children and their grandfather are the main characters. *[2019]*
5. Write an original short story that begins with the words "The day started off well enough, whoever thought it would ...." *[2016]*
6. Write an original story that begins with the words "He was the funniest boy I had ever met. He would make everyone laugh ....". *[2015]*
7. Write an original short story that begins with the words "It's not my fault", he shouted .... *[2014]*
8. Write an original short story that begins with the words "In the background, I could hear an awful commotion, men's voices raised and women screaming ...." *[2013]*
9. Write an original short story that begins with the words "It wasn't going to be easy she knew but somehow she had to confront him. She took a deep breath and walked into the room........." *[2012]*
10. Write an original story entitled "Lost and Found" *[2011]*
11. Write an original short story that begins with the words "This story pertains to ...."
12. Write a short story to illustrate the proverb 'Knowledge is power'.
13. Write a story that concludes with the sentence 'Every cloud has a silver lining.'
14. Write an original short story that begins with the words "I was returning to India after having completed my studies from abroad. The yearning to meet my parents and friends grew ...."
15. Write a short story entitled 'Escaped'.
16. Write a story that ends with the words '......... would not have to go through all this.

Answers

1. **The Best Friends**

Ramu and Suresh were really good friends. They had been classmates since they started school and loved to create mischief. They always pranked teachers but their pranks never hurt anyone. Though they were pranksters of the school, they were loved by all. One could find them playing sports in the field, working on projects together and even participating in debates taking opposite stands.

Once their English Teacher Mr. Sullivan had read the poem 'The Tale of Custard the Dragon' in the class and started a discussion on bravery. The discussion was healthy till a classmate stated that Suresh was not as brave as he showed and told the class that Suresh was sacred of lightening. Suresh who was sitting quietly got upset when Ramu did not defend him. He asked Ramu to do the same but Ramu did not say a word. Thus, it led to a fight between the best friends.

Mr. Sullivan got worried for he did not want the best friends to fight over something as trivial as this. So, he called the boys and explained the situation to them but in vain. The boys did not even want to talk to each other. So, Mr. Sullivan decided to play a small prank on the boys to prove his statement. He called the boys to the banned part of their Convent School which was claimed to be haunted.

When the boys reached the area, the door of the room closed and strand sounds came from the room. The boys were scared and started beating the door so anyone could hear them. But no one came to help them. They even looked out to find a way to escape the haunted room and saw a window with a broken pane. Together they rushed towards it and helped each other escape the room. When they were finally out of the room, they hugged each other for both of them were safe. Outside they saw Mr. Sullivan who was standing with a smile. He told the boys about his plan to reunite them and explained that Ramu had requested him for the discussion so that Suresh learns to defend himself and be bold. Ramu told Suresh how he had heard other call Siuresh a wimp and wanted Suresh to prove them wrong. Suresh easily understood Ramu's explanation and apologised for starting the fight.

2. The Lost Puppy

A little girl named Sophie found a puppy near a tree when she was returning home from school. The puppy looked weak and was afraid of people passing by. She went close to him and he stepped back a little. He tried to hide behind the tree. Seeing this, Sophie took out a water bottle and a packet of biscuits from her bag and offered them to the puppy. The puppy hungrily ate the biscuits and drank the water. Meanwhile, Sophie was patting the puppy. It seemed that he liked it as he started wagging his tail. Sophie found that one of the legs of the puppy was hurt, so she took him to a veterinary clinic and got him medicines and band aids. Suddenly, Sophie noticed a name written on puppy's collar indicating that he was someone's pet.

She went to nearby homes where she found the puppy but could not find his owner. Since no one was there to look after the puppy, she decided to take him home.

On reaching home, she gave him a bath, cleaned him thoroughly and put medicine on his injury. She took great care of him. Meanwhile, she also put up an advertisement in the locality so that Tabby the puppy's name as written on his collar, could reach his real owner. After a few days of advertisement, an old lady came up to Sophie and told her that she was Tabby's owner. The lady told her that she went out for a couple of days and left her puppy with the neighbours.

But he ran from their house and ended up meeting Sophie. Tabby also started licking the lady's face happily. Seeing this, Sophie was sure that Tabby belonged to the lady. He happily went away with her. Sophie would visit the old lady's house whenever she missed him.

3. The Secret

Rohan was a fun-loving teenager. He was fourteen years old and a student of eighth standard in a reputed school. His happy family included his parents and his seven years old sister, Rhea. His father was a doctor and mother was a homemaker. One day, Rohan found a diary in their storeroom while playing with his sister. The diary had an attractive leather cover with golden border. He took it and kept it in his bookrack.

The next day, Rohan opened the diary and found that it was an old secret diary that belonged to his mother. He started reading it. It contained beautiful description of his mother's childhood, her village, ancestral home, etc. Next he found the description of the marriage ceremony of his parents and their new life. But the real surprise waited for him. After a few pages, it was written that he was the adopted child of his parents. They adopted him from an orphanage five years into their marriage. This secret left him absolutely shattered. He felt betrayed and ran away from home immediately.

Rohan roamed for many hours. Being exhausted, he sat on a bench in a park. There, he saw an old lady coming with a large tiffin-box. She distributed puri-aloo to all poor children. All the children called her 'Amma' (mother). After finishing their meal, they started reading. Again, the old lady helped them.

Suddenly, Rohan realised that his parents were so caring and loved him unconditionally. They never differentiated between him and his sister, who was their biological child. They always fulfilled his every wish. He realised his mistake and returned home. His anxious mother asked him where he had gone for such a longtime. He replied that he was very busy with his cricket match and didn't pay heed to the time. She served his favourite meal, Rajma-chawal. Rohan realised it was his real home and decided that he would never think about the 'secret' anymore.

4. What Sarita Did with Grandfather's Coins

Every month, Sarita and her younger cousins would go for Sunday lunch at their grandparents' house.

The children would always wait excitedly for the moment their grandfather would give them a few coins, so that they could buy something for themselves. Then, all the children would run off to buy chewing gum, ice cream or potato chips. The adults in the family felt that the children would never learn to manage their money. So, they told the children that they would have to show, over a period of one year, just what they could manage to get with those few coins.

The two smallest children paid no attention to this and continued spending the coins on sweets. However, Ajit, who was ten years old, had a will of iron. He saved all the coins he was given. At the end of the year, he had collected more money than anyone. He won the competition hands down. His cousins learnt from him the advantages of knowing how to save and be patient.

The eldest cousin was 12-year-old Sarita. Poor Sarita didn't enjoy the end of the competition because even though she had had a wonderful secret plan, she had spent her money without giving her plan enough time to work. But that didn't stop her from continuing with her plan.

When she was about to complete the second year of her plan, Sarita surprised everyone by turning up at her grandparents' house with a guitar and a lot of money. Her playing was even more impressive. She did it really well.

Then, Sarita told how she did it. She had got to know a poor guitarist who played in the park. She offered him all the coins her Grandfather had given her if he would teach her how to play. On seeing Sarita's excitement, the guitarist agreed, and he taught her happily for months. Then, the guitarist loaned her a guitar so they could play together in the park, as a duo. They were so successful that gradually she managed to buy her own guitar.

Sarita would always tell people how it was possible, with just a few coins well spent, to make your wildest dreams a reality.

5. An Unpredictable Day

The day started off well enough, whoever thought it would end otherwise. We were going to Mumbai to spend a week with my elder sister who was settled there. We had booked the plane tickets in advance. My younger sister and I were very happy and excited, so we reached the airport well in advance. Finally, the flight time approached and the formalities were completed. We were just about to board the plane when a loud announcement terrified us. "All passengers about to board INDIGO/75A flight should immediately deboard and gather in the waiting hall. The flight is cancelled." It was 11 o'clock and I could see the dark airport road outside. Suddenly, an old lady came rushing and said, "There is a time bomb and some terrorists are suspected to be inside the airport." We all were very scared and prayed for our safety. Suddenly, there was a commotion as security personnels were running after someone. As the person was running with great speed, the police was not able to apprehend the suspect terrorist.

He was holding a gun in his hand and as he passed the hall where people had been gathered, he started shooting randomly. An old lady who could not move or act very fast became the first victim. I was extremely terrified but kept my cool and decided to help the police. As the terrorist was shooting and running, it became very difficult to catch him. I just bent down and slowly started crawling towards the suspect. As his back was turned towards me, I pointed the security personnel to come closer.

Still bent down, I pushed him hard in the legs. His gun fell down and immediately he was overtaken by the security personnels. The suspect was very angry and tried to catch hold of me but, because of security personnels, he was captured and taken to a secret place where officers would interrogate him.

I was surrounded by people in the hall, who congratulated for my presence of mind and courage. As our flight was cancelled and we were too terrified to travel the next day, we decided to return home. I was so excited that morning but never knew the adventure I would of live through by the end of the day.

6. Time Heals Everything

He was the funniest boy I had ever met. He would make everyone laugh even in the most trying times. Blessed with a funny nature, Varun would make everyone forget his/her worries in his company. No amount of sadness could dampen his spirit.

I remember once, three of us friends including Varun had failed the chemistry exam badly. Our parents had been called and we were told that we would have to repeat a year. That was a very hard time but even then no look of worry could be spotted on Varun's face or in his behaviour. His cheer remained undiminished even when his father suffered a major financial loss in business. Even during that time, Varun was known to spread cheer around. He always pushed his worries to the backseat and dedicated himself towards making others happy.

However, the loss of Varun's pet Veeto, some months ago, immersed him in grief. That was the only time that robbed him of his smiling face. For days, he did not speak to anyone and shut himself up in his room. We could not see him like that, so all of us friends decided to do something to dispel his gloom.

One day, we all went to his place and rang the door bell of his house. There we kept a little box, slightly open from one side and hid ourselves so that he could not see us. When he opened the door, he was surprised to find no one. He picked up the box with a look of amazement on his face. He took the lid off, and there came out a pug, quite like Veeto. He held it in his hands and started to play with it. It brought his smile back. Then, we all came into the sight and shouted with excitement, 'Surprise!'

Indeed, that little effort from our end helped Varun come out of his sorrow.

7. Misplacing of Camera

"It's not my fault," he shouted as he went across to the opposite bank of the river in the boat. He was very annoyed with his friends, who accused him of forgetting the camera at a coffee shop.

He was a teenage boy, who came with his friends on a school trip. I came here because this place was a famous tourist spot. It was famous for its scenery and numerous water sports besides the folk dance of the locals. It was really fascinating to see how one could enjoy a whole world of entertainment here. However, I was curious to know more about the teenage boy. Several questions came in my mind-Whose camera was it? What made him forget the camera? Did he go to find it?

Therefore, to settle my curiosity, I enquired about him from the children who came on the same school trip. I came to know that his name was Rohan. He belonged to a middle class family. He was passionate about photography. Another child informed me that some of his friends were quite rich. One of his friends named Ankit brought his camera on the trip. Because Rohan clicked beautiful pictures, his friend gave his camera to him. After every click, Rohan used to return the camera to his friend, Ankit. But, Ankit was very irresponsible.

After clicking pictures in the coffee shop, Rohan placed the camera in Ankit's hands. Ankit however kept it out on the table. They sat there for a while and then left the place. When they crossed a beautiful temple, they thought of getting some pictures clicked. It was then that everyone realised that the camera was missing. Ankit and others started blaming Rohan for misplacing the camera. Rohan felt humiliated and left his group.

I felt pity for Rohan and wanted to help him. I went to the coffee shop and narrated the entire incident. The manager of the coffee shop was a genuine man. He ordered his staff to find the camera. Suddenly, one of the staff members remembered that one of those boys went to the washroom while leaving. The camera was found in the washroom. I took it and returned it to Ankit. He then realised his mistake and apologised to Rohan.

8. Tremulous Fire

In the background, I could hear an awful commotion, men's voices raised and women screaming. I was at a loss to understand what the matter was. I tried to ignore and sleep, but the voices became too loud. I could hardly sleep. I was so irritated that I threw my sheet and rushed towards the window. I was aghast to find thick black clouds of smoke emanating in the sky. I was sure that something terrible had happened.

The whole scenario was one of chaos as hundreds of people were rushing in and out of their homes with buckets full of water. They tried to extinguish the fire, but to no avail. Huge flames of fire leapt into the sky making the scene look tremulous and terrifying.

I rushed into my parents' room and woke them up. They were fast asleep, as their room was in the back. They too were totally bewildered after I gave them the news. We rushed downstairs and joined the crowd which was besirk with shrieks and clamours. While some people were running desperately for water, some fainted due to suffocation.

On enquiring, we came to know that the multi-storeyed building was caught in a blazing fire, due to a short circuit. I could see a lot of smoke coming out of its many floors but nothing seemed to be clearly visible.

The entire building was disastrously caught in fire, without any possibility of rescue and escape. Many people were still trapped in the building that was wrapped in a black hideous smoke.

The fire brigade arrived and many fire fighters rushed to the spot. Water was thrown at a tremendous speed and quantity. The people trapped were asked to move to one side of the building. Slowly, they all were rescued from the demolishing fire which was ready to swallow each and everything at sight.

I have never had such a bewildering experience in my life. It was the most devastating and dangerous live experience I witnessed.

9. Confessions

It wasn't going to be easy she knew but somehow she had to confront him. She took a deep breath and walked into the room. She came across a dark corridor that led to her father's room. He was sitting right in front reading the newspaper with his back was towards her. She was nervous as she knew why she was called. Initially, she hesitated but somehow, ignoring the lump in her throat, she called for him. Hearing her voice, he turned towards her and kept the newspaper aside. He was wearing spectacles which he suddenly took out and kept on the table. He asked her about her report card. She kept looking down as she did not have the courage to look him in the eye.

He waited for her response but when there was no answer, he lost his calm and shouted with anger. It made the poor girl fearful. Shiveringly, she dropped her report card on the floor. All the blood vanished from her face making her look completely pale. Her father picked up the report card.

As he opened it, he saw that his daughter had scored all the marks in nineties. A smile came upon his angry face. His eyes turned towards his daughter who was still trembling with fear. He went towards her and hugged her. She was aghast at her father's behaviour. Although out of words, she felt her father's love for her. This was all that she ever desired. Two months before her boards, her father made it very clear that she must score full marks in order to get into the best college in the city. But, when her result came, her score was 92.5 per cent which was not enough to get her a seat in the best college of the city.

She was scared that her father would be disappointed. Thus, she was afraid to reveal her marks to her dad. Her dad, however, jumped with excitement as his daughter had worked hard and scored in nineties. A chill ran down her spine and suddenly all her fear disappeared. Now, she could enjoy her result.

10. Lost and Found

The graveyard was cold, dark and dreary. One weary old oak tree leaned over the entrance gate and broken, battered headstones were scattered all around. I could hear the sound of the howling wind and the creak and groan of branches as they swayed in the storm. The smell of fear and rotting leaves filled my nostrils and I breathed deeply afraid that I would get sick. As I walked towards my brother's grave, I heard another noise. It was of slow heavy footsteps. When I turned back, a tall muscular man was walking towards me. "I don't think this is a good idea", I shouted. "It's too late to change your mind", the man replied in a low threatening voice. "Either we dig him up now or you spend the rest of your life wondering how he died."

"Ok, Ok", I mumbled.

I could still remember the day those two army officers arrived at my house to tell me that my brother was dead. I lost my brother. Their cold hard faces gave little away when I asked how he died. "Killed in the course of duty" was all they would say. Everything else was 'classified'.

They handed me a letter from my brother, saluted, then turned and left. I stood frozen the spot, dazed, confused and devastated. I could not bear the loss of my brother. Finally, I opened the letter with trembling fingers but it only stared back at me.

"I'll always be with you brother, John." What did he mean? How could he be with me ever again? He was dead.

Now, I leaned heavily on the dusty shovel in my hands and started to dig, determined to uncover the truth. The scar-faced man beside me began to dig at the other end of the grave and soon my brother's coffin began to emerge from beneath the layers of sodden Earth. Faced with this moment of truth, I began to panic. What if I was wrong?

I knew John hated the army, I knew he wanted to be out. I looked down at the coffin as my hired helper tugged at the lid with a crowbar. With a loud snap the lid flew back revealing the frozen corpse inside. My whole body was filled with relief when I saw that the dead man in the coffin was not my brother.

11. A Terror Averted

This story pertains to the period when terrorism in Punjab was at its peak. The people in the state lived under the shadow of terror, caused by a professional soldier from across the border. There were daily incidents of murder, bomb blast and other crimes committed by these misguided elements. The police were constantly publishing photographs of dreaded terrorists, offering handsome rewards to the person providing information for their capture dead or alive. One fine day, a clean shaven, muscular built gentleman walked into the studio located in Civil Lines, the main commercial market of Hoshiarpur, carrying a medium size suitcase.

He told the photographer that he had to leave for Delhi the very next day and hence the photograph would be required positively by late evening. He also requested him to keep his suitcase, as he had some urgent shopping to do prior to his departure for Delhi. No sooner had the strange gentleman left the shop, than the photographer's friend Col AK Singh, a soldier in the Indian Army, walked in carrying the local daily newspaper. On the cover page was a photograph of a terrorist, whom the police expected to be behind the terrorist activities.

The photographer was taken aback, for the photograph bore a striking resemblance to the stranger who had just left the shop.

He immediately told Col Singh as to what had happened. Col Singh heard him intently, after which he instructed him to call the local police immediately. The telephone lines were dead. It was then that the Colonel took charge. Fearing the worst, he instructed all the shopkeepers to immediately vacate the building. Col Singh then very cautiously moved towards the suitcase and with his deft fingers opened it. There was indeed a time bomb set off to explode within a minute. With trembling fingers, he set about defusing the deadly device. We all held our breath in nervousness. Finally, the device was defused and we heaved a sigh of relief. The police reinforcement had also come by now and they took the briefcase into their custody. And that's how my friend, Col Singh became a hero.

12. Knowledge is Power

'Vijay Bhaiya Zindabad, Jeet Mubarak', shouted the motley crowd of people assembled at the stadium to welcome their new leader as he walked in to address them. A tall, lean, strikingly handsome man, dressed in spotless white *chooridar pajama kurta*, walked up to the podium, raising his hands to acknowledge the greetings of the people. He was profusely garlanded by the elite of the town who had come to honour their elected representative to the State Assembly.

Vijay's trek to glory was not all that easy. After completing his schooling in the village, Vijay went to Varanasi for higher education. He eventually completed his masters degree in agriculture from Banaras Hindu University. Unlike other youth, Vijay returned to his native village to put his knowledge to practical use for the benefit of the villagers. His scientific method of farming soon caught the attention of the villagers.

His willingness to help others and compassion for the well-being of the villages won their hearts. Having gained their confidence, he formed self-help groups comprising village youth and with the help of an NGO developed a proper drainage system for the village. To reduce the problem of potable drinking water, he drew the attention of the district authorities to install hand pumps in the densely populated parts of the village.

His knowledge of science came in handy to produce gobar gas from cow dung. This became an alternate fuel for the oppressed housewives of the village.

Thus, in a span of five years, he transformed the village into a small town having all the basic amenities.

Vijay's good work soon caught the attention of the opposition party. Seeing a sure winner in him, they gave him a ticket to contest the election as their party candidate. The rest was indeed history, with Vijay emerging victorious in the elections. This very well illustrates the aptness of the proverb 'knowledge is power'.

13. Every Cloud has a Silver Lining

"You are under arrest." I looked back and saw the police officer accompanied by his juniors. I was whisked into a car and taken like a high profile criminal. The car stopped not in front of the police station but at the Crime Branch Headquarters where the SSP and other senior officers were waiting for me. As I stepped out of the car, newsmen flashed their cameras. It was chaos as, I was taken inside a room for interrogation. I was frightened and had no idea about what was happenings and was totally disordered.

At last, someone dressed in civil uniform came and started questioning me, "How do you know Dawood? What are your plans?" The questions pouring in caused a more puzzling environment. The police was already issuing statement mentioning the details of how they had trapped Chetan, Dawood's man in Pune. All kinds of stories were circulated within hours. The evening newspaper had splashed my photograph on the front page and every channel worth its name had a footage of me as breaking news.

I told him that I was innocent but no one paid any heed to it. I also heard some of the police officials talking about using third degree on me so that I would reveal the truth. I was terrified at the thought of it. But the truth was that I was innocent and no one wanted to believe that.

After great difficulty, I understood the entire situation. The much talked about criminal, Dawood was sending orders to his counterparts in India. These orders were given on a mobile number which was similar to mine. The police intercepted some messages and played them for me. I said the voice was not mine. They recorded my voice and sent the record for the audio and voice forensic analysis. Finally, it was proved that the voice was not mine. Then, they went into the details of the number again and enquired whether it was 98919XXXXX. I told them that my number was 989981XXXX. Only then, they realised their folly.

Eventually, I was allowed to go and all the charges levelled against me were dropped. I was also interviewed by many news channels. I became a star overnight. After it was all over, I realised that 'Every cloud has a silver lining'.

14. The Hijacking

I was returning to India after having completed my studies from abroad. The yearning to meet my parents and friends grew with every passing minute as I boarded the plane. Seated next to me was a boy who was about five years old. He was going to visit his grandma in India and was travelling alone. Next to him were two old ladies in their late fifties, who despite their gray hair were bubbling with excitement and chattering excitedly causing some distraction. No sooner had the plane taken off from London Airport, than the boy jumped out of his seat removing his seat belt and started roaming about in the plane.

He was very candid and spoke to every one in the plane. The old ladies called the boy and gave him two chocolates. The air-hostess brought some snacks and tea, which was indeed very tempting. After having my refreshment, I settled down to complete a novel that I had brought with me. I had almost completed my novel when I heard the captain requesting passengers to fasten the safety belts, as we were about to land at the Palam airport. Just then, a young man seated behind me got up and caught hold of the boy, placing a knife on his neck. He warned us to stick to our chairs. Entering the cockpit, he ordered the pilot not to land the plane. Suddenly, one of the old ladies collapsed on the floor. Seeing this, the other lady shouted at the hijacker for having caused a heart attack.

The hijacker's attention was momentarily diverted. Sensing this, a well built young man sitting in the front passage just near the hijacker, knocked the knife out of his hand. Wild and noisy disorder prevailed for a while, as the others pounced on the unarmed hijacker, freeing the boy in the process. He was overpowered and everybody heaved a sigh of relief. The plane finally landed at the airport and the hijacker was promptly arrested.

We were all accorded a warm welcome from the waiting crowd which had gathered at the airport as news of the hijacking had spread. The child leaped into the open arms of his grandma who hugged him lovingly. It was indeed a very eventful homecoming for all of us.

15. Escaped

John wanted to escape from the world. He had nobody in the world. One day, he went to the city to get some food. On his way, he shot 16 zombies who wanted to attack him. Then, he saw a girl who was being followed by a zombie. When she saw him, her eyes glanced. There was hope in her eyes. John shot the zombie that was following the girl. She got scared. He stopped the car and the girl ran to him. John took her home. Her name was Jane. She had lost her whole family to the zombies. But, now she felt safe with John. One day, John went to the forest but while he was coming home to the farm, he saw thousands of zombies at the farm. He ran as fast as he could but he couldn't do anything.

The zombies had got Jane. He screamed and cried. His new found hope was gone as he lost Jane in the zombie invasion. The zombies got attentive because of John's screams. But his eyes were closed. He opened them when he heard some strange noises in front of him. He saw all the zombies coming towards him. He ran to his car and turned on the engine. He drove away from the farm, crying. After hours of driving, he didn't know where he was. He drove along a lonely highway. Every hundred metres, there were some crashed cars with dead persons or zombies. He knew he was lost.

After days of driving around, he stopped the car on the highway. He took his gun and held it to his head. His eyes hurt and red. There was no other way to escape the zombies. He lost his only hope and he had no food for days and as a result, he began to get crazy and started talking to himself.

He pulled the trigger. A loud noise came out of the gun and he escaped the world. He took his life, when he was only two miles from the military base where he could have been safe with other people who gave up on their hope. But he didn't make it and escaped his life.

16. Advice not Taken

The ability to make effective decisions is a fundamental requirement for both professional success and personal happiness. A teenager is restless, keen to learn, willing to try new flavours of life and finally aggressive in behaviour. As a teenager, we feel that our decisions are right and perfect and so we do not prefer to listen to advice of our elders.

Teenagers are friendly and so am I. I would prefer to be in a park with all my friends than in Mauritius with my family. Once, my friends and I decided to go out and watch a movie at PVR. On the other hand, there was a family function that day. I asked my mother if I could go out with my friends that day and the clear and obvious answer was, No! "How can you be out when there is a family event?" she said. I stood hard on my decision and compelled her to stand with it.

The difficult part was over as I had convinced my mother and did not have any pressure of missing the event. Like all mothers, my mother advised me not to go out to crowded places and insisted on carrying a cell phone. We all left before the scheduled time as we decided to roam around and spend some time in the gaming centre. After that, we went to book tickets for the movie. Luckily, we got the tickets of the show and all our seats were in the same row. But, little did we know that our luck would stay with us just for a short while. Hardly had the movie begun, than a group of men barged into the theatre hall and started creating a chaos.

They asked all of us to leave the screening hall. Then, they began damaging the chairs, lights and were creating a rampage. All of us were suddenly taken aback. Some panicked, some rushed out, some stayed in their places and some were confused like us. The exit doors got jammed as all the audience started rushing out. It was almost like a panic scene.

Soon, the police arrived and the situation was under control. They took us aside and made sure that we were safe. They asked us why we had come without our parents and advised us not to go to alone to such places. Disappointed, I came home and also felt guilty for not taking my mother's advice. If I had taken my mother's advice, I would not have to go through all this.

SELF ASSESSMENT

1. Relate a short story which has as its theme 'Regret but Too Late to Repent'.
2. Write a story with the theme 'A friend in need is a friend indeed'.
3. Draft a story that ends with the words "I haven't got what I have wanted in my life". Put your own experience in it if possible.
4. Write a short story in which the conclusion has the following proverb 'A stitch in time saves nine.'
5. Write an original story that begins the words "She was the very beautiful and charming I had ever met. She would make everyone amazed...."
6. Write a short story on the theme 'Sweet are the uses of adversity'.
7. Write a story with the following beginning and give a suitable title to it "Rahul was alone at home. Suddenly the phone rang......... ."
8. Write a story with the following beginning and give a suitable title to it. It had been over two hours waiting for the train. Ruhi was getting restless. Sudddenly she ....
9. You went to your aunt Mary's house for her blessings on your birthday. She asked you to do one good thing everyday. The next day when you were going to your school, you helped an old woman. Write a story how you helped an old woman when you remembered your aunt's advice.
10. "Meena is staying with her mother. One day, a stranger came to Meena's house. Her mother was not in the house at that time. The man caught hold of Meena. She began to cry loudly. But no one was there to hear her ...." Complete the story.

CHAPTER

5

Picture Composition

Picture composition is usually divided into three patterns. A student is asked to describe a given picture, to make a story out of it or to express and elaborate upon the thoughts and feelings suggested by the given picture. The picture can be a photograph, an action scene, a quote written over a picture or a scene or a sketch of a famous personality. The composition is written in three different forms so as to highlight this uniqueness.

It requires a wide range of imagination, creativity, good hold on vacabulary and the ability to sequence all events together. In the examination, word-limit for the picture composition is 300-350 and its weightage is 20 marks.

Following points should be followed while writing picture composition

- The student should look at the picture carefully to ascertain the basic plot or the theme.
- If the picture doesn't suggest anything evidently, the student is advised to invent a theme which bears a direct connection with the picture.
- After identifying or deciding the theme, major attention should be paid to the designing of the characters of the story.

Description of the Picture

- The picture should be studied carefully with a view to identify the specific and minute details.
- The focus should be widened to take into account the other or peripheral details, given in the picture, i.e. facial expressions, postures, clothes, etc.
- Design the factors or causes which have an impact on the details.
- A strong conclusion is required at the end of the composition.

Points to be Kept in Mind While Writing a Picture Composition

- The content chosen must be directly related to the given picture.
- The student must maintain the connection and the focus between the picture and the content.
- The full structure of the composition should be analysed in the mind before starting the writing based on picture.
- As the word-limit is going to range between 300-350 words, the student must try to spread out their ideas so that there is variety of ideas in his composition.
- Use of simple language and imagination is required.
- Logical expression of the entire idea based on the picture will make it an effective composition.

Sample 1

Study the picture given below. Write a story or a description or an account of what it suggests to you. Your composition may be about the subject of the picture or you may take suggestions from it; however, there must be a clear connection between the picture and your composition. *[2018]*

Ans. While I agree that girls from all corners of the nation are coming out of shells and taking positions that were denied to them, I had never expected to see a women's cricket match cheered by all. But I did see the image.

Last week, a cricket match was held in Muzaffarnagar, my friend's village. I was in his village because both of us were going on a road trip together and I had to pick him up. While there, he told me about the match and I went to watch the game him thinking it to be an all- boys cricket match. But I was in it for a surprise when I saw three girls playing with the bat and ball as if warming up. I thought maybe they were just kidding. But no, the girls were actually parts of the team that were paying the match that day.

My shock was just wearing off when I found another shock in the forms of the entirety of the villages coming forward to support the girls. My friend, looking at my face, told me that this was how it was in their village. Girls were not discriminated. In fact, Girls were told to go to school, get educated, work and participate in all extracurricular activities, especially sports.

Soon, the teams were ready to play the game and what a game it was. The girls were astounding. The first teams totaled at 215 runs in 15 overs while the second team took the lead by 218 runs in 12 overs. While the girls were playing, the village elders were cheering and complementing the girls for their improvement and performance. I was stoked. The image of Indian villages being orthodox, limiting and traditional was completely shattered by the village. Contrary to my opinion, my friend's village was more open and accepting of its female population than many communities residing in cities.

Sample 2

Study the picture given below. Write a story or a description or an account of what it suggests to you. Your composition may be about the subject of the picture or you may take suggestions from it; however, there must be a clear connection between the picture and your composition. *[2017]*

Ans. Ramesh lives in a small house on the outskirts of a jungle near Bengaluru. Herds (a large group) of elephants are seen in jungles and Ramesh is employed at a plantation where an elephant's job is to root out stumps with its heavy feet. Mohini, one of the female elephants at the plantation where Ramesh works, died of an unknown disease leaving her six month old baby elephant Kamu to his fate. Being alone and without the company of his mother, Kamu's health started deteriorating as there has been no one to take care of him. Ramesh brought him to his home thinking that the change of environment might have a positive impact on him. Ramesh's twelve year old daughter Kavya's happiness knew no bound seeing this baby elephant at her house. Kamu who seemed to be uneasy in the beginning, gradually started liking Kavya as she was around him all the time and took care of his food and fondled him.

Soon, Kamu started forgetting his mother and Kavya became the only center of his attention. Now Kavya and he have become inseparable souls. As long as Kavya is around him, his eyes twinkle and seem to be dancing with her activities; but the moment she is out of his sight, he becomes restless and keeps moving here and there till she reappears before him. Kavya too is very fond of Kamu. She is a bit proud of him too as no child of her village can boast of having an elephant as pet. She takes Kamu for a walk daily in the evening. Sometimes, she walks along with him and sometimes she rides on his back.

Who says man is an enemy of animals. Kavya and baby elephant are living example of close bonding between man and animals. What animals need is love and sincerity and they will prove more faithful and helpful than other human beings. This bonding proves the words 'Haathi Mera Sathi', which means the elephant is my friend.

EXAM PRACTICE

1. Study the picture given below. Write a short story or a description or an account of what it suggests to you. Your composition may be about the subject of the picture, or you may take suggestions from it; however, there must be a clear connection between the picture and your composition. *[2023]*

2. Study the picture given below. Write a short story, description or an account of what it suggests to you. Your composition may be about the subject of the picture or you may take suggestions from it. *[Sem II 2022]*

3. Study the picture given below. Write a story, a description or an account of what it suggests to you. Your composition may be about the subject of the picture or you may take suggestions from it; however, there must be a clear connection between the picture and your composition. *[2020]*

4. Study the picture given below. Write a story, a description or an account of what it suggests to you. Your composition may be about the subject of the picture or you may take suggestions from it; however, there must be a clear connection between the picture and your composition. *[2019]*

5. Study the picture given below. Write a story or a description or an account of what it suggests to you. Your composition may be about the subject of the picture or you may take suggestions from it; however, there must be clear connection between the picture and your composition. *[2016]*

6. Study the picture given below. Write a short story or description or an account of what the picture suggests to you. Your composition may be about the subject of the picture or you may take suggestions from it; however, your composition must have a clear connection with the picture. *[2015]*

7. Study the picture given below and write a short story or description or an account of what the picture suggests to you. Your composition may be about the subject of the picture or you may take suggestions from it; however, your composition must have a clear connection with the picture. *[2014]*

8. Study the picture given below and write a story or a description or an account of what it suggests to you. Your composition may be about the subject of the picture or you may take suggestions from it; however, there must be a clear connection between the picture and your composition. *[2013]*

9. Study the picture given below and write a story or a description or an account of what it suggests to you. Your composition may be about the subject of the picture or you may take suggestions from it; however, there must be a clear connection between the picture and your composition. *[2012]*

10. Study the picture given below and write a story or a description or an account of what it suggests to you. Your composition may be about the subject of the picture or you may take suggestions from it; however, there must be a clear connection between the picture and your composition. *[2011]*

11. Study the picture given below and write a story or a description or an account of what it suggests to you. Your composition may be about the subject of the picture or you may take suggestions from it; however, there must be a clear connection between the picture and your composition. *[2009]*

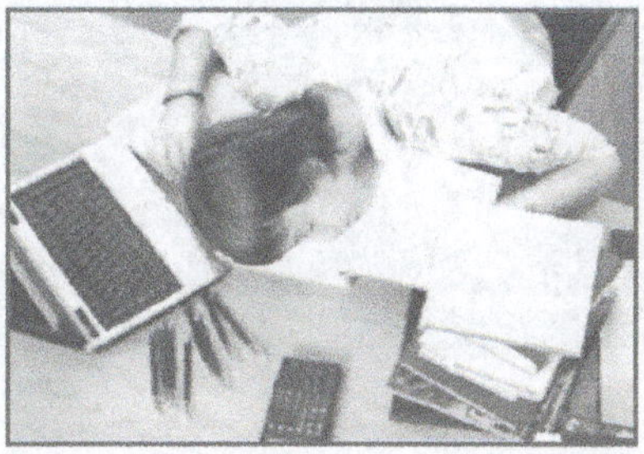

12. Study the picture given below and write a story or a description or an account of what it suggests to you. Your composition may be about the subject of the picture or may take suggestions from it; however, there must be a clear connection between the picture and your composition. *[2007]*

13. Study the picture given below and write a story or a description or an account of what it suggests to you. Your composition may be about the subject of the picture or may take suggestions from it; however, there must be a clear connection between the picture and your composition. *[2006]*

14. Study the picture given below and write a short story or description or an account of what the picture suggests to you. Your composition must have a clear connection with the picture.

15. Study the picture given below and write a short story or description or an account of what the picture suggests to you. Your composition must have a clear connection with the picture.

16. Study the picture given below and write a short story or description or an account of what the picture suggests to you. Your composition must have a clear connection with the picture.

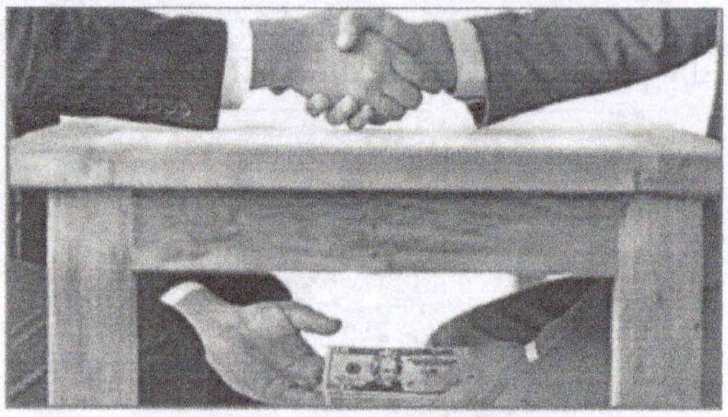

Answers

1. Dog was the first animal that humans tamed when they settled down and started practicing agriculture. They have been rightfully called 'man's best friend'. Dogs have always been very helpful to humans and have always shared a special relationship with us. The cure fluffy creatures protect us from dangers, are the most loyal creatures and stand by our side from thick and thin.

Regardless of their role in helping humans over the generations, a lot of dogs are stray and lonely in the streets. They often don't have anyone to help them. People even behave rudely to them at times. Since they can't voice their emotions, it is important for humans to try to understand them and help them by providing any sort of assistance they may need, as is shown in the given picture. It is important to be compassionate towards them and all other animals because they are living beings and need help, just like humans. Just by treating the dogs well, we can make sure that those animals who on the streets are able to survive and lead a good life. Even the little acts of kindness such as protecting them from the rain or the cold can act wonders.

Dogs are amongst the most loyal animals and would go to any length to protect the people they care about. They don't need money or any material possessions, only to be treated with kindness, care and compassion and they would be some of the best companions. Their symbiotic relationship with humans is the reason why we have co-existed together for many years and the dogs on the streets have survived for many years even without proper resources. It is our duty, as humans, to help them, to do our part and preserve the bond that exists between our species, the foundations of which were laid thousands of years ago when the first dog became a part of the human community.

2. I was passing by a motor garage when I saw him working. I was stunned to see a 12-year-old boy, covered in dirt and car oil trying to repair a car. I went to him and asked him his name. He told his name was 'Chhotu' as his employer used to call him that. I asked him why he was not at school at that time and was instead working there. Chhotu got emotional and told me his story. He told me that a few months age he also went to a nearby government school. But one day, his father died in a road accident and his mother had no money left to send him to school. He had to become the bread earner of the family to support his mother and 3 younger siblings. As a result, he dropped out of the school and started doing menial works, and then joined this garage a few months ago.

   I was so touched by his story that I wanted to do something for him. I held his hands and told him that he would be going to school from the next day and that he could work in the garage part-time. I also told his employer the same and he agreed. Next day, I went to Chhotu's house and talked to his mother and got him ready along with his siblings to get them admitted in the nearby school.

   They felt so happy knowing that they would be going to school. Their mother thanked me a million times. I tried to help their mother by getting her associated with a famous NGO who helps women in distress. They impart them vocational trainings free of cost to make them self-reliant. Chhotu also promised me that he would work hard to become a respectable and learned man in future. I felt so content after helping the child. My soul was filled with happiness.

3. The given picture shows five children, seemingly from a humble background trying to click a selfie. The only difference is that they don't have a mobile phone. But there is one thing that they have that strikes out invariably irrespective of the fact that they are just pretending to take a selfie. That thing is the genuine smile on their face. They may not have the perfect tool for clicking a selfie but they have smile that indicates their joy. In this century, no one can refuse that money has become a deciding factor for the quality of life we are leading. But the problem is that nowadays people have started linking money with happiness. We will have to understand that money helps us in acquiring the comforts and luxuries of life but it does not guarantee happiness.

   Money doesn't make you laugh when you are lonely. Indeed, money can help you buy a mansion, a fancy car or branded clothes that might make you happy, but these things don't last for long. Soon, you will start seeing that your neighbours have a better house, more cars and many other things that you don't have. At that moment, money will no longer be a source of happiness.

   Happiness isn't a quality like height, weight or income that can be measured easily. It is a complex, indistinct state that is developed by momentary simple pleasures. It is the tendency to feel positive emotions and holding a sense of purpose.

   Happiness is not having a lot of privilege or money. It's a broader thing. It is our ability to connect with others, to have meaningful relationships and to have a better community. People who say they are happy have strong connections and communications with other people. That is a sort of recipe for happiness.

   This picture of these children smiling with pure innocence reflects their happy souls and gives us the clear message that we should stop searching for happiness in materialistic things. All we need is a big smile from within the heart and the world will be a happy place.

4. When I went to the local market outside my office during the lunch break to eat something, I observed a very common sight at the nearby small shop which sold all kinds of packaged food items such as chips, sweets, etc. The nearby primary school had just got over and there was a crowd of students around this shop, who were jostling each other to buy food items. I realised that the children were simply wasting their pocket money on such snacks which are tasty but have very little nutritional value. In fact, such snack items are harmful to the health of children. This is because they are generally deep fried and spiced heavily, thus being high in calories, fat, sugar and salt. Children and teenagers these days are more prone to eat such foods daily while they neglect homemade food. They are leading their lives towards danger through their unhealthy lifestyle.

   These foods affect their health adversely, whatever may be their age group, weight and health condition. The foods are considered as high in calories; however, one who eats them ends up getting easily exhausted and needs more food frequently. These items do not provide an appropriate level of energy which is required by children of this age. Thus, the child develops the tendency of craving for food more frequently. What the children acquire from these foods are unhealthy fats, but not healthy nutrients. Thus, they feel a lack of oxygen, which causes poor functioning of the brain. They absorb cholesterol from such types of foods. The cholesterol causes plaque formation in the arteries and creates problems for the heart to pump its normal amount of blood. That's why they feel fatigue.

A high level of bad cholesterol damages their liver and also increases their weight. According to research, such children are overweight or obese and are highly prone to heart and liver disorders. They are more prone to become diabetic and lethargic because of the high amount of sugar collecting in their body. They also get high blood pressure because of the high amount of sodium in the salt. Thus, such children should be trained by their parents to follow healthy eating habits and not waste their pocket money on such items.

5. Everybody is waiting for the rains to arrive. The city has already had a long dry spell. The weather has been very hot, the power cuts and water shortage have added to the misery. A lot of people have fallen ill due to the intense heat and few have died also.

Not only the humans, but the animals also are having a hard time in this burning heat. The monsoons were scheduled to arrive in the city, but the wait is still on for the season's first rain. A few people are organising *havans* so as to please the rain god. Some have left the city and gone to the mountains to get respite from the heat.

Finally, the rain came when we least expected it. It seemed that people had lost hope after waiting for too long. It was afternoon time and suddenly it started raining. The downpour was very heavy and lasted for 2 hours.

I was studying for my class test when it rained when I saw a girl and a boy playing in the rain from my window. Although they had umbrellas, they threw it away and were enjoying getting wet. Everyone was joyous and enjoyed the rain. Children were dancing and playing in the rain. They also made paper boats and floated them in the water. This reminded me of my childhood days. I also used to come out in the rain and play with my friends. The weather had become cool after the rain. When I finished studying, I had a cup of tea with *pakoras*. Everyone in my home was very happy as finally, it had rained after a long wait. It was such a great relief for everyone!

6. The picture shows a tiger asleep on a tree. Through it, it aims to highlight an important concern of today that is the loss of habitat for tigers.

The world's population of tigers have some basic necessities in order to survive. These are water, food (which comprises of only preys as tigers are carnivores) and forests where these animals can conceal themselves. When any of the above-mentioned requirements is not available, their chances of survival diminish naturally. Today, world over, tigers face this situation.

As human population and exploitation continue to grow, the forest cover tends to shrink. As more and more space is needed by the human population and the infrastructure they require – towns, roads, buildings, etc., more and more forests and other natural habitats are being destroyed to make room.

Human beings are rapidly encroaching into wild areas which were once ruled exclusively by the tigers. Loss of habitat is only driving this animal to the verge of extinction. Without tall trees or grass, this animal can be easily hunted down by anyone. Moreover, as without the forests, even the tiger's prey cannot survive, so the former will ultimately die of starvation.

However, the government has taken a view of the grim situation and has reserved some essential forest covers as wildlife sanctuaries and national parks. This particular percentage of the reserved area is not to be touched by man and his activities. Thus, we as humans must realise our social responsibility and make an effort to let the tigers and other wild animals have their natural habitat intact. For if they are robbed off their home, the ecological balance gets disturbed.

7. Lakshmi was the third child in the family of five children. Her mother was a poor labourer who worked at the nearby construction site along with her father. Lakshmi was 7 years old and used to accompany her parents to the construction site. One day, the manager at the construction site offered to employ Lakshmi at a meagre pay. Her parents accepted, considering it an additional income for their family.

The small girl was forced to do hazardous work without proper compensation. She was risking her life just to keep her family's body and soul together. So tragic is her condition that she had turned into a physical and mental wreck. Her weak and fragile body seemed to suffer from disease.

Lakshmi would keep breaking stones in a corner, crying and regretting her fate. Such was her misery that in the days when she should be going to school and playing, she had to work hard. Such was her irony that instead of smiles and carefreeness, her face was writ large with a worry for earning her bread.

Child labour is another name which can be given to this picture. It is a serious blot in the efforts to project our nation as a dynamic country. The root cause of child labour is poverty and to some extent ignorance.

This girl Lakshmi has become symbolic of all child labourers who are exposed to the difficulties of the world at such a tender age. It is a pity to see her shouldering the responsibilities of her family.

The government should thus, realise the grimness of the situation and take strict actions to ban child labour. Additionally, adopting a multi-prolonged problem-solving approach is required.

Furthermore, this should be incentivised by the provision of education and vocational based skills training for each child in the poor families. The combination of the right information complemented by the right rewards will combat child labour and in the longer run, poverty.

8. School is perhaps one of the best experiences of life. This makes me recall an incident from my life. An excursion was planned by my school when I was in the 9th standard. The news came as a surprise to me. We all were too excited to go. We were informed that we were going to Jaipur for two nights and three days. When I went home, I very cautiously told this to my mother who did not stir a bit. I had to try very hard to convince her. Finally, she gave her consent and advised me not to do anything reckless on the trip.

Once we were in Jaipur, we visited beautiful forts. We also saw peacocks and could not stop ourselves from admiring their beauty. As we were about to click some pictures of the peacocks, we heard some school kids screaming. The noise was so loud that we moved towards the direction from where screams were coming. To our surprise, we saw three of our school children sitting on an elephant. That was not the usual scene of an elephant ride because the animal was crossing the lake with all these four people sitting on it. The lake surrounded the fort and was deep. The water was also quite cold that day and so the elephant was slightly uncomfortable crossing the lake.

The elephant was losing its balance and this was the reason that the kids were screaming. Everybody present there was only looking at the helpless kids as even the elephant's master was unable to control the balance of the animal. Although the kids were holding each other, they seemed to be very afraid. Suddenly, the elephant lost its balance and all its passengers fell in the water.

All the children started yelling for help. My friends and I knew swimming, so we jumped into the lake to their rescue. By God's grace, we were successful in saving their lives. On coming back from the trip, we were praised by our school Principal and were also awarded with the bravery award. Our parents felt so proud of us.

9. The intense and clear study of the picture in question describes a girl's poor state. She is sitting with her younger sister at a popcorn stall. There are a lot of packets spread around her and a heap of popcorn is under the process of roasting and cooking in the pan. While the girl is roasting the popcorn, her younger sister is anxiously waiting for the customers. They look quite innocent and poor.

It is the story of a 9-year-old deprived girl child, Gudiya. According to her friends and teachers, she was extremely good in studies. Unfortunately, she could not go to school anymore because she had to earn money for the family after the sudden demise of her father. Her father was the sole bread earner of the family. His demise led her to choose between her books and starvation. The choice was obvious. She decided to help her mother by earning a livelihood to support her family.

The second time, I met Gudiya after 6 months of our first meeting. This time was different from the last time. I was disturbingly shocked to see the adverse changes that had forced her into such an ill fate. Those little eyes that once twinkled with the gleam of becoming a doctor, sparkled no more. She now worked at a roadside popcorn stall, selling popcorn with her younger sister, only to earn a square meal for her struggling family.

Childhood should be a time of enjoyment, discovery and learning. Child labour is a reprehensible practice that steals children of their childhood. Like Gudiya, many others are out there, who are forced and exploited due to circumstances.

Poverty, hunger, starvation etc turn them into child labourers. They are considered useful as labourers because they are easier to manage and control and perhaps, most importantly, could be paid less than adults. Child labourers are often made to work for long hours in dangerous conditions. This practice is considered exploitative and is illegal.

However, India itself is a home to a quarter of the world's working children. Although Indian law prohibits the employment of children under 14 years of age, child labour remains widespread in India. This is all due to public indifference, poverty and lack of political will and proper implementation of law.

10. Due to the heavy downpour, the city of Kolkata is completely flooded. All the streets are waterlogged which makes commuting hazardous.

Life in Kolkata seems to move pretty smoothly for everyone till the rains descend. The rains are the only time when vehicles lose their power of transporting people from one end to the other end of the city. The best and the only available mode of conveyance is the cycle or hand-rickshaw. When most of the people are seen stranded in the city, believe it or not, in these trying times the rickshaw pullers come to their rescue.

The hand rickshawalas actually call it their season.

Everyone is eager to get a ride on a hand rickshaw and is even eager to pay more. Thus, the rickshaw pullers earn more than 8 to 10 times of their usual wages during this period and some of them thank the rain Gods for this bounty.

Sujit, a hand-rickshaw puller, had been out of luck for many days. He was not able to make enough money for there was much competition on his route. He was a native of Kolkata but he always found that people from outside came and dominated the rickshaw pulling trade. Sujit needed money and he knew that things were getting tough.

Although it had rained and the roads were flooded, he was not getting many customers. At the corner of the road, he saw two ladies stranded. They looked poor with an umbrella and had a worried look on their faces. They had left their home and were going to meet their family. When the auto driver dislodged them from his vehicle, they could not wade the flooding waters.

Sujit offered to help them and allowed the ladies to sit in his rickshaw. One of the ladies said that she would pay, but Sujit just wanted to help them. It took him more than an hour to take them through the flooded water to their house. There family members were waiting anxiously for ladies to arrive. The family members had tried all means of communication to contact them.

On seeing the ladies, their families were extremely happy. Sujit did not expect anything, but the delighted father gave him a five hundred rupee note with tears in his eyes and expressed his gratefulness to Sujit. Sujit realised that 'God rewards the noble people'.

11. Today, the world has become so competitive that it has caused a sharp rise in the expectations of parents. Expectations always cause pressure and this pressure is borne by the child. This pressure sometimes acts as a catalyst but very often it proves fatal, resulting in a child trying to eliminate himself or developing an inferiority complex. This in turn causes them to withdraw into a shell. The picture depicts an overburdened student.

Very often, children are found falling off to sleep while studying due to sheer exhaustion. The parents expect their child to wake up at 4 am and get down with their studies, get ready and then attend school, again get down with their books at night and prepare their subject for the next day.

During the examination period, it gets even worse. The child is expected to perform miracles and is goaded to despair in a quest for obtaining a high rank and percentage. The child, on their part, tries hard to live up to the high expectations of their parents and in doing so, mentally and physically wears themselves out. Some succeed while others are not so fortunate.

Parents are only concerned with their expectation but have no time to understand the psyche of their child. They don't take out time to understand their child's mentality, their weaknesses or strengths and their interests. They don't even know if their child would be able to cope up. At times, they try to fulfil their unfulfilled ambitions through their child and here lies the problem. Every child is a gift of God and is born to achieve greatness in their own way. Children should be nourished properly in order to prepare them for the burden of studies.

It is, therefore, strongly recommended that the parents should understand the fact that a child must be allowed to grow up according to their natural instincts. Parental discretion and direction is definitely a must, but to mould a child according to your own ambitions is wrong.

12. The Delhi Race Course is getting all geared up for the summer racing season. People fly from all over the country to witness the glitter and glamour that surrounds the great spectacle. As the great day arrives, the race course is decorated with cheerful crowd comprising fashionably dressed men and women. It becomes the central hub of activity. Owners, participants, jockeys, fans and the green grounds before them make it a perfect picture. I visited the race course and was amazed with the magnitude of what I beheld as I walked along with my uncle. He is the owner of a large number of horses. I was directed to the 2nd row of seats with a great view. I glanced around in amazement to see ladies with umbrella to protect them from the afternoon sun. Men were in three piece suits. The fragrance and aroma, a blend of flowers and perfumes filled the air. Finally, the pistol fired in the air, the gates flew open and the 10 massive creatures broke free in a mad chase. There was cheering and an indescribable excitement in the air. The jockeys were taking the race well and were tightening every muscle to make every stride of their horse with ease and perfection. These riders are thorough professionals and the animals are extremely well bred. The first race is won by 'Watergate'. The experience was gripping and it left me speechless. 'Watergate' is paraded in along with its rider and the owner. They receive a big trophy and also a cash prize. I was so thrilled at the spectacle that I settled down for the next race.

At this moment, a thought passed through my mind. I have heard wild stories of people betting on horses and becoming millionaires in a day. Even my uncle is a multi-millionaire. I secretly wish in my heart to be able to earn a fortune by betting on these horses. However, my thoughts are quickly rejected by the moral values of hardwork and honesty inculcated in me by my father.

13. The light of the dying Sun was shimmering on the sand. The beaches of Lakshadweep Islands were illuminated by the showers of beautiful and peaceful light. My grandpa lived at Kadmat island in Lakshadweep and we visited him along with my younger brother, Vaasu.

This season as well, the Lakshadweep Adventure Sports Championship was going to be organised. I like wind surfing a lot and so I got my name registered immediately. At last, the day arrived. I had practised for it day and night and thus, was quite confident of winning it. Vaasu also infused a lot of confidence in me.

The day dawned bright and clear as I took my grandpa's blessings and set out for the starting point with Vaasu on my tail. The spectators crowded the beach, moving their handkerchiefs and throwing flowers.

At last, the trumpet sounded and the whistle blew up. I trapped the wind in my sail and the board lurched forward. I could hear Vaasu, 'Di, you can do it!' Hearing this, I zipped through all the contestants. Everybody was dumbstruck but cheered madly. The track was not an easy one. After 2 km, I saw a boy approaching me very fast. It appeared as if he was determined enough to overtake me. The last 3 km route was the toughest part of the race. Sometimes, he left me behind and sometimes I left him behind. Then, there came a steep turn and unfortunately for him, a lot of turtles clogged his way.

He was a bit confused and tried to scrap past them. However, he could not control the speed and crashed down. Before he could recover from the blow, I crossed the finishing line.

My grandpa and Vaasu came walking through the water and hugged me. The first prize was a real big trophy and along with that I got a beautiful new surfboard and gear.

14. Delhi Metro has been the greatest gift to Delhi's residents. It has not only made travel easier but has also helped a great deal in reducing traffic in Delhi. Most importantly, the pollution level in Delhi has gone down because of the reduced usage of cars and bikes. Delhi Metro Rail Corporation Ltd was set up on 3rd May, 1995 in equal equity participation from the Government of India and the Government of National Capital Territory. Delhi Metro is the world's 12th longest metro system in length and 16th largest in ridership. It is the second oldest metro in India after Kolkata Metro.

There are many upcoming projects under DMRC and it is said to connect many other far away distances. The metro train runs at a speed of 30 km per hour.

There are three types of coaches, the 8-coach, the 4-coach and the 6-coach. The 8-coach metro runs successfully on the Yellow and Blue Line but it is yet to reach the violet line because the violet line is in dire need of more metro trains and with more coaches, keeping in mind the number of commuters on that line.

All corridors are centrally air-conditioned and there are various interchanging stations. Rajiv Chowk, Central Secretariat, Kashmiri Gate are some of the interchanging stations in Delhi Metro.

We are really thankful to our government for blessing us with the Delhi Metro.

15. Statue of Liberty is one of the seven wonders of the world. It represents America in the world and is the pride of America. The story behind the Statue of Liberty is that it was a gift from the French to the United States in honour of the first hundredth anniversary of American Independence in 1886. It was designated as an American National Monument. This masterpiece was created by Frederic Auguste Bartholdi, who got the idea about the design of Liberty when he was on a visit to the US. He got a creative thought about designing a statue which will represent freedom all over the world.

It is located in the New York Harbour on Liberty Island. The Statue of Liberty is 46 m (151 ft) tall and the surface of the statue is composed of hammered copper sheets that were riveted to an iron framework. The statue is made up of concrete; therefore, its base and pedestal increase the height of the monument to 93m (305 ft) high. 'Liberty Enlightening the World' is the second name of the Statue of Liberty.

The statue depicts a woman escaping from the chains. Her right hand holds a burning torch in order to represent liberty. The Liberty has seven rays on the top of her head which symbolise the seven seas and continents.

Even in the fluctuating climate of The United States, Liberty's body remains unaffected from any unexpected change in nature because its green patina (a green or brown film on the surface of bronze or any other metals) gives the Liberty an excellent copper exterior which lasts for a long time and does not get affected by weather. Lady Liberty is built and placed in order to give immigrants arriving from abroad a welcoming signal. In conclusion, the Statue of Liberty is really famous around the world as it represents the basic principle of freedom.

16. The word 'corruption' is not something we hear only these days. It has existed in our society since long. History reveals that it was present even in the Mauryan period. Great scholar Kautilya mentions the existence of forty types of corruption in his contemporary society. It was practised even in the Mughal and Sultanate period. When the East India Company took control of our country, corruption reached new heights.

Now-a-days, corruption in India has become so common that people are averse to thinking of public life without it. Corruption means illegal or dishonest behaviour, especially by people in positions of power.

In other words, undue favour for anyone for some monetary or other gains is corruption. Simultaneously, depriving the genuinely deserving of their right or privilege is also a corrupt practice. Giving up of one's duty is also a form of corruption. Besides, thefts and misuse of public property constitute varieties of corruption.

Dishonesty, exploitation, malpractices, scams and scandals are various manifestations of corruption. It has spread its wings in every sphere of life namely business, administration, politics, officialdom and services. In fact, there is hardly any sector which can be called non-corrupt. Corruption is evidently present in every segment and every section of our society, barring the social status attached to it.

To root out the evil of corruption from society, we need to make a comprehensive code of conduct for politicians and bureaucrats. Judiciary should be given more independence and initiatives on issues related to corruption.

Law and order machinery should be allowed to work without political interference. NGOs and media should come forward to create awareness against corruption in society and educate people on combatting this evil.

A non-corrupt society is a moral responsibility of every citizen and we are morally bound to stand against corruption and fight against it and save our system from collapsing.

SELF ASSESSMENT

1. Study the picture given here. Write a story or description or an account of what it suggests to you. Your composition may be about the subject of the picture or you may take suggestions from it. However, there must be a clear connection between the picture and your composition.

2. Study the picture given here. Write a story or description or an account of what it suggests to you. Your composition may be about the subject of the picture or you may take suggestions from it. However, there must be a clear connection between the picture and your composition.

3. Study the picture given here. Write a story or description or an account of what it suggests to you. Your composition may be about the subject of the picture or you may take suggestions from it. However, there must be a clear connection between the picture and your composition.

4. Study the picture given here. Write a story or description or an account of what it suggests to you. Your composition may be about the subject of the picture or you may take suggestions from it. However, there must be a clear connection between the picture and your composition.

5. Study the picture given here. Write a story or description or an account of what it suggests to you. Your composition may be about the subject of the picture or you may take suggestions from it. However, there must be a clear connection between the picture and your composition.

6. Study the picture given here. Write a story or description or an account of what it suggests to you. Your composition may be about the subject of the picture or you may take suggestions from it. However, there must be a clear connection between the picture and your composition.

7. Study the picture given here. Write a story or description or an account of what it suggests to you. Your composition may be about the subject of the picture or you may take suggestions from it. However, there must be a clear connection between the picture and your composition.

8. Study the picture given here. Write a story or description or an account of what it suggests to you. Your composition may be about the subject of the picture or you may take suggestion from it. However, there must be a clear connection between the picture and your composition.

9. Study the picture given here. Write a story or description or an account of what it suggests to you. Your composition may be about the subject of the picture or you may take suggestions from it. However, there must be a clear connection between the picture and your composition.

10. Study the picture given here. Write a story or description or an account of what it suggests to you. Your composition may be about the subject of the picture or you may take suggestions from it. However, there must be a clear connection between the picture and your composition.

CHAPTER 6

Letter Writing

Letter is a written message which we send to persons who are far away from us. It is meant to convey our message to them in a clear manner. We usually write letters to our friends and relatives. Although the advent of IT–Telephones, Mobile SMSs and chat has reduced the importance of personal letter writing, this art is still required when there is a need for formal communication. Art of letter writing is no more an ornamental accomplishment but something that every educated person must acquire for practical purposes. In the examination, its weightage is 10 marks.

Types of Letters

Letters can be broadly classified into two main categories

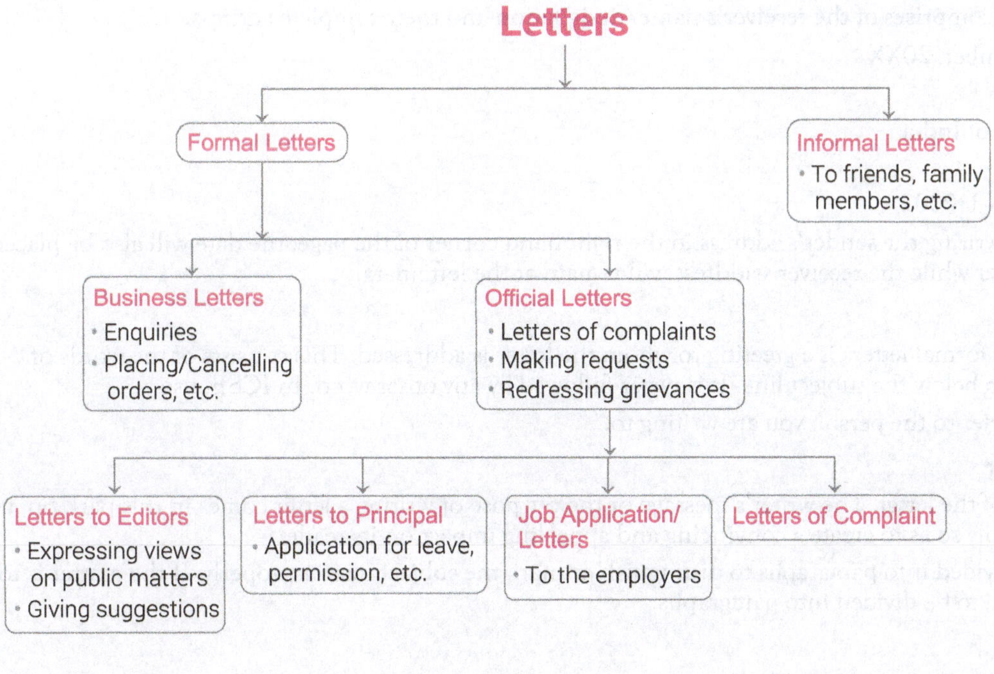

Formal Letters

Formal letters are meant to be addressed to the heads or managers of civil, public or private companies, such as the Police Commissioner, Director, Branch Manager, Chairman, Mayor, etc. Hence, the language used to write such letters must be positive, polite and formal. Also, the message must be to-the-point and short. Informal language and jargons should be avoided in these types of letter.

Formal letters are written to serve the following purposes

- To ask or give information
- To register complaints
- To apply for job
- To apply for leave
- To redress grievances (to bring into notice public/social issues)
- To persuade customers, etc.

Steps to Write a Formal Letter

1. **Sender's Address**

   Make sure that the sender's address is clear, precise and complete. It is written at the top on the left hand corner or right hand corner of the page. Specify the house number first, followed by the street, town/state and pincode.

   Example 2334/31, Mangal Pandey Nagar
   Ekta Park
   Meerut-250002

   Note While writing the address, one must **NOT** use a comma at the end of each line.

2. **Date and Receiver's Address**

   While writing the date, always remember that the day is written in figures, month in words and year in full figures. The receiver's address comprises of the receiver's name/designation and their complete address.

   Example 12th December, 20XX
   The Editor
   The Times of India
   Daryaganj
   New Delhi-110002

   Note When you are writing the sender's address in the right hand corner of the page, the date will also be placed at the right hand corner while the receiver's address will remain at the left margin.

3. **Salutation**

   The salutation used in formal letters is a greeting to whom the letter is addressed. This consists of the words of greetings and is written below the subject line. It is never followed by any other word. In ICSE, use **Dear Sir/Madam** to refer to the person you are writing to.

4. **Body of the Letter**

   This is the main part of the letter. The writer's message or the purpose of writing a letter comes in this part. So, it must be drafted carefully so as to create a convincing and appealing impact on its reader.

   The message can be divided into paragraphs to distinguish or mark the subject matter properly. If the matter is too short, it is not required to be divided into paragraphs.

The body of the letter can be divided into the following parts

- **Introductory Paragraph/Sentence** State the purpose of writing.
- **Information Paragraph** Give details of the issue (cause, effect, solution, etc.)
- **Concluding Paragraph** States your hopes, request, comment, etc.

5. Subscription/Leave-Taking

A letter should not be ended abruptly with only the writer's name or signature as that may look rude. So, there should be proper leave-taking followed by one's name.

It is a courteous way of ending the letter. The expression used must match the salutation.

Example Yours sincerely, Yours faithfully,

Note: The first letter of the second word (here 's', 'f') is never written in capital letter.

6. Name and Signature

It is written just below the subscription and includes the sender's name and his/her signature. If applicable, the sender's designation can be added in brackets.

Points to be Kept in Mind While Writing a Letter

- Read the question carefully to understand it properly.
- Write the key points for establishing good content and make sure that the body of the letter is in sync with the main theme.
- A letter must be coherent and not begin or end abruptly.
- Keep the letter brief and to-the-point.
- Use simple language so that the letter is easy to understand.
- These letters are written in a crisp and clear pattern, and in a matter-of-fact style.

Formats of Formal Letter

The ICSE Board had published two formats of writing a formal letter.

Format 1

Write a letter to the Police Commissioner of your city drawing his/her attention to the menace of hawkers outside your school. Tell him/her what dangers they pose and offer solutions for their rehabilitations.

Flat 236, Block C,
Hill Crest View Apartments,
Salem Street,
Coonoor-26 — Sender's Address

23rd February, 2018 — Date

The Police Commissioner,
Police Commissioner's Office,
6 Cavalry Road,
Coonoor-3 — Receiver's Address

Dear Sir/Ma'am, — Salutation

I write to draw your attention to the menace of hawkers outside St. Paul's school in Nehru Nagar of our town. I am the Secretary, Swach Bharat Club, St. Paul's School. — Introduction

The hawkers sell open food and cheap toys. A number of our school students cluster around them and the lane in front of our school is blocked, dirty and congested.
I would request you to look into this problem and have the hawkers move into the field behind our school. This would ensure that they are not deprived of their livelihood and the area in front of our school is kept clean and congestion fee.
The hawkers must also be warned about the importance of necessary hygiene and the sale of clean food. This will ensure that students do not fall sick after eating food sold by the hawkers. — Informative Paragraph

I trust that you will consider my suggestion and take the necessary steps as outlined in my letter to you to deal with the menace of hawkers outside the school. — Conclusion

Thanking you,

Yours truly,/Yours faithfully
Santosh Haldar — Complimentary Closure

Specimen of Formal Letter, ICSE 2019

Format 2

Write a letter to the Police Commissioner of your city drawing his/her attention to the menace of hawkers outside your school. Tell him/her what dangers they pose and offer solutions for their rehabilitations.

Ans.

Flat 236, Block C
Hill Crest View Apartments,
Salem Street,
Coonoor-26

23rd February, 2018

The Police Commissioner,
Police Commissioner's Office,
6 Cavalry Road,
Coonoor-3

Dear Sir/Ma'am,

I write to draw your attention to the menace of hawkers outside St. Paul's school in Nehru Nagar of our town. I am the Secreatary, Swach Bharat Club, St. Paul's School.

The hawkers sell open food and cheap toys. A number of our school students cluster around them and the lane in front of our school is blocked, dirty and congested.

I would request you to look into this problem and have the hawkers move into the field behind our school. This would ensure that they are not deprived of their livelihood and the area in front of our school is kept clean and congestion fee.

The hawkers must also be warned about the importance of necessary hygiene and the sale of clean food. This will ensure that students do not fall sick after eating food sold by the hawkers.

I trust that you will consider my suggestion and take the necessary steps as outlined in my letter to you to deal with the menace of hawkers outside the school.

Thanking you

Yours truly,/Yours faithfully

Santosh Haldar

Specimen of Formal Letter, ICSE 2019

Marking Scheme

Format : 3 marks

Body : 1 mark–Two complaints (½ accumulation of garbage + ½ drains remain waterlogged)

1 mark–Two suggestions (½ drains need to be cleaned + ½ setting up of health camp)

Expression : 5 marks

Business Letters

Business letters are a basic means of communication between companies or even among the different departments in a company. They are written to keep permanent records of communication. These letters are written to professionals and hence, proper care must be taken about its language. Business letters must be drafted in

- formal language
- in a straightforward manner (to-the-point).
- with a polite and positive tone even while making a complaint

These letters include

- letters of enquiry (seeking or giving information)
- placing orders and sending replies
- cancelling orders
- complaint against wrong/late delivery of goods, inferior quality of goods, etc.
- acknowledgement regarding the receipts of goods/payments, etc.

Samples of Business Letter

1. You are Sakshi/Saksham living in Vellore. Your family plans to go for a vacation to Udaipur. Write a letter to the Front Office Manager of a five-star hotel seeking information about the types of rooms, tariffs, facilities, availability, etc. in their hotel.

Ans. H. No. 495,
Gautam Villa,
Pragati Colony,
Vellore, Karnataka
9th December, 20XX

The Manager,
Front Office,
The Oberoi Udayvilas,
Udaipur, Rajasthan

Dear Sir/Ma'am,

This is in reference to an online advertisement regarding the commendable services provided by your hotel. I wish to enquire regarding the same.

My family plans to visit Udaipur for sight-seeing in the month of June this year. We may stay at your esteemed hotel, provided your tariff plans suit our budget. We are four people including two adults and two children, and will be staying from the 2nd of June to the 6th of June, 20XX. We will prefer 'premier rooms' and will be requiring two of such rooms.

Kindly let me know your tariff plans and availability for the above mentioned room type and also give details of the facilities provided by your hotel. Also, please let me know whether you provide pick-and-drop service and sight-seeing facilities.

I would request you to mention any special concession offers, if going on.

Looking forward to your reply.

Thanking you,

Yours faithfully,
Sakshi Arora

2. You are the Librarian of Amla Public School. You had placed an order for textbooks with Dhanpati & Sons. As the books did not arrive on time, you have decided to cancel the order. Write a letter to the Manager, Dhanpati & Sons, Chennai, cancelling the order.

Ans. Amla Public School
24, Ooty Road
Coimbatore-641001
13th April, 20XX

The Manager,
M/s Dhanpati & Sons,
12/A Anna Salai,
Chennai-600001

Dear Sir/Ma'am,

Kindly refer to our above order dated 7th March, 20XX for various textbooks for our school students, in which the last date of delivery was 31st March, 20XX.

We regret that the books ordered have not been received by us.

As the new term of the school has already started, we are constrained to cancel the above order, as you did not comply with the delivery date and also have not informed us when you expect the books to be delivered.

Kindly acknowledge the receipt of this letter.

Yours faithfully,
KC Mohapatra
(Librarian)

SELF ASSESSMENT

1. Write a letter from a business firm to a customer in reply to his complaint that the goods sent were received in damaged condition.
2. You are Praveen/Renu Gupta, Sales Manager of Shoe Emporium, Lucknow. You have placed a bulk order for various kinds of shoes (for both ladies and gents) with Riverside Shoe Manufacturers, Kanpur. Due to changes in demand, you want to amend the order by reducing the quantity of one type of gents shoes and increasing the quantity of one type of ladies shoes. Write a letter to the supplier mentioning the changed quantities. Invent the necessary details.
3. You are Anoop/Aakriti Mourya, Baden Powell Senior Secondary School, Delhi. Write a letter to the Sales Manager, Aparana Publishing House, Delhi placing an order for books (minimum four titles) for your school library. Invent the necessary details.
4. Write a letter to Lightways Sports, Amrapalli, Thane placing an order for sports articles (minimum 4) to be supplied to your school, ABC Matriculation School, Civil Lines, Pune. Sign as Ravi/Raveena Mohan, Sports Secretary.
5. You are Sushil Kumar, the Sports Secretary of your school. Write a letter to Rishabh Enterprises, New Delhi, a leading firm dealing in sports goods, requesting them to supply their trade catalogue. Mention the items you intend to buy and ask for a discount on the catalogue prices.

Official Letters

These letters include letters of complaint, enquiries, requests and are generally written to the heads of various private, public, civil departments. For example, Chairman of Municipal Corporation, Mayor, Police Superintendant, etc. Therefore, they must be written in formal language with polite and positive attitude.

These letters are written to

- bring into notice traffic jam, breakdown of electricity, etc.
- request for opening of school, library, hospital, park, etc.
- requesting eminent personalities to become chief guests, etc.

Samples of Official Letter

1. Write a letter to the Chief Minister of your state drawing his attention to the urgent need for a government hospital in your district.

Ans. 16, Gol Bazar,
Yamunanagar,
Madhya Pradesh,
17th June, 20XX

The Honourable Chief Minister,
Government of Madhya Pradesh,
Bhopal

Dear Sir/Ma'am,

This is to bring to your kind notice that five tehsils comprising fourteen villages in the Yamunanagar district are devoid of primary healthcare facilities. Many valuable lives are becoming victims of death everyday due to the insufficiency of hospitals and doctors in our area. There are only two government hospitals in our district.

In case of minor ailments, the poor people have to rely on private clinics in their or nearby villages. But when there are serious cases or casualties, it is not only very difficult, but also risky to take the patient to the hospitals which are far away from their residence. Even these hospitals are not equipped with adequate facilities. Nor do they have sufficient number of capable doctors. Private hospitals charge very high fees which the poor peasants can't afford.

To check the increasing mortality and deteriorating health conditions in the district, a government hospital with all modern equipment is urgently required. It will cater to the basic needs of healthcare and medicine.

I hope you understand the gravity of the matter and take necessary steps in this regard as requested.

Thanking you,

Yours faithfully,
KL Mishra

2. You are Arun Maheswari. Write a letter to the Dean of Indira Gandhi National Open University enquiring about a course in Mass Communication.

Ans.

H. No. 453, Sector 15
Gurugram
Haryana-122001

17th December, 20XX

The Dean,
Indira Gandhi National Open University,
Maidan Garhi, New Delhi-110030

Dear Sir/Madam,

This is in reference to your advertisement in the Indian Express. I would like to enquire about a course that your university offers.

I have completed my graduation in English with 55% and am interested in joining the Masters Programme in Mass Communication in your university. I would like to know the eligibility criteria for the same and also request you to send me the details regarding cost, hostel facilities and other relevant information.

A self-addressed envelope is being enclosed herewith. Looking forward to an early response.

Yours faithfully,
Arun Maheshwari

SELF ASSESSMENT

1. Write a letter to the Director of the Archaeological Survey of India complaining about the damage caused to a historical monument in your city due to negligence. Suggest steps that the civic authorities should take to preserve the monument.
2. Due to insanitary conditions in the colony, the population of rodents has been multiplying, exposing the residents to multiple diseases. Write a letter to the Municipal Commissioner bringing the problem to his notice and urging him to take urgent action in the matter. You are Suraj/Supriya Kumar, 12 MG Road, Chennai.
3. Write a letter to the Manager of a local bus depot pointing out that there are very few buses plying on the route you use in the morning and these are invariably late, causing great inconvenience to the daily passengers.
4. You are Akshat Singhania, a resident of 39, Mayur Vihar, New Delhi. You are interested in joining the course in Advanced Techniques of Digital Photography advertised by Iconic Image Institute of Photography, Laxmi Nagar, Delhi. Write a letter of enquiry for the same.
5. Write a letter to the President of the Municipal Corporation for a scholarship to enable you to join a college.

Letters to the Editor

These letters are written to the Editor of a newspaper. The main purpose of writing these letters is to draw the attention of public and related authorities towards the said problem through the newspaper.

These letters are written to

- express agreement or disagreement with the news items or articles published in a newspaper.
- redress social issues or problems and give suggestions or seek solutions.

While writing letters to Editors

- be specific and clear in order to make your purpose be understood.
- always remember that the Editor can give your opinions, suggestions or questions 'a voice'. He/She cannot give you a solution, so don't ask for it.

Samples of Letter to the Editor

1. Write a letter to the Editor of a newspaper about the insanitary conditions prevailing in your locality and the indifference of the Municipal authorities in spite of repeated letters of complaint.

Ans. 102, Rai Mansion,
Bajrang Nagar,
Kanpur
4th April, 20XX
The Editor,
The Times of India,
Kanpur, Uttar Pradesh
Dear Sir/Ma'am,

Through the column of your prestigious daily, I wish to draw the attention of the concerned authorities towards the extremely pitiable conditions in Gokul Dham Colony. Sanitation is the cornerstone of public health and our colony drastically lacks it. Improper disposal of domestic waste and open sewages have been causing catastrophic effects on the health of the children as well as the adults in our colony.

This, in turn, is giving rise to serious diseases like diarrhoea, cholera, etc. Waterlogging and open manholes are other sources of diseases like malaria. They have also posed a risk before parents who are scared of sending their children out for playing. Yet, the local authorities are indifferent to such a grave concern. This is not only astonishing but also shameful on their part.

I would like to request the civil authorities to show their concern in this regard and take necessary steps immediately.

Thanking you,
Yours sincerely,
Abhay Jha

2. You are Nita Sharma, residing at A-406, Vasundhra Apartments, Ghaziabad. You are disturbed to watch the portrayal of women in TV serials. Write a letter to the Editor, The Times of India, BSJ Marg, New Delhi, expressing your views on the issue.

Ans. A-406, Vasundhra,
Apartments,
Ghaziabad-211007
14th December, 20XX

The Editor,
The Times of India,
BSJ Marg, New Delhi -110002

Respected Sir/Ma'am,

Through the column of your esteemed daily, I would like to draw the attention of the concerned authorities towards the skewed portrayal of women in TV serials. Most of the TV channels telecast family soaps which do not show women in proper light. A woman is portrayed as either Kaikeyi or Sita. The serials advocate values which are against Indian culture. There is no respect for values in these serials. The women are being portrayed as a house breaker, conspirator or vamp. The Indian woman, known for her kindness, tolerance and sacrifices, is being portrayed as just the opposite.

I am of the opinion that the content of TV serials should be regulated and put under observation. This is the right time to check the trend before the image of the Indian woman is tarnished.

Yours faithfully,
Nita Sharma

SELF ASSESSMENT

1. The government has decided to cut off subsidy on cooking gas which has resulted in creating tremendous pressure on budgeting household expense for middle class people. Write a letter to the Editor of a local daily expressing your views.
2. As a regular commuter by bus from Noida to Delhi, you have been witnessing rash driving by the bus drivers daily without an exception. Write a letter to the Editor, The Times of India drawing the attention of the General Manager, Delhi Transport Corporation to this problem. You are Priti/Prakash Yadav, 15 Udyog Vihar, Noida.
3. You are Kamini/Kamal Sinha of 10, Civil Lines Extension, Chanakyapuri, Agra. The main road leading to your locality has three open manholes, causing frequent accidents at night, especially during the rainy season. Write a letter to the Editor, The Times of India drawing attention of the Municipal Commissioner to this problem of the residents.
4. You have noticed many stray animals on the road during the busy hours of the day. These animals cause traffic jams as well as accidents. You have already written to the concerned authorities but no action has been taken so far. Write a letter to the Editor, The Hindu drawing attention of the Municipal Commissioner, Chennai. You are Shantha/Suresh Nathan, 12, MG Road, Chennai.
5. The youth of the country is very vigilant these days and feels concerned about the problems being faced by the people. Write a letter to the Editor of a national daily urging them to highlight the role of the youth in eradicating the problems of poverty, unemployment and corruption.

Letters to Principal

In this type of letters, you need to convince the Principal of your school/college regarding something. There should be a logical order to arguments that you provide in favour of your request.

These letter are written to

- change of subject, granting leaving/character certificate, etc.
- organising an event/guest lecture for the benefit of students, etc.
- taking the students to some fair, seminar, etc.
- providing or increasing certain facilities
- fee concessions and scholarships

Note *Letters to the librarian, accounts department of your school/college may also come under this category.*

Samples of Letter to Principal

1. Write an application to your Principal to make arrangements for extra classes of Mathematics as the teacher was on a long leave and the course could not be completed.

Ans. The Principal
DAV Inter College
Kanpur,
2nd September, 20XX

Dear Ma'am/Sir,

On behalf of all the students of Class XA, I request you to arrange for extra classes of Mathematics after school timings.

Our honourable teacher is making a sincere effort to complete the syllabus. But, since he was on long leave, it is lagging far behind. I am sure you can understand that Mathematics is a subject that requires a lot of practice after learning once. Therefore, we all are ready to attend extra classes in the evenings.

We shall be highly obliged to you for your kind consideration.

Thanking you,

Yours obediently,

Naina Malik

(Class Xth A)

2. Write a letter to the Principal of your school requesting him to allow you and a few of your friends to take Economics in place of Biology for Board Examination. Your school is a Science school that conducts/runs no classes for Economics as it's an Arts subject. Convince your Principal as to why you want to opt for this subject and request him to make necessary arrangements.

Ans.

The Principal,

St Francis School,

Rohini, New Delhi,

21st February, 20XX

Dear Sir/Ma'am,

This is to inform you that I am a student of Class X, Section A. I find Biology a little difficult. I score pretty well in Mathematics, Physics, Chemistry and languages. But, I fear that my overall score in the Board Exam may be affected due to getting less percentage in Biology. Moreover, when I discuss my future career plans with my parents, they tell me that I can take up a graduation course in Economics, Mathematics and Statistics, since I have a greater inclination towards Economics than Science subjects. Also, this has become a rewarding career these days. Therefore, I want to change Biology to Economics. A few of my classmates also want to take up this subject.

I know Economics is not taught in our school. But, if you kindly give us permission to opt for it, we will be taking private coaching for this subject.

I would be highly obliged to you if you allow us the same.

Yours obediently,

Rahul Roy

(Class Xth A)

SELF ASSESSMENT

1. There is a book fair going on in your city. Write a letter to the Principal of your school on behalf of your class, requesting him to make arrangements for a visit to the fair.
2. You have just been admitted to a new school. Write a letter to the Principal complaining about excessive ragging being done by the senior students and requesting him to look into the matter.
3. Write a letter to the Principal of your school, requesting him to make regular arrangement for evening games.
4. Write a letter to the Principal of your school requesting him to issue your transfer and character certificates as your father has been transferred to another city, and you have to go along and join another institute.
5. Write a letter to the Principal of your school requesting him to make arrangement for some more furniture for your classroom. Also, give reason for your demand.

Job Applications

Job applications or cover letters are letters written to prospective employers pointing out suitability for an advertised vacancy. These letters must be written in a strictly formal and precise manner. In such letter you must include

1. reference if you are replying to an advertisement/call
2. the post you want to apply for
3. Your interest in the job
4. Your suitability/qualifications
5. Your experience, if any
6. Mention your enclosure of biodata/testimonials/certificates

Samples of Job Application

1. You are Anvay/Anaaya Bamrutwar living in 362, Mayur Vihar, New Delhi. You saw an advertisement in the newspaper for the post of an 'Electrical Engineer' in Bharat Heavy Electricals Limited (BHEL). Write an application to the Human Resource Manager, BHEL giving details of your qualifications and experience.

Ans.

362, Poonam Apartments,
Mayur Vihar,
New Delhi

21st November, 20XX

The Manager,
Human Resource Department,
Bharat Heavy Electricals Ltd,
New Delhi

Dear Sir/Ma'am,

With reference to your advertisement in The Times of India dated 20th November, 20XX, I would like to apply for the post of Electrical Engineer in your esteemed organisation.

I have completed engineering in Electrical Technology with an aggregate of 77% marks from Chennai University. I have also done a one-year diploma in Network Analysis in addition to a basic course in computer. I have worked with Bajaj Electricals for 3 years and was awarded twice for my best contributory work by my employer. I was the winner of 'Student of the year' in 2010 during the second year of my college. I have also been an active participant in various extra-curricular activities and delivered seminars and projects on various topics successfully.

I have attached my testimonials herewith for your kind consideration. I will be available for the interview at any time of your convenience provided you find a suitable candidate in me.

Thanking you,

Yours faithfully,

Anaaya Bamrutwar

Encl : Testimonials

2. You are Anand/ Arti Singh Sidhu of 14, Model Town, Delhi. You have seen an advertisement in 'The Hindu' for the post of Chief Chef in a 5-Star Hotel. Apply for the job with a complete resume.

Ans.

14, Model Town,
Delhi-110009

12th August, 20XX

The HR Manager,
Hotel Meridian,
10, Raisina Road,
New Delhi-110001

Dear Sir/Ma'am,

This is in response to your advertisement in 'The Hindu' dated 10th August, 20XX. I would like to apply for the post of Chief Chef.

I have a 3-year Diploma in Hotel Management from the Pusa Institute, one of the best institutions of the country in this field. In addition, I have a total of 10 years of experience in various 5-Star Hotels. Currently, I am working as Deputy Chief Chef in another 5-Star hotel.

I am enclosing my resume, one testimonial and attested copies of my certificates with this letter for your consideration.

Looking forward to hearing from you.

Yours faithfully,
Anand Singh Sidhu
Encl : Resume, testimonial and certificates

SELF ASSESSMENT

1. You have seen an advertisement in the newspaper for the post of teacher. Write an application to the Manager, ABC Public School, applying for the post of TGT (English).

2. You wish to apply for the post of a Cashier to a local bank. Write a letter to the Branch Manager applying for the job. Also ask him which of the documents you should take along for his reference.

3. You saw an advertisement in a local newspaper regarding the vacancy of an Assistant Manager. Write a letter to the HR Manager, in response to the advertisement to apply for the same post. You are Anup Sharma and you have done MBA from Kanpur University.

4. There is a vacancy for a Front Office Assistant in a 3-Star Hotel in your town. The requirements for the post are as follows

- Young, unmarried females of age 19-24.
- Candidates must be a graduate.
- Good communication skills in English and Hindi.
- Height at least 5' 4" and a pleasing personality.

Write a letter to the HR Manager to apply for the post.

5. You are Prem/Parul Gupta of 16, TT Nagar, Bhopal. You would like to apply for the post of Marketing Manager in a reputed firm in Mumbai. Write a letter to the Public Relations Officer, Chantac Enterprises, Mumbai, applying for the job.

Letters of Complaint

This type of letters is written to the addressed person to draw their attention towards the problem that has arisen with a product or service. In such letters, a person is asked to provide the solution as per their jurisdiction.

Though this type of letters demands strong persuasive force in one's words, it should be drafted in formal language as other official letters. No personal influence or threats should be reflected in the letter.

Samples of Complaint Letter

1. Write a letter to the Manager of the showroom from where you have recently purchased an LED TV, complaining that it is not functioning properly. Give details of the model of the TV and your purchase date. Also, ask for its replacement.

Ans.

10, Apna Ghar Society,
Vikhroli,
Allahabad
17th October, 20XX
The Manager,
Golchha Electronics,
Sagarpur,
Allahabad

Dear Sir/Ma'am,

This is to bring to your notice that I had purchased an LED TV from your showroom last month on the 5th September, 20XX receipt no XLYV26. It has been only a period of a month and the TV is not functioning properly. There are some problems in its sound system. Also, it sometimes gets switched off automatically. The model of the television set I purchased is 40" Full HD LED TV K/V-40r-562 C–(2015 Model–Semi Smart).

I request you to replace the set with a new one as it is in warranty period.

Thanking you,
Yours faithfully,
Sumit Patel

2. Write a letter to the Commissioner of Police complaining about the loud music being played by some people in your locality and requesting to stop it. This is disturbing students who are preparing for their annual examination.

Ans.

'Shreyas' Niwas,
Raman Colony,
Gail Industrial Area,
Pune

1st January, 20XX

The Commissioner of Police
Gail Industrial Area Police Station, Pune

Respected Sir/Ma'am

Most respectfully, I wish to bring to your notice the deplorable condition of the students preparing for their exams in our colony. February to May is a crucial period for studies as most of the exams in schools and professional colleges take place during this period. The students in our area are not able to concentrate on their studies because of the loud music being played by the nearby marriage halls.

Most of the time, the music keeps on playing till late night. This distracts the students from their studies a lot. Also, since last week, there have been many rallies and roadshows in our area which use loudspeakers at high volume. If the situation persists, the students will not be able to make productive use of their time and their future will be at stake.

I request you to put a ban on the use of loudspeakers and playing of loud music during the examination months.

Hope you take kind consideration and effective measures to stop this practice as early as possible.

Yours faithfully,
Shailaja Verma

SELF ASSESSMENT

1. Write a letter to the Station Incharge of your area, requesting him to take action against some undesirable persons who are disturbing the public peace in your locality.
2. You are the Manager of a book store. You had ordered books for various sections of your store from a wholesale dealer in another city. The number of books delivered by the wholesale dealer is less than that ordered by you. Write a complaint letter to the dealer regarding this.
3. While you were returning from office last evening, somebody snatched your handbag from you and ran away. Write a letter to the local police station complaining about this theft. Also, give the details of the man's appearance as much as you could observe.
4. You were on a business tour to Sikanderabad for four days. During your stay at a local hotel, you had given your clothes to the laundary department for cleaning. After returning home, you noticed that one of your blazers was missing. Write a letter of complaint to the Front Office Manager of the hotel regarding your missing blazer. Also ask him to send it by courier as soon as it is found.
5. There is a big market near the area in which you reside. There is a parking area near the market. Yet, many people park their vehicles in front of shops and on roads. This creates traffic jam and makes it difficult for people to walk through. Write a letter to the Police Commissioner complaining about illegal parking by people and also suggest some disciplinary measures to be implemented in the city.

EXAM PRACTICE

(Based on All Categories)

1. A certain book/chapter has been included in your syllabus. You have heard that a film version is now available. Write a letter to the Manager of a film theatre near your school, requesting that the film be shown. Tell him/her why it will be beneficial to the students. *[2023]*
2. You are being considered for a Head boy/Head girl position in the school. Write a letter to the Principal explaining why you think you would make a good Head boy/Head girl. Why does the role interest you? Describe ways in which you would carry out your responsibilities. *[Sem II 2022]*
3. Some taps in your locality are left open all day resulting in a tremendous waste of water. Write a letter to the Municipal Commissioner of your town / city, complaining about the problem. Suggest ways in which this waste of water can be prevented. *[2020]*
4. You want to start a new club in your school. Write a letter to your Principal requesting permission to start the club. Explain your role in it and give reasons to prove that the club will be beneficial for the school. *[2019]*
5. The traffic outside your school is very heavy and chaotic.

   Write a letter to the Deputy Commissioner of Police (Traffic) pointing out the dangers of such heavy and chaotic traffic in a school zone. Suggest possible solutions for the problem. *[2018]*
6. Being the Secretary of Live Happy Youth Club of your town/city, you are going to organise a charitable camp for eye and dental check-up and treatment for the poor people. You wish to get a sponsor and hence decide to write a letter to the Managing Director, Persistence Technologies Pvt Ltd for the sponsorship. Write a letter giving full details of your mission.
7. Many areas near your school have been affected by flood. You are the President of your school's Social Service Club. Write a letter to the Mayor of your town/city telling him/her what you plan to do for the relief of the victims. Suggest ways in which you can join with other organisations to bring about better distribution of relief items. *[2012]*
8. You are the President of the school's Nature Club. Write a letter to a well-known Social Worker or Environmentalist inviting him/her to be the Chief Guest at the Annual Function of your club. Give some details about your club and the Annual Function.
9. A company has been marketing spurious medicines behind claims that its product could be effective in preventing the avian flu or other forms of influenza. Write a letter to the Drug Controller General of the Directorate of Health Services, examining the claim of the company and explaining the harm these kind of claims could cause.
10. Status of women in India is not as satisfactory as it could have been in the twenty first century. Women are working in almost every sector and proving their calibre. Yet, their dignity is at stake since some people do not respect them. Write a letter to the Editor of a local daily expressing your views on this issue.
11. You are the Manager of a Private Sector Bank in Noida. A newspaper has published an inaccurate account of a robbery in your branch. Write a letter to the Editor detailing what actually happened.
12. Write a letter to the Director of a television channel complaining about the quality of the programmes telecast on it. Suggest ways to improve the quality of programmes. *[2010]*
13. Your class wants to visit a well-known historical monument in a nearby town. Write a letter to your Principal seeking permission and say how you would benefit from the visit. *[2016]*
14. A number of loose electric wires are hanging from a lamp post near the main gate of your school. Write a letter to the Municipal Commissioner explaining the problem, the danger it poses and also suggest a quick solution. *[2017]*
15. You are Rajat Kumar, a resident of 79, RK Puram, New Delhi. You are interested in joining a course in Communication Skills advertised by the Elite School of Language, South Extension. Write a letter to the director enquiring for the same.

16. You are interested in pursuing a short-term course in computer graphics during your holidays. Write a letter to the Director, Easy Computers, enquiring about their short-term courses and asking for all the necessary details. You are Naresh/Nandini Kumar.

Answers

Based on Format 1

1. XYZ School
PQR city
21st September, 20XX
The Manager,
Cinepolis,
PQR City
Dear Sir/Ma'am,

It is to inform you that I am a student of the ABC school, PQR city. Recently, our syllabus has been altered and the book *Pride and Prejudice* by Jane Austen has been added to it. Since it is a new addition to the syllabus, most of the students have very little idea about the novel.

It has recently come to my knowledge that the film version of this book has also become available. The movie is considered to be a good adaptation of the book and has received positive reviews. It has also been commended for its brilliant performances, great direction and above all its great portrayal of the late nineteenth century England. I feel that the movie would be helpful to most of the students in understanding the culture, customs and norms of those times. By watching the movie, they would also be able to learn the pronunciation of the words that they find in the book. Also, a lot of the students prefer to watch movies over reading books. They confess that watching a movie makes them concentrate much more and it would be helpful to them in understanding the novel and doing well in the exams.

Therefore, I request you to show this movie for the students of our school in your film theatre. It would be extremely helpful for the students and it would increase their knowledge of the story considerably.

Thanking you,
Yours sincerely,
Abhishek

2. The Principal,
XYZ School,
New Delhi
22nd July, 20XX
Dear Sir/Ma'am,

This is to inform you that, I, Neha Sharma, of Class X I have been nominated as the Head Girl of the school. A Head Girl is a mature, hard-working and talented person who is seen as someone with a friendly and positive approach to work. It is a role that requires patience, respect, care, the ability to work well in a team and to support the reputation of the school. Being open-minded and being able to talk to the younger students on a one-on-one the level are also important qualities required.

I firmly believe I have the skills and qualities necessary to represent the school as the Head Girl. As can be seen by my contribution in the last term, I was able to continue all of my extra-curricular activities both during and after school, in addition to completing my homework on time and performing well in the Mock examinations. Moreover, I would personally benefit by becoming the Head Girl. It would give me an opportunity to develop my public speaking and leadership skills, which will be useful later on in life.

Therefore, I am confident that I will be able to balance additional school activities with schoolwork.

Thank you for the consideration.

Yours obediently,
Neha Sharma
Class X-A

3. House No. 222,
Shakti Nagar
Amritsar, Punjab

15th September, 20XX

The Municipal Commissioner,
Punjab

Dear Sir/Ma'am,

This is to bring to your notice the tremendous wastage of water occurring in our area. The Municipality has installed various public taps to facilitate the water supply. It is especially helpful for those households which do not have submersibles at their homes. But this facility has now become a source of trouble for the people. Due to lack of maintenance, most of the taps have worn out and as a result they keep on running. This has caused two problems : first, there is a lot of wastage of water and second, this water gets collected along the roads leading to waterlogging. This has caused a lot of inconvenience for the residents.

I, therefore, request you to look into the matter and get the taps repaired. Also, to prevent the excessive wastage of water, these public taps could be replaced by underground water pipelines with connection to every household. This would provide people water twice a day and there would not be any wastage of water. Until then, these public taps should be repaired and replace at regular intervals.

I hope you will take the matter into consideration and act accordingly as soon as possible.

Thanking you,
Yours faithfully,
Pragya Sharma

4. The Principal,
Sunlight Public School,
Ghaziabad

8th July, 20XX

Respected Sir/Ma'am,

This is to inform you, I, Rahul Singh, along with, the students of Class 9, want to start a Nature Club in our school. The objective of the club will be to inform as many students as possible about our environment, and to study animals, birds, flowers and plants and how to conserve them. We plan to hold weekly excursions and meetings on Saturday afternoons when school gets over. I myself have experience of running such a club in my previous school last year. It will help in increasing our general knowledge about these and will also benefit the school by enabling students to do better in the examinations.

We hope you will permit us to start the Nature Club for the students. Their activities can be monitored by a teacher whom we request you to nominate.

Thanking you,
Yours obediently,
Rahul Singh
Class IX, Section A

5. Brahma Public School,
Hindu Colony, Dadar,
Mumbai - 400014

17th October, 20XX

The Deputy Commissioner,
Mumbai Police (Traffic),
Mumbai – 400009

Dear Sir/Ma'am,

This is to bring to your kind attention the problems our school students face on Bhadkamkar Marg due to regular traffic jams at the time when school opens in the morning and when it closes in the afternoon.

We all are aware that the number of vehicles and commuters on the roads is continuously increasing and that there is no proportional increase in the width of the roads to accommodate this increased traffic. Consequently, traffic jams are bound to happen if the traffic is not disciplined.

We observe that jams occur because of all kinds of vehicles being parked irresponsibly for long periods of time on the road near our school. Then, we can see drivers getting into ugly arguments, indulging in rash driving, etc. Further, as this is a school area, it is a Silence Zone, as some signboards put up by your department proclaim. However, there is no silence, as some motorists continuously honk when there is a traffic jam.

If your department arranges two traffic constables on duty at the time of the school's opening and closing, they can create awareness among the drivers about traffic rules and regulations. Further, they can regulate the traffic at that time to improve the situation. If the necessary action is not taken from your side very soon, it may lead to accidents also.

We have faith in the Police Department. I believe that the Police Department will fulfil its duties to combat this problem of traffic jams in our school zone.

Thanking you,

Yours sincerely,

Ramcharan Mohapatra
(Head Boy)

6. 16, Dwarka Apartments
Shankar Nagar,
Nashik

1st June, 20XX

The Managing Director,
Persistence Technologies,
Nashik

Dear Sir/Ma'am,

It is with great pleasure that I have written this letter to inform you on behalf of 'Live Happy Youth Club' that we are organising a charity mission for the poor of our town. I wonder if your esteemed organisation could raise a hand towards charity and add to its goodwill.

We will be conducting a 'Health Camp' for three days at Nehru Nagar. There will be free eye and dental check-ups followed by the required treatment on the subsequent days. The patients will also be provided with the necessary medicines. Experienced doctors and nurses from the government and private hospitals of the city will be treating the patients. There will also be an arrangement of all modern equipment necessary for proper diagnosis and cure of the ailments. The government multi-speciality hospital of the city has shown its modesty to offer the best equipment it has.

I request you to offer your sponsorship for the event. In turn, we will give publicity to your company by printing its name on the pamphlets and banners. Awaiting your prompt reply.

Thanking you,

Yours faithfully,

Neelam Patil
(Secretary, Live Happy Youth Club)

7. Dronacharya School
Rajendra Nagar
Kolhapur

10th August, 20XX

The Mayor
District Office
Kolhapur

Dear Sir/Ma'am,

With all due respect, I would like to draw your kind attention towards the grievous situation of the flood victims of our district. The flood has completely devastated the houses as well as the fields of the people residing in our area. Many have been injured and there is an acute shortage of food and clothes.

The government as well as the Armed Forces are working towards providing fast relief to the victims. But, the loss is so severe and large that this effort is falling short. It is of course our duty to help our brethren in such a woeful situation. Therefore, the Social Service Club of our school has decided to provide a helping hand for speedily relief. We would be appealing to various organisations and NGOs to raise funds to assist us by offering their manpower for this mission. Our teams would join the relief camps to assist them in evacuating people and treating the casualties. We would also be buying food items and clothes from the funds collected.

I hope, with the cooperation of other organisations and your kind consent, we will be able to help our unfortunate brothers and sisters to relieve them from this grim problem.

Thanking you,

Yours faithfully,

Harshita Motwani

(President, Social Service Club)

8. Vidya Niketan School,

New Delhi,

6th February, 20XX

Ms. Madhu Bhatnagar

The Head of Environmental Department,

Sri Ram School,

New Delhi

Dear Ma'am,

It gives me a great honour to invite you on behalf of my school to be the Chief Guest on the Annual Day Celebration of our Nature Club. We established the Nature Club in our school on 20th February three years ago. Since then, we have been organising various activities such as 'Planting Tree Campaign', 'Cleanliness Campaign', 'Save Our Planet Campaign', etc., every year. By organising such events, we hope to instil in our students as well as the whole society love and respect for our planet and humanity.

It would be an honour for us if you adorn the function by your gracious presence and also enlighten all of us with your experiences.

Looking forward to welcoming you.

Thanking you,

Yours faithfully,

Ashwin Patel

(President, Nature Club)

Based on Format 2

9.

24/7, Charkhop Pharmacy Stores,

Andheri West,

Mumbai

2nd December, 20XX

The Drug Controller General,

Directorate of Health Services,

Mumbai

Dear Sir/Ma'am,

This is to draw your attention towards the marketing of a spurious medicine, 'Oxeprazole capsules and injections', by XYZ India Ltd. It claims that these medicines are effective in preventing the avian flu and other forms of influenza. Such huge claims have attracted the doctors who are readily prescribing these medicines to their patients.

Many patients of the avian flu have used these medicines and their condition has further deteriorated. Some of them have developed severe side effects. Many have even been on the brink of losing their lives.

I, therefore, request you to examine the claims of this company thoroughly and prevent any more such medicines from flooding the markets so that innocent lives may be spared. Moreover, a ban should be issued on the production of such medicines. Your immediate action in this regard would be highly appreciated.

Yours faithfully,
Rakesh Kumar

10. 12, Garima Enclave,
Indralok Society,
Abhyankar Nagar, Nagpur

13th May, 20XX

The Editor,

The Hitavada ,

Civil Lines,

Nagpur

Dear Sir/Ma'am,

Through the column of your esteemed daily, I would like to draw the attention of the people towards the plight of women in our country. Women have been working in almost every field and walking abreast with their male counterparts. They have shown an evolutionary rise from a housewife to a working professional and to an entrepreneur. Yet, the menace of dowry, domestic violence, eve-teasing, female foeticide, etc. has not left them. The dignity of women is still not safeguarded. They are still becoming prey to the lust of men. To satisfy their much fanned 'ego' and to be authoritative and powerful, men still dominate and humiliate women.

Inspite of shouldering the responsibility of family and also contributing to the growth of the nation, women have not got an equal status in India. Supreme Court's latest verdict on the law against molestation of women is relieving. Similar steps on the part of local administrators and police departments of every state and city are expected. Unless the activities of atrocities against women are strictly monitored and controlled, women cannot consider themselves safe.

I will strongly admire your newspaper raising voice for women's honour.

Yours sincerely,
Vaibhav Tendulkar

11. Arunodaya Bank,
Bank Colony,
Noida

22nd September, 20XX

The Editor,

Jagruti Express,

Noida–07

Dear Sir/Ma'am,

This is in reference with the press report in your newspaper on 21st September, 20XX, that highlighted 'The senior officer's connivance leads to bank robbery of ₹ 10 crores'. The news report published by your daily was not only far from truth but also attacked the goodwill of the officers as well as the bank. I would like to bring to your kind notice the discrepancies in the report by your correspondents.

The robbers looted the bank in the middle of the night whereas the report states it to have occurred at around 8 in the evening. The report also states the robbery of ₹ 10 crores, whereas the exact loss incurred was ₹ 7 crore and gold worth ₹ 20 lakh, as mentioned in the FIR No. 768. Moreover, our security guard was so mercilessly beaten while he tried to resist them that he is in ICU at City Hospital. It is disgusting that the news report has mentioned of him being merely threatened on the tip of the revolver. This creates a very bad impression among the public whose faith is shaken.

I request you to publish a rectified news report stating bare facts, so that the harm is compensated.

Yours faithfully,
Jay Narain (Manager)

12. Flat No. 704, A–Wing,
Nexus Apartments,
Tardeo, Mumbai,
13th November, 20XX

The Director,
ABC Entertainment Channel,
Mumbai

Dear Sir/Ma'am,

This is to bring to your kind notice the deteriorating quality of programmes that are being telecast on your channel. It is surprising to note that the channel 'ABC' that was once famous for being thoroughly entertaining and educative has now deteriorated to the level of only family serials where often the women are portrayed as the villains. These serials are undoubtedly having an adverse effect on human relationships within the household.

Youngsters watching this programme are inspired to use filthy language, scheming and plotting against their own family members. Besides this, degradation of values and too much of wealth and opulence teaches youngsters to acquire quick wealth through fair or foul means.

It will be much appreciated if you would take note of the above mentioned complaint and change the outlook of the programmes that are being telecast. I would suggest adding on some variety in the programmes by introducing some–Quiz/GK programme, comedies, cookery shows, interviews and some educative programmes to make the channel more interesting.

I am sure that this letter will not go unheeded. I sincerely look forward to better aired programmes in future.

Yours faithfully,
Shraddha Nigam

13. The Principal
Happy School
Daryaganj
New Delhi-110002
21st November, 20XX

Dear Sir/Madam,

With all due respect, I would like to inform you that I am a student of Class X-B at your school. Our class wants to visit Taj Mahal, Agra as part of an educational trip. We have chosen the destination by conducting a voting among the students. The trip would take two days and would be organised on a weekend so that the classes are not affected. Our class teacher has agreed to accompany us on the trip.

The trip would help us in learning about our cultural heritage. We would also be able to see one of the seven wonders of the world. We are very excited for this visit and have been reading about Taj Mahal and Agra.

Hence, I most humbly request you to permit us to visit.

Yours obediently,
Saloni Mishra
(Class X-B)

14. Apeejay School,
New Delhi,
20th April, 20XX

The Municipal Commissioner,
South Delhi

Dear Sir/Madam,

This is to bring to your notice the precarious situation all school students and staff members face everyday when they enter the gates of Apeejay School, Saket where I am a student. Near the main gate of our school, a lamp post has been there for a number of years. But recently, some loose electrical wires are hanging out of it and wires are extending to the main gate of our school. We have requested the local authorities to repair these loose hanging wires as they pose a literal threat to the lives of students or staff members. There is always a fear of getting electrocuted if any one unintentionally or intentionally touches those wires.

Inspite of repeated requests, nothing has been done so far. It is requested therefore to treat the matter urgently and get the wires set at their proper place to avoid any calamity or loss of life.

Yours faithfully,
Mukesh Sahu
(Head Boy, Class X)

15. 79, RK Puram,
New Delhi - 110045
12th August, 20XX

The Director,
Elite School of Language,
South Extension-II
New Delhi-110048

Dear Sir/Madam,

This is with reference to your advertisement in the Times of India dated 10th August, 20XX announcing a new course in Communication Skills. I am a graduate and plan to take up a part-time job as a Customer Care Executive in a reputed Call Centre. For this, I shall need to improve my communication skills and would appreciate it if you could forward me the details of the course.

Please let me know the duration of the course for beginners and the advanced course as well as the fees charged for both courses. I would like to know if the courses are recognised by any university and whether they are diploma or certificate courses.

Kindly furnish the details at the address mentioned above as early as possible, so that I can decide about enrolling myself for one of them.

Yours sincerely,
Rajat Kumar

16. 79, RK Puram,
New Delhi-110045
12th April, 20XX

The Director,
Easy Computers,
South Extension II,
New Delhi-110048

Dear Sir/Madam,

This is in reference to your advertisement in the Times of India dated 10th April, 20XX informing about the short-term computer courses you are conducting.

I am a graduate in Science and plan to take up a job in the line of software. Specifically, I am interested in the course on computer graphics and similar other courses in this field. Please send me details of the short-term courses you are conducting, particularly those that start around 1st May.

I will appreciate if you could forward me more details of the computer graphics course, including curriculum, duration, fees, etc.

Yours sincerely,
Naresh Kumar

Informal Letters

Informal letters include the letters written to family members, relatives, friends and acquaintances. There are no formal rules as such on how to write these types of letters. Since they are intended to express feelings and share some life events, they are written in a friendly manner. The style of writing may depend upon an individual's nature and mood. If you are writing to an elderly person, you should use the language which is respectful and courteous. While writing to friends, one can use casual, friendly language.

Purpose of Writing Informal Letters

- To express feelings and emotions
- To stay connected with relatives and friends
- To ask their whereabouts and howabouts
- To send invitations and to give thanks
- To describe an event or incident

Steps to Write an Informal Letter

Informal letters consist of following parts

1. Sender's Address and Date

Sender's address and date of writing the letter (sender's name is never written in the heading part)

2. Greeting/Salutation

This consists of greeting and name of the recipient or the sender's relation with the recipient, e.g. Dear Ashi.

(a) **For Parents**
Dear/My dear father/mother, etc.

(b) **For Relatives**
Dear uncle/aunty, etc.

(c) **For Brother/Sister/Cousin, etc.**
Dear/My dear (name), etc.

(d) **For Acquintances**
Dear Mr (last name)/Ms (name)

3. Body of the Letter/Message

(a) **Introduction/Opening**

- This may begin with enquiring howabouts, e.g. 'How are you?', 'How are you (Akshay/Rahul)?' or 'I hope you are hale and hearty', 'I hope you are doing well', or 'It's been a long time since I have heard from you.'
- The letter may also begin with acknowledging/thanking for the previous letter/gift received, e.g. 'Thank you for such a precious gift of yours' or by apologising if you are writing/replying after too long.
e.g. "Hi Preeti. I received your letter, but I was so busy with my new project that I could not reply earlier."

(b) **Main Body of the Letter**

- Here, you write about the actual purpose of your letter, sharing the current events happening in your life, school, college, etc.
- Try to write your message according to the theme of the question asked.
- While you share your experiences, your feelings, ask questions in between to arouse interest of the reader. This will give your letter a touch of live conversation.
- Also, give replies to the questions of the recipient if he/she has written to you earlier.

4. Closure/Concluding Sentence

Even if you are writing an informal, friendly letter, you cannot end it abruptly. So, give your letter a proper closure with the consent of the reader. e.g. 'Hope to see/hear from you soon'.
Also, you may convey love to family members, and good wishes to friends and acquaintances. e.g. 'Convey my regards to aunty and uncle', 'Love to little Chinu', etc.

5. Subscription or Leave-Taking

As in formal letters, informal letters too need to be courteous and respectful to the person you are writing to. Below the subscription, comes the signature or name of the writer as e.g.

- **Family Members and Relatives** Your affectionate/loving son/daughter/ brother/ sister/ nephew, etc.
- **Close Friends** Yours lovingly/loving friend
- **Acquaintances** Yours faithfully/sincerely

Formats of Informal Letter

The ICSE board has prescribed two formats for informal letter.

Format 1

Image that you are in boarding school and have performed poorly in your terminal examination. Write a letter to your mother, explaining the reasons for your poor performance, and tell her how you plan to do better in the forthcoming examinations.

Jingle Bells
Residential School
Igatpuri–422 402 — *Sender's Address*

10th October, 2018 — *Date*

My dear Mummy/Mother, — *Salutation*

I know that you are very disappointed with my half yearly report that you must have received last week. I am truly sorry for a poor performance and I am feeling very depressed at having let you down so badly. I do not want to make excuses, but this last term I have been in and out of the infirmary several times. I had a bad attack of malaria and was unable to attend classes for about a week. Barely had I got over this when I broke out in a rash because of the medication and I had to go back into the infirmary. As result of this I missed many classes and I scored very poorly in three subjects.

I have now picked up health and have requested my teacher to give me some extra assignments. I also plan to do group study with some of the other boarders of my class.

I am sure that these will help me to catch up with my studies and I promise you I will score much better marks in the next unit tests. — *Body of the Letter*

Please do not be worried about my health, I am much better. I look forward to meeting you during the mid-term break. — *Closing Expression*

Yours lovingly, /Yours affectionately, /Your loving son,
Sanjiv — *Subscription and Signature*

Specimen of Informat Letter, ICSE 2019

Format 2

Imagine that you are in a boarding school and have performed poorly in your terminal examination. Write a letter to your mother, explaining the reasons for your poor performance and tell her how you plan to do better in the forthcoming examinations.

Jingle Bells Residential School,
Igatpuri-422402

10th October, 2018

My dear Mummy/Mother,

I know that you are very disappointed with my half yearly report that you must have received last week. I am truly sorry for a poor performance and I am feelling very depressed at having let you down so badly. I do not want to make excuses, but this last term I have been in and out of the infirmary several times. I had a bad attack of malaria and was unable to attend classes for about a week. Barely had I got over this when I broke out in a rash because of the medication and I had to go back into the infirmary. As result of this I missed many classes and I scored very poorly in three subjects.

I have now picked up health and have requested my teacher to give me some extra assignments. I also plan to do group study with some of the other boarders of my class.

I am sure that this will help me to catch up with my studies and I promise you I will score much better marks in the next unit tests.

Please do not be worried about my health, I am much better. I look forward to meeting you during the mid-term break.

Yours lovingly, /Yours affectionately, /Your loving son,
Sanjiv

Marking Scheme

Format	:	2½ marks
Body	:	2½ marks
Expression	:	5 marks

Samples of Informal Letters

1. You were part of an organising committee for an inter-school event which was very successful. You and the other committee members were congratulated and praised at the school assembly by the Principal. Write a letter to your grandmother telling her about the event and your feelings at being recognised and praised in front of the school. *[2017]*

Ans. St. Thomas Boys Hostel,
Roorkee

20th April, 20XX

Dearest Grandmother,

How are you? I miss you everyday. I am very excited and happy right now. Last week, my school had organised an Inter-School Quiz Competition in which six schools had participated. An organising committee was formed by our school principal. The committee's function was to chalk out the programme and to look after the participants and accompanying teachers coming from other schools. I was also selected as a member of that organising committee. The event went off smoothly and the guests were looked after properly. Timely distribution of snacks, water and serving of lunch was all responsibilities of the members of the organising committee which were taken care of with minutest details.

Next day during morning assembly, the principal congratulated all the members of this organising committee. The principal praised our efforts in front of the whole staff and students. It was a proud moment for all of us. As I was also a part of it, I was very happy as everyone appreciated our work. It was a great feeling to be recognised and praised in front of the whole school and staff members.

I wanted to share this proud moment with you. I know you would also feel very proud of me and bless me for future.

With loving regards,

Mukesh

2. Imagine yourself as Gaurav Mallya. Your roommate Tejas' right hand is plastered as it got fractured while playing badminton in the school. Write a letter to his father informing him about the accident and also asking him not to worry.

Ans.

Shri Ram Boys Hostel,
Mall Road,
Shimla-171001

17th October, 20XX

Dear Uncle,

At first, let me introduce myself to you. I am Gaurav Mallya, a student of Shri Ram School in Shimla and I stay in the school hostel with your son, Tejas. He is my roommate.

I am writing to inform you that last evening, while playing badminton in the school, Tejas fractured his right hand which has been plastered. He himself is not able to write because of the plaster. I know you and aunty will get worried, but it is only a hairline fracture.

Let me assure you that there is nothing to worry about and I am here to look after him. We are like brothers and I will help him with everything. There is no need for you to rush here to see him. I will keep you informed about Tejas periodically.

Regards,
Gaurav Mallya

EXAM PRACTICE

1. You have had to shift to a new house recently. Write a letter to your grandmother telling her what you miss about your old house. Tell her also what you like about your new house and what you plan to do to make it comfortable for yourself. *[2023]*

2. Your favourite aunt/uncle has asked you what you would like as a gift for your birthday. What gift would you choose (specify) and why would you choose this? Write a letter to your aunt/uncle thanking her/him for the kind thought. *[Sem II 2022]*

3. You changed your school recently. Write a letter to your friend in your old school telling him/her not only what you like about your new school but also what you miss about your old school. *[2020]*

4. Your friend has not fared well in the recent examinations.

Write a letter to him/her expressing your concern. Give him/her some advice on how to score better marks and offer to help him/here to improve his/her performance. *[2019]*

5. Your uncle has offered to get you a pet for your birthday. Write a letter to him telling him what you like, give reasons for your choice and tell him how you take care of your pet. *[2018]*

6. Your school recently held a silver jubilee celebration. Write a letter to your friend who was unable to attend, giving details of the function and your role in it. *[2016]*

7. You are to be awarded a special prize at the Annual Prize Day Ceremony of your school. Write a letter to a female relative giving her the news. Be sure to include details of the prize that you are to receive and tell her why you have been chosen for this honour. *[2015]*

8. Your uncle has promised to give you a gift of ` 1000. Write a letter thanking him for the offer and tell him how you plan to spend the money and why you wish to spend it in that way. *[2014]*

9. You will soon have to make a decision about the subjects that you wish to study in Classes XI and XII. Write a letter to your grandfather telling him about the subjects that you plan to take up. Be sure to explain the reason for your choice and how you think these subjects would help you in the future. *[2013]*

10. You were taken by your school to visit a place of historical interest. Write a letter to your classmate who was unable to go on the trip telling him/her about the trip. Also share why it was important and what you gained from the experience. *[2012]*

11. Write a letter to your landlord asking him to undertake repair work in your rented house.

Answers

Based on Format 1

1. 3-397/B, Kavita Vihar,
New Delhi,

17th November, 20XX

Dearest grandmother,

I hope you are in the best of health and taking your medication on time. I miss you and the rest of the family more than I can describe in words. Ever since I left our house, I have always felt alone. When I was there with all of you, I was always having fun. It was good to always have some company. In our house, I enjoyed walking the spacious corridors, spending time sipping tea in the balcony with the family members and playing on the roof with my siblings. One could always find food in the kitchen and it was possible to watch television with the rest of the family.

In my new house, there is no television, roof or balcony. While I do miss those things, I have found that not having these distractions helps me focus on my work. The house is tiny and that makes it easier to take care of. I can clean it pretty easily too. Also, I have a personal bedroom and study, as well as an entire wall that I can use for posters without having to share it with my siblings. However, the house still needs a lot of work to make it more comfortable. I am planning to install a kitchen chimney, which helps with the smoke from cooking. I also have to buy new covers, cushions and blankets for my bed to have a comfortable sleep. I am also planning to have a window installed so that the house could have some much needed sunlight. I hope you would visit me once I have made the house more comfortable.

Yours lovingly,
Anuj

2. 25/89-B, Ground Floor,
Laxmi Nagar,
Delhi

1st June, 20XX

Dear uncle,

First of all, how are you? I hope you are healthy and fit. Second, a big thank you for sending me the gift I asked for. It is such a beautiful camera.

I know you couldn't attend my birthday party due to your busy schedule but I missed you the most. I was overjoyed at receiving blessings and the DSLR Camera on my birthday. It is the best present I have ever received. All my friends have also liked it very much. The camera works so well. I took a lot of pictures on my birthday with the camera which I will show you on your next visit. I have a keen interest in photography and would like to pursue it as my professional career. I am planning to join a professional course in photography during summer vacations for which I have already taken permission from mummy and papa. I'm so excited that I'll be able to learn to use the camera in a professional way. Pursuing photography is my dream career.

Once again, thank you very much for the gift. It is a really lovely present.

I am looking forward to your visit.

Yours lovingly,
Prateek

3. House No. 125,
Sector 1, IMT,
Manesar, Gurugram
Haryana

24th March, 20XX

Dear Yug,

Hope this letter finds you in good health. I am writing this letter to tell you about my new school. It has been a month since I joined this school after my father transferred here. The name of my new school is Modern Public School. It is a lot bigger than my old school. It has the playground twice the size of the one we had in our old school. Even the library is bigger. There is also a spacious cafeteria that serves good quality food. The teachers are extremely knowledgeable and teach very well. Every Saturday, we have house activities in which the students compete with each other in various sports, literary and cultural competitions. I have also made some new friends.

But I still remember the fun I used to have in my old school. I especially miss those hobby classes that were conducted every Thursday. What fun we used to have during the dance class! I also miss Sangeeta ma'am and am grateful to her for teaching English so well. (But most of all, I miss you). Although I have made new friends, nobody can replace you.

I hope I will be able to see you soon. Eagerly waiting for you!

Yours affectionately,
Harshit

4. B-103, Sajeevani Society,
MG Road,
New Delhi–110019

27th March, 20XX

Dear Mohit,

How are you? I came to know from your brother, who I met yesterday, that you had not fared well in your Class IX final exams. I am very concerned about this because you were always serious about your studies and I did not expect this.

I miss you so much now that you are away at boarding school. When you come here to spend the summer holidays, we will have lots to talk over.

I am sure you can do much better in the Boards next year if you learn to study without help from coaching. I feel you had adjusted yourself to coaching till you studied here upto Class VIII. In boarding school, I know that there is no coaching and thus. I don't attend any coaching either. I study by myself every day in the evening and revise each lesson taught in class that day. This keeps the lessons fresh in my mind. At the time of exams, I just need to go through my notes to refresh my memory. You can study using my method when you come here and obtain as good results as I get.

More news when we will meet. Take care of yourself. I look forward to meeting you in the second week of May.

Your loving friend,
Ravi

5. House 365 - E,
Malviya Nagar,
Patna - 800003

15th February, 20XX

Dear Uncle,

Namaste. How are you? I am sure you are healthy and fine. Even I am doing well here.

As you know very well, next week is my birthday. You know your gifts are always valuable to me and delightful.

I remember you were telling me, when you visited our home last month, that you were planning to give me a puppy as my birthday gift.

Uncle, I am eagerly waiting for this give from your side. I am quite excited about it. Since a long time, I have been interested in looking after a puppy and you are fulfilling my wish. As you very well know, dogs are very faithful pets and can also guard a home against intruders. I can train up the puppy to be a good guard dog.

I understand that keeping pets in the house is not easy. We have to take good care of them. I assure you that I will take good care of it. I will keep writing to you regularly about its training and progress.

I am eagerly awaiting its arrival. I am making preparations for its stay in my room.

Thanks once again.
Please convey my respects to Aunty and regards to Sunny.
Yours affectionately,
Arvind

6. WZ-1263,
Nangal Raya,
New Delhi-46

5th March, 20XX

Dear Rashi,

How are you? I hope that you are recuperating from your illness. While you were on leave, we celebrated the Silver Jubilee of our school.

A special function was organised to celebrate the Silver Jubilee. We gathered in the auditorium for the function. The principal gave a small speech before the function started. He told us about the history and the founders of our school. The function started with a cultural programme. It was organised by the students of Class XII and depicted the diverse culture of our country.

The next programme was a fashion show. I also participated in that show and represented our class. Everyone cheered for me when I went on the stage. I was adjudged the best dressed female by the judges. The party was followed by a small snacks where we also got a chance to meet the honourable Chief Minister of Delhi, who was the Chief Guest on the occasion. We enjoyed the celebrations a lot. It would have been more fun if you also had been present on that day.

I hope that you get well soon and join school.

Your loving friend,
Nisha

Based on Format 2

7. 120, 'Girish Sadan',
Kingsway, Gokul Vihar,
Benaras,

3rd December, 20XX

Dear Anu Aunty,

I received your letter last week and was quite overwhelmed with your words of immense love. It is this love and faith of yours that keep inspiring me to work with utmost sincerity and persistence in achieving the goals of my life. And I am always at a loss for words to express my gratitude to you.

Today, I wish to share with you an exciting experience that may come my way. Next week is going to be the week for annual celebration in our school. And I have been nominated for the Award For Extraordinary Work for Humanity. In fact, I have been finalised for this award. Very exciting, right!

Our school had started a campaign for educating the girls and the boys of poor and destitute families on Sundays. It was open for everybody that liked to voluntarily render the service to the socio-economically backward fellowmen of ours. I always had a desire to do some or the other social work of my capacity. And this was a golden opportunity for me. So, I spent 3-4 hours every Sunday towards fulfilling the mission.

There were other classmates and colleagues of mine who volunteered for this programme but only I would be honoured with this prize because I spent the maximum hours in teaching them. I am very happy to have contributed to this noble work.

I hope you too must be very happy to hear this.

With my warmest regards,

Yours affectionately,
Simran Gurung

8.

25/247, Bagla Kunj,
Khandari,
Agra
12th December, 20XX

Dear uncle,

I wish to thank you for the gift of ₹ 1000 that you have promised to give me if I score above 80% in my final exams. It is really very thoughtful of you. I am thrilled that I would be able to spend the money as I like. Moreover, this incentive is pushing me to study harder and give my hundred per cent.

There is a book, 'The Alchemist' by Paulo Coelho, which I have been wanting to buy for a long time. Everybody is praising this book. One of my friends has read it and she found it truly inspiring. It costs about ₹ 450 and I would buy it once I get your gift. So, I will still be left with ₹ 550 to spend on other things.

The other day when I went shopping with my mom, I found a beautiful set of painting colours. You know how fond I am of painting. My art teacher has always praised my sense of colour and wants me to join her workshop for five days in the winter vacation. Although the workshop is free of cost, I need painting material. So, I will use the rest of the money for this. Once again, thanks for your kind gesture and the thoughtfulness behind it. I hope you will be happy to hear the way I plan to spend the money.

I am looking forward to your visit.

Yours lovingly,
Shruti

9.

808, Galleria Apartments
DLF Phase-IV,
Gurgaon, Haryana
30th March, 20XX

Dear grandpa,

My final examinations have just got over and I was thinking about the stream of subjects which I would have to pursue in Classes XI and XII. I am still very confused regarding the same. Although the subjects in Science and Humanities stream are more or less the same in number, the difficulty graph would definitely increase manifold. On the other hand, Commerce stream offers a new range of subjects about which I have no idea.

I did not know which stream would suit me the best. So, I decided to opt for the one-week trial classes. After attending them, I thought I should go for Commerce with Maths stream.

Although the subjects are new, they are quite interesting and offer a practical approach. It is quite fun to solve accountancy questions, draw balance sheet, etc. There is so much to explore in Business Studies and Economics as well.

I feel that I have taken the correct decision because it will enhance my interests and aptitude towards becoming an entrepreneur in the future. Moreover, you and dad are always there to guide and assist me in my future endeavours.

I am sure with a lot of diligence and motivation from both of you, I will do very well and will realise my ambition soon. This stream would greatly benefit me in the future.

Hope to see you soon.

Yours affectionately,
Armaan

10.

H.No. 01
New Era Colony
Ghaziabad
8th February, 20XX

Dear Kapil,

I hope you are fine now. I missed you a lot during the tour. I know you must be very curious to know about it.

It was an amazing trip. We started from our school at 6 am and got there at around 8 : 30 am. We enjoyed a lot during our travel, eating chips, cakes, etc., and singing songs and mimicking. Our teachers were also very sportive and shared many jokes.

The real euphoria of the exploration began when we reached Fatehpur Sikri. A guide accompanied us there. As and when he told us the history associated with each place, we felt like having entered into the Mughal period. The Buland Darwaza which is a huge massive gate to the Jama Masjid proved to be a 'Time Machine' for me. I found myself transported to the Mughal Empire and could visualise 'Akbar, the great with his Beghums and courtiers'.

Every building is an example of grandeur and marvellous art. The buildings are constructed using red sandstones which give them a unique lustre. The Panch Mahal, Jama Masjid, Diwaan-e-Aam (the hall of public audience) and Diwaan-e-Khas (the hall of private audience) capture one's wit.

We had our lunch in the garden. Amidst jokes and songs, all became fully satiated. Then, we played 'Dumb-Charades' which was a very nice experience. A few of us danced too. There were bursts of laughter in between. Everyone enjoyed themselves greatly.

Had you been there, it would have been more exciting.

Take care and get well soon!

Yours lovingly,
Gurpreet

11.

311, Kohat Enclave
Pitampura,
New Delhi-110088

21st May, 20XX

Dear Mr. Singh,

I wish to draw your kind attention to our meeting held last week in which I requested you to carry out the repairs in your house now rented out to me.

The rainy season is going to set in soon. I am afraid, if the necessary repairs are not carried out, it will cause much inconvenience to us. I request you, therefore, to take immediate steps to carry out these repairs at the earliest. The roof is leaking and the wall plaster has come out at almost all the places. Window panes are broken and need to be replaced. The floor of the roof has potholes. The switches at many places have got loose. The entire house needs whitewashing and its doors and windows need painting. I am quite willing to share the cost of repairs to be carried out in the house. The costs may be adjusted towards the rent of the house.

If you so desire and permit, I can carry out the necessary repairs on your behalf. The costs, of course, will be deducted from the rent.

I request you to give priority to this.

Yours sincerely,
Vishu Taneja

SELF ASSESSMENT

1. You are very fond of adventure. You were on a tour to Gulmarg in Jammu and Kashmir a few days ago. Write your thrilling experience of ice-skiing in a letter to your best friend.
2. Write a letter to your high-school English teacher, thanking him/her for teaching you English so well that you are confident in speaking as well as writing in English on any topic easily. You are Anuj/Anuja Sharma of Class X.
3. Your younger brother/sister has recently won a football championship match on district level, wherein a great number of schools participated. Write a letter to congratulate him/her and also motivate him/her for further practice to pursue it as a profession.
4. You are Abhishek/Abhilasha Kumar, a final-year MCA student. You had lost/misplaced important documents including your marksheets of previous years. An unknown person has posted you the documents. He was of a great help to you. Write a letter expressing your gratitude to him/her.
5. As a member of the School Environment Society, you developed a park in your school compound with a team of 10 volunteers. Write a letter to your friend Nitin telling him about your experience.
6. There was a fancy dress competition in your niece's school. Write a letter to your best friend telling her/him how you prepared your niece for this event. Also, tell her/him what all efforts you had to take for the selection of the theme and buying her dress and accessories.
7. One of your relatives is going to shift with his/her family to a city where you had spent a few years. He/She seeks your advice on which schools in the city are good for his/her children. Write a letter in reply giving the desired information.
8. Rahul/Radha is a good friend of yours and you are very well aware of his/her likes and dislikes. Also, you know what subjects he/she has a knack for. He/She seeks your help in choosing a right career option for himself/herself. Write a letter suggesting some good options and your views for those options.
9. Write a letter to your cousin who stays abroad asking him/her about the country, its culture, people, etc. and also, what his/her personal experiences in the country are.
10. You are studying in Class X and you stay in a hostel. Your Mathematics teacher suggests some good books for the better preparation for board exams. Write a letter to your father asking him for the money to buy the books.

CHAPTER 7

Notice

A notice is an important form of written communications used by individuals and organisations to convey information about functions, events and occasions or to announce something that has happened or is about to happen. It is direct and formal in language. Its style is straightforward. . In the ICSE Board examinations, its weightage is 5 marks.

A notice contains the following

- Heading (Subject of the notice)
- Contents include
  - Target group (to whom it is addressed)
  - What it is about.
  - Why the notice is issued.
  - Details of the event like date, time, venue and other details

Points to be kept in mind while writing a Notice

- The language used must be lucid and in third person, i.e. pronouns like I, me, you, mine, your, etc. should not be used.
- Usually present tense or future tense is used.
- Adhere to the word limit, if given in the question.
- A notice should include some value points (necessary details) in order to make it precise and effective.

Format of Notice

The ICSE board has prescribed two formats of writing a notice.

Format 1

Your school is hosting an intershool debate competition. Write a notice for the students, informing them of the event.

War of Words *[1]*

Inter-school Debate Competition *[1]*

on 8th December, 2017 *[½]*

from 9:00 a.m to 12 noon *[½]*

at Centenary Hall, St. Hilda's School *[½]*

All pupils from classes IX and X who wish to participate are to *[½]*
give their names to Mrs. T Baker on or before 1st December, 2017. *[½]*

Specimen of Notice, ICSE 2019

Format 2

Your school is organizing a charity drive for the flood victims. Write out a notice to be put up in your school informing students about the event and inviting them to participate in the charity drive.

GIVE TILL IT HURTS!

Charity Drive for the Flood Victims

Date: Friday, 3rd August, 20XX

Time: 8 a.m. to 11 a.m.

Venue: The Assembly Area, SMJ School

All the students from Class 5 to 10 kindly contribute to make the charity drive a success. food, clothes, medicines and other things may be handed over to your class prefect.

Be as generous as possible. Give Till It Hurts!

Specimen of Notice, ICSE 2019

Type 1 Notice for Meeting

While writing a notice for a meeting, the details that need to be furnished are

- Purpose of the meeting or agenda
- Date and time/duration of the meeting
- Details of persons to attend/departments to attend
- Venue, specific instructions for the persons called for the meeting

Sample of Type 1 Notice

You are Abhishek/Avantika Kumar of Class X, Translam Academy, Kanpur. Being an Activity Coordinator, draft a notice to all the other Activity Council members to discuss and plan the activities for Christmas Day celebration.

Ans.

IT'S CHRISTMAS TIME!

Meeting regarding activities for Christmas Celebration

on 23rd December, 20XX

at 10:30 a.m

in Biology Lab, Translam Academy, Kanpur

All the Activity Council Members are hereby informed to attend the meeting with the purpose of discussing activities for Christmas Day celebration.

SELF ASSESSMENT

1. You are Tripti/Trilok Lahiri, Secretary, ABI, School Cricket Association. It has been decided that a meeting of all the members of the school cricket team will be held to discuss plans and strategies for the coming Zonal Tournament. Write a notice informing the members of the team about the meeting and requesting them to attend it.
2. You are the Secretary of Sri Parthasarathy Sabha, Salem. Draft a notice to be sent to the members of the Sabha requesting them to attend an extraordinary meeting. Invent necessary details such as items on the agenda, date, time, etc. Sign as Kamal/Komal Agnihotri.

3. Your are Anuj/Anita Shah, Head Boy/Girl of your school. Draft a notice inviting all the house captains to discuss the coming annual day function.
4. You are Nikhil/Nikita Shah, Secretary of 'Help Poor Child Club' of your school. Draft a notice to be sent to all the members to attend the meeting regarding fund collecting for flood affected poor children.
5. You are Manoj or Monika Gupta of Class X. You are the captain of your school hockey team. Draft a notice towards all the players calling for an urgent meeting to discuss the next days's match.

Type 2 Notice for Events/Excursions

These notices include competition/tour/celebration/annual sports/cultural event, etc.

- Name of the event
- Who can participate in it.
- Occasion if any
- Number of days (in case of tours/visit)
- Expenditure estimate (tour/visit)
- Fare cost and other costs included (tour/visit)
- Last date for depositing the advance (tour/visit)
- Any specific instructions

Sample of Type 2 Notice

You are the Cultural Secretary of Delhi Public School, Roorkee. You have been asked to inform students of Classes VI to XII about an Inter-House Dramatics Competition. Draft a notice in not more than 50 words with necessary details.

Ans.

ACT! ACTING! ACTION!

Inter-House Dramatics Competition

Date 31st January, 20XX

Time : 11:00 a.m. onwards

Venue : Auditorium, Delhi Public School, Roorkee

All the House Captains must submit the scripts of the play being enacted by their House to the Cultural Secretary by 25th January, 20XX.

SELF ASSESSMENT

1. Your club is going to organise an Inter-Class Singing Competition. Write a notice inviting names of the students who want to participate in it. Give all the necessary details. You are Naveen/Navita Aggrawal, Secretary, Music Club, Akash Public School, Agra.
2. Every year, in the central park of the city, a Flower Show is held in February. Your school has received a circular from the District Collector inviting your students to visit it. Write a notice informing the students about the show and advising them to go and enjoy it. You are Amit/Amita Kulkarni, Head Boy/Head Girl, Sunrise Public School, Surat.
3. An Inter-School Kabaddi Competition is being organised by your school. Write a notice requesting the students to be present at the venue to encourage the players. Invent all the necessary details. You are Arjun Agrahari, the Sports Captain of your school.

4. You are Mohan/ Mohini Bagga, Secretary, Social Activities Club of ABC School, Gokulpuri. The club has decided to launch a cleanliness drive in a slum colony near your school during the Dussehra holidays. Write a notice informing Class X students of your school about the drive and urging them to volunteer their names for the programme. Give all the necessary details.
5. Your school has planned an excursion to Lonavala near Mumbai during the autumn holidays. Write a notice for your school notice board, giving detailed information and inviting the names of those who are desirous to join. Sign as Naresh/Namita Singh, Head Boy/Head Girl, DV English School, Thane, Mumbai.

Type 3 Notice for Lost or Found

- Article/Object lost or found
- Where you lost or found it
- Description of the article like colour/size/model, etc
- Date/Time/Day when you lost it/found it
- Whom to contact
- A suitable gift/reward for the person who returns that article/product
- Writer's name and designation/class

Note Format for this type of notice cannot be modified.

Sample of Type 3 Notice

You are a student of Class X of Vanasthali Public School, Ludhiana. You have lost your hall ticket for the Board Examination. You have to put up a notice on your school notice board.

Ans.

Vanasthali Public School, Ludhiana

1st March, 20XX

Loss of Hall Ticket

Students are informed that a Board Examination hall ticket was lost in the school playground. It contains a photograph along with the Roll No. 1234567. Anybody, who finds it, is requested to give it to the Administrative Officer. The person finding it and handing it over will be rewarded.

SELF ASSESSMENT

1. You lost your Titan wrist-watch in your school. Draft a notice, in not more than 50 words, to be placed on your school notice board. You are a student of Class X of Rani Ahalya Devi Senior Secondary School, Gwalior. Sign as Rani/Ram Prasad.
2. You have lost your leather wallet, containing your examination entry ticket for Class X, while travelling by bus from Banshankari to MG Road in Bengaluru. Write a notice, to be published in 'Deccan Herald'. You are Pranav/Parveen Shukla, 12 Gandhi Road, Bengaluru.
3. You are Ashok/Simi Khanna. You have lost your water bottle in the playground of your school. Draft a notice for the school notice board giving details.

4. You are Vikas/Vinita Verma. You have found a bracelet near the washroom of your school. Draft a notice for the school notice board. Give details for the same.
5. You are Neha/Abhinav Sethi. You have found a gold earing in the canteen of your school. Write a notice for the school notice board.

Type 4 Notice for Seminar/Workshop/Debate or any other Literary Event

- Body organising it
- Who can attend it
- Subject of the seminar/debate/workshop
- Duration of the programme
- Speakers/Chief Guest/Honourable Persons
- Date/Time
- Specific instructions

Sample of Type 4 Notice

You are the School Captain of Mccrut Public School, Shastri Market, Varanasi. Write a notice informing the students of Class X about a guest lecture by Mr Rajiv, an environmentalist, on the topic 'Conservation of Water'.

Ans.

SAVE WATER!

Guest Lecture on Conservation of Water

on 3rd November, 20XX
from 10:30 a.m. to 11:30 a.m.
in the Auditorium, Meerut Public School, Varanasi
Chief Guest–Mr. Rajiv, a renowned environmentalist

Attendance of Class X students is compulsory. For more information, contact the school captain.

SELF ASSESSMENT

1. Chennai Book Society is going to organise a week-long book fair in the city during the coming autumn vacation. It has requested your school for volunteers to manage various counters. As Secretary, Cultural Club, Chennai Public School, write a notice inviting the names of those students who want to help. You are Lalith/Latha Sinha.
2. You are Rameshwaram/ Rameshwari Kumar, Secretary, Literary Club of ABC School, Vikaspuri. Your schoolmate, Gautam Adhikari, a budding writer, has won the first prize in the State Story Writing Competition. The club has decided to organise a function to felicitate him on his laudable achievement. Write a notice, informing all the students of your school about the function and urge them to attend it to make the occasion memorable. Give all the necessary details.
3. As Student Editor, draft a notice for your school notice board inviting articles from the students for your school magazine. You are Rohan/Rupini Saket of Vasant Vihar School, Pune.
4. You are Nakul/Aashi Mehta, Head Boy/Head Girl of Jawahar Navodya Vidyalaya, Vadodra. You have been asked to draft a notice inviting the students to attend Career Counselling Workshop Organised by the Students' Council of your school. Give details for the same.
5. You are Head Boy/Girl of your school. You have been asked to inform students of Class IX and X about an Inter-School Debate Competetion. Draft a notice for the notice board with all necessary details.

Type 5 Notice for Appeal/Warning

- Whom to appeal/warn
- Issuing authority (if different from the person signing the notice)
- A slogan or message
- Important instructions
- Courteous way to appeal
- Name and designation of the issuing person
- Any punishment (if required, in case of warning type only)

Sample of Type 5 Notice

Recently, it was in the news that a hurricane hit Odisha and around 13 districts were affected. Being the Head of Environment Society of your school, draft a notice for the students and staff appealing for donations of relief products like clothes, money, books and other articles.

Ans.

GIVE TILL IT HURTS!

Appeal for Donations

Date : 5th December, 20XX

Time : 10:00 a.m. to 1:00 p.m.

Venue : Auditorium, Deewan Public School, Mysore

Students can donate money, clothes, books, articles like blazers, etc. for the victims of the hurricane. Certificated will be given to the highest contributors.

SELF ASSESSMENT

1. Sarvodaya Education Society, a charitable organisation, is coming to your school to distribute books among the needy students. As the Principal of Sunrise Public School, Surat, write a notice asking such students to drop the list of books they need in the box kept outside your office.
2. Very soon, your school is going to be a centre for CBSE examinations. You have seen that during lunch break, students of junior classes keep going around the examination rooms and making all kinds of noises. You are Tutorial Head of Akash Public School, Ajmer. Write a notice warning such students not to go near the examination rooms.
3. You are Kavita/Kavish Jha, Head Boy/Girl of your school. Write a notice warning all the students of classes VI to XI not to bring mobile phones in school premises.
4. There have been many accidents just outside your school lately. As the Secretary of Awareness Society of your school, write a notice informing all the students of your school to be careful while driving their vehicles or walking along the road.
5. Cancer has been spreading very rapidly in our country. Tabacco products are the main reasons that cause this disease. You are the Head of the Medical Welfare Club of your society. Write a notice making the people of your society aware of the bad effects of tabacco products.

Type 6 Notice for Change of Name/Residential/Company Address, etc.

- Whom to inform about the change
- Reason for change
- Existing Name/Current Residential/Company Address
- New Name/Residential/Company Address
- Your name and signature

Note Format of this category of notices cannot be modified.

Sample of Type 6 Notice

You are proprietor of a company which has changed its office address from 2A, Phool Bagh Colony to 334/3, Mangal Pandey Nagar. Draft a notice to be inserted in the local newspaper informing about the change in address.

Ans.

NOTICE

25th March, 20XX

Change in Address

This is to inform all that we have changed our office address from 2A, Phool Bagh Colony to 334/3, Mangal Pandey Nagar. All are requested to contact us at our new address.

Our phone no. 0121-248276X remains unchanged.

Vinay Sharma

SELF ASSESSMENT

1. You are Tanvi/Tarun Pandey. Draft a notice informing the students of Class X about the change of name in Board form. Invent all the necessary information.
2. You are the owner of 'Green Garden'. Due to construction work in your restaurant, it has been shifted to a new building. Draft a notice informing your customers about the shifting of your restaurant and its new address.
3. You are Rohit/Rohini Singh. You are the Head of the service centre of a mobile company. The office has been shifted to the third floor from the ground floor. Draft a notice informing all the employees and customers about the change.
4. You are the Manager of a football club. Your team is to leave for Delhi to participate in a tournament tomorrow. Due to some reasons, two players have been replaced with new players. Write a notice informing all the members about the change.
5. You are the main coordinator at your office. You have recently moved to Western Delhi from South Delhi. Draft a notice informing all your colleagues about the change of your residence with full detail of the new address.

EXAM PRACTICE

(Based on All Types)

1. Write a notice to be put up in your school informing the pupils of Classes IX and X about the Remedial Classes to be held after the school hours and asking them to register their names for it. *(2023)*
2. March 22nd is World Water Day. The school Dramatics Club is planning to stage a one-act play to mark the occasion and create awareness. Write a notice to be put up on the school notice board, giving details of the event. *(Sem II 2022)*
3. Your school is organising a fete/carnival to raise funds for victims of the recent floods in your state. Write a notice to be put up on the school notice board giving details of the event. *(2020)*
4. Your school is hosting an Inter-School Quiz Competition. Write out a notice to be displayed in your school giving all details for the event. *(2019)*
5. You are the Secretary of Tours and Trips Society of Translam Academy International, Meerut. The school is organising a 10-days historical tour to some important places in South India. You have been asked by the Activity Coordinator to put up a notice inviting students interested in visiting those places. Write this notice to be put up on the school notice board.
6. You are the Secretary of AVM Housing Society. You are going to organise a Blood Donation Camp. Write a notice urging the members of your society to come in large numbers for this noble cause. Invent all the necessary details.
7. You are the President of a children's club in your locality. You and your team are planning to organise a programme to celebrate Teachers' Day. Write a notice, to be put up in the local Supermarket, giving details of the programme to create an awareness of the event.
8. Draft a notice as Secretary of Lion's Club, Dwarka to inform all the members about the Diwali Mela and sale of items.
9. As the Librarian of Crescent International School, Gwalior, draft a notice asking all the students and teachers to return the library books they have borrowed, two days before the commencement of the examination.
10. Your school is conducting an Inter-class Talent Search. Write out a notice to be put up in your school informing students about the event and inviting them to participate.
11. You are the Principal of St. Thomas School. Write a notice informing students and parents about the 'Obesity Camp' to be organised by Jessa Ram Hospital.
12. Young astronauts have to be selected for 'Mission NASA'. The preliminary round will be conducted in Modern School. Write a notice inviting students who wish to become astronauts to take the preliminary round for final selection. You are the Director of Science Research Centre.
13. You are the Cultural Secretary of RM Public School, Alkapuri, Vadodara. You have been asked to inform students of classes IX to XII about an Inter-School Dramatics Competition. Draft a notice for the students' notice board with all necessary details.
14. You are the Games Captain at school. The school is organising an Inter-house Basketball Competition. Write out a notice to be put up in your school informing students about it.
15. You are the Secretary of the English Literary Association of Tagore Memorial School, Patna. Write a notice for notice board inviting names of those who would like to participate in the proposed Inter-House Debate, Oratorical and Elocution contest.
16. You are the President of the Literary Club of your school. You have organised an Inter-School Debate Competition on the occasion of the Silver Jubilee celebrations of your school. Write a notice informing the students of your school about the competition.

Answers

Based on Format 1

1.

Remedial Classes
For Classes IX and X

Days : Monday to Friday

Timing : 2:30 a.m. to 4:00 p.m.

Venue : Respective Classes

Register your names with your class teacher.

2.

Save Blue. Live Green.
World Water Day Celebration

On 22nd March, 20XX (World Water Day)

from 1:30 p.m. to 3:00 p.m.

in Auditorium, Delhi Public School, Meerut

All the students are hereby invited to the one-act play, to mark the occasion and create awareness. The play will be followed by an interactive session.

3.

For the Ones in Need
Fund Raising Carnival

on 8th April, 20XX

from 11:00 a.m. onwards

in Vidyasagar Public School, Bihar

Students are requested to be a part of the fest, and bring their parents and friends. There will be various food stalls, games and rides. A lucky draw will also be organised. The coupons for the luky draw can be obtained from the reception.

4.

Puzzlers
Inter-School Quiz Competition

on 5th September, 20XX

4 p.m. onwards

in Auditorium, Sunlight Public School, Ghaziabad

The events of the function is as follows

- Welcome to the Chief Guest, Ms. R Shastri, MLA
- Announcement of the rules, introduction of the teams and the Quiz Master
- Actual conduct of the quiz
- Presentation of prizes to the winners and runners-up
- Address by Chief Guest
- Vote of Thanks by the Principal
- Refreshments

All faculty, staff and students are requested and welcome to attend.

5.

Learn Better!

Historical Tour

from 17th to26th December, 20XX

to Chennai, My sore, Rameshwaram and Bengaluru

Interested students must submit their parents' acceptance letter along with ₹ 2500 by 15th November, 20XX to their respective class teachers. The tour is only for students of classes IX to XII.

6.

DONATE BLOOD! GIVE LIFE!.

Blood Donation Camp

on 15th March, 20XX from 11 a.m. onwards in

Community Hall AVM Housing Society, Ghaziabad

Residents above the age of 18 and below 50 years with good medical health are urged to volunteer in large number for this noble cause. Qualified doctors will be available to carry out the procedure.

7.

Thank you Teacher!

A cultural programme to celebrate Teachers' Day

on 5th September 20XX

from 5.00 p.m. to 7.00 p.m.

at Community Centre, South City Mall

All teachers who are residents of the South City Complex are cordially invited

8.

HAVE FUN!

Diwali Mela

on 13th October, 20XX

from 10 :00 a.m. to 8 : 00 p.m.

in the Lion's Club Ground, Dwarka

Members are hereby informed that there will be a sale of various items like sweets, toys, etc. along with snacks and beverages. Registration for stalls is open till 12th October, 20XX.

Based on Format 2

9. **Crescent International School, Gwalior**

Last Date for Returning of Library Books

Students are reminded to return the library books issued to them latest by 1st March, 20XX to avoid the undesirable situation of being debarred from sitting for the final examination. Teachers are also requested to return the books on time to help in completing the stock-verification of library books. Your prompt action will be appreciated.

Vimal Pathak

(Librarian)

10. **EVERYBODY'S GOT TALENT**

Inter-class Talent Search

Date: Tuesday, 24th July, 20XX

Time: 9 a.m. to 4 p.m.

Venue: The Auditorium of St. Agnes' School

Interested students from Classes 8, 9 and 10 may register with the Vice Principal on or before 14th July, 20XX.

11. **SHRED THE FAT**

Obesity Camp

Date : 30th March, 20XX

Time : 9:00 a.m. to 5:00 a.m.

Venue : MI Room, St. Thomas School, Hyderabad

Renowned Dr. Ajay Gupta will be the Chief Guest of the camp and will share knowledge on obesity and its ill effects. All students should inform their parents about this event.

12. **CHASE YOUR DREAM!**

Preliminary Round for Mission NASA

Date 19th July, 20XX

Time

Phase I Timings 8:30 a.m. to 9:30 a.m.

Phase II Timings 10:00 a.m. to 11:00 a.m.

Venue : Modern School, Barakhamba Road

A fee of ₹ 800 should be deposited by 15th July at the Centre's Fee counter in Modern School. Interested students should enrol themselves with the Science Club Manager at Modern School and receive a copy of the sample papers and a CD for preparation. All the students appearing for Class XII ISC exam this year are eligible.

13. **Opportunity for Budding Actors**

An Inter School Dramatics Competition

Date : 25th December, 20XX

Time : 11:30 a.m. onwards

Venue : Auditorium, RM Public School, Alkapuri, Vadodara

Students of Classes IX to XII are eligible to take part in competition. Last date for giving names is 24th December, 20XX.

14.

DRIBBLE STARS

Inter- House Basketball Competition

Date: Wednesday 4th July, 20XX

Time: 9 a.m. to 1 p.m.

Venue: The Main Basketball Court, Berkeley High Sports Complex

The Match schedule is as follows

Ruby vs Emerald

Sapphire vs Topaz

The Battle- Match for third place

The Grand Finale- The Final Match

All House Captains are requested to keep their respective House teams ready and submit the names to the Games Captain before 25th June,20XX.

15.

GOLDEN CHANCE

Inter-House Competitions

The English Literary Association invites participants in the following contests to be held in the school auditorium

(a) Debate competition : 20th August, 20XX at 11 : 00 a.m.

(b) Oratorical skills : 21st August, 20XX at 11 : 00 a.m.

(c) Elocution contest : 2st 1 August, 20XX at 2 : 00 p.m.

Each House can send a team of two students per item. Last date for submission of names is 7th August, 20XX

16.

SPEAK YOUR MIND!

Debate Competition

Date 18th December, 20XX

Time : 11: 00 a.m. onwards

Venue : Saraswati Auditorium, Sophia International, Kanpur

Topic : 'Nuclear Armament is India's Best Defence against Cross-border Terrorism'

Last date for submission of names is 10th December upto 4:30 pm in the Activities Room.

CHAPTER

8

E-Mail

E-mail or electronic mail is a message distributed through electronic means from one computer user to one or more recipients *via.* a network. With the advent of the digital age, e-mail plays an important part in everybody's life. It is the most popular and fastest way of sending messages anywhere in the world and is generally used in formal situations.

So, a student should be well-versed with the e-mail technology. He/She should be familiar with the various features of an e-mail program. The knowledge of e-mail and Internet makes a student up-to-date with today's technologies and prepares him/her to be ready for the future. In the examination, its weightage is 5 marks.

Parts of an E-mail

Recipient's Address

The first thing you need to enter when composing an e-mail is the recipient's address. An example of e-mail address is: sakshiwrites@gmail.com. When sending a message to multiple recipients, be sure to separate all addresses with a comma.

Cc and Bcc

Another option when sending a message to multiple recipients is to use the Cc, or carbon copy, and Bcc or blind carbon copy fields. When using the Cc feature, all recipients can see the e-mail addresses of everyone the message was sent to. If you want your communication to be more private, choose the Bcc option and the identities of the other recipients will not be shown.

Subject Line

The subject line is the first part of your e-mail that the recipient will see. When entering the subject line, write what the e-mail is about.

Body

The body is where you actually write the message that you want to send.

Attachments

Attachments are similar to enclosures in traditional mail. If you have files that you want to share with your recipient(s), you can include them as attachments in the e-mail.

Signature

Some e-mail systems allow you to enter a signature that will appear automatically at the bottom of every mail you send. This feature is optional and can be turned off and on as needed.

E-mail Etiquettes

It refers to the dos and donts of the things to do while writing e-mails.

1. **Do not leave the Subject line blank** The subject of the e-mail states what your e-mail is about. So, it should be brief and accurate and must not be left blank.
   A few examples of a good subject line are
   (i) Assignment for Class X-English (ii) Time Table for Class IX-B (iii) Subscription Enquiry
2. **Include Proper Salutation as per the E-mail type** One must include proper salutation before starting to write an e-mail.
   Examples
   Respected Sir/Ma'am
   Sir/Ma'am
   Dear Sir/Ma'am
3. **Avoid using Capital Letters** One should avoid using capital letters in e-mail. Words written in capital letters are interpreted as if the sender is angry or shouting at the recipient(s).
4. **Use of Abbreviations and Acronyms** One should avoid using abbreviations and acronyms in formal e-mails.
5. **Add Appropriate Closing** One should use proper closing of the e-mail before hitting the send button. The closing of the e-mail should be appropriate.
   Examples
   Your obediently
   Yours sincerely
   Yours faithfully

Formats of An E-mail

Format 1

Write an e-mail to the Principal of a neighbouring school informing her of the event and requesting her to send a team to participate in the interschool debate competition being held in your school.

Ans.

To : principalbluebellschool@gmail.com [½]
Subject : Inter-school Debate Competition [½]

Dear Madam, [½]
Our school is celebrating its 50th anniversary this year. As part of the celebrations we are hosting a series of competitions and we are beginning with 'War of Words', an inter-school debate competition. Opening Sentence [½]
It will be held on 8th December, 2017 from 9.00 a.m. till 12 noon in the Centenary Hall of St. Hilda's School.
Please do send your senior debate team to participate in the event.
The topic will be given to the participants an hour before the start of the competition.
They may bring their laptops for use during the preparation time.
We look forward to your school's participation in the competition.
Thanking you,
Yours faithfully,
Ashish Roy
Debating Secretary

Format 2

Write an e-mail to the General Manager of the Supermarket seeking permission to display the notice and requesting a sponsorship for the event of Teacher's Day.

Ans. To : rmsouthcity@gmail.com

Subject : Teachers' Day Celebration

Dear Sir,

Teachers' Day is around the corner and we, the residents of the South City Complex, would like to express our gratitude to our teachers by hosting a brief cultural programme on the 5th September between 5.00 p.m. to 7.00 p.m.

There are about 25 teachers in our complex and we would be grateful if you allow us the use of the foyer in the Supermarket for the celebration.

We also request you to please sponsor a cup of tea and light refreshments for the teachers and a few guests, about 40 in all.

We look forward to a favourable response.

Thanking you,

Yours faithfully,

Ashish Roy

Secretary, Youth Club, South City Society.

EXAM PRACTICE

1. Write an e-mail to the Principal of a neighbouring school inviting their pupils to attend the classes if they so wish. Give all details of the classes to be held. *[2023]*
2. Write an e-mail to the Principal of a neighbouring school requesting him/her to send a team of children to participate in the interactive session which will follow the play on 'World Water Day' celebration. *[Sem II 2022]*
3. Write an e-mail to the Principal of a neighbouring school, inviting him/her to send their students to attend a fete/carnival. *[2020]*
4. Write an e-mail to the Principal of a neighbouring school requesting him/her to send a team of three members to participate in the Quiz Competition. *[2019]*
5. Write an e-mail to the Principal of a neighbouring school requesting him / her to send a team of teachers to judge the interclass talent search.
6. You are the President of the Nature Club of your school. You wish to subscribe to the 'Nature for All' magazine for the school library. Write an e-mail to the Subscription Department of the magazine requesting them to send the details of the subscription plans.
7. Write an e-mail to a prominent basketball coach of your city who has agreed to be the referee at the Inter-house basketball competition in your school, giving all relevant details.
8. You purchased a pair of shoes from an outlet of a well-known brand. The sole of the shoes cracked within a month of your using them. Write an e-mail to Customer Care Department of the company asking them to replace your shoes.
9. Write an e-mail to an English Daily requesting them to sponsor the Debating Competition to be held at your school. You are Jeevan/Jasper Kaur of Class X, Air Force School.
10. Write an e-mail to your School Counsellor requesting him/her to take a session on the topic 'How to choose the right stream in Class XI'. Invent necessary details.
11. You are Saurabh/Saumya of Class X of Happy School, Daryaganj, New Delhi. You wish to participate in a Robotics Contest being organised by a Infocom Private Company. Write an e-mail to your Principal requesting him to nominate your name for the Class IX-X level, giving him the detail of the Robot that you want to display in the contest.
12. As a member of your residential society, write an e-mail to the Inspector of Local Police Station, Mr. Sharma informing him about miscreants who ride their bikes rashly every evening outside your society.
13. Write an e-mail to the Manager of Smart Automotive Company, Mr. Ahmed regarding the poor quality of service facility available in the city.
14. Write an e-mail to the General Manager of a local hospital requesting him/her to send a senior doctor to talk to the participants at the event about the quality of mask which would give them the best protection.
15. As an intern at ABC Consulting Pvt. Ltd., write an e-mail to your Internship Project Manager, Mr Ram informing about the progress that you are making and difficulties that you are encountering.
16. Write an e-mail to the Principal of the neighboring school informing him/her of the event and requesting him/her to send a team to participate.

Answers

1. **To** : principal.dps.2013@yahoo.com

Subject : Invitation for students to attend foreign language classes

Dear Sir/Ma'am

The school is going to organise Spanish, German and French classes for the students of Classes IX to XII from the 20th of September, 20XX. The school has invited teachers and language experts from multiple countries to teach the languages. The classes would last three months and would take place after school hours (2 p.m. to 4 p.m.) from Monday to Friday.

This is a great opportunity for the students to get acquainted with foreign languages. They can be really helpful for the students in the future as being multilingual can be a great advantage for their careers. They can also be helpful to them if they choose to study abroad or work in a foreign country. Also, having the understanding of multiple cultures enhances their overall worldview.

The students of your school are welcome to attend these classes if they wish. Each student can pick one language to learn from the three given languages. Kindly send the interested students to our school for the same.

Thanking You,

Yours faithfully,

Anita Kumar (Head Girl)

Vidya Public School

2. **To** : principal.abc@xyzschool.com

Subject : Interactive Session on World Water Day

Dear Sir/ Ma'am,

Delhi Public School, Delhi is going to organise a one-act play on World Water Day, i.e. 22nd March, 20XX in the School Auditorium to mark the occasion and create awareness. The play will be followed by an interactive session on the same.

You are requested to send a team of children to participate in the interactive session. It will be a great opportunity for students of both the schools to interact with one another and improve their knowledge.

Kindly send the names of the participants by 4th March, 20XX.

Thanking you,

Regards,

PQR

(Principal)

Delhi Public School

3. **To :** principalgloriaschool@gmail.com

Subject : Invitation for attending the carinval

Dear Sir/Ma'am,

We feel an immense pleasure in inviting you to attend the carnival being organised by our school on 8th April, 20XX. The carnival will begin at 11 o'clock in the morning. The purpose of this carnival is to raise funds to help the victims of the recent floods in our state. There will be a lot of interesting games and rides. Attractive food stalls have also been arranged.

We request you to kindly grace the occasion with your presence.

Thanking You,

Yours Obediently,

Sarita Sethi

(Head Girl)

Vidyasagar Public School

4. **To** : principal@ bhairavschool.com
Subject : Invitation for Sending Team for Inter-School Quiz Competition

Dear Sir/Ma'am,

Our school has been honoured to host the Inter-School Quiz Competition of the district this year. Ms. R. Shastri, MLA, has kindly consented to be the Chief Guest.

A notice giving details of the event is enclosed. You are requested to send a team of three students to participate on behalf of your school.

You are requested to convey the contact details of the undersigned given below to any of your staff members for any further inquiry about the competition.

Thanking you
With Regards,
Ravi Saroha
(Head Boy)
Sunlight Public School
Mobile no. 99885XXXXX
Encl. a/a

5. **To** : principal@stflorence.org
Subject : Request to appoint judges for a talent search event.

Dear Sir/ Madam,

I am Maya Gilani, the Cultural Secretary of the Student Council, St. Agnes' School. We are conducting a talent search contest for the students of Classes 8, 9 and 10. This is to be held on the 24th of July, 2018, from 9 a.m. to 4 p.m. in Music, Art, Dance, Magic, Acrobatics and Stand-up Comedy.

We request you to send a team of three teachers from your school to judge the talent search, Everybody's Got Talent.

Anticipating a positive response,
Yours faithfully,
Maya Gilani
Cultural Secretary, Student Council
St. Agnes' School

6. **To** : theweek@subscriptionenquiring.com
Subject : Subscription enquiring for 'Nature for All'

Dear Sir/Ma'am,

I am the President of the Nature Club of Springdales School, Dhaula Kuan, New Delhi. I happened to go through a copy of your magazine at your stall in the recently concluded Book Fair at Pragati Maidan.

I found your magazine very interesting and wanted to subscribe to it for our school library so that students can benefit from it. Kindly send me the details of the cost of its subscription and the various plans available for the same. I would appreciate if you could give us some discount over and above the regular subscription rates as we would be using it for educational purposes.

Looking forward to your correspondence.
Yours faithfully,
Naveen Kaul
(President, Nature Club)
Springdales School

7. **To :** coachformidable123@gmail.com

Subject : Invitation to Referee Dribble Stars – Inter House Basketball Competition.

Dear Sir,

I am Sam Sequeira of Berkeley High and I write with reference to my telephone call to you earlier. We are conducting an inter- house basketball competition on 4th July, 2018 from 9 a.m. to 1 p.m. on the Main Basketball Court, Berkeley High Sports Complex. Thank you for having accepted our request to referee the event.

The schedule is as follows

- Ruby v/s Emerald Match 1
- Sapphire v/s Topaz Match 2
- The Battle – For third place – Match 3
- The Grand Finale – The Final Match

We will arrange to pick you up by 8.15 a.m. from your residence and you will be dropped back after the Basketball Competition.

We look forward to seeing you at Berkeley High.

Thanking you,

Yours faithfully,

Sam Sequeira

Games Captain

Berkeley High

8. **To :** cfl@customercare.com

Subject : Complaint for faulty shoes

Dear Sir/Madam,

This is to inform you that I had purchased a pair of ACTION PRO-LITE shoes from your store located in Pacific Mall, Subhash Nagar, New Delhi. The date of purchase and bill no. is 24/11/2017 and A-423, respectively.

Within a month of its usage, the sole of the shoes has cracked, making them unwearable. I have been a regular customer of your ACTION brand of shoes and have never experienced such an issue earlier. Therefore, I request you to look into this issue and replace the faulty shoes with a brand new one of the same type.

Please feel free to contact me in case you need any further details.

Looking forward to your e-mail.

Yours sincerely,

Jesika Desai

Contact no. 98184XXXXX

9. **To :** englishdaily@gmail.com

Subject : Sponsor the debating competition

Dear Sir/Ma'am,

I am a Class X student of Air Force School, Subroto Park, New Delhi. Our school is organising a debating competition in the last week of November. A total number of 51 schools from the Delhi region are going to participate in the contest.

Being a leading newspaper of Delhi, I request you to sponsor the event. We would be placing your name in the pamphlets for the event and on the banner for the debating competition.

Looking forward to your reply.

Yours sincerely,

Jasper Kaur

Class X-A

Air Force School

10. **To** : Pqr@gmail.com

Subject : Session on choosing the right stream in Class XI

Dear Sir/Ma'am

I am a student of Class X-D of your school. After a few months, we would be promoted to Class XI and face the dilemma of choosing the right stream that is suitable to our aptitude. Making a wise decision at that stage is very important for a student and their future career prospects.

Therefore, I request you to conduct a session on 'How to choose the right stream in Class XI' for us in our free period. This would help us in getting prepared in advance for the process and thus, avoid making a last minute blunder in the crucial decision-making process.

Thanking you,

Yours obediently,

Camilla Roy

Class X-D

11. **To** : principalhappyschool@gmail.com

Subject : Nomination for entry in Robotics Contest

Respected Sir,

I am a student of Class X-B of your school. I most humbly request you to nominate my name in the Class IX-X category of the upcoming Robotics Contest being organised by Infocom Pvt. Ltd.

The Robot that I have made for the contest can mimic a human's voice. It is also capable of reciting a few nursery rhymes. I am quite confident that my entry would bag the first prize in the contest.

Kindly nominate my name on the behalf of our school.

Thanking you,

Yours obediently,

Saurabh Grover

Class X-B

12. **To** : inspectorsharma10@yahoo.com

Subject : Miscreants in the area

Dear/Mr. Sharma,

I am a resident of Siddhartha Nagar. I would like to bring to your notice that a few guys are riding their bikes very rashly in the evening hours in the main road of the colony. As you know that this is the time when children play on the road and the elderly go for an evening walk. In the recent times, we have observed that due to this rash driving, many accidents have happened and several people have been injured. This is creating a constant nuisance for all. So, I would like to request you to take necessary action to curb these activities.

Thanking you,

Yours sincerely,

Vaibhav Kumar

13. **To** : ahmedsac@gmail.com

Subject : Poor service quality in the city

Dear Mr. Ahmed,

I recently bought Fiat Palio from "Sridhar Fiat Showroom" in Nagole. However, I faced a small problem with car AC and brought the car for maintenance. But to my utter surprise, the showroom staff told me that service is not available in their showroom and they asked me to take the car to the nearby service center. I found that there are very few service centers available compared to sales showrooms and there are many complaints regarding this. This in turn is causing many pending problems and increased maintenance cost, time and delivery time.

I would like to suggest to you that if more service centers are opened in the city, customer satisfaction also goes up which finally convert into more sales.

Thanks and regards,
Kamlesh Chopra

14. **To** : GMHospital@sthospital.com
Subject : request to send a team of doctors to discuss the Mask quality.

Dear Sir/Ma'am,
This is to request you to kindly send a team of doctors to our area for health meeting against Covid-19 protection including mask quality. People here are living below the poverty line and are unable to afford a health checkup. This health checkup would be very beneficial for them because then they may approach their concerned doctors and get their treatment done. This initiative of yours would be appreciable
Anticipating a positive response.
Thanking you,
Yours faithfully,
ABC
Principal
(ABC School)

15. **To** : ramjoshiabcpl@gmail.com
Subject : A mix of progress and problem

Dear Mr. Ram,
Thank you for allotting a challenging project for my internship. I am making steady progress and learning many new things. The project is due next month and we are on tight schedule. I need some additional support with regard to the reporting of analytics. Your guidance helped me access the database with ease but I have several doubts regarding the requirements of the design. I am facing little problem in reporting.
Thanks and regards,
Brajesh
(Intern)

16. **To** : principal.dps.2013@yahoo.co.in
Subject : Request to send a team for participation in the Interschool Music Competition
Dear Sir/Ma'am,
The school is going to organize an Interschool Music Competition on the 20th of September, 20XX. Five schools from the city will be participating in the competition. The winning team will be honoured with Gold Medals and prize money.
Kindly send a team from your school to participate in the event.
Thanking you,
Yours faithfully
Anita Kumar (Head Girl)
Vidya Public School

SELF ASSESSMENT

1. Write an e-mail to the Principal of Ramjas School, Anand Parbat, New Delhi requesting him to send his team for the Inter-School Cricket Tournament to be held in your school on 28th November, 20XX.
2. You are Vikas/Vaishnavi Saha of Class X-C of Sanskriti School, Chanakyapuri, New Delhi. Write an e-mail to Director, School of Foreign Languages, New Delhi asking him/her to send the e-catalogue of the books published by the school.
3. Write an e-mail to The Online store to update you about the status of the order placed by you. Invent necessary details.
4. You are the Secretary of your school's Dramatics Club. Compose an e-mail to Akshara Theatre, New Delhi enquiring about the availability of the theatre in the last week of December, so that you can stage your play there.
5. You are Chetan/Drishti Dhanraj, a student of a reputed school. Send an e-mail to the Tutorial Head of the secondary wing of your school requesting him/her to arrange a workshop on 'School Safety' for the students of your school.
6. You have recently visited the Delhi zoo. Write an e-mail stating your views about the miserable condition of birds and animals there to the curator of the zoo.
7. Write an e-mail to the Manager of the Community Centre in your area seeking permission to display the drawings made by the underprivileged children residing in the nearby slum on Children's Day.
8. Write an e-mail informing the office-bearers of a school's Science Society about their meeting with the Principal, to chalk out details about the forth-coming Science Fair.
9. Write a e-mail instructing the residents of a colony to maintain cleanliness in the park in their neighbourhood. E-mail is to be addressed to the senior and prominent citizens and civic bodies operating in the area.
10. Write a e-mail, addressed to the principals of different schools located in the district/zone and informing the students of a school about a three-day inter-school campaign for tree plantation, organised by the district administration. Assuming that you're the head of the campaign, request them to participate in the campaign, and refer to some award to be given to the schools represented by most active participants.

CHAPTER

9

Comprehension

Comprehension involves a thorough understanding of the given passage consisting of one or more paragraphs. It is meant to test the comprehending (understanding) skills of a student.

In the examination, there will be a passage followed by different types of questions that are to be answered on the basis of the information given in passage.

Format of Questions

This question comprises a passage of about 450 words followed by three types of questions as follows

1. **Vocabulary Based Questions** The first question is based on vocabulary. It includes choosing the correct synonym or meaning of the given word.
2. **Short Answer Type Questions** The second question contains 5 subjective or short answer type questions which are to be answered in the context of the passage.
3. **Summary Based Questions** The third question is based on summary or characterisation. The students are required to answer the question in about 50 words.

Important Steps to Follow While Attempting the Question

(i) Read the passage quickly so as to get the main theme of the passage.

(ii) At this stage, do not worry about the difficult words that you encounter.

(iii) Now, go through the questions once. This will facilitate the process of comprehending the passage.

(iv) Now, read the passage carefully and comprehensively.

- This time you should read the passage slowly so as to grasp the minute details of every point talked about in the passage.
- If you try to read the passage hurriedly, you will not be able to discover every detail and will end up wasting your time in repeated readings.
- Try to make out the meanings of the words you have underlined.
- Do not try to attempt the questions, before you have completely read the passage.

Points to be Kept in Mind While Answering the Questions

- The answers must be in complete sentences.
- The answers must be relevant and to-the-point.
- No information from outside the passage should be included in the answer even if that information is related to the topic.
- The answers must be written using
  - one's own language.
  - simple, appropriate words.
  - correct grammatical English.
- The tense of the answers must be the same as that of the questions.
- Avoid using the language of the passage.

Sample Passage

Passage 1

Read the following passage carefully and answer the questions that follow.

Every Monday, on his way back from work, Bipin Chowdhury would drop in at New Market to buy books. He had to buy at least five at a time to last him through the week. He lived alone, was not a good mixer, had few friends and didn't like spending time in idle chat. Those who called in the evening got through their business quickly and left. Those who didn't show signs of leaving would be told around eight o'clock by Bipin Babu that he was under doctor's orders to have dinner at eight-thirty. After dinner, he would rest for half an hour and then turn in with a book. This was a routine which had **persisted** unbroken for years.

Today, Bipin Babu had the feeling that someone was observing him from close quarters. He turned round and found himself looking at a round-faced, meek-looking man who now broke into a smile.

'I don't suppose you recognise me.'

Bipin Babu felt ill at ease. It didn't seem that he had ver encountered this man before. The face seemed quite unfamiliar. 'Have we met before?' asked Bipin Babu.

The man looked greatly surprised. 'We met every day for a whole week. I arranged for a car to take you to the Hundroo Falls. My name is 'Parimal Ghosh'. 'Ranchi?'

Now Bipin Babu realised this man was making a mistake. Bipin Babu had never been to Ranchi. He smiled and said, 'Do you know who I am?'

The man raised his eyebrows and said, 'Who doesn't know Bipin Chowdhury?'

Bipin Babu turned towards the bookshelves and said, 'You'r making a mistake. I've never been to Ranchi.' The man now laughed aloud.

'What are you saying, Mr. Chowdhury? You had a fall in Hudroo and cut your right knee. I brought you iodine. I had fixed up a car for you to go to Netarhat the next day, but you couldn't because of the pain in the knee. Can't you recall anything? Someone else you know was also in Ranchi at that time, Mr Dinesh Mukherjee. You stayed in a bungalow. You said, you didn't like hotel food. I'll tell you more : you always carried a bag with your books in it on your sightseeing trips. Am I right or not?'

Bipin Babu spoke quietly, his eyes still on the books. 'Which month in Nineteen fifty-eight are you talking about?' The man said, 'October'.

'No, sir,' said Bipin Babu. 'I spent October Nineteen fifty-eight with a friend in Kanpur. You're making a mistake. Good day'.

But the man didn't go, nor did he stop talking.

'One evening, I had tea with you on the veranda of your bungalow. You spoke about your family. You said you had no children and that you had lost your wife a **decade** ago.'

When Bipin Babu had paid for the books and was leaving the shop, the man was still looking at him in utter disbelief.

Bipin Babu's car was safely parked in Bertram Street. He told the driver as he got into the car,

'Just drive by the Ganga, will you, Sitaram.' Driving up the Strand Road, Bipin Babu regretted having paid so much attention to the **intruder**. He had never been to Ranchi. He had an excellent memory.

Unless he was losing his mind! ***(2017 Modified)***

Questions

1. Choose the correct meaning of the following words as used in the passage.
   (i) persisted (line 13)
   (a) moved on (b) carried on
   (c) fleeting (d) All of these
   (ii) decade (line 55)
   (a) a period of ten hours
   (b) a period of ten days
   (c) a period of ten months
   (d) a period of ten years
   (iii) intruder (line 63)
   (a) trespasser (b) encroacher
   (c) robber (d) Both (a) and (b)
2. Answer the following questions briefly using your own words.
   (i) How did Bipin Chowdhury find time to read five books a week?
   (ii) How did he get rid of visitors who stayed late?
   (iii) Which sentence tells you that Bipin was uncomfortable?
   (iv) What strong argument did Bipin Babu give to prove that he was not in Ranchi at that time?
   (v) What does Bipin Babu regret?
3. What memories of the trip does Parimal Ghosh evoke to prove that Bipin Babu was indeed in Ranchi? Describe in your own words and answer in not more than 50 words.

Answers

1. (i) (b) carried on
   (ii) (d) a period of ten years
   (iii) (d) Both (a) and (b)
2. (i) Bipin Chowdhury found time to read five books a week because he lived all alone in his house. He was not a good mixer and hadn't many friends. He did not like spending time in idle chat.
   (ii) He got rid of the visitors who stayed late by telling them that he was under doctor's order to have dinner at eight-thirty and he could no longer spend time with them.
   (iii) The sentence 'Bipin Babu fell ill at ease' tells us that he felt uncomfortable.
   (iv) The strong argument given by Bipin Chowdhury to prove that he was not in Ranchi at that time was that in October 1958, he was with a friend in Kanpur. He said that he never been to Ranchi.
   (v) Bipin Babu regrets having paid so much attention to the stranger who was making false claims of having met him.
3. Parimal Ghosh tried to remind Bipin Babu that it was he who had arranged a car for Bipin Babu when he was in Ranchi in October 1958. He also reminded Bipin that he had brought iodine for him when he had a fall in Hudroo and had cut his right knee. Someone known as Dinesh Mukherjee was also in Ranchi. Parimal reminded Bipin of his dislike for hotel food and that he always carried a bag containing books on sightseeing trips.

Passage 2

Read the following passage carefully and answer the questions that follow.

Ann Davison, the first woman to sail single-handedly to the Atlantic Ocean, was all set to begin her journey of hopes, aspirations and of troubles, when she received a gift pack. It was a Christmas gift from her friends. It contained greeting cards and small gifts that, instead of cheering her, made her feel more lonely.

Ann Davison had a passion for aviation and was among the few Americans to become a pilot. Her marriage to Frank Davison had changed her life. They had bought a motorsailer named Reliance. Ann lost her husband in a tragedy with 'Reliance'. After that, she got a job and a boat 'Felicity Ann' which created in her the desire to sail across the Atlantic Ocean.

That day the boat was making only a half knot. So, she ran the engine for a while and this improved her spirits. She decided to run it a little everyday, while the ocean was calm. It kept the engine from corroding and the sound was good for her **morale**.

She was waiting for a little wind to blow. But, there was a squall and the boat, Felicity Ann was heeled over, dangerously. She was discovering the learning of many other long-distance sailors : the single hander's main enemies were lack of confidence, discouragement and loneliness.

Ann tried hard to reef the mainsail but was unsuccessful. She groped her way on deck and rested. She gave up trying and instead of getting nervous, she **consoled** herself by reading poetry in the cabin and discovering memory games. In the afternoon, a little desirable wind blew and she could cover a short distance towards her goal. The lowering mark of fuel in her boat was alarming her. She knew she would not be able to sail everyday. Squalls had actually filled in her way more than calms. She kept her morale high, calculated miles and days. She knew she was only about seven hundred miles from Barbados.

Now, she was experiencing fatigue though the twin staysails were working again and she was slowly heading towards the goal. She suspected that it was due to the **deficiency** of vitamin, though she had faithfully taken her vitamin tablets. As a consequence, she decided to head for Barbados, the nearest West Indies island, though she had originally planned for Antigua. This was also due to her mental depression which was another big concern. She struggled a lot to sail to the North-West reefing and changing sails constantly, usually in the middle of the night. Now, there was one more reason for Ann Davison to worry about. She had crossed the estimated sixty-day mark for her voyage. And the store of both food and water was going to be short. She tried heavy ropes astern to make Felicity Ann steer better. But, the ropes got tangled up as the directions of squalls were changing constantly. She had to pull the ropes into cockpit and untangle them. This exhausted her even more and her eyes were getting so swollen that her eyesight was getting poorer. Finally, on 18th January, weak and dispirited, she made out a faint shape on the horizon, the mountainous outline of Barbados.

Questions

1. Choose the correct meaning of the following words as used in the passage. One word answers or short phrases will be accepted.

(i) morale (line 21)
(a) The level of a person's self-confidence and enthusiasm at a particular time.
(b) The level of a person's self-doubt and depreciation at a particular time.
(c) The level of a person's self-hatred and anger at a particular time.
(d) All of the above

(ii) consoled (line 31)
(a) aggravated or angered someone
(b) cared for and look after someone
(c) comfort or sympathise with someone who is unhappy or disappointed
(d) Both (b) and (c)

(iii) deficiency (line 44)
(a) abundance of something
(b) surplus of something
(c) lack of something
(d) All of the above

2. Answer the following questions briefly in your own words.

(i) What was Ann Davison discovering about the learnings of other long-distance sailors?
(ii) Why do you think the author says, "the sound was good for her morale"?
(iii) What did Ann Davison do when squall struck and she could not sail anymore?
(iv) Why did Ann Davison decide to head for Barbados although she had originally planned for Antigua?
(v) What exhausted her even more?

3. Give a character sketch of Ann Davison in your own words. Do not exceed 50 words.

Answer

1. (i) (a) The level of a person's self-confidence and enthusiasm at a particular time
   (ii) (c) comfort or sympathise somebody who is unhappy or disappointed
   (iii) (c) lack of something

2. (i) Ann Davison discovered that other long-distance sailors had learnt that the single-hander's main enemies were lack of confidence, discouragement and loneliness.
   (ii) Since Ann's boat was not working properly, she had decided to sail a little everyday. This would help her not to lose confidence and keep her motivated. Hence, I think the author says, ".......... the sound was good for her morale".
   (iii) When a squall struck her boat, Ann gave up trying to sail and consoled herself by reading poetry in the cabin.
   (iv) Ann was suffering from fatigue which she suspected was as a result of a vitamin deficiency. Therefore, owing to her deteriorating physical health and mental depression, she decided to head for Barbados instead of Antigua, as it was nearer.
   (v) For steering better, Ann tried to stream heavy ropes backwards. But, due to the changing directions of the violent wind, the ropes got tangled up and she had to pull them to the cockpit to untangle them. This exhausted her even more.

3. Ann Davison was a very courageous woman with strong determination. She was also very emotional as the gift pack by her friends made her feel lonely. The sudden strong and violent winds stopped her for a while but could not discourage her. Instead of being demoralised, she busied herself in reading and playing memory games. This shows her self-motivation. Deficiency of fuel and deteriorating health disheartened her a little but could not deviate her from reaching her goal.

EXAM PRACTICE

Passage 1

Read the following passage carefully and answer the questions that follow. ***(2023)***

That huge bell never stopped ringing. It got us out of bed, it **summoned** us for meals, it rang between class periods, it sent us unwillingly to bed.

One morning it failed to ring, or rather, there was no bell to ring. Someone had removed it and it wasn't found till late in the afternoon.

What a glorious day! As there was no bell to rouse us, everyone got up late, and there was no morning PT. Some of us missed breakfast too. The teachers got confused and mixed up their classes. How could the school manage without it? Confusion reigned.

Of course, no one owned up. It could have meant expulsion. Some suspicion fell on the Sports Captain because of our **aversion** to morning PT, but nothing could be proved.

No one was very anxious to find the bell- we were quite happy without it-but it was finally discovered hanging from a branch of one of the trees.

'It may have been Mr. Sharma', surmised Brian. Mr. Sharma, our Maths teacher, was known to walk in his sleep. And sleepwalkers did funny things sometime.

'It could be Mool Chand himself', suggested Cyrus Satralkar.

Mool Chand was the school chowkidar, who also had the job of banging the brass bell at appointed times.

'Why would he throw it away?'

'He must be as fed up with ringing it as we are of hearing it.' This was my theory. 'Perhaps he wants a rise in salary.'

The identity of the culprit remained a mystery. Happily, the senior hockey team went on a winning spree against all corners, and our month-end exits were **restored**.

But soon there was another sensation.

A girl was admitted to our class!

The boys were scandalised. No girl ever studied in our school before. We protested.

'What's the problem?' asked Mr. Knight, our class master. 'Haven't you seen a girl before?'

'But-but. Sir.....' Tata was our spokesman. 'How will we concentrate on our studies?'

'When did you ever concentrate on your studies, Tata'.

'Are we going co-ed, sir?' Adams wanted to know.

'No at all', said Mr. Knight. 'This is a special case. She is the school accounts manager's daughter, and he can't afford the girls shool fees. So, I,m sure you'II make her feel very welcome.'

The accountant was a popular man also ran the shcool's tuck shop and allowed most of us a certain amount of credit. All our objections faded away.

At first, Sunita, our new entrant, was a bit of a distraction because, although she was very shy and demure, she had lovely curly hair, bright eyes, pink cheeks and a smile for everyone. All the boys were very polite and attentive to her and Brian in particular was always ready to help her.

–Collection of Stories, Ruskin Bond

Questions

1. Choose the correct meaning of the following words as used in the passage. ***[3]***

(i) summoned (line 2)

(a) totalled (b) ordered
(c) requested (d) shout

(ii) aversion (line 16)

(a) hatred (b) fear
(c) politeness (d) creation

(iii) restored (line 38)

(a) helped (b) returned
(c) permit (d) victory

2. Answer the following questions briefly in your own words.

(i) Why did no one confess to having removed the missing bell?

(ii) Why did suspicion fall on the Sports Captain?

(iii) What made Brian think that it was Mr. Sharma?

(iv) Which sentence in the passage tells you that Mr. Knight thought poorly of Tata's academic performance?

(v) Why was the accountant a popular man?

3. In not not more than 50 words describe the effects of the lost bell.

Passage 2

Read the following passage carefully and answer the questions that follow: ***(2020 Modified)***

Attending classes inside a railway carriage seemed unusual enough, but the seating arrangements turned out to be unusual, too. At Totto-chan's previous school each pupil was **assigned** a specific desk. But here they could sit anywhere they liked at any time. The most unusual thing of all about this school, however, was the lessons themselves.

Schools normally schedule one subject, for example history, during the first period, when everyone in the class just did history; then say, arithmetic in the second period, when you just did arithmetic. But here it was quite different. At the beginning of the first period, the teacher made a list of all the problems and questions in the subjects to be studied that day. Then she would say, "Now, start with any of these you like".

So, whether you started on history or arithmetic or something else didn't matter at all. Someone who liked composition might be writing something, while behind you someone who liked chemistry might be boiling something in a flask over an alcohol burner. This method of teaching enabled the teachers to observe as the children progressed to higher grades, what they were interested in as well as their way of thinking and their character.

It was an **ideal** way for teachers to really get to know their pupils.

As for the pupils, they loved being able to start with their favourite subject, the fact that they had all day to cope with the subjects they disliked meant they could usually manage them somehow. So, study was mostly **independent**, with pupils free to go and consult the teacher whenever necessary. Then pupils would be given further exercises to work at alone. It was study in the truest sense of the word, and it meant there were no pupils just sitting inattentively while the teacher talked and explained.

The first-grade pupils hadn't quite reached the stage of independent study, but even they were allowed to start with any subject they wanted. Some copied letters of the alphabet, some drew pictures, some read books, and some even did physical exercises. Just then the boy sitting behind her got up and walked toward the blackboard with his notebook, apparently to consult the teacher.

Totto-chan stopped looking around the room and fixed her eyes on his back as he walked. The boy dragged his leg, and his whole body swayed from side to side. Totto-chan wondered at first if he was doing it on purpose, but she soon realised the boy couldn't help it.

The boy said brightly, "My name's Yasuaki. What's yours?" She was so glad to hear him speak that she replied loudly, "I'm Totto-chan."

Adapted from Totto-chan

1. Choose the correct meaning of the following words as used in the passage:

(i) assigned (line 4)

(a) declared (b) allotted
(c) decried (d) None of these

(ii) ideal (line 28)

(a) attainable (b) concrete
(c) appropriate (d) superfluous

(iii) independent (line 34)

(a) follow the right way to do something
(b) redundant
(c) Both (a) and (d)
(d) not bound by any schedule

2. Answer the following questions briefly in your own words.

(i) What was unusual about the seating arrangement?

(ii) How did the method of teaching help the teacher?

(iii) Why did the pupils enjoy their lessons at this school?

(iv) What different things did the first-grade pupils do?

(v) Which sentence in the passage tells us that the boy had difficult walking like other children?

3. In not more than 50 words, describe how the children were taught.

Passage 3

Read the following passage carefully and answer the questions that follow. ***(2019 Modified)***

Billy Weaver had travelled down from London and by the time he arrived it was nine O'clock in the night and the moon was coming up.

"Excuse me," he asked a porter. "but is there a cheap hotel nearby?"

"Try The Bell Hotel," the porter answered, pointing down the road.

Billy thanked him, picked up his suitcase and set out to walk the distance to The Bell Hotel. He had never been to Richmond before. But the man at the Office had told him it was a **splendid** city.

Billy was seventeen years old. He was wearing a new navy-blue overcoat, a new brown hat, and a new brown suit, and he was feeling fine. He walked briskly down the street. He was trying to do everything briskly these days. The big shots up at the Head Office were fantastically brisk all the time. They were amazing.

The road was lonely and dark with a few scattered houses.

Suddenly, in a downstairs window Billy saw a printed notice propped up against the window glass. It said Bed and Breakfast.

He moved a bit closer and peered through the window into the room, and the first thing he saw was a bright fire burning in the hearth. On the carpet in front of the fire, a little dog was curled up asleep with its nose tucked into its belly. The room in half-darkness was filled with pleasant furniture. There was a Piano and a big sofa and several plump armchairs; and in one corner he **spotted** a large parrot in a cage. Animals were usually a good sign in a place like this, Billy told himself and it looked to him as though it would be a pretty decent house to stay in.

Then a queer thing happened to him. He was in the act of stepping back and going away from the window when he felt a strange urge to ring the bell!

He pressed the bell. He heard it ringing , and then at once the door swung open and a woman was standing there.

She gave him a warm welcoming smile.

"Please come in," she said pleasantly. Billy found himself **automatically** moving forward into the house.

"I saw the notice in the window," he said, holding himself back.

"Yes, I know."

"I was wondering about a room."

"It's all ready for you, my dear," she said. She had a round pink face and very gentle blue eyes.

"How much do you charge?"

"Five dollars a night, including breakfast."

It was fantastically cheap. He could easily afford it.

1. Choose the correct meaning of the following words as used in the passage.

(i) splendid (line 11)
 (a) expendable (b) excellent
 (c) modest (d) dreadful

(ii) spotted (line 32)
 (a) noticed (b) speckled
 (c) brindled (d) dappled

(iii) automatically (line 45)
 (a) instinctively (b) escapable
 (c) evident (d) uncertain

2. Answer the following questions briefly in your own words.

(i) How did the porter assist Billy?
(ii) Why did Billy want to do everything briskly?
(iii) Why did Billy think animals were a good sign in a place like that?
(iv) Which sentence tells you that something strange happened to Billy?
(v) How much did the room cost?

3. In not more than 50 words, give a brief account of what Billy saw as he looked through the window of the room.

Passage 4

Read the following passage carefully and answer the questions that follow. ***(2018 Modified)***

Granny knew I'd been in the train for two nights, and she had a huge breakfast ready for me.

Later she told me there'd been a letter from Uncle Ken.

'He says he's the manager in Firpo's hotel in Simla,' she said. 'The salary is very good. It's a steady job and I hope he keeps it'.

Three days later Uncle Ken was on the veranda steps with his bedding roll and **battered** suitcase.

'Have you given up the hotel job?' asked Granny.

'No,' said Uncle Ken. 'They have closed down.'

'I hope it wasn't because of you.'

'No, Aunt Ellen. The bigger hotels in the hill stations are closing down.'

'Well, never mind. Come along and have your lunch.'

Over lunch, Uncle Ken talked very seriously about ways and means of earning a living.

'There is only one taxi in the whole of Dehra', he **mused**. 'Surely there is business for another?'

'I'm sure there is,' said Granny. 'But where does it get you? In the first place, you don't have a taxi. And in the second place, you can't drive.'

'I can soon learn. There's a driving school in town. And I can use Uncle's old car.'

'I don't think it will run now,' said Granny.

'Of course, it will. It just needs some oiling and greasing and a spot of paint.'

'All right, learn to drive.'

So, Uncle Ken joined the driving school.

After a month, Uncle Ken announced that he could drive and that he was taking the car out for a trial run.

'You haven't got your license yet,' said Granny.

'Oh, I won't take it far,' said Uncle Ken. 'Just down the road and back again.'

He spent all morning cleaning up the car. Granny gave him money for a can of petrol.

After tea, Uncle Ken said, 'Come along, Ruskin, hop in and I will give you a ride. Bring Mohan along too.' Mohan and I needed no urging. We got into the car beside Uncle Ken.

'Now don't go too fast, Ken,' said Granny anxiously. 'You are not used to the car as yet.'

Uncle Ken nodded and smiled and gave two sharp toots on the horn. He was feeling pleased with himself.

Driving through the gate, he nearly ran over a cat.

Miss Kellner, coming out for her evening rickshaw ride, saw Uncle Ken at the wheel of the car and ran indoors again.

Uncle Ken drove straight and fast tootling the horn without a break.

At the end of the road, there was a roundabout.

'We'll turn here,' said Uncle Ken, 'and then drive back again.'

He turned the steering wheel, we began going round the roundabout, but the steering wheel wouldn't turn all the way, not as much as Uncle Ken would have liked it to……

So, instead he went on and straight through the Maharaja of Jetpur's garden wall.

It was a single-brick wall, and the car knocked it down and **emerged** on the other side without any damage to the car or any of its occupants. Uncle Ken brought it to a halt in the middle of the Maharaja's lawn.

Running across the grass came the Maharaja himself. When he saw that it was Uncle Ken at the wheel, the Maharaja beamed with pleasure.

'Delighted to see you, old chap!' he exclaimed. 'Jolly decent of you to drop in again. How about a game of tennis?'

Questions

1. Choose the correct meaning of the following words as used in the passage.

(i) battered (line 9)
   (a) gave up (b) worn out
   (c) turn up (d) left out

(ii) mused (line 20)
   (a) said impulsively
   (b) thought angrily
   (c) thought whimsically
   (d) said thougtfully

(iii) emerged (line 65)
   (a) came out (b) came up
   (c) came after (d) came across

2. Answer the following questions briefly in your own words.

(i) Why did Granny hope Uncle Ken would keep his job at Firpo's hotel?

(ii) When Uncle Ken arrived with his luggage, Granny remarked that she hoped the hotel had not closed down because of him. What does this remark tell you about Uncle Ken?

(iii) Why did Uncle Ken think that driving a taxi in Dehra would be profitable?

(iv) Which sentence tells you that the narrator and his friend were waiting to be invited for a drive in a car?

(v) Why did Miss Kellner run indoors when she saw Uncle Ken at the wheel of the car?

3. In not more than 50 words, describe what happened after the car went through the wall.

Passage 5

Read the following passage carefully and answer the questions that follow.

Rudyard Kipling, the great achiever of the honourable Nobel Prize for Literature in 1907, was a **versatile** writer with an articulate style of writing. He was an English short story writer, poet and novelist.

He was the first English language writer to receive Nobel Prize for Literature. On one hand, his writings depicted an aureate style of writing. On the other hand, his works have also shown careless and colloquial styles.

Rudyard Kipling was born in Mumbai, on 30th December, 1865 to John Lockwood Kipling and Alice Kipling. His father who was a professor of archaeological sculptor, was appointed curator of the Government Museum in Lahore. So, his family had to move to Lahore, soon after his birth. At the age of six, he was sent to England for schooling. He did his further education from United Service College, Devon. When he returned to India, he was a reporter for the Lahore Civil and Military Gazette and the Allahabad Pioneer. After this, he sailed back to England and also travelled through China, Japan and the United States.

Kipling was a versatile personality and had many qualities that made him extremely popular.

He was more than a writer or journalist. His works include stories of Indian people, of children and of animals. His articles also talked about the value of the machine, his belief in progress, benefits of civilisation to the rest of the world. All these things carved him a niche in the hearts of many readers. He wrote about everything from adventure to supernatural activities, to romance and instilled in everything a special feeling. Although many of his writings were very much different from those of the **contemporary** writers, he won the popularity of readers. He put a new life into the literature of 1890s.

After his daughter's death, Kipling collected stories for what became 'Just so Stories for Little Children' published in 1902. This was the year when he gained highest popularity. Till the first decade of the 20th century, he was at the height of popularity.

One critic described Kipling as "a versatile and **luminous** narrative gift". Henry James, the well known writer once said, "Kipling strikes me personally as the most complete man of genius that I have ever known."

In 1936, when Kipling was 70, he underwent a surgery; a few days after which he died.

Questions

1. Choose the correct meaning of the following words as used in the passage.

(i) versatile (line 3)
  (a) all rounder
  (b) very artistic
  (c) able to do many different things
  (d) Both (a) and (c)

(ii) contemporary (line 37)
  (a) of or belonging to the same time (or era) as one lives in
  (b) modern time (or era)
  (c) the current time period or age
  (d) a time long gone and forgotten

(iii) luminous (line 47)
  (a) easily understood
  (b) complicated or complex
  (c) unnecessary
  (d) None of the above

2. Answer the following questions briefly in your own words.

(i) What contrasting features of Rudyard Kipling's writings does the author talk about in the first paragraph?

(ii) What are the names of the Kipling's parents?

(iii) Why did Kipling's family move to Lahore?

(iv) Why, according to you, does the author say that Rudyard Kipling was a versatile personality?

(v) What all was the work of Kipling based on?

3. Write the summary of the above passage in your own words. Do not exceed 50 words.

Passage 6

Read the following passage carefully and answer the questions that follow. ***(2011 Modified)***

I rested for a moment at the door of Anand Bhavan, on Market Road, where coffee drinkers and tiffin eaters at their tables sat **transfixed** uttering low moans on seeing me. I wanted to assure them.

"Don't fear, I am not out to trouble you. Eat your tiffin in peace, don't mind me... You, nearest to me, hugging the cash box, you are craven with fear, afraid even to breathe. Go on, count the cash, if that's your pleasure. I just want to watch, that's all...

If my tail trails down to the street, if I am blocking your threshold : it is because, I'm told, I'm eleven feet tip to tail. I can't help it. I'm not out to kill...I'm too full—found a green pasture teeming with food on the way. Won't need any for several days to come, won't stir, not until I feel hungry again. Tigers attack only when they feel hungry, unlike human beings who slaughter one another without purpose or hunger..."

To the great delight of children, schools were being hurriedly closed. Children of all ages and sizes were running **helter-skelter** screaming joyously, 'No school, no school, Tiger, tiger!' They were shouting and laughing, and even enjoyed being scared. They seemed to welcome me.

I felt like joining them and bounded away from the restaurant door and trotted along with them, at which they gleefully cried, 'The tiger is coming to eat us; let us get back to the school!'

I followed them through their school gate while they ran up and shut themselves in the school hall securely. I ascended the steps of the school, saw an open door at the far end of a veranda and walked in. It happened to be the headmaster's room, I believe, as I noticed a very dignified man jumping on his table and heaving himself up into an attic. I walked in and flung myself on the cool floor, having a partiality for cool stone floors, with my head under the large desk—which gave me the feeling of being back in the Mempi cave...

As I drowsed, I was aware of cautious steps and hushed voices all around. I was in no mood to bother about anything. All I wanted was a little moment of sleep; the daylight was dazzling.

In half sleep, I heard the doors of the room being shut and bolted and locked. I didn't care. I slept. While I slept, a great deal of consultation was going on. I learnt about it later through my master, who was in the crowd—the crowd which had gathered after making sure that I had been properly locked up—and was watching.

The headmaster seems to have remarked some days later, "Never dreamt in my wildest mood that I'd have to yield my place to a tiger ......" A wag had retorted, "Might be one way of maintaining better discipline among the boys."

'Now that this brute is safely locked up, we must decide', began a teacher. At this moment, my master pushed his way through the crowds and admonished. 'Never use the words 'beast' or 'brute'. They're ugly words coined by humans in their arrogance. The human being thinks all other creatures are 'beasts', Awful word!

Questions

1. Choose the correct meaning of the following words as used in the passage.

(i) transfixed (line 3)

(a) unable to move because of great shock

(b) unable to move because of great horror

(c) running around in fear

(d) running around in utter shock

(ii) helter-skelter (line 22)

(a) now and then

(b) up and down

(c) here and there

(d) right and left

(iii) admonished (line 60)

(a) reprimanded

(b) shocked and scared

(c) to anger and enfuriate someone

(d) to caution against something

2. Answer the following questions briefly in your own words.
   (i) What reassurance did the tiger give to the coffee drinkers?
   (ii) In what way are tigers different from human beings?
   (iii) Why were the children delighted?
   (iv) What did the headmaster say some days later?
   (v) What was the wag's response to the headmaster's words?
3. Describe the tiger's activities from the time it followed the school children till it slept in your own words. Do not exceed 50 words.

Passage 7

Read the following passage carefully and answer the questions that follow.

It was a dull autumn day and Jill Pole was crying behind the gym. She was crying because they had been **bullying** her. This is not going to be a school story, so I shall say as little as possible about Jill's school, which is not a pleasant subject. It was co-educational, a school for both boys and girls, what used to be called a 'mixed' school; some said it was not nearly so mixed as the minds of the people who ran it. These people had the idea that boys and girls should be allowed to do what they liked.

And unfortunately what ten or fifteen of the biggest boys and girls liked best was bullying the others.

All sorts of things, horrid things, went on which at an ordinary school would have been found out and stopped in half a term, but at this school they weren't.

Or even if they were, the people who did them were not **expelled** or punished. The head said they were interesting psychological cases and sent for them and talked to them for hours. And if you knew the right sort of things to say to the head, the main result was that you became rather a favourite than otherwise.

That was why Jill Pole was crying on that dull autumn day on the damp little path which runs between the back of the gym and the shrubbery. And she hadn't nearly finished crying when a boy came round the corner of the gym whistling, with his hands in his pockets. He nearly ran into her.

"Can't you look where you're going?" said Jill Pole. "All right", said the boy, "you needn't start—" and then he noticed her face, "I say, Jill", he said, "what's up?"

Jill only made faces; the sort you make when you're trying to say something but find that if you speak you'll start crying again. "It's them, I suppose—as usual", said the boy grimly, digging his hands further into his pockets. Jill nodded. There was no need for her to say anything, even if she could have said it. They both knew. "Now, look here", said the boy, "its no use..."

He meant well, but he did talk rather like someone beginning a lecture. Jill suddenly flew into a temper (which is quite a likely thing to happen if you have been interrupted in a cry). "Oh, go away and mind your own business", she said. "Nobody asked you to come **barging** in, did they? And you're a nice person to start telling us what we all ought to do, aren't you? I suppose you mean we ought to spend all our time sucking up to them and currying favour and dancing attendance on them like you do." 'Oh, Lord!' said the boy, sitting down on the grassy bank at the edge of the shrubbery and very quickly getting up again because the grass was soaking wet. His name unfortunately was Eustace Scrubb, but he wasn't bad sort.

"Jill!" he said. "Is that fair?"

"I don't know and I don't care," sobbed Jill.

Eustace saw that she wasn't quite herself yet and very sensibly offered her a peppermint. He had one too. Presently Jill began to see things in a clearer light. "I'm sorry, Eustace", she said presently.

Questions

1. Choose the correct meaning of the following words as used in the passage.
   (i) bullying (line 3)
      (a) to use strength to harm someone
      (b) to intimidate those who are weaker
      (c) to harm people inferior to you
      (d) All of the above
   (ii) expelled (line 20)
      (a) made them take leave
      (b) made them to leave school
      (c) made them to return to school
      (d) None of these

(iii) barging (line 49)
(a) to bump into someone
(b) to meet someone after long
(c) to say goodbye to someone
(d) Both (b) and (c)

2. Answer the following questions briefly in your own words.
(i) Why do you think Jill was crying behind the gym?
(ii) Who is the 'them' referred to in the line 10.
(iii) Why did Jill fly into a temper?
(iv) Which sentence tell us that both Jill and Eustace Scrubb had suffered similarly?
(v) When did Jill begin to see things differently?

3. What kind of school did the children go to in above passage? Write your answer in your own words and not more than 50 words.

Passage 8

Read the following passage carefully and answer the questions that follow. ***(2016 Modified)***

Lying in bed, Swami realised with a shudder that it was Monday morning. It looked as though only a moment ago it had been the last period on Friday; already Monday was here. He hoped that an earthquake would reduce the school building to dust, but that good building—Albert Mission School—had withstood similar prayers for over a hundred years now.

At 9 o'clock, Swaminathan wailed, "I have a headache."

His mother said, "Why don't you go to school in a bullock cart?"

"So that I may be completely dead at the other end? Have you any idea what it means to be **jolted** in a cart?"

"Have you any important lessons today?"

"Important ! Bah ! That geography teacher has been teaching the same lesson for over a year now. And we have arithmetic, which means for a whole period we are going to be beaten by the teacher .... Important lessons !"

And mother generously suggested that Swami might stay at home.

At 9:30, when he ought to have been lining up the school prayer hall, Swami was lying on the bench in mother's room. Father asked him, "Have you no school today?"

"Headache," Swami replied.

"Nonsense ! Dress up and go."

"Headache."

"Loaf about less on Sundays and you will be without a headache on Monday."

Swami knew how **stubborn** his father could be and changed his tactics. "I can't go so late to class."

"I agree, but you'll have to; it is your own fault. You should have asked me before deciding to stay away."

"What will the teacher think if I go so late?"

"Tell him you had a headache and so are late."

"He will beat me if I say so."

"Will he? Let us see. What is his name?"

"Mr. Samuel."

"Does he beat the boys?"

"He is very violent, especially with boys who come late. Some days ago a boy was made to stay on his knees for a whole period in a corner of the class because he came late and that after getting six cuts from the cane and having his ears twisted. I wouldn't like to go late to Mr Samuel's class."

"If he is so violent, why not tell your headmaster about it?"

"They say that even the headmaster is afraid of him.
He is such a violent man."

And then, Swami gave a lurid account of Samuel's violence; how when he started caning he would not stop till he saw blood on the boy's hand, which he made the boy press to his forehead like a vermilion marking.

Swami hoped that his father would be made to see that he couldn't go to his class late. But father's behaviour took an unexpected turn. He became excited. "What do these people mean by beating our children? They must be driven out of service. I will see........."

The result was he proposed to send Swami late to his class as a kind of challenge. He was also going to send a letter with Swami to the headmaster.

No amount of protest from Swami was of any **avail** : Swami had to go to school.

By the time he was ready, father had composed a long letter to the headmaster, put in an envelope and sealed it.

"What have you written, father?" Swaminathan asked apprehensively.

"Nothing for you. Give it to your headmaster and go to your class."

Swami's father did not know the truth, that actually Mr. Samuel was a very kind and gentle man.

Questions

1. Choose the correct meaning of the following words as used in the passage.

(i) jolted (line 15)
(a) shaken up badly (b) bring to light
(c) removed (d) to awake someone

(ii) stubborn (line 33)
(a) one who refuses to change one's opinion
(b) one who changes one's opinion
(c) one who falters frequently
(d) None of the above

(iii) avail (line 71)
(a) convert (b) bring
(c) buy (d) use

2. Answer the following questions briefly in your own words.

(i) What did Swami wish for on a Monday morning? Why was his wish unlikely to be answered?
(ii) Which sentence tells us that Swami's father was completely unsympathetic to his son's headache?
(iii) In what way was Swami's mother's response different from his father's?
(iv) Why did Swami give a colourful account of Mr. Samuel to his father?
(v) In what way did father's behaviour take an unexpected turn?

3. Describe how Swami tries to prove that Mr. Samuel is a violent man in your own words and not more than 50 words.

Passage 9

Read the following passage carefully and answer the questions that follow.

A panther was terrorising the Khulna district of Bangladesh, just outside the Sundarbans. It had recently carried off a little girl. She was the seventh person killed in two months by the animal. And it was growing bolder. The previous victim was a man who had been attacked in broad daylight in his field. The beast dragged him off into the forest and his **corpse** was later found hanging from a tree. The villagers kept a watch nearby that night, hoping to surprise the panther and kill it, but it never appeared.

The Forest Department hired a professional hunter. He set-up a small, hidden platform in a tree near a river where two of the attacks had taken place. A goat was tied to a stake on the river's bank. The hunter waited several nights. He assumed the panther would be an old, wasted male with worn teeth, incapable of catching anything more difficult than a human. But it was a sleek tiger that stepped into the open one night : a female with a single cub.

The goat bleated. Oddly, the cub, who looked to be about three months old, paid little attention to the goat. It raced to the water's edge, where it drank eagerly. Its mother followed it. Of hunger and thirst, thirst is the greater urge. Only once the tiger had **quenched** her thirst did she turn to the goat to satisfy her hunger.

The hunter had two rifles with him : one with real bullets, the other with immobilising darts. This animal was not the man-eater, but so close to human habitation she might pose a threat to the villagers, especially as she was with a cub. He picked up the gun with the darts. He fired as the tiger was about to attack the goat. The tiger **reared** up and snarled and raced away. But immobilising darts don't bring on sleep gently-they knock the creature out without warning. A burst of activity on the animal's part makes it act all the faster. The hunter called his assistants on the radio. They found the tiger about two hundred yards from the river.

She was still conscious. Her back legs had given way and her balance on her front legs was shaky. When the men got close, she tried to get away but could not manage it.

She turned on them, lifting a paw that was meant to kill. It only made her lose her balance. She collapsed and the Pondicherry zoo had two new tigers. The cub was found in a bush close by, meowing with fear.

The hunter, whose name was Richard Parker, picked it up with his bare hands and remembering how it had rushed to drink in the river, named it Thirsty. But the shipping clerk at the Howrah train station was evidently a man both confused and diligent. All the papers received with the cub clearly stated that its name was Richard Parker, that the hunter's first name was Thirsty and that his family name was none given. Richard Parker's name stuck. I don't know if the hunter was ever called Thirsty None Given!

Questions

1. Choose the correct meaning of the following words as used in the passage.
   (i) corpse (line 8)
   (a) dead animal (b) decomposed human
   (c) dead body (d) decomposed insects
   (ii) quenched (line 27)
   (a) thirst (b) increased
   (c) satisfied (d) decreased
   (iii) reared (line 36)
   (a) to put down
   (b) to raise itself upright on hind legs
   (c) to fall down
   (d) None of these
2. Answer the following questions briefly in your own words.
   (i) Why does the author say that the panther 'was getting bolder'?
   (ii) Why did the Forest Department hire a professional hunter?
   (iii) What did the hunter expect to encounter? What did he actually encounter?
   (iv) What did the tiger do before turning to attack the goat? Why did it do that?
   (v) What name did the hunter give to the cub? Why?
3. Narrate how the hunter and his assistants captured the tiger and her cub, in your own words and not more than 50 words.

Passage 10

Read the following passage carefully and answer the questions that follow.

There were other boys in Manjari village, but Bisnu was the only one who went to school. His mother would not have fussed if he had stayed at home and worked in the fields. That was what the other boys did; all except lazy Chittru, who preferred fishing in the stream or helping himself to the fruit of other people's trees. But Bisnu went to school. He went because he wanted to. No one could force him to go and no one could stop him from going.

He had set his heart on receiving good schooling. He wanted to read and write as well as anyone in the big world and so he walked to school everyday.

A colony of langoors lived in the forest. They fed on oak leaves, acorns and other green things and usually remained in the trees, coming down to the ground only to play or sun themselves. They were beautiful, supple-limbed animals, with black faces and silver-grey coats and long, sensitive tails. They leapt from tree to tree with great **agility**. The young ones wrestled on the grass like boys.

A dignified community, the langoors did not have the cheekiness or dishonest habits of the red monkeys of the plains; they did not approach dogs or humans. But they had grown used to Bisnu's comings and goings, and did not fear him. Some of the older ones would watch him quietly, a little puzzled. They did not go near the town; because the boys threw stones at them. And anyway, the forest gave them all the food they required.

Coming from another direction was a second path and at the junction of the two paths Sarru was waiting for him. Sarru came from a small village about three miles from Bisnu's and closer to the town. They **hailed** each other and walked along. They often met at this spot, keeping each other company for the remaining two miles.

'There was a panther in our village last night,' said Sarru.

This information interested but did not excite Bisnu.

Panthers were common enough in the hills and did not usually present a problem except during the winter months, when their natural prey was scarce.

'Did you lose any animals?' asked Bisnu.

'No, It tried to get into the cowshed but the dogs set off the alarm. We drove it off.'

'It must be the same one that came around last winter. We lost a calf and two dogs in our village.'

'Wasn't that the one the shikaris wounded? I hope it hasn't become a cattle-lifter.'

'It could be the same. It has a bullet in its leg. These hunters are the people who cause all the trouble. They think it's easy to shoot a panther. It would be better if they missed altogether, but they usually wound it.'

...............'And then the panther's too slow to catch the barking-deer and starts on our own animals'.

We're lucky it didn't become a man-eater. Do you remember the man-eater six years ago? I was very small then. My father told me all about it. Ten people were killed in our valley alone.'

'What happened to it?'

'I don't know. Some say it poisoned itself when it ate the headman of the village.'

Bisnu laughed. No one liked that old **villain**. They linked arms and scrambled up the stony path to school.

Questions

1. Choose the correct meaning of the following words as used in the passage.
   - (i) agility (line 22)
     - (a) to move around slowly
     - (b) the ability to move about quickly and easily
     - (c) to stay stationary for a long time
     - (d) All of the above
   - (ii) hailed (line 38)
     - (a) to call and attract attention of someone
     - (b) to enchant someone in a spell
     - (c) to praise someone without stopping
     - (d) All of the above
   - (iii) villain (line 71)
     - (a) a joyous hero
     - (b) an anti-hero
     - (c) a murderer
     - (d) a wicked man
2. Answer the following questions briefly in your own words.
   - (i) How was Chittru different from other boys?
   - (ii) What was Bisnu's ambition?
   - (iii) What information did Sarru give Bisnu?
   - (iv) How did the information affect Bisnu?
   - (v) What joke did Sarru make?
3. Describe what the narrator tells us about the behaviour of the langoors, in your own words and not more than 50 words.

Passage 11

Read the following passage carefully and answer the questions that follow.

They pass me everyday, on their way to school—boys and girls of the surrounding villages and the outskirts of the hill station. There are no school buses plying for these children; they walk.

For many of them it's a very long walk. Ranbir, who is ten, has to climb the mountain from his village, four miles distant and two thousand feet below the town level. He comes in all weathers, wearing the same pair of cheap shoes until they have almost fallen apart.

Ranbir is a cheerful soul. He waves to me whenever he sees me at my window. Sometimes, he brings me cucumbers from his father's field. I pay him for the cucumbers; he uses the money for books or for small things needed at home.

Many of the children are like Ranbir—poor, but slightly better off than what their parents were at the same age. They cannot attend the expensive residential and private schools that abounded here but must go to the government-aided schools with only basic facilities. Not many of their parents managed to go to school.

They spent their lives working in the field or delivering milk in the hill station. The lucky ones got into the army. Perhaps Ranbir will do something different when he grows up.

He has yet to see a train but he sees planes flying over the mountains almost everyday.

"How far can a plane go?" he asks.

"All over the world," I tell him. "Thousands of miles in a day. You can go almost anywhere."

"I'll go round the world one day," he vows. "I'll buy a plane and go everywhere!"

And maybe he will. He has a determined chin and **defiant** look in his eyes.

Up to a few years ago, very few girls in the hills or in the villages of India went to school. They helped in the home until they were old enough to be married, which wasn't very old. But, there are now just as many girls as there are boys going to school.

Bindra is something of an extrovert-confident fourteen years old who chatters away as she hurries down the road with her companions. Her father is a forest guard and knows me quite well. I meet him on my walks through the deodar woods behind Landour. And I had grown used to seeing Bindra almost everyday.

When she did not put in an appearance for a week, I asked her brother if anything was wrong. 'Oh nothing,' he says, "she is helping my mother cut grass.

Soon the monsoon will end and the grass will dry up. So, we cut it now and store it for the cows in winter."

"And why aren't you cutting grass too?"

"Oh, I have a cricket match today," he says and hurries away to join his teammate. Unlike his sister, he puts pleasure before work!

Cricket, once the game of **elite** has become the game of masses. On any holiday, in any part of this vast country, groups of boys can be seen making their way to the nearest field or open patch of land, with bat, ball and any other cricketing gear that they can cobble together. Watching some of them play; I am amazed at the quality of talent, at the finesse with which they bat or ball. Some of the local teams are as good, if not better, than any from the private schools, where there are better facilities. But boys from these poor or lower middle-class families will never get the **exposure** that is necessary to bring them to the attention of those who select state or national teams. They will never get near enough to the men of influence and power. They must continue to play for the love of the game or watch their more fortunate heroes exploits on television.

Questions

1. Choose the correct meaning of the following words as used in the passage.
   (i) defiant (line 35)
   (a) conformist
   (b) agile
   (c) daring
   (d) encumberant

   (ii) elite (line 60)
   (a) the richest people in a society
   (b) the poorest people in a society
   (c) the weakest people in a society
   (d) the strongest people in a society

   (iii) exposure (line 72)
   (a) the fact of experiencing something
   (b) being exposed to toxic things
   (c) being vulnerable to the environment
   (d) None of these

2. Answer the following questions briefly in your own words.
   (i) In what way are the children better off than their parents?
   (ii) What was Ranbir's ambition?
   (iii) How has the fate of the girls changed?
   (iv) In what way was her brother different from Bindra?
   (v) Why is the narrator amazed?

3. Relate the difficulties that the children face in their daily lives. How does the author feel about it? Write your answer in your own words and not more than 50 words.

Passage 12

Read the following passage carefully and answer the questions that follow.

The boy was idling in the market place on the look out for mischief. All at once, he saw it beckoning him. Workmen had been slating the church spire and their ladders stretched invitingly from Earth to steeple. All children like scrambling up to high places to see if the world looks any different from an apple tree or a stable loft. Over and above his love for climbing, Michael had a longing to do things that had never been done before.

As he gazed at the spire, crowned by a golden ball and weather-vane, an idea crept into his mind he would be the first person in flushing to stand on the golden ball beneath the weather-vane!

He glanced around. No one was looking; Michael began to swarm up the ladder. At the top of the tower, there rose a slated spire crowned by a golden ball and a weather-vane. At last, Michael found himself squatting on top of the ball holding on by the vane. Presently, he heard workmen moving below.

He did not peer over or speak. He was not going to be hauled down. The voices died away and Michael sat resting. At last, he felt ready to **startle** the town. He pulled himself to his feet and keeping tight hold of the weather-vane, managed to stand on top of the ball. It was well that he had a cool head and iron nerves. Someone must have cast a **casual** glance up at the vane and seeing his little figure, cried out. In a minute or two, Michael was delighted to see the market place full of people who had rushed out of their shops and houses to gaze at the dizzy sight.

It was splendid to have all those eyes and hearts glued upon you! But Michael did not intend to stay there until he was fetched down, to be handed over to his father and cuffed before the crowd. After a while, he prepared to descend of his own free will. He leaned over the ball. The ladder was gone. The workmen had taken it away! A sudden feeling of sickness and giddiness came over Michael. He mastered it.

To wait for rescue was a humiliating way to end his escapade. He would come down alone, even if it cost him his life.

The spire at the base of the ball was only half slated and Michael saw some hope of gaining a foothold on the old part. He clasped his arms round the top of the ball and let his body swing down; he was just able to feel the first slate with his toes. Those toes were shod with iron toe-caps, for Michael was hard on his shoes.

Michael kicked with his armoured toes till the slate crashed and fell in; then he got a foothold on the wooden laths beneath. He rested for a minute, with aching arms and a stiff body. He must change his grip on the ball which was too big to slide his arms down; he must get clear of it and somehow **grasp** the spire beneath. One false move and he would be hurled to death on the cobbles below. Slowly, he began to slide his hands together on the top of the ball and then downward over its bulging face. Every inch was packed with peril; every inch pushed him backward towards his death. It seemed to him that he would be too weak to hold on when the time came for him to grasp the spire.

But at last, the steady, deadly creeping of his fingers brought him to a point where he could bend forward.

With a sudden snatch, he caught the base of the ball. The next moment he was kicking out a stairway in the old tiles and swarming swiftly down.

He reached the foot of the spire, lifted the trapdoor of the tower, ran down the steps and was caught by his father in the organ loft.

Questions

1. Choose the correct meaning of the following words as used in the passage.
   (i) startle (line 25)
   (a) surprise (b) recall
   (c) behave (d) forget
   (ii) casual (line 29)
   (a) serious (b) not planned
   (c) planned (d) permanent
   (iii) grasp (line 60)
   (a) catch (b) let loose
   (c) run swiftly (d) hold firmly
2. Answer the following questions briefly in your own words.
   (i) What was Michael doing in the market place? What attracted his attention?
   (ii) What did Michael long to do? What did he plan to accomplish this?
   (iii) What sight filled Michael's heart with delight?
   (iv) Why did Michael not wait for rescue?
   (v) Use the word 'face' in a sentence of your own such that it has a different meaning from that it carries in the passage.
3. With close reference to the last five paragraphs of the extract, trace Michael's descent from the top of the ball to the foot of the spire. Describe in your own words and not more than 50 words.

Passage 13

Read the following passage carefully and answer the questions that follow.

At school, everybody seemed to be overwhelmed by the thought of the examinations. It had been weeks since anybody saw a smile on Shankar's face. Somu had become brisk and businesslike. Pea took time to grasp jokes and seldom made any either. And as for Rajam, he came to school at the stroke of the first bell, took down everything the teacher said and left at the stroke of the last bell, hardly uttering a dozen words to anybody.

Mani was beginning to look worried and took every opportunity to take Shankar aside and have his doubts (that arose from time to time as he **plodded** through his texts) cleared. He dogged the steps of the school clerk. There was a general belief in the school that the clerk was omniscient and knew all the question papers of all the classes. One day Mani went to the clerk's house and laid a neat bundle containing fresh brinjals at his feet. The clerk was pleased and took Mani in and seated him on a stool.

The clerk looked extremely **amiable** and Mani felt that he could ask anything at that moment and get it. The clerk was murmuring something about his cat, a lank ill fed thing, that was nestling close to him. Most of what he was saying did not enter Mani's head. He was waiting feverishly to open the topic of question papers. The clerk had meanwhile passed from cats to eye-flies; but it made little difference to Mani, who was waiting for the other to pause for breath to launch his attack.

'You must never let these eye-flies buzz near your eyes. All cases of eyesore can be traced to it. When you get eyesore, the only thing you can do is to take a slice of raw onion ......' Mani realised that the other would not stop and butted in, 'There is only a week more for the examinations sir......'

The clerk was slightly puzzled : 'Yes. Indeed, a week more ... You must take care to choose only the juicy variety, the large juicy variety, not the small onion ......' ' Sir,' Mani interrupted, ignoring the juicy variety.

'I am much worried about my examination.' He tried to look pathetic.

'I am glad. If you read well, you will pass,' said the Oracle.

'You see, sir, I am so worried, I don't sleep at nights, thinking of the examination......' If you could possibly tell me something important... I have such a lot to study. I don't want to study unnecessary things that may not be necessary for the examination. He meandered thus the clerk understood what he was driving at, but said, 'Just read all your portions and you will pass.' Mani realised that diplomacy was not his line. He asked bluntly, 'Please tell me, sir, what questions are we getting for our examination?'

The clerk denied having any knowledge of the question papers. Mani flattered him by asking, he did not know the questions, who else would. By just a little more of the same judicious flattery the clerk was moved to give what Mani believed to be valuable hints.

In spite of the fact that he did not know what the first form texts were, the clerk ventured to advise 'you must pay particular' attention to Geography. May be you will have to practice map-drawing a lot. And in Arithmetic make it a point to solve at least five problems every day and you will be able to tackle Arithmetic as easily as you swallow plantains.'

'And what about English?'

'Oh, don't worry about that. Have you read all your lessons?'

'Yes, sir,' Mani replied without **conviction**. 'It is all right then. You must read all the important lessons again and if you have time, yet again and that will be ample.' These answers satisfied Mani greatly. On his way home, he smiled to himself and said that the four annas he had invested on brinjals was not after all a waste.

Questions

1. Choose the correct meaning of the following words as used in the passage.

(i) plodded (line 14)

(a) to work slowly and continously without interest
(b) to push and poke at something
(c) to ruin something by excessive disturbance
(d) All of the above

(ii) amiable (line 22)

(a) hastily
(b) angrily
(c) frustratingly
(d) friendly

(iii) conviction (line 78)
(a) belief that someone is wrong
(b) belief that what someone said is true
(c) belief that what someone said is false
(d) Both (a) and (c)

2. Answer the following questions briefly in your own words.
(i) What effect did the coming examination have on Shankar, Somu, Pea and Rajam?
(ii) Which word in the passage describes the clerk as all knowing?
(iii) Why did Mani give the clerk fresh brinjals?
(iv) What did the clerk believe was the reason for eyesore? What was the remedy?
(v) Why did Mani ask the question bluntly?

3. What did Mani really want to know? What valuable hints was he given? Write your answer in your own words and not more than 50 words.

Answers

Passage 1

1. (i) (b) ordered (ii) (a) hatred
(iii) (b) returned

2. (i) No one confessed to having removed the missing bell because it could have meant expulsion.
(ii) Suspicion fell on the Sports Captain because of the students' aversion to morning PT.
(iii) Brian thought that it was Mr. Sharma because he was known to walk in his sleep and sleepwalkers did funny things sometimes.
(iv) The sentence in the passage that tells us that Mr. Knight thought poorly of Tata's academic performance is: 'When did you ever concentrate on your studies, Tata?'
(v) The accountant was a popular man because he also ran the school's tuck shop and allowed most of the students a certain amount of credit.

3. When the bell was lost, it was a glorious day for the students. As there was no bell to rouse them, everyone got up late, and there was no morning PT. Some of them missed breakfast too. The teachers got confused and mixed up their classes. Since the school couldn't manage without it, there was a lot of confusion.

Passage 2

1. (i) (b) allotted (ii) (c) appropriate
(iii) (d) not bound by any schedule

2. (i) In contrast with normal seating arrangement where every student is allotted a designated place to sit, the students in this school could sit wherever they liked.
(ii) As the children studied their favourite subjects, the teachers had a lot of time to observe them and find out more about their interests, their way of thinking and their character. In this way, the teachers got to know students well enough to help them go ahead with their studies.
(iii) The pupils enjoyed their lessons at this school because they could begin their day by studying their favourite subjects. In this way, they could also save the rest of the day to cope with the subjects they found difficult. The pupils could go and discuss their problems with the teachers whenever they liked. In this way, no pupil sat inattentively wasting their time.
(iv) The first grade pupils were not allowed to study independently but were allowed to start with the subject of their choice. So, some of them wrote alphabet, some drew pictures, the others read books and some of them did physical exercises.
(v) 'The boy dragged his leg, and his whole body swayed from side to side'.

3. The teacher made the list of all the topics to be studied that day. The children were then allowed to begin the day with the subject of their own choice. They could discuss their difficulties with the teachers anytime they liked. The first grade pupils also followed the same practice.

Passage 3

1. (i) (b) excellent (ii) (a) noticed
(iii) (a) instinctively

2. (i) The porter assisted Billy by guiding him to The Bell Hotel when Billy asked him whether there wes any cheap hotel nearby.
(ii) Billy wanted to do everything briskly because he admired the senior officers at the Head Office who also did everything briskly.
(iii) Billy thought that animals were a good sign in a place like that because the road was lonely and dark, and pet animals there made him feel that it would be a decent place to live in.
(iv) The sentence which tells us that something strange happened to Billy begins in line 24 with the words, "Then a queer .... ."
(v) The room cost five dollars a night, with breakfast.

3. When Billy looked through the window, he saw a bright fire burning in the hearth with a little dog asleep on the carpet in front of it. The room's furniture included a piano, a big sofa and several plump armchairs. A large parrot was in a cage in one corner.

Passage 4

1. (i) (b) worn out
   (ii) (d) said thoughtfully
   (iii) (a) came out
2. (i) Granny hoped that Uncle Ken would keep his job at Firpo's hotel as it was a steady job with a good salary.
   (ii) This remark tells us that Uncle Ken was not good at work or has faced situations where he had messed up badly, and Granny knew him very well. Granny was doubtful of him and wanted to point out that Uncle Ken should be serious about earning a living.
   (iii) Uncle Ken thought that driving a taxi in Dehra would be profitable because there was only one taxi in the whole of Dehra; thus, there was enough business for another.
   (iv) The sentence which tells us this is : Mohan and I needed no urging.
   (v) Miss Kellner had seen Uncle Ken nearly running over a cat, so she was afraid for her own safety. Thus, she ran indoors when she saw Uncle Ken at the wheel of the car.
3. Uncle Ken stopped the car in the middle of Maharaja of Jetpur's lawn. Seeing this, the Maharaja became alarmed and came running to see what had happened. When he saw that it was Uncle Ken, whom he knew, he remarked that he was delighted to see his friend and expressed his desire to play a game of tennis with him.

Passage 5

1. (i) (d) Both (a) and (c)
   (ii) (a) of or belonging to the same time (or era) as one lives in
   (iii) (a) easily understood
2. (i) The author says that some of Kipling's works exhibit a very decorative and expressive style of writing, while a few of his works have been written in informal and careless style.
   (ii) John Lockwood Kipling and Alice Kipling are the names of Rudyard Kipling's father and mother, respectively.
   (iii) Kipling's father was appointed curator of the Government Museum of Lahore. Hence, they moved to Lahore from Mumbai.
   (iv) Rudyard Kipling had many qualities that made him popular. He was not only a writer but also a journalist. His works include short stories, novels and poems all written in different styles of writing. Therefore, the author says he was a versatile personality.
   (v) Kipling's works included stories of Indian people, of children and of animals. His works also depicted the value of the machine, benefits of civilisation to the world.
3. Rudyard Kipling was born in Mumbai in 1865 and soon after, his family moved to Lahore. He received his education from England. He was a prolific writer and a versatile personality.

   His works include short stories, novels and poetry; based on Indian people, children and animals. He gained immense popularity though he wrote in different styles. He was the first writer in English to receive Nobel Prize for Literature. He died in 1936, a fews days after undergoing a surgery.

Passage 6

1. (i) (b) unable to move because of great horror
   (ii) (c) here and there
   (iii) (d) to caution against something
2. (i) The tiger reassured the coffee drinkers that he was there to enjoy the sight and would not trouble them.
   (ii) Human beings kill one another, even their brethren without any reason or hunger, whereas tigers attack only when they are hungry.
   (iii) The children were delighted because the schools were being closed hurriedly.
   (iv) Some days later, the headmaster remarked that he had never dreamt of giving his office up to a tiger.
   (v) A wag cracked a joke, saying that the tiger's presence is better for maintaining discipline among the boys.
3. The tiger watched the children cheering and cherishing the joy coupled with fear. He watched them scream joyously and followed them.

   He took himself to the steps of the school, saw an open door at the other end of the veranda. He entered the room of the headmaster.

   The headmaster jumped to the attic out of fear. The tiger lay down on the cool floor with his head under the table and went to sleep.

Passage 7

1. (i) (d) All of the above
   (ii) (b) made them to leave school
   (iii) (a) to bump into someone
2. (i) Jill was crying on the little damp path that ran between the gym and the shrubbery because she was being bullied by malicious students.

(ii) 'Them', in line 10 refers to the malicious students of Jill's school who liked to frighten and harm others.

(iii) Jill flew into a temper because Eustace seemed to preach her not to be saddened because of those bad students' behaviour.

(iv) The sentence "I suppose you mean we ought to spend all our time sucking up to them and currying favour and dancing attendance on them like you do" indicates that both Jill and Eustace had suffered similarly.

(v) Jill began to see things differently when Eustace, understanding the delicacy of the situation, offered her a peppermint. She realised that he was not a bad fellow.

3. The children went to a co-educational school. The people who ran the school were indifferent to the problems of the students. They had a strange and wicked idea that boys and girls should be allowed to do what they liked.
Some senior students who liked to harm and frighten others took advantage of this. They were immune to any fear of being expelled. But the other students suffered a lot due to being bullied by them.

Passage 8

1. (i) (a) shaken up badly
(ii) (a) one who refuses to change one's opinion
(iii) (d) use

2. (i) Swami wished there had been an earthquake and the school building had collapsed. His wish was unlikely to be fulfilled because calamities do not take place as a response to human wishes.

(ii) The sentence "Nonsense! Dress up and go" shows that Swami's father was unsympathetic to his headache.

(iii) When Swami informed his mother of his headache, she asked him to stay home and miss school. In this way, his mother's response was different from his father's who seemed adamant on sending his son to school.

(iv) Swami knew that his father was bent on sending him to school. So, he gave a colourful account of Mr. Samuel to convince him that he was very cruel and would punish him severely.

(v) Swami's father was quite annoyed hearing about Mr. Samuel and his behaviour. He decided to send Swami to school late as a challenge. He also decided to write a letter to the headmaster.

3. Swami gave a colourful account of Mr. Samuel to his father as he did not want to go to school. He said that if he reached late to school, his teacher Mr. Samuel would beat him. He added that his teacher was very violent, especially with boys who came late. He also narrated an incident of a boy who was made to stay on his knees for a whole period in a corner of the class because he came late and that too only after beating him with the cane and twisting his ears.

Passage 9

1. (i) (c) dead body
(ii) (c) satisfied
(iii) (b) (of an animal) to raise itself upright on its hind legs

2. (i) The panther was getting bolder as it had killed seven people in two months. Very recently, it carried off a little girl and the previous victim had been a man who was attacked in broad daylight in his field.

(ii) The villagers kept a watch for the panther hoping to surprise and kill it, but it never appeared. So, the Forest Department hired a professional hunter to track and kill it.

(iii) The hunter expected that the panther would be an old, wasted male with worn teeth, incapable of catching anything more difficult than a human. But what he actually encountered was a sleek tigress with a cub.

(iv) The tiger followed the cub to the water's edge and drank water before she turned to the goat to satisfy her hunger because thirst is a greater urge than hunger.

(v) The hunter named the cub 'Thirsty' as he remembered how the cub had rushed to drink water in the river.

3. The hunter shot an immobilising dart at the tiger as she was about to attack the goat. The tiger rose and ran away. The hunter called his assistants. They found the tiger about two hundred yards from the river. She had lost balance. She tried to attack the men as they got close but collapsed. Then, the men captured her.

Passage 10

1. (i) (b) the ability to move about quickly and easily
(ii) (a) to call and attract attention of someone
(iii) (d) a wicked man

2. (i) While other boys worked in the fields, Chittru did fishing in the stream or engaged himself in plucking fruits from other people's trees. This is how he was different from other boys.

(ii) Bisnu aspired to receive good schooling. He wanted to be known in the big world. So, he went to school regularly.

(iii) Sarru informed Bisnu that a panther had entered his village the previous night. He also told that they didn't lose any animal.

(iv) The information interested Bisnu but did not excite him. This was so because panthers were common in the hills and they did not present any problem except during the winter months, when their natural prey was scarce.

(v) Bisnu asked Sarru what happened to the panther that purportedly killed ten people. Sarru joked that it ate the headman of his village and got poisoned to death.

3. A colony of langoors lived in the forest. They fed on oak leaves, acorn and other green things. They lived on trees and moved quickly from one tree to another. They came down only to play in the Sun. The young ones of the langoors wrestled on the grass like boys.The langoors were honest and didn't approach dogs or humans. They would however watch Bisnu quietly when he passed through the forest where the langoors lived.

Passage 11

1. (i) (c) daring
   (ii) (a) the richest people in a society
   (iii) (a) the fact of experiencing something
2. (i) The children are better off than their parents because they can attend school. Their parents never got a chance to go to school and spent their lives working in the fields or delivering milk in the hill station.
   (ii) Ranbir's ambition was to buy a plane one day and go all around the world.
   (iii) In earlier days, very few girls had the privilege of attending school. They had to do household work and would be married soon. But, the fate of girls has changed now because the number of girls going to school has equalled that of boys.
   (iv) Bindra was a hardworking and dutiful girl but her brother put pleasure before work. He preferred playing cricket to helping his mother cut the grass.
   (v) The narrator is amazed at the quality of talent and fineness with which the boys bowled or batted. He observed that some of the local teams were as good as those from the private schools with better facilities.
3. The children do not get buses to go to school. They have to walk. Some children walk up the hills. However, their condition is better than their parents who could not get the opportunity to study. Girls, earlier, didn't get education and got married at an early age. Now, they are getting education. Many children are talented enough to get selected for state and national teams but don't get exposure. Yet, they are better off than their parents.

Passage 12

1. (i) (a) surprise (ii) (b) not planned
   (iii) (d) hold firmly
2. (i) Michael was freely wandering in the market place and was looking out to do some mischief. The ladders stretched from Earth to the steeple of the church and the workmen slating the church spire attracted his attention.
   (ii) Michael longed to do the things that had never been done before. He planned to be the first person in flushing to stand on the golden ball at the top of the spire of the church which was beneath the weather-vane.
   (iii) The market was full of people who had rushed out of their shops and houses to gaze at the precarious view of Michael standing at such a giddy height. His heart was delighted to see all eyes centred at him.
   (iv) Michael did not wait for rescue because he did not want to be handed over to his father and rebuked before the crowd for his escapade.
   (v) 'Bold people do not hesitate to face the challenges of destiny'.
3. Michael clasped his hands around top of the ball and let his body swing down. His toes, somehow reached the first slate. He kicked the slate with his iron toecaps and got a foothold on the wooden laths beneath.
   Slowly sliding his hands downward over the bulging face of the ball, he finally reached its base, where he got a stairway to run down.

Passage 13

1. (i) (a) to work slowly and continuously without interest
   (ii) (d) friendly
   (iii) (b) belief that what someone said is true
2. (i) The coming examination made everyone grave about studies. Shankar had not smiled for weeks. Somu had become confident and serious. Pea didn't indulge in cracking jokes and took time to understand them. Rajam came to school exactly at the first bell, took down everything that the teacher said, without wasting time in chatting and left at the stroke of the last bell.
   (ii) The word 'omniscient' in the passage describes the clerk as all knowing.
   (iii) There was a general belief in the school that the clerk knew everything. Therefore, Mani took fresh brinjals to please him and wheedle him into telling him what questions would appear in the examination.
   (iv) The clerk believed that the eyeflies were mainly responsible for eyesore and the only remedy for it was a large juicy variety of onion.
   (v) Mani wanted to extract the exact information about the questions and was not satisfied with the clerk's diplomatic and wandering replies. So, he asked the question bluntly.
3. Mani wanted to know which questions would appear in the exam in order to do selective study and avoid reading unnecessary things.
   After giving a diplomatic reply first and then being flattered by Mani, the clerk told him that he should practise map-drawing more for Geography and solve five problems everyday for Mathematics. For English, he advised Mani to read all lessons; asserting more emphasis on important lessons.

SELF ASSESSMENT

Passage 1

Read the following passage carefully and answer the questions that follow.

Writing is HARD, and it's not with just a capital H, it's with capital ARD too, or maybe even longer words like challenging or difficult or problematic with all their alphabets in capitals, underlined and in bold. It's been a week since I decided to be amongst the 0.33 per cent people who finish writing a book every year, but all I can think of are the beautiful books I have read, of how I will let them down if I write something **pathetic** and unreadable. It's like performance pressure when **drowning** under the watchful eyes of a gaggle of coaches and parents.

I have just written half a sentence and it goes like, 'As he entered ...' Post that I felt like death, stationary, stuck in place, and all pervasive. I felt light and disgusted, and soon, I was in a pit of inconsolable despair, clawing to get out. Staring at a blank computer screen is distressing, unromantic, and in stark contrast to feeling imprinted sheets of paper, yellowed by age and use, between your fingers.

There are 298 listed writers in the Wikipedia page under the category 'Writers who committed suicide', and like every list, I'm sure it's incomplete. I shudder to think of the pressure writers are under to not write something that's hated.

I have just finished reading Fahrenheit 451, a novel set in the future, when houses and buildings are fireproof, and firemen don't stop fires, they start them. Their job is to burn all the books and stoke the fires that consume them, one page at a time, one story at a time.

451 Fahrenheit is the temperature at which the printing paper catches fire and I am that temperature. Anything that I write should catch fire and burn before anyone reads it, because reading it would destroy them. And I hope not to destroy.

I shut down my laptop, dump my register and the solitary printed sheet with half a sentence in my bag, and storm out of the library. I have come to realise that trying to write is the single fastest path to feeling worthless. But also, there is a little joy.

I take the Metro to college, which is conveniently located, at a ten-minute distance from Dad's library. Today we have Advanced JAVA, C++ and IT security, but I'm not worried about the classes, I'm worried about not descending down the slippery slope of depression and nihilism. I am reading a hardback and walking towards the class, wondering if the author battled with **mediocrity** like I am, trying not to fall in my own eyes. Often deep in my thoughts, my writing is shallower than the script of Pokemon.

The book I am reading is so brilliant that I want to cry and throw it away. Instead, I just keep reading, not thinking of writing a book, and soon enough I do crash into a stupid lamp-post, the book flies out of my hand and I am sprawled on ground with my legs wide open. My chest hurts and a few girls start giggling from a distance. In all the years I have been ..... walking, a perfect upright homo-sapiens-type walk, this is when they choose to notice me, in my brightest hour.

'Are you okay?' a voice says from behind. I turn around to see Archana, my ex-girlfriend, and she's not imaginary. Our relationship was brief but it happened. 'I' am fine, I say. 'This lamp-post here. Stupid lamp-post, always there, never moving'. She giggles, like she always does, and covers her mouth with her slender fingers.

Questions

1. Choose the correct meaning of the following words as used in the passage.

(i) pathetic (line 10)

(a) pitiful (b) comical

(c) cheerful (d) uncanny

(ii) drowning (line 11)

(a) cannot breathe under water

(b) cannot see under water

(c) being overwhelmed by something

(d) being underwhelmed by something

(iii) mediocrity (line 53)

(iii) mediocrity (line 53)
- (a) the state of being the best
- (b) the state of being average
- (c) the state of being the worst
- (d) None of the above

2. Answer the following questions briefly in your own words.

(i) What attempts has the writer made to convince the reader that writing is not an easy task? What does he want to express by saying 'with all their alphabet in capitals, underlined and in bold'?

(ii) What was the author's situation after being unable to write anything more than half a sentence?

(iii) What thoughts horrify the author?

(iv) What is the job of the firemen in the book 'Fahrenheit 451'?

(v) What is tragic, in the author's opinion, about being noticed by the girls?

3. Describe the author's state of distress and despair due to not being able to write something good, using your own language. Do not exceed 50 words.

Passage 2

Read the following passage carefully and answer the questions that follow.

I believe forgetting can be an art. I would like to say

I forgot my family's past. It would make my task (and my life) much easier. But I didn't forget my family's past, I was ignorant of it. And this ignorance bothered me. Not in itself, mind you. It wasn't as if they had all died before I had a chance to talk to them. No, I would see my mother every day, and my grandparents almost as often, and not once did I ask them a single question about the past.

To put it more precisely then: it wasn't my ignorance that **bothered** me, it was the fact I wasn't bothered. I grew up in a small mining town in the coalfields of the Hunter Valley, in what at the time was an exotic family, and I couldn't give a stuff.

It came to me sometime in High School. I couldn't work it out then, but I think I can understand a little now of what was going on. As an adolescent, I hated the child I had been. I could have sympathised with him if he'd failed to learn his mothertongue (how often had I been told what a 'hard' language Russian was?), but he didn't fail because he didn't even try. It was the absence of desire I could never forgive myself; and though I couldn't put it into words, I knew that it had something to do with cowardice, a fear of something too large (and dark) to grasp: A fear of being **swamped**.

Now, as I write, I'm not so sure. Perhaps there was something heroic in my desire not to know, or at least something positive—something necessary.

And how could I know that my grandfather might have conspired in this ignorance, happy, for his own reasons, that I showed no **inclination** to push beyond what he had given? Because the truth is, the few stories I had were enough.

During the first twelve years of my life I knew almost nothing about the Ukraine and while, on the surface at least, I cared little for its actuality, as a fabled place it became for me the source of almost all my romance. I understand now that it was precisely because I knew so little that this could be so.

Like almost all second generation Australians, I lived in two worlds as a child. And somehow that child sensed intuitively that it was essential to avoid actual knowledge; that by knowing just a little, not only was he able to establish his own sense of self, he could also, and more importantly, make himself however he wanted. Without knowledge, without language, there was no deceit and certainly no self-consciousness: it was the easiest thing in the world to see the forests of the Ukraine, to listen at night to the howl of the wolves, in the backyards of Cessnock.

Questions

1. Choose the correct meaning of the following words as used in the passage.

(i) bothered (line 12)
- (a) inconvenienced
- (b) comforted
- (c) angered
- (d) infuriated

(ii) swamped (line 29)
(a) buried under ground
(b) overwhelmed with an excessive amount of something
(c) stuck in a swamp
(d) stepped on

(iii) inclination (line 36)
(a) a hatred for something
(b) an indifferent attitude towards something
(c) an obsession for something
(d) an interest in or liking for

2. Answer the following questions briefly in your own words.

(i) What advantage did the writer see in being ignorant about his family's history?
(ii) Whom does the author refer to as 'him' in the second paragraph? When could the author have sympathised with 'him'?
(iii) Why does the author say that he could never forgive himself?
(iv) Why does the author feel that his grandfather might have conspired?
(v) What was the easiest thing in the world for the author?

3. Write down in your own words, what kind of feelings did the author experience about not trying to know the past of his family. Do not exceed 50 words.

Passage 3

Read the following passage carefully and answer the questions that follow.

Ashfaqulla Khan was a loyal friend, a great revolutionary, a real martyr who sacrificed his life for the cause of freedom. By his unique sacrifice, Ashfaqulla Khan became an **immortal** revolutionary, an unforgettable name in the Indian freedom struggle history.

Born in Shahjahanpur, Uttar Pradesh, Ashfaqulla Khan was the son of Shafiqulla Khan. In 1921, Mahatma Gandhi had called on all Indians not to pay taxes to the government or cooperate with the British.

This Non-Cooperation Movement **kindled** the fire of freedom in the hearts of all Indians. However, with the Chauri Chaura violence which resulted into setting ablaze of a police station and death of some policemen, Mahatma Gandhi called off the Non-Cooperation Movement in February, 1922. The youth of the country were greatly disappointed with this calling off the movement and they themselves resolved that the country should become free as early as possible. Ashfaqulla Khan joined the band of such revolutionaries.

Ramprasad Bismil who also hailed from Shahjahanpur was the leader of the militant group of these revolutionaries. A friendship was cultivated between Ashfaqulla Khan and Ramprasad Bismil. He was an Aryasamaji whereas Ashfaqulla Khan was a devout Muslim. They were so devoted to the cause of the nation that their religion did not come in the way of their firm resolve to join together for the freedom struggle.

Their friendship was so strongly fastened that they always moved together, ate together and worked together. They were called two bodies but one soul. An incident in this connection is worth mentioning. Once Ashfaq had severe fever and under the very high temperature he was **muttering** Ram, my dear Ram. Ashfaq's parents became much perturbed and thought Ashfaq had been overpowered by some evil spirit since he was uttering the name of Ram, the Lord of Hindus.

They called their neighbour. The neighbour assured them, explaining that Ashfaq was remembering Ramprasad Bismil, his friend, whom he was in the habit of addressing as Ram. Bismil was called. Asfaq's muttering came to a stop and both embraced each other.

They formed the Hindustan Republican Association. Shachindra Nath Sanyal was the founder of this organisation. Their objective was to win freedom for the country through armed revolution.

The association published a manifesto called Krantikari in 1925, advocating the elimination of inequality and slavery. For the purpose of carrying out the revolution, they needed money. The famous Kakori train robbery was conceived with the sole objective of getting money for carrying out their revolutionary activities. The train robbery was conceived by Ramprasad. Once while travelling from Shahjahanpur to Lucknow, he noticed money bags being taken into the guard's van and dropped into an iron safe. Ashfaq opposed the idea saying that it would be a hasty step and will expose the revolutionaries to direct attack by strong government that will use the entire machinery to crush the revolutionary activities.

However, the revolutionaries decided to go ahead with the plan. Like a disciplined soldier, Ashfaq vowed to join.

Questions

1. Choose the correct meaning of the following words as used in the passage.
   (i) immortal (line 4)
   (a) memorable (b) obscure
   (c) legendary (d) Both (a) and (c)
   (ii) kindled (line 12)
   (a) aroused (b) induce
   (c) douse (d) extinguish
   (iii) muttering (line 38)
   (a) talking very loudly
   (b) talking to one's soul
   (c) talking under one's breath
   (d) talking to one's friend
2. Answer the following questions briefly in your own words.
   (i) Who called the Indians for non-cooperation movement? How was it to be carried out?
   (ii) Why was the non-cooperation movement called off ?
   (iii) Why were Ashfaq's parents perturbed?
   (iv) What plan was proposed by Ramprasad Bismil in order to materialise the mission of revolution?
   (v) What epithet did the friendship of Ashfaq and Ramprasad win them?
3. Describe the character and life events of Ashfaqulla Khan based on the passage in your own words. Do not exceed 50 words.

Passage 4

Read the following passage carefully and answer the questions that follow.

In Banaras District, there is a village called Bira in which an old, childless widow used to live. She was a Gond woman named Bhungi and she didn't own either a scrap of land or a house to live in. Her only source of livelihood was a parching oven. The village folk customarily have one meal a day of parched grains, so there was always a crowd around Bhungi's oven. Whatever grain she was paid for parching, she would grind or fry and eat it.

She slept in a corner of the same little shack that sheltered the oven. As soon as it was light she'd get up and go out to gather dry leaves from all around to make her fire. She would stack the leaves right next to the oven, and after twelve, light the fire. But on the days when she had to parch grain for Pandit Udaybhan Pandey, the owner of the village, she went to bed hungry. She was obliged to work without pay for Pandit Udaybhan Pandey. She also had to fetch water for his house.

And, for this reason, from time to time the oven was not lit. She lived in the Pandit's Village, therefore, he had full authority to make her do any sort of odd job. In his opinion, if she received food for working from him, how could it be considered as work done without pay? He was doing her a favour, in fact, by letting her live in the village at all. It was spring, a day on which the fresh grain was fried and eaten and given as a gift. No fire was lit in the house. Bhungi's oven was being put to good use today.

There was a crowd worthy of a village fair around her. She had scarcely any opportunity to draw a breath. Because of the customer's impatience, **squabbles** kept breaking out. Then two servants arrived, each carrying a heaped basket of grain from Pandit Udaybhan with the order to parch it right away. When Bhungi saw the two baskets, she was alarmed. It was already after twelve and even by sunset, she would not have time to parch so much grain.

Now she would have to stay at the oven parching until after dark for no payment. In despair, she took the two baskets. One of the **flunkeys** aided menacingly, 'Don't waste any time or you'll be sorry.' With this command, the servants went away and Bhungi began to parch the grain.

It's no laughing matter to parch a whole **maund** of grain. She had to keep stopping from the parching in order to keep the oven fire going. So, by sundown not even half the work was done. She was afraid Panditji's men would be coming. She began to move her hands all the more frantically. Soon the servants returned and said, "Well, is the grain parched?'

Feeling bold, Bhungi said, "Can't you see? I'm parching it now.' 'The whole day's gone and you haven't finished any more grain than this! Have you been roasting it or spoiling it? This is completely uncooked! How's it going to be used for food? It's the ruin of us!

You'll see what Panditji does to you for this.' The result was that that night the oven was dug up and Bhungi was left without a means of livelihood.

Questions

1. Choose the correct meaning of the following words as used in the passage.
   - (i) squabbles (line 36)
     - (a) a noisy quarrel about something important
     - (b) a quiet disagreement about something trivial
     - (c) a quiet disagreement about something important
     - (d) a noisy quarrel about something trivial
   - (ii) flunkeys (line 45)
     - (a) woman servant
     - (b) man servant
     - (c) goon
     - (d) None of these
   - (iii) maund (line 49)
     - (a) a unit of height
     - (b) a unit of weight
     - (c) a unit of width
     - (d) a unit of breadth
2. Answer the following questions briefly using your own words.
   - (i) How did Bhungi earn her livelihood?
   - (ii) Why was Pandit Udaybhan against paying Bhungi?
   - (iii) Which word in the passage shows that the old woman started working hastily in a disorderly manner out of anxiety?
   - (iv) What did one of the servants of Pandit warn Bhungi?
   - (v) What does the author mean by 'She had scarcely any opportunity to draw a breath'?
3. Describe the hard work and the plight of Bhungi, in your own words not exceeding 50.

Passage 5

Read the following passage carefully and answer the questions that follow.

Lucie, a student from the United States, has just arrived at Charles de Gaulle in Paris, the airport that greets a million visitors to Paris every day. Paris; finally. It's always been a dream of Lucie to live in the city of light, the city of fine arts, of the Latin Quarter, of wine, and who knows, perhaps the city of a little love story.

She plans to study in France for one year, to get her degree in Computer Science at the University of Versailles St Quentin-en-Sveline. It's the university that offered her a **scholarship** to study. Plus, her friend Josephine studies there and Lucie can live with her in a small apartment.

She takes the RER which brings her straight to the St Lazare station at the city center. After arriving there, she looks for the platform that will take her to the train for Versailles. She boards the train and soon it's heading into a black tunnel toward Versailles.

Lucie is a little **disappointed** because she has to stay in Versailles when she'd like to live in Paris. But, she tells herself that Versailles is only a few minutes by train from the big city of Paris, and moreover, there are several attractions in Versailles.

The train exits the tunnel, and while passing the big city, she sees a large cemetery, the Eiffel Tower, and Montmartre with the Sacre Coeur cathedral nearby. A few moments later she arrives at Versailles station.

She has arrived. This is her **destination**. In front of her is the grand Chateau of Versailles where Lucie 14th, the Sun king, had parties and lived the high life with his mistresses. To the right is the avenue St Cloud where the apartment that she'll live in with Josephine is tired, but joyful. She starts looking for the address of the apartment. "All alone in a new country, knowing no one, future, I' m ready!" Lucie says to herself. Lucie has arrived at the Versailles train station. She has already seen the Chateau of Versailles but she wants to come back later for a more in-depth visit. But, first she walks along avenue St Cloud to find her apartment. She finds the address in front of the police station in a little brick house. She sets her bags down in front of the gate of the little pathway that leads to the sidewalk of the house. She rings the yellow doorbell next to 'Josephine Gerard'.

Her friend, Josephine, whom she met on the web, opens the door. Josephine gives her two kisses. Shocked Lucie asks why she did that. "That's how it's done in France. Girls give each other two kisses, guys give two kisses to girls and guys shake each other's hands. We do all this to say hello". Josephine says.

"Come with me", says Josephine. "I'll show you the apartment. It's small but it's our own little place." Silently Lucie follows her. Awed, she looks at the apartment's entryway. She can't believe her eyes, she enters the hallway and sees the walls are painted red, completely red. The floors are wood, beautiful and possibly oak. The ceiling is painted black. On the left is an iron table with the telephone on it.

She goes on and to the left is a bathroom, which is across from Josephine's room. A little farther, to the right is Lucie's room. She puts all of her things in the corner, jumps into the bed, and stretches her arms and legs. "Finally at my own place," she says to herself.

Questions

1. Choose the correct meaning of the following words as used in the passage.
   (i) scholarship (line 11)
   (a) grant (b) learning
   (c) culture (d) All of these
   (ii) disappointed (line 20)
   (a) saddened (b) dismayed
   (c) disheartened (d) All of these
   (iii) destination (line 31)
   (a) the beginning of a journey
   (b) the end of a journey
   (c) the last station of a train
   (d) the middle of a journey
2. Answer the following questions briefly in your own words.
   (i) What are the two reasons for Lucie to take admission to the University of Versailles?
   (ii) How does Lucie console herself about living in Versailles? What is her sorrow?
   (iii) What is Lucie ready for?
   (iv) How do people say 'hello' in France?
   (v) Why does Lucie say "Finally, at my own place", according to you?
3. Describe the apartment, in which Lucie goes to stay, right from the entry in your own words. Do not exceed 50 words.

Passage 6

Read the following passage carefully and answer the questions that follow.

Curious as it may sound, I have always felt I am an Indian by accident. Let me explain why I say this.

I was born in Bhagalpur. This ought to make me a Bihari. But I am not because my mother was a Bengali whose family had settled in Bihar. Within weeks of being born I came to Calcutta, where I spent all my growing up years. My school was founded by a Frenchman, a soldier of fortune. And though I scored far better marks in Bengali and Hindi there, the only language I learnt was English. How and why I have no clue since we all spoke Bengali at home. My first English article appeared in the Statesman when I was 13. Soon I published my first book of poems, again in English. I dropped out of college.

Wrote more books till the desire to change the world (yes, in those days we actually thought we could) brought me to what was then Bombay, to be a journalist. Mumbai is where I have lived for most of my life.

In between, for what seemed like six long years, I also lived in Lutyens' Delhi. In a charming bungalow just opposite the BJP office on Ashoka Road, eating subsidised meals in Parliament and representing Maharashtra's interests on a Shiv Sena ticket. So am I a Mumbaikar? Or a Bengali from Calcutta? A Bihari? Or a born again Anglophile like Nirad C Chaudhuri? I have no clue. Most Indians are like me, put together by accident.

That's the magic of being a migrant in your own land, trying to discover yourself through your many identities.

My mother's maiden name seemed to suggest that someone in her family in the past had a Muslim connect though her first name was Hindu (or Bengali, depending on how you see it). The only place of worship I ever saw her visit was the St Paul's cathedral on New Year's eve more out of convention than faith. My father was born a Hindu and his family home was in Kalighat. His father remarried and **chucked**. them out.

My father, his mother and two sisters found themselves on the street trying to fend for themselves when a passing Jesuit took pity on them. He gave them shelter in Bishnupur where he ran a school. The freedom struggle brought my parents together.

They married and we three brothers were born. Never did it once strike me what my religion was, which state I belonged to, what my language ought to be, which culture I should fight for. (My adolescent years went in protesting against the Russians **invading** Czechoslovakia and the Americans, in Vietnam. My Bengali DNA I guess.)

If you look around you, you will find many people like me who in the midst of their many identities, accidentally chanced upon their Indianness. Each of them will **swear** by their regional culture, the language they speak, the faith they follow or (like me) do not. And, as they wander through all these, and discover themselves, they also discover the magic of being Indian.

Questions

1. Choose the correct meaning of the following words as used in the passage.

(i) chucked (line 44)

(a) threw (b) retained
(c) kept close (d) beat

(ii) invading (line 56)

(a) looting (b) attacking
(c) murdering (d) massacring

(iii) swear (line 62)

(a) curse (b) vow
(c) damn someone (d) All of these

2. Answer the following questions briefly using your own words.

(i) Why does the author say that he is an Indian by accident?

(ii) What brought the author to Bombay?

(iii) What pity a passing Jesuit on road took on the author's family?

(iv) What similarity does the author seem to have with Nirad C Chaudhuri as mentioned in the passage?

(v) What quality in himself does the author attribute to his Bengali DNA?

3. Write in your own words, how the author discovers magic in being Indian. Do not exceed 50 words

Passage 7

Read the following passage carefully and answer the questions that follow.

Nails provide vital clues to the state of your health. Made up of protein, keratin and sulphur, they grow about one centimetre every 3 months and protect the highly sensitive nerve endings at the fingertips. It is not surprising, then, that nails can highlight very important changes in the body. What sort of complaints show up in fingernails? One problem, anaemia, is **betrayed** by spoon-shaped nails and often by a brittle texture and a whitish hue.

Psoriasis, a skin problem, which affects two per cent of the population, can appear in the primary stages as yellow marks on the nails. Alopecia (circular patterns of hair loss, most commonly on the scalp) may be signified by multiple sunken pits on the nails.

The colour of the nails can also act as an indicator of a general health problem. A dysfunction in the lung, for **instance**, can be signalled by a bluish tinge to the nails accompanied by clubbing or excessive roundness and spreading of fingertips and nail tips.

Heart disease is often revealed by reddish nails with white half moons. Yellowed nails, on the other hand, are a telltale sign of liver problems, while the appearance of brown streaks on the nail could indicate a melanoma, a type of cancer, under the nail.

Although nails can highlight serious illness, they are far more likely to show up nutritional or vitamin and mineral deficiencies. e.g. zinc deficiency is to blame for the white spots often wrongly **attributed** to a lack of calcium.

Brittle, splitting nails could also be due to a lack of hydrochloric acid in the system, a deficiency often caused by stress. We know that vitamin deficiency can render the hair dull and lifeless, so it is only natural it should affect the nails, which are similarly composed. A person with weak nails is also often lacking in Essential Fatty Acids (EFAs). Of course, brittleness can be hereditary, or even the product of external factors such as overexposure to detergents.

One of the more intriguing conditions you can discern from the nails is arsenic poisoning which may be disclosed by white lines across their surface. But before you go running off to the doctor the next time you break a nail or spot a strange marking, you should remember that the state of the nails varies greatly from individual to individual. John Eastman, a naturopath in London, points out: There may be ten separate reasons why ten different people have nails problem.

Questions

1. Choose the correct meanings of the following words as used in the passage.
   - (i) betrayed (line 8)
     - (a) given up
     - (b) given off
     - (c) given out
     - (d) given away
   - (ii) for instance (line 18)
     - (a) for example
     - (b) exemplar
     - (c) a bad example
     - (d) None of these
   - (iii) attributed (line 32)
     - (a) ascribed
     - (b) given
     - (c) laid upon
     - (d) provided
2. Answer the following questions briefly in your own words.
   - (i) What are the symptoms of anaemia that can be seen in nails?
   - (ii) What changes are found in fingernails when there is a dysfunction in lungs?
   - (iii) What is the common misconception about white spots in nails?
   - (iv) Which part of the body is told to be similar to the fingernails in the passage? In what respect are they similar?
   - (v) What are the different causes of weak nails that are discussed in this passage?
3. In your own words, describe all the diseases or disorders the symptoms of which can be seen in nails, as discussed in the passage. Do not exceed 50 words.

Passage 8

Read the following passage carefully and answer the questions that follow.

Apollo Hospital group installed the world's most advanced Cyberknife robotic radio surgery system at the Cancer Speciality Centre in Chennai, India. Although it meant substantial price for the hospital, Apollo decided to go ahead with the project due to the new-found enthusiasm for robotics in India.

From the Chandrayaan I project for sending robots to Moon, to biomedical engineering and the auto industry, India has been using robotics on a wide scale.

In an increasingly technology-driven country, robotics has fast assumed **significance** not only for industrial applications, but also in various day-to-day human activities. According to the Oxford Dictionary, robotics is the branch of technology that deals with the design, construction, operation, structural disposition, manufacture and application of robots.

The word robotics was derived from the word robot.

The word robotics was first used in print by Isaac Asimov, in his science fiction published in May 1941, in Astounding Science Fiction. Today it is a confluence science using the continuing advancements of mechanical engineering, material science sensor fabrication, manufacturing techniques and advanced algorithms.

Presently, robotics is the **pinnacle** of technical development. Though robotics in India is at a nascent stage, but industrial automation in India has opened up huge potential for robotics. Innovation coupled with consolidated research and development has catapulted India's scientific position in robotic technology. Analysts claim that the Indian manufacturing industry has been growing at an average rate of 10 per cent to 12 per cent per year and the global market for robots is projected to rise by an 5 average of 4.2 per cent, while in India, the industry is expected to grow at a rate 2.5 times that of the global average.

In medicine, the importance of robotics has been growing. Robotic surgery is a new and exciting emerging technology that holds significant promise. Robotics are increasingly being used in a variety of clinical and surgical settings for increasing surgical accuracy and decreasing operating times and often create better healthcare outcomes than standard current approaches. Robotic technology will have a tremendous social and cultural impact on the future of healthcare.

In providing healthcare, robots are expected to augment traditional treatment, resulting in humans and robots working side by side.

It has been proven that robotic systems have benefited in many ways. For instance, few robots have helped children with developmental disabilities, others have improved the health status of people with different **deficiencies.** People who have experienced therapy robots in their lives have commented that robots brought confidence in their lives as well as solved problems related to health.

The other fact is that in some industrial countries robots are helping children with deficiencies to develop faster and have positively influenced their behaviour. Experts predict that by 2020, robots will become more intelligent and irreplaceable as they would perform most household chores like laundry and home maintenance and would provide valuable services for children and elderly people. Thus, future robots promise important role in our lives.

Questions

1. Choose the correct meanings of the following words as used in the passage.

(i) significance (line 13)
(a) trivial (b) importance
(c) mediocre (d) minute

(ii) pinnacle (line 29)
(a) peak (b) pit
(c) nadir (d) midair

(iii) deficiencies (line 64)
(a) insufficiency (b) surplus
(c) abundance (d) profusion

2. Answer the following questions briefly in your own words.

(i) In which sectors has India been using robotics?
(ii) What does 'robotics' mean?
(iii) Which word in the passage denotes that setting up a radio surgery system was an expensive deal for Apollo Hospital group?
(iv) What is the current scientific position of India in robotic technology?
(v) Why are robotics being increasingly used in clinical surgeries?

3. Describe in your own words, the present scenario of robotic technology in India and its growing influence in medicine. Do not exceed 50 words.

Passage 9

Read the following passage carefully and answer the questions that follow.

"If a country is to be corruption free and become a nation of beautiful minds, I strongly feel there are three key societal members who can make a difference. They are the father, the mother and the teacher."

These golden words are remembered by the people of the country as they mourn the death of Dr A P J Abdul Kalam; the great scientist and former President of India. Throughout his lifetime, he had been an inspiration for the students, the youth who are the aspirants of great India. And these '**ignited** minds' illuminated by the character and influence of this great soul will keep spreading the light of their wisdom and virtues across the world. Kalam was born into a poor South Indian family in Rameshwaram. His family lived a very frugal life and could hardly make their both ends meet. It was difficult for his father to pay even the school fees on time.

So, Kalam had a habit of sparingly using his resources. Despite all unfavourable circumstances, he worked very hard and continued with his education and **consequently** became a highly respected aerospace scientist in the country.

His journey to success was not an easy affair. India's 'Missile Man' also had some failure stories. He had narrowly missed his dream of becoming a fighter pilot as he ranked 9th in the list and there were only eight positions in the IAF.

Also, when he was pursuing aerospace engineering in Madras Institute of Technology, his Dean was dissatisfied with the lack of progress that he exhibited in a project. It is another fact that he later accomplished it within the deadline of three days and impressed the Dean.

Abdul Kalam received Honorary doctorate from 40 universities. The Government of India awarded him the Padma Bhushan in 1981, and the Padma Vibhushan in 1990 for his work with ISRO and DRDO and as a scientific advisor to the government. The government also awarded him the highest civilian award 'Bharat Ratna' for his contribution to the Missile Programme in 1997.

Kalam's message for the youth was that they should have the courage to think differently, to travel the unexplored path, discover the impossible and to overcome the problems and succeed. Above all they should work towards achieving 'excellence' was his most important lesson for the youth of the country.

He didn't believe in doling out advice about the things he didn't do himself. It is said that amidst his tight schedule, Kalam found time to put pen to paper, almost everyday. His urge for excellence and fear of intellectual **stagnation** always provoked him to stretch his schedule beyond the daily routine.

When Kalam was President, a reporter who was interviewing him was referring to him as 'Your Excellency'. Kalam cut him short, saying, 'call me Kalam'.

This is the key to Kalam's personality. He was modest to the core.

This great philosopher and scientist who spread the message of spirituality, inspiration, and hardwork in the country passed away due to a cardiac attack while he was delivering a lecture on 'Creating a livable Planet Earth' at Indian Institute of Management in Shillong on the 27th July, 2015.

Questions

1. Choose the correct meanings of the following words as used in the passage.
   (i) ignited (line 10)
   (a) dampened (b) triggered
   (c) cause to catch fire (d) put to use
   (ii) consequently (line 21)
   (a) as a drawback of (b) as a catalyst for
   (c) as a failure of (d) as a result of
   (iii) stagnation (line 54)
   (a) lack of activity (b) lack of growth
   (c) lack of development (d) All of these
2. Answer the following questions briefly in your own words.
   (i) What is Dr Kalam's view regarding a nation of beautiful minds?
   (ii) How did Kalam acquire a habit of using his resources sparingly?
   (iii) Why could Dr Kalam not become a fighter pilot in the IAF?
   (iv) What according to Dr Kalam should the youth of the country strive for?
   (v) Why did Abdul Kalam stretch his schedule beyond the daily routine? What did he do?
3. Give the character sketch of APJ Abdul Kalam using your own language. Do not use more than 50 words.

Passage 10

Read the following passage carefully and answer the questions that follow.

At the end of my first year at Hampton, I was confronted with another difficulty. Most of the students went home to spend their vacation. I had no money with which to go home, but I had to go somewhere. In those days very few students were permitted to remain at the school during vacation. It made me feel very sad and homesick to see the other students preparing to leave and starting for home. I not only had no money with which to go home, but I had none with which to go anywhere.

In some way, however, I had gotten hold of an extra, second-hand coat which I thought was a pretty valuable coat. This I decided to sell, in order to get a little money for travelling expenses. I had a good deal of boyish pride and I tried to hide as far as I could, from the other students the fact that I had no money and nowhere to go. I made it known to a few people in the town of Hampton that I had this coat to sell and after a good deal of **persuading**, one coloured man promised to come to my room to look the coat over and consider the matter of buying it. This cheered my drooping spirits considerably. Early the next morning my **prospective** customer appeared. After looking the garment over carefully, he asked me how much I wanted for it. I told him I thought it was worth three dollars. He seemed to agree with me as to price, but remarked in the most matter-of-fact way: "I tell you what I will do; I will take the coat and will pay you five cents, cash down and pay you the rest of the money just as soon as I can get it." It is not hard to imagine what my feelings were at the time.

With this disappointment I gave up all hope of getting out of town of Hampton of my vacation work. I wanted very much to go where I might secure work that would at least pay me enough to purchase some much needed clothing and other necessities. In a few days, practically all the students and teachers had left for their homes and this served to depress my spirits even more. After trying for several days in and near the town of Hampton, I finally secured work in a restaurant at Fortress Monroe. The wages, however, were very little more than my board. At night and between meals, I found considerable time for study and reading and in this direction I improved myself very much during the summer. One day, during the last week of my stay in the restaurant, I found under one of the tables a crisp, new ten-dollar bill.

I could hardly contain myself, I was so happy. As it was not my place of business, I felt it to be the proper thing to show the money to the proprietor. This I did. He seemed as glad as I was, but he coolly explained to me that, as it was his place of business, he had a right to keep the money and he proceeded to do so. This, I confess, was another pretty had blow to me. I will not say that I became discouraged. I have begun everything with the idea that I could succeed.

I determined to face the situation just as it was. At the end of the week, I went to the treasurer of the Hampton Institute, General J F B Marshall and told him frankly my condition. To my **gratification**, he told me that I could reenter the institution and that he would trust me to pay the debt when I could.

When I left school at the end of my first year, I owed the institution sixteen dollars that I had not been able to work out. It was my greatest ambition during the summer to save money enough with which to pay this debt. I felt that this was a debt of honour and that I could hardly bring myself to the point of even trying to enter school again till it was paid. I economised in every way that I could think of, did my own washing and went without necessary garments, but still I found my summer vacation ending and I did not have the sixteen dollars.

Questions

1. Choose the correct meanings of the following words or phrases as used in the passage.

(i) persuading (line 21)
(a) instigating someone (b) angering someone
(c) convincing someone (d) motivating someone

(ii) prospective (line 25)
(a) potent
(b) potential
(c) previous
(d) All of these

(iii) gratification (line 68)
(a) dissatisfaction
(b) satisfaction
(c) engrossment
(d) indignation

2. Answer the following questions briefly in your own words.

(i) What did the author hide from the other students? Why?

(ii) What did the customer say regarding the deal of the author's second-hand coat?

(iii) Which word in the passage expresses that the author was getting depressed?

(iv) How did the author improve himself during the summer?

(v) What did the proprietor of the restaurant do when the writer showed him the money?

3. What kind of a personality do you visualise the author has? Write the answer in your own words not exceeding 50 words.

CHAPTER 1

Functional Grammar

Tenses

(Verb Forms)

Tenses are the forms of verb that tell about the time and state of an action.

According to this, there are three kinds of tenses, which are

1. **Present** (the time that is running)
2. **Past** (the time that is gone)
3. **Future** (the time that is to come)

These tenses indicate the time at which an action is taking place. Each tense has four sub-types. They are

(i) Simple Tense
(ii) Continuous Tense
(iii) Perfect Tense
(iv) Perfect Continuous Tense

Present Tense

1. Simple Present Tense

Type of Sentence	Structure	Example
Affirmative	Singular Subject + V1 + s/es + Object I/Plural Subject + V1 + Object	She **goes** for a walk. They **go** for a walk.
Negative	Singular Subject + does not + V1 + Object I/Plural Subject + do not + V1 + Object	She **does not go** for a walk. They **do not go** for a walk.
Interrogative	Does + Singular Subject + V1 + Object? Do + I/Plural Subject + V1 + Object?	**Does** she **go** for a walk? **Do** they **go** for a walk?

This tense is used to denote

(i) **Habitual/Regular/Periodic Actions, e.g.**

(a) Maria plays basketball in the evening.
(b) Riddhi reaches office at 9 am everyday.

(ii) **Universal/Eternal Truths, e.g.**

(a) The Sun rises in the East.
(b) Plants produce their own food by photosynthesis.

(iii) **General Facts, e.g.**

(a) Every cloud has a silver lining.
(b) People elect their own representatives in a democratic set up of government.

(iv) **Actions Happening in Near Future, e.g.**

(a) The government launches new schemes for poor students next month.

(b) The next train comes in 10 minutes.

2. Present Continuous Tense

Type of Sentence	Structure	Example
Affirmative	Singular Subject + is/am + V1 + -ing + Object	She **is going** for a walk.
	Plural Subject + are + V1 + -ing + Object	They **are going** for a walk.
Negative	Singular Subject + is/am + not + V1 + -ing + Object	She **is not going** for a walk.
	Plural Subject + are + not + V1 + -ing + Object	They **are not going** for a walk.
Interrogative	Is/Am + Singular Subject + V1 + -ing + Object?	**Is** she **going** for a walk?
	Are + Plural Subject + V1 + -ing + Object?	**Are** they **going** for a walk?

It is used to denote actions

(i) that are progressive or going on at the time of speaking, e.g.

(a) She is plucking flowers from the plant.

(b) Mansi is searching her book.

(ii) that are taking place but not at the exact time of speaking, e.g.

(a) Rumpa is looking for a job. (Not now, but these days)

(b) I am reading 'The Blue Hour'. (these days)

(iii) that are going to happen in near future, e.g.

(a) The Prime Minister is visiting the flood affected areas of Assam tomorrow.

(b) The actor is getting married in December this year.

3. Present Perfect Tense

Type of Sentence	Structure	Example
Affirmative	Singular Subject + has + V3 + Object	She **has gone** for a walk.
	I/ Plural Subject+ have + V3 + Object	They **have gone** for a walk.
Negative	Singular Subject + has + not + V3 + Object	She **has not gone** for a walk.
	I/ Plural Subject+ have + not + V3 + Object	They **have not gone** for a walk.
Interrogative	Has + Singular Subject + V3 + Object?	**Has** she **gone** for a walk?
	Have + I/ Plural Subject+ V3 + Object?	**Have** they **gone** for a walk?

It is used to denote actions

(i) that are recently completed.

These sentences generally contain adverbs like just, recently, this week, this month, this year, etc., e.g.

(a) I have just had my lunch.

(b) The organisation has recently completed 1 year.

(ii) that were started in past, continued for some time and are complete now, e.g.

(a) They have lived in this city for 30 years. (action started 30 years ago and recently completed).

(b) Ms Reena has worked here since 1999.

4. Present Perfect Continuous Tense

Type of Sentence	Structure	Example
Affirmative	Singular Subject + has been + V1 + -ing + Object	She **has been going** for a walk.
	I/ Plural Subject+ have been + V1 + -ing + Object	They **have been going** for a walk.
Negative	Singular Subject + has + not + been + V1 + -ing + Object	She **has not been going** for a walk.
	I/ Plural Subject+ have + not + been + V1 + -ing + Object	They **have not been going** for a walk.
Interrogative	Has + Singular Subject + been + V1 + -ing + Object?	**Has** she **been going** for a walk?
	Have + I/ Plural Subject + been + V1 + -ing + Object?	**Have** they **been going** for a walk?

It is used to denote action that started at some point of time in the past, continued for some time and is still going on at the time of speaking.

Use of 'For' and 'Since' in Present Perfect Continuous Tense

(i) 'Since' is used when the 'point of time' is given, e.g.
  (a) Abhay has been reading a novel since morning/since 9 o'clock in the morning.
  (b) Ms Aditi has been teaching History since 2003.

(ii) 'For' is used when the 'period of time' is given, e.g.
  (a) Kamal has been writing articles for a magazine for 2 years.
  (b) Garima has been working in the kitchen for many hours.

Past Tense

1. Simple Past Tense

Type of Sentence	Structure	Example
Affirmative	Singular/ Plural Subject + V2 + Object	She **went** for a walk.
Negative	Singular/ Plural Subject + did not + V1 + Object	They **did not** go for a walk.
Interrogative	Did + Singular/ Plural Subject + V1 + Object?	**Did** they go for a walk?

It is used to denote actions

(i) that were completed in the past, e.g.
  (a) They reached Goa yesterday. (when time is given)
  (b) I called you many times. (When time is not given, but it is implied that the action was completed in the past.)

(ii) that were past habits, e.g.
  (a) Sagar wore T-shirts earlier. (doesn't wear now)
  (b) I played badminton in my college. (don't play now)

2. Past Continuous Tense

Type of Sentence	Structure	Example
Affirmative	Singular Subject + was + V1 + -ing + Object	She **was going** for a walk.
	Plural Subject+ were + V1 + -ing + Object	They **were going** for a walk.
Negative	Singular Subject + was + not + V1 + -ing + Object	She **was not going** for a walk.
	Plural Subject+ were + not + V1 + -ing + Object	They **were not going** for a walk.
Interrogative	Was + Singular Subject + V1 + -ing + Object?	**Was** she **going** for a walk?
	Were + Plural Subject+ V1 + -ing + Object?	**Were** they **going** for a walk?

It is used to denote an action that was progressive in the past, e.g.
  (a) Naina was watching a movie at 6 pm yesterday.
  (b) The teacher suddenly entered the class while the students were mimicking him.

3. Past Perfect Tense

Type of Sentence	Structure	Example
Affirmative	Singular/ Plural Subject + had + V3 + Object	They **had gone** for a walk.
Negative	Singular/ Plural Subject + had + not + V3 + Object	She **had not gone** for a walk.
Interrogative	Had + Singular/ Plural Subject + V3 + Object?	**Had** they **gone** for a walk?

It is used when

(i) Two actions occurred one after the other in the past.
- The action that happened earlier (i.e. Ist action) is expressed in **Past Perfect tense.**
- The action that happened later (i.e. IInd action) is expressed in **Simple Past tense.**

  e.g.
  (a) The tiger had run away before the hunter reached the forest.
  (b) All had settled down before the director arrived.

(ii) Desires in the past that have not been fulfilled,
  e.g.
  (a) I wish I had taken the 3 o'clock train.
  (b) Madhuri wishes she had studied a little more seriously.

(iii) For conditional sentences (If......then), for actions which were possible but could not happen,
  e.g.
  (a) If he had spoken politely, he would not have borne the consequences.
  (b) Had they started earlier, they would have caught the train.

4. Past Perfect Continuous Tense

Type of Sentence	Structure	Example
Affirmative	Singular/ Plural Subject + had been + V1 + -ing + Object	She **had been** going for a walk.
Negative	Singular/ Plural Subject + had + not + been + V1 + -ing + Object	They **had not** been going for a walk.
Interrogative	Had + Singular/ Plural Subject + been + V1 + -ing + Object?	**Had** they **been** going for a walk?

It is used to denote an action that began before a certain point in the past and continued upto that time, e.g.

(a) When we met in Pune last year, she told me that she had been working in Wipro since 1995.
(b) When Mr Mukerjee came to school in 1995, Mr Anand had already been teaching there for five years.

Future Tense

1. Simple Future Tense

Type of Sentence	Structure	Example
Affirmative	Singular/ Plural Subject + will/ shall + V1 + Object	She **will go** for a walk.
Negative	Singular/ Plural Subject + will/ shall + not + V1 + Object	They **will not go** for a walk.
Interrogative	Will/ Shall + Singular/ Plural Subject + + V1 + Object?	**Will** they **go** for a walk?

(i) It is used to denote actions happening in future, e.g.
(a) I will tell you a story tomorrow.
(b) If it rains, our bus will halt in the village. (Subordinate clause of a conditional sentence in Simple Present tense).

Note The use of 'shall' with I/we has become archaic now. So, in general 'will' is used with all subjects (Ist/IInd/IIIrd person singular/plural). When there is determination/obligation/threat, etc., then with I/we-will and you/he/she/it-shall is used, e.g.
(a) You shall obey my orders.
(b) We will pass the UPSC exam this year.
(c) Trespassers shall be executed.
(d) The students shall follow the rules and regulations.

2. Future Continuous Tense

Type of Sentence	Structure	Example
Affirmative	Singular/ Plural Subject + will/ shall be + V1 + -ing + Object	They **will be going** for a walk.
Negative	Singular/ Plural Subject + will/ shall not be + V1 + -ing + Object	She **will not be going** for a walk.
Interrogative	Will/ Shall + Singular/ Plural Subject + be + V1 + -ing + Object	**Will** they **be going** for a walk?

It is used to indicate an activity that will be in progress over a period of time in future, e.g.
(a) The famous tennis star will be inaugurating the sports day events.
(b) The doctor will be coming in an hour.

3. Future Perfect Tense

Type of Sentence	Structure	Example
Affirmative	Singular/ Plural Subject + will/ shall have + V3 + Object	She **will have gone** for a walk.
Negative	Singular/ Plural Subject + will/ shall + not + have + V3 + Object	They **will not have gone** for a walk.
Interrogative	Will/ Shall + Singular/ Plural Subject + have + V3 + Object?	**Will** she **have gone** for a walk?

It expresses an action that will be completed by a certain time in future, e.g.
(a) Ruhi will have completed MA by 2017.
(b) India will have become a superpower by 2025.

4. Future Perfect Continuous Tense

Type of Sentence	Structure	Example
Affirmative	Singular/ Plural Subject + will/ shall have been + V1+ -ing + Object	They **will have been going** for a walk.
Negative	Singular/ Plural Subject + will/ shall + not + have been + V1 + -ing + Object	She **will not have been going** for a walk.
Interrogative	Will/ Shall + Singular/ Plural Subject + have been + V1 + -ing + Object?	**Will** they **have been going** for a walk?

It expresses an action that will be continuing over a period of time and then end in future, e.g.
(a) On Lydia's birthday, we will have been decorating the hall since morning.
(b) When Sharad returns to home country, his parents will have been waiting for him for many years.

EXAM PRACTICE

Multiple Choice Questions (MCQs)

In the following passages, fill in each of the numbered blanks with the correct form of the word given in the brackets by choosing the correct option.

1. Pablo Picasso (0) showed (*show*) his truly exceptional talent from a very young age.

   His first word (i) ……… (*be*) lapiz (Spanish for pencil) and he (ii) ……… (learn) to draw before he could talk. He was the only son in the family and was very good looking, so he was thoroughly (iii) ……… (*spoil*). He (iv) ……… (*hate*) school and often (v) ……… (*refuse*) to go unless his doting parents (vi) …… (*allow*) him to take one of his father's pet pigeons with him.

   Once, he painted his father's half completed painting so beautifully that his father (vii) ……… (*give*) him his own palette and brushes, and never (viii) ……… (*paint*) again. He was 13 then.

   (i) (a) is (b) was (c) were (d) had

   (ii) (a) had learn (b) learned (c) had learnt (d) has learnt

   (iii) (a) spoilt (b) spoil (c) is spoiling (d) spoils

   (iv) (a) has hated (b) hated (c) is hating (d) was hating

   (v) (a) refuse (b) is refusing (c) refused (d) had been refusing

   (vi) (a) is allowed (b) was allowed (c) has allowed (d) allowed

   (vii) (a) give (b) gives (c) has given (d) gave

   (viii) (a) paint (b) paints (c) painted (d) was painting

2. As heart disease *(0)* is **continuing** *(continue)* to be the number one killer in the United States, researchers (i) ……… (*become*) increasingly (ii) ……… (*interest*) in identifying the potential risk factors that (iii) …….. (*trigger*) heart attacks. High-fat diets and 'life in the fast lane' have long (iv) ….. (*know*) to contribute to the high incidence of heart failure.

   Heart failures (v) ……… (appear) to have seasonal and temporal patterns. Many heart failures (vi) ………… (occur) in cold weather, and more people (vii) ………….(experience) heart failure on Monday than on any other day of the week. Cardiologists (viii) ……… (observe) more morning phenomena of heart attacks than in afternoons or evenings.

   (i) (a) has become (b) have become (c) became (d) becomes

   (ii) (a) interest (b) interests (c) interested (d) was interesting

   (iii) (a) trigger (b) triggers (c) has triggered (d) had triggered

   (iv) (a) was known (b) been known (c) know (d) known

   (v) (a) appears (b) appeared (c) is appearing (d) appear

   (vi) (a) occurs (b) occurred (c) occur (d) None of these

   (vii) (a) experience (b) experiencing (c) experienced (d) was experienced

   (viii) (a) has observed (b) have observed (c) observed (d) is observing

3. The term 'traditional medicine' (0) **refers** (*refer*) to ways of protecting and restoring health that (i)……… (*exist*) before the arrival of modern medicine. As the term (ii) ……… (*imply*), these approaches to health belong to the traditions of each country and (iii) ……… (*hand*) down from

generation to generation. Traditional systems in general have had to meet the needs of the local communities for many centuries. China and India (iv) ...... (*develop*) very sophisticated systems such as acupuncture and ayurvedic medicine. A genuine interest in various traditional practices now (v) .... (*exist*) among practitioners of traditional, indigenous or alternative systems. They (vi) .... (*begin*) to accept and (vii) .... (*use*) some of modern technology. This (viii) .... (*help*) foster teamwork among all categories of health workers within the framework of primary health care.

(i) (a) exist (b) existed
(c) exists (d) None of these

(ii) (a) imply (b) has been implying
(c) implies (d) had implied

(iii) (a) has been handed (b) was handed
(c) have been handed (d) handed

(iv) (a) developed (b) developing
(c) has developed (d) have developed

(v) (a) exist (b) exists
(c) is existing (d) existed

(vi) (a) is beginning (b) are beginning
(c) has begun (d) was beginning

(vii) (a) used (b) use
(c) uses (d) All of the above

(viii) (a) is helped (b) help
(c) will help (d) helped

4. Eye donors can (0) **belong** (*belong*) to any age group or sex. People who (i) .... (*use*) spectacles, or those (ii) .... (*operate*) for cataract, can still donate the eyes. People who (iii) .... (*be*) diabetic, have hypertension, asthma and those without communicable diseases can also (iv) .... (*donate*) eyes. Eyes must (v) .... (*remove*) within 4-6 hours after death. The eye bank team if (vi) .... (*inform*) immediately (vii) .... (*remove*) the eyes at home of the deceased or at a hospital. Eye removal (viii) .... (*take*) only 10-15 minutes. It is a simple process and does not lead to any disfigurement.

(i) (a) is using (b) uses
(c) use (d) used

(ii) (a) operate (b) operates
(c) operated (d) None of these

(iii) (a) is (b) was
(c) were (d) are

(iv) (a) donate (b) donates
(c) donated (d) has donated

(v) (a) was remove (b) be removed
(c) is removed (d) was removing

(vi) (a) inform (b) informs
(c) informed (d) All of the above

(vii) (a) remove (b) removes
(c) removed (d) Both (a) and (b)

(viii) (a) take (b) takes
(c) taken (d) took

5. I (0) **climbed** (*climb*) into bed and (i) ...... (*roll*) myself in my blankets, first extinguishing the light that (ii) .... (*burn*) steadily near the door. I lay still trying to get to sleep, but my fear (iii) .... (*make*) that impossible and soon I (iv) .... (*sit*) up in bed peering into the darkness and occasionally (v)......... (*glance*) at the round window in the side of the ship which (vi) .... (*seem*) like a plate suspended in the darkness. For an hour I must have sat like this, and (vii) ....(*rouse*) by a drought of cold air. I (viii) .... (*jump*) out of the bed; not having allowed for the motion of the ship,
I was instantly thrown violently across the room.

(i) (a) roll (b) rolls
(c) rolled (d) was rolling

(ii) (a) is burning (b) burnt
(c) was burning (d) had burnt

(iii) (a) make (b) makes
(c) made (d) was made

(iv) (a) sit (b) sat
(c) sits (d) has been sitting

(v) (a) glances (b) glanced
(c) is glancing (d) glancing

(vi) (a) seem (b) seems
(c) seemed (d) seeming

(vii) (a) roused (b) rouse
(c) has been rousing (d) will have roused

(viii) (a) jump (b) will jump
(c) had jumped (d) jumped

6. Mobile phones (0) **have become** (*become*) the greatest necessity in today's age. They (i) .... (*be*) no longer a means of mere communication but serve many other purposes. Mobiles (ii) .... (*take*) the form of a mini PC. Apart from making calls and sending texts, they (iii) .... (*facilitate*) you to schedule your work, take photographs, browse data, store as well as share data, etc. They (iv) .... (*connect*) you to your friends miles away in minutes through WhatsApp and Facebook. Moreover, they can (v) ....(*use*) anytime and anywhere without electricity unlike landline phones. GPS and GPRS (vi) .... (*add*) to the advantages of mobile phones. But youngsters (vii) .... (*tend*) to purchase costliest phones to (viii) .... (*show*) off their status and prestige.

(i) (a) are (b) is
(c) was (d) were

(ii) (a) has taken (b) have taken
(c) took (d) had taken

(iii) (a) facilitated (b) is facilitating
(c) facilitate (d) has facilitated

(iv) (a) connect (b) connects
(c) Both (a) and (b) (d) None of these

(v) (a) was used (b) be used
(c) has been used (d) is used

(vi) (a) has added (b) will have added
(c) have added (d) added

(vii) (a) tends (b) is tending
(c) has tended (d) tend

(viii) (a) show (b) shows
(c) showed (d) None of these

7. After 68 years of independence, it is a necessity that we (0) **measure** (*measure*) our gains and losses. We need (i) .... (*consolidate*) our gains and prevent further losses. While (ii) .... (*do*) so, we must also introspect on what we did for the country and for ourselves. Only then will we be able (iii) .... (*take*) steps towards the benefit of the country and of our own. It's time we (iv) .... (*define*) our goals. Also remember that if you (v) .... (*aim*) to reach the top of the mountain, you will reach the top of the tree. If you aim for the top of the tree, you (vi) .... (*reach*) the height of the tip of the top of the grass. If you aim for the tip of the top of the grass, (vii) .... (*imagine*) where you will (viii) .... (*go*).

(i) (a) consolidate (b) to consolidate
(c) had consolidated (d) consolidate

(ii) (a) do (b) did
(c) does (d) doing

(iii) (a) to took (b) to taken
(c) to take (d) had taken

(iv) (a) defined (b) define
(c) defines (d) is defined

(v) (a) aim (b) aims
(c) have aimed (d) All of the above

(vi) (a) will have reached (b) will be reaching
(c) will reach (d) will have been reaching

(vii) (a) imagines (b) has imagined
(c) will imagine (d) imagine

(viii) (a) gone
(b) has gone
(c) was gone
(d) have gone

Subjective Question

In the following passage, fill in each of the numbered blanks with the correct form of the word given in the brackets. ***(2023)***

1. Fill in each of the numbered blanks with the correct form of the word given in brackets. Do not copy the passage but write in correct serial order the word or phrase appropriate to the blank space.

Example:

(0) One night four college students ________ (be) out partying late and did not study for the test scheduled for the next day.

Ans were

In the morning, they (i) ________ (think) of a plan. They (ii) ________ (make) themselves look dirty with grease and dirt. Then they (iii) ________ (go) to the Dean and (iv) ________ (say) they (v) ________ (go) out to a wedding last night and on their way back the tyre of their car burst and they had to push the car all the way back.

The Dean thought for a minute and said that they could have the re-test after three days. They (vi) ________ (thank) him and said they would be ready. On the day of the test, they were made to sit in separate rooms. They agreed as they (vii) ________ (prepare) well. But they (viii) ________ (get) a rude shock!

2. By the time she was three, Matilda had (0) **taught** (*teach*) her to read by (i) ……… (*study*) newspapers and magazines (ii) ……… (throw) *around the house. At the age of four, she* (iii) ……… (*read*) fast and well and she naturally began (iv) ……… (*hanker*) after books. The only book in the whole of enlightened household was something called Easy Cooking, (v) ……… (*belong*) to her mother and when she had read this cover-to-cover and had (vi) ……… (*learn*) all the recipes by heart, she (vii) ……… (*decide*) she (viii) ……… (*want*) something interesting. ***[2020]***

3. Once upon a time, in the days when genies and giants (0) **roamed** (*roam*) the land, there (i) ……… (*live*) a farmer (ii) ……… (*name*) Baba Ayub. He lived with his family in a little village by the name of Maidan Sabz. Because he had a large family to feed, Baba Ayub (iii) ……… (*see*) his days (iv) ……… (*consume*) by hard work. Every day, he (v) ……… (*labour*) from dawn to sundown, (vi) ……… (*plough*) his field and (vii) ……… (*turn*) the soil and (viii) .... (*tend*) to his meagre pistachio trees. ***[2019]***

4. Alice was (0) **beginning** (*begin*) to get very tired of (i) ……… (*sit*) with her sister on the bank and of having nothing to do : once or twice, she had (ii) ……… (*peep*) into the book her sister was reading, but it (iii) ……… (*have*) no pictures or conversations in it, "and what is the use of a book," (iv) ……… (*think*) Alice, "without pictures or conversations?" Alice wondered whether the pleasure of (v) ……… (*make*) a daisy-chain would be worth the trouble of getting up and picking the daisies, when suddenly a White Rabbit with pink eyes (vi) ……… (*run*) close by her. Alice did not think this was very remarkable, until the Rabbit actually (vii) ……… (*take*) a watch out of its waistcoat-pocket, and (viii) ……… (*look*) at it and then hurried on. ***[2018]***

5. My mother (0) **started** (*start*) school when she (i) .... (*be*) six and (ii) .... (*stop*) the same term. She was unusual in the village as she had a father and brother who (iii) .... (*encourage*) her to go to school. She was the only girl in a class full of boys and claims she was brighter than them. But every day, she (iv) .... (*will*) leave behind her girl cousins (v) .... (*play*) at home and, she (vi) .... (*envy*) them. There (vii) .... (*seem*) to be no point in (viii) .... (*go*) to school just to end up doing housework. ***[2017]***

6. The other days we (0) **discussed** (*discuss*) the attitudes of people in our country. Why (i)........... (*be*) most of them arrogant and aggressive? Akash asked. Rachna (ii) .... (*say*) that it (iii)............. (*be*) because there (iv) .... (*be*) too many people and one had to fight for everything. Nirode (v) .... (*insist*) that it (vi) .... (*be*) the climate. We (vii) .... (*be*) as efficient and polite as Canadians if only our weather (viii).......... (*be*) better. ***[2017]***

7. He had been zero (0) **sitting** (*sit*) on the bank of a small irrigation canal. He was (i)........... (*gaze*) at a couple of heron (ii) .... (*fish*) in the muddy water, when he (iii) .... (*feel*) something bump his elbow. (iv) .... (*look*) around, he

(v) .... (*find*) at his side a little goat, jet black and soft as velvet with lovely grey eyes. Neither her owner nor her mother (vi).......... (*be*) around. She continued to (vii)...........(*nudge*) Mukesh, so he (viii) .... (*look*) in his pocket for nourishment. ***[2016]***

8. One morning, I (0) **saw** (*see*) a python curled up on the dressing table. It was (i) .... (*gaze*) at its own reflection in the mirror. I (ii) .... (*go*) for grandfather but by the time we (iii) .... (return) to the room, the python (iv) .... (move) on. He was seen in the garden and once the cook saw him (v) .... (*crawl*) up the ladder to the roof. Then, we (vi) .... (*find*) him on the dressing table again (vii) .... (*admire*) himself in the mirror. "He's trying to look better for Aunt Mabel", I said. I (viii) .... (*regret*) this remark immediately because grandmother overheard and held up my pocket money for the rest of the week! ***[2015]***

9. From his perch behind the clock, Hugo could (0) **see** (*see*) everything. He rubbed his fingers nervously against the small notebook in his pocket and (i) .... (*tell*) himself to be patient. The old man in the toy booth (ii) .... (*argue*) with the girl. She (iii) ....(*be*) about Hugo's age and he often saw her go into the booth and (iv) .... (*disappear*) behind the counter. The old man (v) .... (*look*) agitated today. Had he figured out that some of his toys were (vi) .... (*miss*)? Well, there was nothing to be (vii) .... (*do*) about that now. The old man and the girl argued some more and finally she closed her book and (viii) ....(*run*) off. ***[2014]***

10. A woman (0) **was waiting** (*wait*) at an airport one night, with several long hours before her flight. She (i) .... (*hunt*) for a book in the airport shops, (ii) .... (*buy*) a bag of cookies and found a place to sit. She (iii) .... (*engross*) in her book, when she happened to see that the man sitting beside her, bold as could be, grabbed a cookie or two from the bag in between, which she tried to ignore to avoid a scene. So, she (iv) .... (*munch*) on the cookies and watched the clock, as the gutsy thief diminished her stock. She (v) .... (*get*) more irritated as the minutes ticked by, thinking, "If I wasn't so nice, I (vi) .... (*blacken*) his eye." With each cookie she took, he took one too. When only one was left, she wondered what he would do. With a smile on his face, a nervous laugh, he (vii) .... (*take*) the last cookie and broke it in half. He offered her half, as he ate the other. She had never known she could be so angry and turned to gather her belongings. As she reached for her baggage, she gasped with surprise, there was her bag of cookies, in front of her eyes. If mine are here, she moaned in despair, the other were his, he (viii) .... (*try*) to share. ***[2013]***

11. My guide (0) **told** (*tell*) me that if I wanted to meet these people, I would have to walk two miles. We finally (i) .... (*reach*) a village where I (ii) .... (*meet*) a lady whose age I (iii) .... (*can*) not immediately make out. My translator (iv) .... (*find*) it difficult to interpret the lady's words because her dialect was quite different. She (v) .... (*be*) a dark-skinned and dark-haired lady. She must have been around 70 years old, but there was no grey in her hair. She obviously could not afford to dye her hair. So, what was her secret? Nobody (vi) .... (*know*). It must have been a 'secret' common to all for not one person in that whole village (vii) .... (*has*) a trace of grey hair! I (viii) .... (*think*) about it for a long time.***[2012]***

12. We were not (0) **allowed** (*allow*) to talk during the lecture. The children (i) .... (*sit*) in a neat circle and (ii) .... (*begin*) (iii)........ (*copy*) their multiplication tables. Most (iv) .... (*scratch*) in the dirt with sticks they had (v) .... (*bring*) for that purpose. The more fortunate (vi) .... (*has*) slate boards that they (vii) .... (*write*) on with sticks (viii) .... (*dip*) in a mixture of mud and water.***[2011]***

13. But just when I had almost (0) **given** (give) up hope, I was (i) .... (*strike*) with a brilliant idea : my birthday was due fairly soon and if I (ii) .... (*deal*) with the family skilfully, I (iii) .... (*feel*) sure, I could not only get a boat but a lot of other equipments as well. I (iv) .... (*suggest*) to the family that, instead of (v) .... (*let*) them choose my presents, I (vi) .... (*may*) tell them the things that I (vii) .... (*want*) most. In this way, they could be sure of not (viii) .... (*disappoint*) me. ***[2010]***

14. As she (0) **spoke** (*speak*), I (i) .... (*rise*) and (ii) .... (*go*) to the centre blackboard. I (iii) .... (*find*) the chalk (iv) .... (*write*) in block letters the title of the book. Then, I (v) .... (*put*) the chalk down and went to (vi) .... (sit) beside her, to (vii) .... (*hold*) her hand. The day had barely (viii) .... (*begin*). ***[2010]***

15. I (0) **am convinced** (*convince*) that my father (i) .... (*remember*) by all those who value integrity. He (ii) .... (*be*) a man of learning and also saw to it that he (iii) .... (*teach*) his pupils with passion and patience. He, at times, (iv) .... (*use*) to lose his temper but that was because he always (v) .... (*want*) his pupils to learn and learn well. As a person, he was honest and simple. His greatness (vi) .... (*lie*) in the fact that he (vii) .... (*have*) a pure heart, devoid of malice. Such a man is always valued and (viii) .... (*be*) very rare to find. ***[2010]***

16. There (0) **was** (*be*) some confusion in the doorway. A man (i) .... (*get*) into the compartment (ii) .... (*stammer*) an apology. Then, the door bell (iii) .... (*rang*) and the world was (iv) .... (*shut*) out again. I (v) .... (*return*) to my berth. The guard (vi) .... (*blow*) his whistle and we (vii) .... (*move*) off. Once again, I (viii) .... (*has*) a game to play.

17. Mid-afternoon while (0) **giving** (give) my report to Mrs Biggs, I (i) .... (*hear*) a loud thumping (ii)........... (*come*) from the direction of her store room. "What (iii) .... (*be*) all that noise downstairs?" I asked. "Probably a rat. I don't hear anything", she replied. I ran downstairs and (iv) .... (*open*) the store room door. There was Mr Biggs (v) .... (*look*) very dusty and very disgruntled; he wanted to know why Mrs Biggs (vi) .... (*shut*) him up for hours. He had gone into the store room in search of a walking stick and Mrs Biggs, (vii) .... (*see*) the door open, had promptly (viii) .... (*bolt*) it.

18. Malala Yousafzai, a Pakistani activist for female education, (0) **was born** (*born*) in 1997.

She (i) .... (*know*) for her advocacy of Human Rights for education. Her family (ii) ....(*run*) a chain of schools in the Swat Valley of Pakistan. So, the devotion for education (iii) .... (*receive*) by Malala in heritage. At the very young age of 13, she (iv) .... (*write*) a blog for the BBC, regarding the right for education, in the pseudonym. Her movement (v) ....(*grow*) international when she gave interviews in print and on television. And she (vi) .... (*nominate*) for 'International Children's Peace Prize' by South African activist Desmond Tutu. After Malala was attacked in 2012 and safely recovered, the UN special Envoy for Global Education, Gordon Brown (vii) .... (*launch*) a UN petition in her name, demanding that all children worldwide be in school by the end of 2015. It (viii) .... (*help*) lead to the ratification of Pakistan's first Right to Education Bill.

19. "My father (0)**will get** (*get*) ahead of me in everything and will leave nothing great for me to do".

These were little Alexander's words when he (i) ....(*come*) to know about the conquests of his father, the King Philip of Macedonia. Action and glory, rather than pleasure and wealth (ii) .... (*be*) what Alexander (iii) .... (*want*) from life. Fame was his passion. One of the greatest rulers in history, Alexander (iv) ....(*conquer*) much of what was then the civilised world. He was born in Pella, Macedonia. Even as a boy, Alexander was fearless and strong. He (v) .... (*tame*) the beautiful and spirited Bucephalus, a horse that no one else (vi) ....(*dare*) to touch or ride. His father was so proud that he said, "Oh my son, (vii) .... (*seek*) out a kingdom worthy of thyself, for Macedonia is too little for thee." And, he (viii) .... (*fulfil*) his father's wishes.

20. Roald Dahl, a famous children's writer, (0) **was born** *(born)* on 13th September, 1916 in Wales. His colourful experiences as a student in boarding schools (i) .... (*be*) the inspiration for his books 'Boy' and 'Danny Champion of the World'.

Dahl (ii) .... (*become*) a writer during World War II, when he (iii) ....(*recount*) in a short story his adventures as a fighter pilot for the Royal Air Force. The story (iv) .... (*buy*) by the Saturday Evening Post and a long, illustrious career was born. He (v) .... (*marry*) a film actress with whom he (vi) .... (*have*) five children. After (vii) .... (*establish*) himself as a writer for adults, Dahl (viii) .... (*begin*) writing children stories in 1960.

21. After Christopher Columbus (0) returned (*return*) from his famous voyage across the Atlantic, the King of Spain (i) .... (*wish*) to celebrate the great event and do honour to the man who (ii)...... (*make*) himself a hero. He (iii) ...... (*do*) so by holding a banquet, in honour of the explorer. To this banquet, he (iv) ...... (*invite*) many of the nobles of the king's court. Some of them (v) ...... (*be*) jealous of the success Columbus (vi) ...... (*achieve*). One of them sat next to Columbus. He turned towards Columbus and said, "Of course you (vii) ...... (*be*) a brave man but anyone can take a ship and sail on and on till he (viii) ...... (*reach*) land."

Answers

Multiple Choice Questions (MCQs)

1. (i) (b) was (ii) (c) had learnt
(iii) (a) spoilt (iv) (b) hated
(v) (c) refused (vi) (d) allowed
(vii) (d) gave (viii) (c) painted

2. (i) (b) have become (ii) (c) interested
(iii) (a) trigger (iv) (b) been known
(v) (d) appear (vi) (c) occur
(vii) (a) experience (viii) (b) have observed

3. (i) (b) existed (ii) (c) implies
(iii) (c) have been handed (iv) (d) have developed
(v) (b) exists (vi) (b) are beginning
(vii) (b) use (viii) (c) will help

4. (i) (c) use (ii) (c) operated
(iii) (d) are (iv) (a) donate
(v) (b) be removed (vi) (c) informed
(vii) (b) removes (viii) (b) takes

5. (i) (c) rolled (ii) (c) was burning
(iii) (c) made (iv) (b) sat
(v) (d) glancing (vi) (c) seemed
(vii) (a) roused (viii) (d) jumped

6. (i) (a) are (ii) (b) have taken
(iii) (c) facilitate (iv) (a) connect
(v) (b) be used (vi) (c) have added
(vii) (d) tend (viii) (a) show

7. (i) (b) to consolidate (ii) (d) doing
(iii) (c) to take (iv) (a) defined
(v) (a) aim (vi) (c) will reach
(vii) (d) imagine (viii) (d) have gone

Subjective Questions

1. (i) thought (ii) made
(iii) went (iv) said
(v) had gone (vi) thanked
(vii) had prepared (viii) got

2. (i) studying (ii) thrown
(iii) read (iv) hankering
(v) belonging (vi) learnt
(vii) decided (viii) wanted

3. (i) lived (ii) named
(iii) could see (iv) being consumed
(v) laboured (vi) ploughing
(vii) turning (viii) tending

4. (i) sitting (ii) peeped
(iii) had (iv) thought
(v) making (vi) ran
(vii) took (viii) looked

5. (i) was (ii) stopped
(iii) encouraged (iv) would
(v) playing (vi) would envy
(vii) seemed (viii) going

6. (i) are (ii) said
(iii) was (iv) were
(v) insisted (vi) was
(vii) will be (viii) is

7. (i) gazing (ii) fishing
(iii) felt (iv) Looking
(v) found (vi) was
(vii) nudge (viii) looked

8. (i) gazing (ii) went
(iii) returned (iv) had moved
(v) crawling (vi) found
(vii) admiring (viii) regretted

9. (i) told (ii) was arguing
(iii) was (iv) disappear
(v) looked (vi) missing
(vii) done (viii) ran

10. (i) hunted (ii) bought
(iii) was engrossed (iv) munched
(v) was getting (vi) would blacken
(vii) took (viii) was trying

11. (i) reached (ii) met
(iii) could (iv) found
(v) was (vi) knew
(vii) had (viii) thought

12. (i) sat (ii) began
(iii) copying (iv) were scratching
(v) brought (vi) had
(vii) were writing (viii) dipped

13. (i) struck (ii) dealt
(iii) felt (iv) suggested
(v) letting (vi) might
(vii) wanted (viii) disappointing

14. (i) rose (ii) went
(iii) found (iv) to write
(v) put (vi) sit
(vii) hold (viii) begun

15. (i) will be remembered (ii) was
(iii) taught (iv) used
(v) wanted (vi) lay
(vii) had (viii) is

16. (i) got (ii) stammering
(iii) rang (iv) shut
(v) returned (vi) blew
(vii) moved (viii) had

17. (i) heard (ii) coming
(iii) is (iv) opened
(v) looking (vi) had shut
(vii) seeing (viii) bolted

18. (i) is known (ii) ran
(iii) was received (iv) wrote
(v) grew (vi) was nominated
(vii) launched (viii) has helped

19. (i) came (ii) were
(iii) wanted (iv) conquered
(v) had tamed (vi) dared
(vii) seek (viii) fulfilled

20. (i) were (ii) became
(iii) recounted (iv) was bought
(v) married (vi) had
(vii) establishing (viii) began

21. (i) wished (ii) had made
(iii) did (iv) invited
(v) were (vi) had achieved
(vii) are (viii) reaches

CHAPTER

2

Active and Passive Voice

In grammar, the voice of a verb describes the relationship between the verb and the subject in a sentence. There are two voices in English

1. Active Voice

A sentence is said to be in **active voice** when the subject is the agent or doer of the action.

Sentence Structure in Active Voice: Subject + verb+ object

Example

(i) I identified the errors in the program.
The given sentence is in active voice because the action is performed by the subject, i.e. 'I'.

(ii) Someone stole my pencil yesterday.
The given sentence is in active voice because the subject 'someone' performs the action 'stole'.

2. Passive Voice

A sentence is said to be in **passive voice** when the subject is the receiver of the action.

Sentence Structure in Passive Voice: Object +verb+ by + subject (optional in some cases)

Example

(i) The errors in the program were identified by me.
The given sentence is in the passive voice because the action of identifying is received by the subject 'me'.

(ii) My pencil was stolen (by someone).
The given sentence is in passive voice because the focus is on the action of a pencil being stolen and not on the subject.

To understand the process of changing an active verb into a passive verb, let us understand the transformation of sentences from active to passive and vice versa.

Change of Persons

Subject	Object
I	me
we	us
you	you
he	him
she	her
they	them
Name (Jay/Mayur)	Name remains as it is (Jay/Mayur)

Change of Verb According to Tense

Tense or Modal + Base	Active Voice	Passive Voice
Simple Present Past Future	beat/beats beat shall/will beat	am/is/are beaten was/were beaten shall /will be beaten
Continuous Present Past Future	am/is/are beating was/were beating shall/will be beating	am/is/are being beaten was/were being beaten Not applicable
Perfect Present Past Future	have/has beaten had beaten shall/will have beaten	have/has been beaten had been beaten shall/will have been beaten
Perfect Continuous Present Past Future	Not applicable	Not applicable
Can/may/must, etc. + base	can/may/must, etc. beat	can/may/must, etc. be beaten

Transformation of Active Voice Into Passive Voice

Present Tense

Simple Present Tense

Active : S + V_1 + O

Passive : 'O' + am/is/are + V + by + 'S'

(a) I bake a cake today. (*Active voice*)
A cake is baked by me today. (*Passive voice*)

(b) NDTV launches gadgets360.com soon. (*Active voice*)
Gadgets360.com is launched soon by NDTV. (*Passive voice*)

Present Continuous Tense

Active : S + am/is/are + V_1 + ing + O

Passive : O + am/is/are + being + V_3 + by + S

(a) Rishabh is painting the portrait of a lady. (*Active voice*)
The portrait of a lady is being painted by Rishabh. (*Passive voice*)

(b) The police are investigating the matter. (*Active voice*)
The matter is being investigated by the police. (*Passive voice*)

Present Perfect Tense

Active : S + has/have + V_3 + O

Passive : O + has/have + been + V_3 + by + S

(a) Ovi has changed the channel on TV. (*Active voice*)
The channel on TV has been changed by Ovi. (*Passive voice*)

(b) Anurag Basu has made a few very good movies. (*Active voice*)
A few very good movies have been made by Anurag Basu. (*Passive voice*)

Past Tense

Simple Past Tense

Active : S + V_2 + O

Passive : O + was/were + V_3 + by + S

(a) We submitted the assignments last week. (*Active voice*)
The assignments were submitted last week by us. (*Passive voice*)

(b) Sakshi cracked GRE at the very first attempt. (*Active voice*)
GRE was cracked at the very first attempt by Sakshi. (*Passive voice*)

Past Continuous Tense

Active : S + was/were + V_1 + ing + O

Passive : O + was/were + being + V_3 + by + S

(a) He was practising Hinduism. (*Active voice*)
Hinduism was being practised by him. (*Passive voice*)

(b) Sumi was counting stars in the sky. (*Active voice*)
Stars in the sky were being counted by Sumi. (*Passive voice*)

Past Perfect Tense

Active : S + had + V_3 + O

Passive : O + had been + V_3 + by + S

(a) I had already done this. (*Active voice*)
This had already been done by me. (Passive voice)

(b) He had tolerated much before coming to this city. (*Active voice*)
Much had been tolerated by him before coming to this city. (*Passive voice*)

Future Tense

Simple Future Tense

Active : S + shall/will + V_1 + O

Passive : O + shall/will + be + V_3 + by + S

(a) He will manipulate her. (*Active voice*)
She will be manipulated by him. (*Passive voice*)

(b) We will find out a solution. (*Active voice*)
A solution will be found out by us.(*Passive voice*)

Future Perfect Tense

Active : S + shall/will have + V_3 + O

Passive : O + shall/will have + been + V_3 + by + S

(a) Mother will have prepared delicious lunch. (*Active voice*)
Delicious lunch will have been prepared by mother. (*Passive voice*)

(b) You will have won the game. (*Active voice*)
The game will have been won by you. (*Passive voice*)

Other Changes

Changes with Modals

(can, could, may, might, should, would, etc.)

be + Past Participle

(a) They **may** change your seat. (*Active voice*)
Your seat **may be** changed by them. (*Passive voice*)

(b) I **can** do this. (*Active voice*)
This **can be** done by me. (*Passive voice*)

Interrogative Sentences

In interrogative sentences, the 'auxiliary' or the 'wh-word' that forms the question remains at its place, the question mark also remains at the end of the sentence. The rest of the changes (like interchange of places of subject and object) take place the same way as in the case of assertive sentences.

Note: Only **'who'** changes to 'by whom' since it acts as the subject itself.

Yes-No Type Questions

Active Voice	Passive Voice
Do you like apples?	Are apples liked by you?
Has she done her homework?	Has her homework been done by her?

Wh-Type Questions

(a) **What** do you need? (*Active voice*)
What is needed by you? (*Passive voice*)
I need a **phone.** (*Active voice*)
A **phone** is needed by me.(*Passive voice*)

(b) Where did she purchase this bag from? (*Active voice*)
From where was this bag purchased by her? (*Passive voice*)
(did + purchase make simple past tense, therefore 'was purchased' and 'by her' also added. Moreover, wh-word remains at its place and the question remains a question)

(c) Who cooked that? (*Active voice*)
By whom was that cooked? (*Passive voice*)

(d) When is she joining office? (*Active voice*)
When is office being joined by her? (*Passive voice*)

(e) Who do you trust? (*Active voice*)
Who is/are trusted by you? (*Passive voice*)

Imperative Sentences

Imperative sentences are of three kinds

(i) **Orders/Commands**
To convert these sentences into Passive voice, 'let' is used followed by 'be + Past participle'.
e.g. (a) Pass the book (*Active voice*)
Let the book be passed. (*Passive voice*)
(b) Close the door (*Active voice*)
Let the door be closed. (*Passive voice*)

(ii) **Requests**
In case of requests, the Passive voice begins with the implicit subject i.e. 'you', as
'You are requested to ....'
e.g. (a) Please, give me some water. (*Active voice*)
You are requested to give me some water. (*Passive voice*)
(b) Please, tell the answer.
You are requested to tell the answer.

(iii) **Advice/ Suggestions**

'Help the poor', 'Love animals' are not orders though they begin with a verb. They are either an advice or a suggestion.

And the implicit subject is 'you', i.e. second person. Therefore, these sentences actually mean

(a) 'You should help the poor.'

(b) 'You should love animals'.

Therefore, their passive voice is

- The poor should be helped (by you).
- Children should be loved (by you).

These can also be done as

- You are advised to help the poor.
- You are advised to love children.

Changes with Prepositions

Prepositions used with the verbs in Active voice are retained in Passive voice.

Active Voice

(a) Yuvi does not listen to the instructions carefully.

(b) Why is everybody staring at her?

Passive Voice

(a) The instructions are not **listened** to carefully by Yuvi.

(b) Why is she being **stared at** by everybody?

Some Important Exceptions

(a) I know her name. (*Active voice*)

Her name is known to me. (Not 'by me') (*Passive voice*)

(b) Her appearance pleases everyone. (*Active voice*)

Everyone is pleased with her appearance.

(Not 'by her appearance') (*Passive voice*)

(c) Such stories interest Janhavi. (*Active voice*)

Janhavi is interested in such stories.

(Not 'by such stories') (*Passive voice*)

(d) The GM's sudden visit shocked all. (*Active voice*)

All were shocked **at** the GM's sudden visit.

(Not 'by the GM's sudden visit') (*Passive voice*)

In Case of Two Objects
(Direct and Indirect)

(a) My friend sent <u>me</u> a <u>gift</u>. (*Active voice*)

↓ me: Indirect object ↓ gift: Direct object

A gift was sent to me by my friend. (*Passive voice*)

Or

I was sent a gift by my friend. (*Passive voice*)

(b) Mr Gandhi teaches <u>us</u> <u>English</u>. (*Active voice*)

↓ us: Indirect object ↓ English: Direct object

English is taught to us by Mr Gandhi. (*Passive voice*)

Or We are taught English by Mr Gandhi. (*Passive voice*)

Points to be Kept in Mind

- Only transitive verbs can be used in the Passive voice. This is because a transitive verb has an object which is the recipient of the action performed by the subject.
- Passive voice is more often used in sentences in which subject is not known/defined.
  e.g. Somebody stole my watch yesterday.
  Sounds better if written as **'My watch was stolen yesterday'** (by someone).

EXAM PRACTICE

Multiple Choice Questions (MCQs)

1. The given sentences have been re-written according to the instructions given after them. Choose the option that contains the correctly written sentence. ***(2023)***

(i) Some boys were helping the wounded man.
(Begin : The wounded ....)
(a) The wounded man was helping some boys.
(b) The wounded man were helping some boys.
(c) The wounded man was being helped by some boys.
(d) The wounded boys were helping the man.

(ii) The examination board is changing its parameters of evaluation rapidly, every year.
(Begin : Its parameters.........)
(a) Its parameters of evaluation is being changed rapidly by the examination board every year.
(b) Its parameters of evaluation are changed rapidly by the examination board every year.
(c) Its parameters of evaluation are being changed rapidly by the examination board every year.
(d) Its parameters of evaluation is changed rapidly by the examination board every year.

(iii) Which all lessons have been prepared thoroughly by you for the coming examination?
(Rewrite using 'have you prepared')
(a) Thoroughly which all lessons have you prepared for the coming examinations?
(b) Which all examinations have you prepared thoroughly for the coming lessons?
(c) Which all lessons have you prepared thoroughly for the coming examinations?
(d) None of the above

(iv) You are requested to oblige me with immediate concern about this matter.
(Rewrite using 'please')
(a) Please oblige me with immediate concern about this matter.
(b) Please obliges me with immediate concern about this matter.
(c) Please obliged me with immediate concern about this matter.
(d) All of the above

(v) The garbage had not been cleared by the scavengers for many days before the Mayor visited the area.
(Begin : The scavengers......)
(a) The scavengers has not cleared the garbage for many days before the Mayor visited the area.
(b) The scavengers had not been cleared the garbage for many days before the Mayor visited the area.
(c) The scavengers had not been clearing the garbage for many days before the Mayor visited the area.
(d) The scavengers had not cleared the garbage for many days before the Mayor visited the area.

(vi) Kangana haigned the film.
(End with : .... 'Kangana)
(a) The film was been signed by Kangana.
(b) The film was being signed by Kangana.
(c) The film has been signed by Kangana.
(d) The film has being signed by Kangana.

(vii) Mother will tie Shipra's ponytail.
(Begin : Shipra's ponytail)
(a) Shipra's ponytail will have been tied by mother.
(b) Shipra's ponytail will be tied by mother.
(c) Shipra's ponytail will be tying by mother.
(d) Shipra's ponytail was tied by mother.

(viii) She had bolted the doors before the alarm rang.
(Begin : The doors)
(a) The doors had been bolted by her before the alarm rang.
(b) The doors have been bolted by her before the alarm rang.
(c) The doors had being bolted by her before the alarm rang.
(d) The doors have being bolted by her before the alarm rang.

2. The given sentences have been re-written according to the instructions given after them. Choose the option that contains the correctly written sentence.

(i) Were all the corners of the hall scanned properly by him?
(Begin : Did he ....)
(a) Did he scan all the corners of the hall properly?
(b) Did he scans all the corners of the hall properly?
(c) Did he scanned all the corners of the hall properly?
(d) Did he had scanned all the corners of the hall properly?

(ii) Why were such stupid questions being bombarded at the speaker by the audience? (End : ……the speaker?)

(a) Why had the audience been bombarding such stupid questions at the speaker?
(b) Why was the audience bombarding such stupid questions at the speaker?
(c) Why were the audience bombarding such stupid questions at the speaker?
(d) Why has the audience been bombarding such stupid questions at the speaker?

(iii) Do you know why this is so boring? (Begin : Is it ………)

(a) Is it know to you why this is so boring?
(b) Is it known to you why this is so boring?
(c) Is it knows to you why this is so boring?
(d) Is it being known to you why this is so boring?

(iv) Vageshwari has been blessed with a sweet and melodious voice. (Begin : God has………)

(a) God has bless Vageshwari with a sweet and melodious voice.
(b) God has blessing Vageshwari with a sweet and melodious voice.
(c) God has been blessing Vageshwari with a sweet and melodious voice.
(d) God has blessed Vageshwari with a sweet and melodious voice.

(v) The poet has maintained a rhythm throughout his poem. (Begin : A rhythm………)

(a) A rhythm has been maintained throughout his poem by the poet.
(b) A rhythm have been maintained throughout his poem by the poet.
(c) A rhythm had been maintained throughout his poem by the poet.
(d) A rhythm was being maintained throughout his poem by the poet.

(vi) This gives a clear reflection. (Begin : A clear)

(a) A clear reflection is given by this.
(b) A clear reflection was given by this.
(c) A clear reflection gives by this.
(d) A clear reflection gave by this.

(vii) Kids are blowing the balloons. (Begin : The balloons)

(a) The balloons are being blown by kids.
(b) The balloons are blown by kids.
(c) The balloons were being blown by kids.
(d) The balloons were blown by kids.

(viii) I have collected a sufficient number of articles. (Begin : A sufficient)

(a) A sufficient number of articles have been collected by me.
(b) A sufficient number of articles are being collected by me.
(c) A sufficient number of articles has been collected by me.
(d) A sufficient articles are being collected by me.

3. The given sentences have been re-written according to the instructions given after them. Choose the option that contains the correctly written sentence.

(i) Last night's dinner was cooked for us by father. (Begin : Father …………) ***[2016]***

(a) Father cooked dinner for us last night.
(b) Father cook dinner for us last night.
(c) Father cooks dinner for us last night.
(d) All of the above

(ii) They are painting a mural on the front wall. (Begin : A mural ……) ***[2015]***

(a) A mural was being painted on the front wall by them.
(b) A mural is being painted on the front wall by them.
(c) A mural is painted on the front wall by them.
(d) A mural was painted on the front wall by them.

(iii) She found the keys in the garage. (Begin : The keys …………) ***[2014]***

(a) The keys was found in the garage by her.
(b) The keys are found in the garage by her.
(c) The keys is found in the garage by her.
(d) The keys were found in the garage by her.

(iv) These windows need cleaning again. (Begin : These windows will …………) ***[2013]***

(a) These windows will clean again.
(b) These windows will have been cleaned again.
(c) These windows will be cleaning again.
(d) These windows will be cleaned again.

(v) The peasants regarded him as a thief and called him a villain.
(End .... the peasants) *[2011]*
(a) He is regarded as a thief and called a villain by the peasants.
(b) He had been regarded as a thief and called a villain by the peasants.
(c) He was regarded as a thief and called a villain by the peasants.
(d) He has been regarded as a thief and called a villain by the peasants.

(vi) Keep your mouth shut.
(Use : Let)
(a) Let your mouth keep shut.
(b) Let your mouth be kept shut.
(c) Your mouth let be kept shut.
(d) Your mouth let be shut.

(vii) Who told you about this?
(Use : by)
(a) By whom were you told about this?
(b) Who were you told about this by?
(c) Whom by told you this?
(d) Both (a) and (b)

(viii) She is watering the plants.
(Begin : The plants)
(a) The plants is being watered by her.
(b) The plants are watered by her.
(c) The plants is watered by her.
(d) The plants are being watered by her.

Subjective Questions

1. Rewrite the following sentences according to the instructions given after each sentence. Make other changes that may be necessary, but do not change the meaning of the given sentence.

(i) What do the workers demand?
(Begin : What is)

(ii) Which religion does he follow?
(Use : followed)

(iii) Please pass the salt.
(Use : requested)

(iv) Convey my message to him.
(Use : Let)

(v) This will cause a great trouble in the future.
(Begin : A great trouble)

(vi) Rahim has learnt a number of proverbs.
(Begin : A number of)

(vii) This will help him in essay writing.
(End with : ....by this)

(viii) Who brought the vegetables today?
(End with : ....brought today)

2. Rewrite the following sentences according to the instructions given after each sentence. Make other changes that may be necessary, but do not change the meaning of the given sentence.

(i) Take your seats quickly.
(use : Let)

(ii) Always respect your parents.
(Begin : Your parents)

(iii) Nobody knows dinosaurs' colour for sure.
(Begin : Dinosaurs')

(iv) Peter Ilyich Tchaikovsky symphonies and many other pieces of music apart from doing ballets.
(Use : written apart)

(v) Don't talk nonsense.
(Use : be talked)

(vi) Vahida has done great acting.
(End with : ....by Vahida)

(vii) The snake was killed with a stick.
(Begin : They)

(viii) Who will give me money?
(Begin : By whom)

3. Rewrite the following sentences according to the instructions given after each sentence. Make other changes that may be necessary, but do not change the meaning of the given sentence.

(i) We are taught grammar by Ms. Sullivan.
(Begin : Ms. Sullivan)

(ii) He was praised by the teacher.
(End with : ....him)

(iii) The injured were taken to the hospital by the fireman.
(End with : ....to the hospital)

(iv) The town was destroyed by an earthquake.
(Begin : An earthquake)

(v) The teacher was pleased with the boy's work.
(Begin : The boy's work)

(vi) The building was damaged by the fire.
(Begin : The fire)

(vii) The Librarian orders books for the school library every year.
(Begin: Books ....) *[2020]*

(viii) The school captain was elected by the students of classes XI and XII.
(Begin : The students ....) *[2019]*

Answers

Multiple Choice Questions (MCQs)

1. (i) (c) The wounded man was being helped by some boys.
(ii) (c) Its parameters of evaluation are being changed rapidly by the examination board every year.
(iii) (c) Which all lessons have you prepared thoroughly for the coming examinations?
(iv) (a) Please oblige me with immediate concern about this matter.
(v) (d) The scavengers had not cleared the garbage for many days before the Mayor visited the area.
(vi) (c) The film has been signed by Kangana.
(vii) (b) Shipra's ponytail will be tied by mother.
(viii) (a) The doors had been bolted by her before the alarm rang.

2. (i) (a) Did he scan all the corners of the hall properly?
(ii) (b) Why was the audience bombarding such stupid questions at the speaker?
(iii) (b) Is it known to you why this is so boring?
(iv) (d) God has blessed Vageshwari with a sweet and melodious voice.
(v) (a) A rhythm has been maintained throughout his poem by the poet.
(vi) (a) A clear reflection is given by this.
(vii) (a) The balloons are being blown by kids.
(viii) (c) A sufficient number of articles has been collected by me.

3. (i) (a) Father cooked dinner for us last night.
(ii) (b) A mural is being painted on the front wall by them.
(iii) (d) The keys were found in the garage by her.
(iv) (d) These windows will be cleaned again.
(v) (c) He was regarded as a thief and called a villain by the peasants.
(vi) (b) Let your mouth be kept shut.
(vii) (a) By whom were you told about this?
(viii) (d) The plants are being watered by her.

Subjective Questions

1. (i) What is demanded by the workers?
(ii) Which religion is followed by him?
(iii) You are requested to pass the salt.
(iv) Let my message be conveyed to him.
(v) A great trouble will be caused in the future by this.
(vi) A number of proverbs has been learnt by Rahim.
(vii) He will be helped in essay writing by this.
(viii) By whom were the vegetables brought today?

2. (i) Let your seats be taken quickly.
(ii) Your parents should always be respected.
(iii) Dinosaurs' colour is known to nobody for sure.
(iv) Symphonies and many other pieces of music were written apart from doing ballets by Peter Ilyich Tchaikovsky.
(v) Let nonsense not be talked.
(vi) Great acting has been done by Vahida.
(vii) They killed the snake with a stick.
(viii) By whom will I be given money?
Or By whom will money be given to me?

3. (i) Ms. Sullivan teaches us grammar.
(ii) The teacher praised him.
(iii) The fireman took the injured to the hospital.
(iv) An earthquake destroyed the town.
(v) The boy's work pleased the teacher.
(vi) The fire damaged the building.
(vii) Books for the school library are ordered by the Librarian every year.
(viii) The students of Classes XI and XII elected the school captain.

CHAPTER

3

Reported Speech

The act of reporting the words of a speaker is called Narration. There are basically two ways in which a speaker can convey the intended message/idea to the listener.

Direct Speech (Direct Narration)

Direct Speech is the speech inside quotation marks. It is used to tell/report the words of a speaker as it is. e.g. Divisha said, "I like to study Geography."

Indirect Speech (Indirect Narration)

While Direct Narration is okay for sharing stories with friends, this is not the best way to report a conversation, either in speech or in writing. Therefore, when we report the words spoken by somebody else in our own words, it is called **Indirect Narration.**

In case of Indirect narration, the pronouns (I, we, you, they, etc.), the tense of the statement, words denoting time (like today, tomorrow, etc.) words denoting place (here, there, etc.) may change as the time and place of the original speech may be different from the time and place of narration.

Therefore, the above statement in indirect narration will be

Divisha said that she liked to study Geography.

Now, before we learn the rules of changing direct narration into indirect narration, let us get to know Reporting verb and Reported speech.

Reporting Verb

The verb that is not part of the speech inside the quotation marks is called the Reporting Verb.

Reported Speech

The words spoken by the speaker and written in quotation marks ("......") are collectively called the Reported Speech.

e.g. Divisha said, "I like to study Geography."

(said → Reporting Verb; "I like to study Geography." → Reported Speech)

Some Basic Rules to Change Direct Speech to Indirect Speech

In Direct Speech

- The reporting verb is separated from the reported speech by a comma.
- The first word in inverted commas begins with a capital letter.

In Indirect Speech

- The comma separating the reporting verb from the reported speech is removed.
- The reporting verb changes according to the sense conveyed by the speech.
- The tense of the reporting verb remains unchanged.
- All kinds of sentences are changed into assertive statements.
- Other changes in the person, verb forms, time and place expressions follow.

Rules for Changing Simple Direct Speech into Indirect Speech

Rules	Direct Speech	Indirect Speech
• Remove separating comma, inverted commas and use the connector 'that'.	He said, "I do not like pasta."	He said that he did not like pasta.
• When there is an object in Reporting verb, change 'said to' into 'told' and 'says to' into 'tells'.	He said to me, "You have been a great help." He says to me, "My teacher is highly educated."	He told me that I had been a great help. He tells me that his teacher is highly educated.
• When there is no object in Reporting verb, 'said' and 'says' remain the same.	Sheeba said, "I work in an MNC." Kamya says, "I will go to the party."	Sheeba said that she worked in an MNC. Kamya says that she will go to the party.

Changes in Reported Speech when Reporting Verb is in Past Tense

Change of Verb Forms	Change of Pronouns	Time, Place Expressions and Other Changes
is, am, are – was, were	1st person → according to the subject	now – then
has, have – had	2nd person → according to the object	ago – before
$V_1 - V_2$	3rd person → unchanged	today – that day
did – had + IIIrd form of the verb	2nd person → changed to 3rd person if the reporting verb has no object	last night–the previous night or the night before
was, were – had been		next week – the following week
will – would		here – there
shall – should		hither – thither
can – could		this – that
		thus – so
		come – go

Note If the reporting verb is in the present form, the tense of the verb in the reported speech remains unchanged. e.g

(i) Riya says, "I stay in a girls' hostel here." *(Direct)*
Riya says that she stays in a girls' hostel here.*(ItalicIndirect)*

(ii) Swara says to Ragini, "I need your help." *(Direct)*
Swara tells Ragini that she needs her help. *(Indirect)*

Tensewise Conversion of Direct into Indirect Speech

Present Tense

Present Simple Changes to Simple Past

	Direct Speech	Indirect Speech
(i)	She said, "I get the first prize."	She said that she got the first prize. ('I' changes to 'she' according to subject)
(ii)	Mohit said to Neetu, "You look very nice in this dress."	Mohit told Neetu that she looked very nice in that dress.
(iii)	Ashi said, "Govind sings bollywood songs."	Ashi said that Govind sang bollywood songs.

Exception If the reported speech is a universal truth or a general fact, then its 'tense' does not change.

	Direct Speech	Indirect Speech
(i)	My father said, "The Earth is round."	My father said that the Earth is round.
(ii)	Our teacher said to us, "Respecting elders is a virtue."	Our teacher told us that respecting elders is a virtue.

Present Continuous Changes to Past Continuous

	Direct Speech	Indirect Speech
(i)	I said to her, "You are doing a good job."	I told her that she was doing a good job.
(ii)	Bhakti said, "I am looking for a good novel to read now."	Bhakti said that she was looking for a good novel to read then.
(iii)	Shamal said, "You are not paying attention to me."	Shamal said that he was not paying attention to her.
(iv)	They said to Gauri, "We are waiting for someone."	They said to Gauri that they were waiting for someone.

Present Perfect Changes to Past Perfect

	Direct Speech	Indirect Speech
(i)	I said, "I have watched this movie earlier."	I said that I had watched that movie earlier.
(ii)	Raman said to Ishita, "You have done it wonderfully."	Raman told Ishita that she had done it wonderfully.
(iii)	Prachi said, "The story has opened my eyes."	Prachi said that the story had opened her eyes.
(iv)	His uncle said to him, "I have got a new bicycle for you **today**."	His uncle told him that he had got a new bicycle for him **that day**.

Present Perfect Continuous Changes to Past Perfect Continuous

	Direct Speech	Indirect Speech
(i)	Aunt said, "Women have been tolerating a lot for years."	Aunt said that women had been tolerating a lot for years.
(ii)	Bunty said to Shipra, "I have been working on this project for two years."	Bunty told Shipra that he had been working on that project for two years.
(iii)	Rishabh said to his mother, "I have been looking for the keys for the last ten minutes."	Rishabh told his mother that he had been looking for the keys for the last ten minutes.

Past Tense

Simple Past Changes to Past Perfect

	Direct Speech	Indirect Speech
(i)	His brother said, "I got the clue."	His brother said that he had got the clue.
(ii)	Ketan said to mother, "You made my day with such a delicious meal."	Ketan told mother that she had made his day with such a delicious meal.
(iii)	"We got here yesterday", said Manu.	Manu said that they had got there the previous day.
(iv)	The doctor said, "The patient lost the will power to live."	The doctor said that the patient had lost the will power to live.

Past Continuous Changes to Past Perfect Continuous

	Direct Speech	Indirect Speech
(i)	Aryan said, "He was calling you."	Aryan said that he had been calling him.
(ii)	Raghu said to Radhika, "You were not answering my calls."	Raghu told Radhika that she had not been answering his calls.
(iii)	Ninad said, "I was playing football in the morning."	Ninad said that he had been playing football in the morning.
(iv)	My father said to me, "India was living in peace before the British came."	My father told me that India had been living in peace before the British had come.

Past Perfect remains Past Perfect

	Direct Speech	Indirect Speech
(i)	She said, "I had finished my job before 5 pm."	She said that she had finished her job before 5 pm.
(ii)	Madhavi said to Manish, "You had borrowed a suitcase from me."	Madhavi told Manish that he had borrowed a suitcase from her.
(iii)	Jeevan said, "I had made the enquiry before their arrival last night."	Jeevan said that he had made the enquiry before their arrival the previous night.

Future Tense

Simple Future (Shall/Will) Changes to (Should/Would)

	Direct Speech	Indirect Speech
(i)	Anurag said, "I will give India a very nice movie next year."	Anurag said that he would give India a very nice movie the coming year.
(ii)	Shaina said to Survi, "You will perform the role of the princess."	Shaina told Survi that she would perform the role of the princess.
(iii)	His uncle said to us, "I will give you a treat tonight."	His uncle told us that he would give us a treat that night. ('you' changes to 'us' according to object.)
(iv)	Shoaib said to his friends, "I will need your cooperation."	Shoaib told his friends that he would need their cooperation. ('Your' changes to 'their' according to object 'friends')

Future Continuous (Shall be/Will be) Changes to (Should be/Would be)

	Direct Speech	Indirect Speech
(i)	Mann said, "You shall be following my orders."	Mann said that he/she/they should be following his orders.
(ii)	Father said, "I will be joining you all at the airport."	Father said that he would be joining us all at the airport.
(iii)	"We will be going there tomorrow", said he.	He said that they would be going there the next day.
(iv)	Pawan said, "We will be getting good crops this year."	Pawan said that they would be getting good crops that year.

Future Perfect (Shall/Will + have) Changes to (Would + have)

	Direct Speech	Indirect Speech
(i)	He said, "I will have completed my MBA by next year."	He said that he would have completed his MBA by the coming year.
(ii)	"We will have purchased a plot on the Mars by the end of 2017", said Alisha.	Alisha said that they would have purchased a plot on the Mars by the end of 2017.
(iii)	Rajan said, "He shall have ended in utter darkness."	Rajan said that he would have ended in utter darkness.
(iv)	Gurmeet said to Manpreet, "I will have taught you good spoken English by next month."	Gurmeet told Manpreet that he would have taught her good spoken English by the next month.

Rules for Changing Interrogative Sentences into Indirect Speech

Interrogative sentences are of two types

(i) Yes-No type questions or verbal questions

(ii) Wh-type questions

Yes-No Type Questions

When the reported speech is a yes-no type question, the conjunction 'if' or 'whether' is used and the interrogative sentence (or question) is converted into an assertive sentence.

The other changes (tense, pronouns, etc.) are made as usual and the question mark is removed.

Most importantly, the reporting verb is changed from 'says' and 'said' to 'asks' and 'asked', respectively.

	Direct Speech	Indirect Speech
(i)	I said to Mayur, "Do you like mangoes?"	I asked Mayur if he liked mangoes.
(ii)	Rohan said to his brother "Are you coming with me?"	Rohan asked his brother whether he was going with him.
(iii)	"Did you pay the electricity bills?", said mother to Parag.	Mother asked Parag whether he had paid the electricity bill.
(iv)	Neha said to Kartik, "Will you marry me?"	Neha asked Kartik if he would marry her.

Wh-Type Questions

- No conjunction is used as the Wh-word itself works as a conjunction to join the reporting verb with the reported speech.
- All other changes are made in the same manner as the yes-no type questions.

	Direct Speech	Indirect Speech
(i)	The man said to the boy, "Where did you come from?"	The man asked the boy where he had come from.
(ii)	Anup said to me, "Which movie do you like most?"	Anup asked me which movie I liked most.
(iii)	Harsh said to his mother, "Who was the first man to travel to the space?"	Harsh asked his mother who the first man to travel to the space had been.
(iv)	I said to her, "How long will you stay here?"	I asked her how long she would stay **here**. (Since the speaker is **'I'**, first person, the place of the speech remains the same)

Rules for Changing Imperative Sentences into Indirect Speech

- In case of imperative sentences, the preposition 'to' is used in place of conjunction after the reporting verb.
- Depending upon the type of imperative sentence (i.e. order, suggestion, advice, request, etc.), the reporting verb is changed into ordered, suggested, advised, requested, etc.
- In case of negative imperative sentences (such as don't play there), 'to' is put after 'not' that follows reporting verb.
- In case of sentences beginning with 'Let's', the reporting verb is changed to proposed or suggested.

	Direct Speech	Indirect Speech
(i)	The teacher said to the students, "Quickly settle down and open your books."	The teacher ordered the students to settle down quickly and open their books.
(ii)	Rati said to Mani, "Please, pass the salt and pepper."	Rati requested Mani to pass the salt and pepper.
(iii)	Pari said to her friend, "Take proper rest."	Pari advised her friend to take proper rest.
(iv)	I said to my sister, "Let's go for a movie tonight."	I suggested my sister that we should go for a movie that night.

Rules for Changing Exclamatory Sentences into Indirect Speech

- We replace the reporting verb with 'exclaimed with joy,' 'exclaimed with sorrow', 'exclaimed with surprise' etc according to the sense of the reported speech.
- The conjunction 'that' is used.

Direct Speech	Indirect Speech
(i) Ritu said, "Wow! That's beautiful".	Ritu exclaimed with joy that it was beautiful.
(ii) He said, "Alas! His heartbeats have stopped."	He exclaimed with sorrow that his heartbeats had stopped.
(iii) She said, "Oops! The power is cut."	She exclaimed that the power was cut.
(iv) Abhay said, "Hurrah! We win."	Abhay exclaimed with extreme happiness that they won.

EXAM PRACTICE

Multiple Choice Questions (MCQs)

1. Rewrite the following sentences according to the instructions given after each sentence. Make other changes that may be necessary, but do not change the meaning of the given sentence. Choose the correct option.

(i) He said to me, "I don't believe you."
(Begin: He said ....) *2023*

(a) He said he doesn't want to believe in me.
(b) He said that he didn't believe me.
(c) He said that he didn't believe in me.
(d) He said I don't believe you.

(ii) Anubhav said to me, "Please lend me your bike for a day."
(Begin : Anubhav requested)

(a) Anubhav requested me to lend me my bike for a day.
(b) Anubhav requested me to lend him his bike for a day.
(c) Anubhav requested me to lend him my bike for a day.
(d) All of the above

(iii) He said, "I shall leave these papers here."
(Begin : He said)

(a) He said that he will leave those papers there.
(b) He said that he shall leave those papers here.
(c) He said that he would leave those papers there.
(d) He said that he would leave those papers here.

(iv) The teacher said, "Gandhiji died in 1948."
(Begin : The teacher)

(a) The teacher said that Gandhiji died in 1948.
(b) The teacher said that Gandhiji had died in 1948.
(c) The teacher told that Gandhiji had died in 1948.
(d) The teacher told that Gandhiji died in 1948.

(v) The mother said to her son, "Change your shoes."
(Begin : The mother)

(a) The mother asked her son to change his shoes.
(b) The mother ordered her son to go and change his shoes.
(c) The mother told her son to change his shoes.
(d) The mother ordered her son to change his shoes.

2. Rewrite the following sentences according to the instructions given after each sentence. Make other changes that may be necessary, but do not change the meaning of the given sentence. Choose the correct option.

(i) The father asked me if I was happy.
(Begin : The father)

(a) The father said, "Are you happy?"
(b) The father told me, "Were you happy?"
(c) The father said to me, "Are you happy?"
(d) The father said to me, "Were you happy?"

(ii) Pravesh asked Seeta whether her brother was playing cricket.
(Use : said to)
(a) Pravesh said to Seeta, "Was your brother playing cricket?"
(b) Pravesh said to Seeta, "Is your brother playing cricket?"
(c) Pravesh said to Seeta, "If your brother is playing cricket?"
(d) Pravesh said to Seeta, "Whether your brother is playing cricket?"

(iii) Kavita asked Minakshi if she watched television.
(Begin : Kavita said)
(a) Kavita said, "Did you watch television?"
(b) Kavita said to Minakshi, "Do you watch television?"
(c) Kavita told Minakshi, "Do you watch television?"
(d) Kavita said to Minakshi, "Did you watch television?"

(iv) The teacher asked Shubham whether he would join extra class the next day.
(Begin : The teacher)
(a) The teacher said to Shubham, "Will you join extra class tomorrow?"
(b) The teacher asked to Shubham, "Would you join extra class tomorrow?"
(c) The teacher told Shubham, "Will you join extra class tomorrow?"
(d) The teacher said to Shubham, "Would you join extra class tomorrow?"

(v) Pushpa asked her teacher respectfully if she might take her book.
(Begin : Pushpa said)
(a) Pushpa said, "Sir, may I take my book?"
(b) Pushpa told her teacher, "Sir, might I take my book?"
(c) Pushpa said to her teacher, "Sir, might I take my book?"
(d) Pushpa said to her teacher, "Sir, may I take my book?"

3. Rewrite the following sentences according to the instructions given after each sentence. Make other changes that may be necessary, but do not change the meaning of the given sentence. Choose the correct option.

(i) Sushma said to Asmita, "Where are you going?"
(Use : asked)
(a) Sushma asked Asmita where she is going.
(b) Sushma asked Asmita where was she going.
(c) Sushma asked Asmita where she was going.
(d) Sushma asked Asmita where had she been going.

(ii) Manmeet said to me, "Why did I fail in my exams?"
(Begin : Manmeet asked)
(a) Manmeet asked me why he failed in his exams.
(b) Manmeet asked me why he had failed in his exams.
(c) Manmeet asked me why had he failed in his exams.
(d) Manmeet asked me why did he fail in his exams.

(iii) They said to us, "Who has broken the wall of the school?"
(Begin : They)
(a) They told us who had broken the wall of the school.
(b) They said to us who has broken the wall of the school.
(c) They enquired from us who had broken the wall of the school.
(d) They enquired from us who has broken the wall of the school.

(iv) Mohit said to his brother, "When will you give me a new shirt?"
(End with : ....a new shirt)
(a) Mohit said to his brother when will he give him a new shirt.
(b) Mohit asked his brother when will he give him a new shirt.
(c) Mohit asked his brother when he would give him a new shirt.
(d) Mohit said to his brother when he would give him a new shirt.

(v) The father said to Apoorva, "Change the dress."
(Begin : The father)
(a) The father ordered Apoorva to change the dress.
(b) The father requested Apoorva to change the dress.
(c) The father urged Apoorva to change the dress.
(d) The father asked Apoorva to change the dress.

4. Rewrite the following sentences according to the instructions given after each sentence. Make other changes that may be necessary, but do not change the meaning of the given sentence. Choose the correct option.

(i) The officer said, "Move fast."
(Begin : The officer)
(a) The officer requested them to move fast.
(b) The officer commanded them to move fast.
(c) The officer asked them to move fast.
(d) The officer asked them to move fast.

(ii) Mahima said to Anubhav, "Please give me a new book."
(Begin : Mahima requested)
(a) Mahima requested Anubhav to give me a new book.
(b) Mahima requested Anubhav to please give her a new book.
(c) Mahima requested Anubhav to please give me a new book.
(d) Mahima requested Anubhav to give her a new book.

(iii) Shardha said, "Keep quiet and listen to my words."
(Begin : Shardha urged)
(a) Shardha urged her to keep quiet and listen to her words.
(b) Shardha urged them to keep quiet and listen to their words.
(c) Shardha urged them to keep quiet and listen to her words.
(d) Shardha urged her to keep quiet and listen to their words.

(iv) I said to my friend, "Take care of your health."
(Use : ………… to take care)
(a) I requested my friend to take care of my health.
(b) I ordered my friend to take care of his health.
(c) I advised my friend to take care of my health.
(d) I advised my friend to take care of his health.

(v) The teacher said to the student, "Do not make a noise."
(Begin : The teacher)
(a) The teacher enquired the student to not make a noise.
(b) The teacher requested the student to not make a noise.
(c) The teacher pleaded the student not to make a noise.
(d) The teacher ordered the student not to make a noise.

Subjective Type Questions

1. Rewrite the following sentences according to the instructions given after each sentence. Make other changes that may be necessary, but do not change the meaning of the given sentence.

(i) He said, "Let us move to the party."
(Begin : He proposed)

(ii) The police said, "Let no one leave this room."
(Begin : The police ordered)

(iii) He said to us, "Let us have some tea."
(Use : we)

(iv) The union leader said, "Let's show the management that we are always together."
(Begin : The union leader urged)

(v) Sarita said to me, "Let you not miss the chance to study." (Remove : Let)

2. Rewrite the following sentences according to the instructions given after each sentence. Make other changes that may be necessary, but do not change the meaning of the given sentence.

(i) Neena exclaimed that the doll was pretty.
(End with : ……….is)

(ii) The doctor wished that Mohan might live long.
(Use : May)

(iii) Kavita exclaimed with sorrow that she was ruined. (Begin : Kavita said)

(iv) Arpit applauded me saying that I had won the match. (Begin : Arpit said)

(v) The captain exclaimed with joy that they had won the match. (Use : Hurrah)

3. Rewrite the following sentences according to the instructions given after each sentence. Make other changes that may be necessary, but do not change the meaning of the given sentence.

(i) He said, "I write a letter."
(Begin : He said that)

(ii) She said, "He goes to school daily."
(Begin : She said)

(iii) They said, "We love our country."
(Begin : They said)

(iv) He said, "He does not like computers."
(Use : that)

(v) She said, "He has finished his job."
(Begin : She said)

4. Rewrite the following sentences according to the instructions given after each sentence. Make other changes that may be necessary, but do not change the meaning of the given sentence.

(i) He said that he had started a job.
(Begin : He said)

(ii) I said that she had eaten the meal.
(Begin : I said)

(iii) They said that they had not gone to New York.
(Begin : They said)

(iv) He said that he had been studying since 3 o'clock.
(Begin : He said)

(v) She said that it had been raining for three days.
(Begin : She said)

5. Rewrite the following sentences according to the instructions given after each sentence. Make other changes that may be necessary, but do not change the meaning of the given sentence.

(i) I said, "She has been working in this office since 2007."
(Use : that office)

(ii) He said to me, "You answered correctly."
(Use : told)

(iii) John said, "They went to the cinema."
(Use : gone)

(iv) He said, "I made a table."
(Begin : He said)

(v) She said, "I didn't buy a car."
(Begin : She said)

6. Rewrite the following sentences according to the instructions given after each sentence. Make other changes that may be necessary, but do not change the meaning of the given sentence.

(i) They said, "We were enjoying the weather."
(Use : had)

(ii) He said to me, "I was waiting for you."
(Use : me)

(iii) I said, "It was raining."
(Begin : I said that)

(iv) She said, "I was not laughing."
(Begin : She said that)

(v) The old women said to Arun, "Can you help me to cross the street?"
(Begin : The old woman asked Arun ......) ***(2019)***

Answer

Multiple Choice Questions

1. (i) (b) He said that he didn't believe me.
(ii) (c) Anubhav requested me to lend him my bike for a day.
(iii) (c) He said that he would leave those papers there.
(iv) (a) The teacher said that Gandhiji died in 1948.
(v) (d) The mother ordered her son to change his shoes.

2. (i) (c) The father said to me, "Are you happy?"
(ii) (b) Pravesh said to Seeta, "Is your brother playing cricket?"
(iii) (b) Kavita said to Minakshi, "Do you watch television?"
(iv) (a) The teacher said to Shubham, "Will you join extra class tomorrow?"
(v) (d) Pushpa said to her teacher, "Sir, may I take my book?"

3. (i) (c) Sushma asked Asmita where she was going.
(ii) (b) Manmeet asked me why he had failed in his exams.
(iii) (c) They enquired from us who had broken the wall of the school.
(iv) (c) Mohit asked his brother when he would give him a new shirt.
(v) (a) The father ordered Apoorva to change the dress.

4. (i) (b) The officer commanded them to move fast.
(ii) (d) Mahima requested Anubhav to give her a new book.
(iii) (c) Shardha urged them to keep quiet and listen to her words.
(iv) (d) I advised my friend to take care of his health.
(v) (d) The teacher ordered the student not to make a noise.

Subjective Type Questions

1. (i) He proposed that they should move to the party.
   (ii) The police ordered that no one should leave that room.
   (iii) He suggested us that we should have some tea.
   (iv) The union leader urged the employees to show the management that they were always together.
   (v) Sarita urged me not to miss the chance to study.

2. (i) Neena said, "How pretty the doll is!"
   (ii) The doctor said to Mohan, "May you live long!"
   (iii) Kavita said, "Alas! I am ruined."
   (iv) Arpit said to me, "Bravo! You have won the match."
   (v) The captain said, "Hurrah! We have won the match."

3. (i) He said that he wrote a letter.
   (ii) She said that he went to school daily.
   (iii) They said that they loved their country.
   (iv) He said that he did not like computers.
   (v) She said that he had finished his job.

4. (i) He said, "I have started a job."
   (ii) I said, "She has eaten the meal."
   (iii) They said, "We have not gone to New York."
   (iv) He said, "I have been studying since 3 o'clock."
   (v) She said, "It has been raining for three days."

5. (i) I said that she had been working in that office since 2007.
   (ii) He told me that I had answered correctly.
   (iii) John said that they had gone to the cinema.
   (iv) He said that he had made a table.
   (v) She said that she had not bought a car.

6. (i) They said that they had been enjoying the weather.
   (ii) He told me that he had been waiting for me.
   (iii) I said that it had been raining.
   (iv) She said that she had not been laughing.
   (v) The old woman asked Arun whether he could help her to cross the street.

CHAPTER

4

Preposition

A preposition is a word which shows the relationship of the nouns (or the pronouns) with another words in the sentence. The word 'preposition' comes from the idea of being positioned before. There are approximately 80 to 100 prepositions in English language. They introduce information to the reader. This information can include where something states place (such as 'at' the store), when or why something takes place (such as 'before' dinner), or general descriptive information (such as the girl 'with' the cool tattoo).

Role of a Preposition

Prepositions are important when constructing sentences. Prepositions are usually short words, and they are normally placed directly in front of nouns. e.g.

1. It is a container for butter.
   (*The preposition 'for' shows the relationship between butter and container*).
2. The eagle soared above the clouds.
   (*The preposition 'above' shows the relationship between clouds and soared*).

Types of Prepositions

There are four types of prepositions. These are as follows

(i) Simple Prepositions They include 'at', 'by', 'for', 'in', 'of', 'off', 'on', 'out', 'through', 'till', 'to', 'up', 'with', etc.

(ii) Compound Prepositions These are usually formed by prefixing a preposition ('a' or 'be') to a noun, an adjective or an adverb.
These include

about	beside	inside
along	below	outside
amidst	beneath	within
among	between	without
aloud	beyond	underneath

(iii) Phrasal/Group Prepositions These are formed by joining two or more words. These include 'according to', 'in front of ', 'by means of', 'on account of', 'in place of ', etc.

(iv) Participle Prepositions When Present participles are used without any noun or pronoun attached to them, these are called Participle prepositions. These include 'concerning', 'passing', 'considering', 'during', 'notwithstanding', 'pending', 'regarding', etc.

Classification of Prepositions

To make a distinction, prepositions can also be divided into three classes

(i) Prepositions of Time and Date These include 'at', 'on', 'in', 'by', 'to', 'till', 'until', 'during', 'for', 'since', 'from', 'within', 'before', 'after', 'afterwards', 'then', etc.

(ii) Prepositions of Place These include 'at', 'in', 'on', 'to', 'behind', 'instead of', 'in', 'into', 'at', 'out' 'out of ', 'off', etc.

(iii) Prepositions of Travel and Movement These include 'from', 'to', 'by', 'on', 'in', 'into', 'at', 'out', 'out of', 'off', etc.

How the Prepositions Should be Placed

Prepositions normally precede nouns or pronouns. However, in certain cases, it is possible to move the preposition to the end of the sentence.

(i) When object of the preposition is an interrogative pronoun like what, who, whom, which, where, etc., the preposition can take the end or the front position.

e.g. (a) What are you thinking **of**?

(b) **To** whom were you talking?

(ii) When object of the preposition is the relative pronoun 'that', the preposition takes end position.

e.g. This is the dish that she is fond **of**.

(iii) When object of the preposition is infinitive (to + verb), the preposition is placed after infinitive.

e.g. It is a beautiful house to live **in**.

(iv) In some sentences, where the relative pronoun is hidden, the preposition takes end position.

e.g. This is the girl (that) I told you **about**.

(v) In some miscellaneous sentences, the preposition is attached with the verb.

e.g. I hate being laughed **at**.

The Use of Prepositions

Prepositions are used with reference to time and to space. With reference to time, they may denote 'a point of time' or 'a period of time'. A point of time will tell you a particular time as 8 o'clock, 8 pm, etc., whereas a period of time as 8 years, 8 months, etc.

With Reference to Time

1. At, In, On

(i) **At** Used for a point of time.

e.g. (a) Meet me at 1 pm.

(b) At noon, at the age of ninety.

(ii) **In** Used for a period of time in which something happens.

e.g. (a) I met him in the morning.

(b) His birthday falls in the month of January.

(iii) **On** Used with particular dates and days.

e.g. (a) Her dog died on Friday.

(b) I will go to Mumbai on 22nd of this month.

2. In, Within, Before , After

(i) **In** Also denotes the end of a period of time.

e.g. (a) Justin will return in a week.

(b) Shalini will leave in a minute.

(ii) **Within** Denotes anytime before the expiry of a period.

e.g. They have ordered him to come back within a week.

(iii) **Before** Used when we refer to a point of time.

e.g. I will come back before 8:00 am.

(iv) **After** Denotes the end of a period of time.

e.g. (a) I will go there after a month.

(b) She gave the book back after I reminded him.

3. By, Till

(i) **By** Denotes not later than.

e.g. (a) We will have vacated this space by 6 o'clock.

(b) She will have done it by this evening.

(ii) **Till** Means up to certain period.

e.g. (a) I will be staying in London till 15th of December.

(b) Wait here till I come back.

4. Since, For, From

(i) **Since** Used for a point of time.

e.g. (a) He has not been in touch since last Monday.

(b) He has been absenting himself since last week.

(ii) **For** Used to define a period of time.

e.g. (a) Nirmala has been ill for two weeks.

(b) I have been struggling in the industry for 3 years.

(iii) **From** Used for a point of time but can be preceded by a verb in any tense.

e.g. (a) I will be busy from tomorrow onwards.

(b) The guest lecture is from 8 to 10 am.

With Reference to Space

1. At, In

(i) **At** Used with the names of places.

e.g. (a) He was waiting at the metro station.

(b) Her friend lives at Nehru Nagar.

(ii) In Used with the names of big cities, states and country.

e.g. (a) He lives at Kalyan in Mumbai.

(b) The Prime Minister lives in Delhi.

2. In, Into

(i) **In** Denotes rest or position inside something.

e.g. (a) They are waiting in the room.

(b) The guests gathered in the auditorium.

(ii) **Into** Denotes motion towards the inside of something.

e.g. (a) He came into the room.

(b) The fisherman jumped into the river.

3. On, Upon

(i) **On** Used to point to something at rest.

e.g. (a) She was made to sit on the floor.

(b) The girl sat on the carpet.

(ii) **Upon** Generally denotes motion.

e.g. (a) The cat jumped upon the table.

(b) The tiger sprang upon the deer.

4. Behind Refers to the position or place signalling at the back of something.

e.g. (a) He hid behind the wall.

(b) Who stood behind Abhinav?

5. Between, Among

(i) **Between** Used for two persons or things.

e.g. (a) Share this biscuit between the two girls.

(b) Shankar and Ravi fought between them selves.

(ii) **Among** Used with more than two persons or things.

e.g. (a) They shared the fruits among themselves.

(b) There is said to be honour even among thieves.

6. Beside, Besides

(i) **Beside** Means 'by the side of' or 'next to'.

e.g. (a) She sat beside him.

(b) His speaking ill about her is beside the point.

(ii) **Besides** Means 'in addition to'.

(a) Besides Mira, all of you are invited.

(b) Besides being rich, she is famous too.

7. Above, Below, Across

(i) **Above** Means 'in a higher position'.

e.g. (a) The bag was kept above the almirah

(b) I was surprised to see my name above his.

(ii) **Below** Means 'a lower level than the other'.

e.g. (a) He is much below me in rank.

(b) I live in the flat below his.

(iii) **Across** Means 'from one side to the opposite'.

e.g. (a) He waited across the road.

(b) I live across the river.

8. Towards Denotes 'in the direction of'.

e.g. (a) They moved towards the setting sun.

(b) She ran towards the police station for help.

9. Through Indicates a piercing action and also the medium or passage.

e.g. (a) The sword ran through him.

(b) I was able to pull through the deal.

10. Around Refers to a surrounding position.

e.g. (a) She looked around the place.

(b) The path around the statue was concrete.

11. Over, Under

(i) **Over** Indicates the position exactly above something or somebody.

e.g. (a) I leaned over my son to explain the sentence.

(b) A new bridge is being constructed over this river.

(ii) **Under** Indicates a position exactly below somebody or something.

e.g. (a) I put my suitcase under the table.

(b) There is something under your chair.

12. Against Indicates opposition of some kind.

e.g. (a) She went against him for Rachna.

(b) He married against his parents' wish.

13. Along Through any part of the length of or from one end to the other end.

e.g. (a) I took a walk along the broken path.

(b) They looked for the gold ring along the edges of the river.

EXAM PRACTICE

Multiple Choice Questions (MCQs)

1. Fill in the blanks with correct prepositions.

(i) Peter is playing tennis ……… Sunday.
(a) on (b) to (c) of (d) for

(ii) My brother's birthday is ……… the 5th of September.
(a) to (b) up (c) on (d) in

(iii) My friend has been living in Canada ……… two years.
(a) of (b) for
(c) from (d) All of these

(iv) The son and the daughter are sitting ……… each other.
(a) behind (b) beside
(c) above (d) besides

(v) The woman is looking ……… her daughter.
(a) up (b) of
(c) above (d) at

(vi) What are you doing ……… Saturday?
(a) up (b) in (c) on (d) an

(vii) I haven't been to the countryside ……… December.
(a) at (b) to (c) since (d) for

(viii) I am leaving ……… the afternoon.
(a) at (b) in (c) to (d) for

2. Fill in the blanks using suitable prepositions.

(i) The people are busy ……… some important work.
(a) with (b) for (c) from (d) by

(ii) The girl was eager ……… show her painting.
(a) for (b) by (c) with (d) to

(iii) He dreamt ……… being a king.
(a) for (b) from (c) at (d) of

(iv) I write letters ……… my parents regularly.
(a) at (b) in (c) to (d) up

(v) Look after the children ……… a while.
(a) of (b) at (c) for (d) by

(vi) He takes a lot ……… interest in music.
(a) for (b) of (c) by (d) from

(vii) Put this ……… place of that.
(a) at (b) in (c) on (d) from

(viii) I learnt about it ……… my friend.
(a) from (b) at (c) with (d) by

3. Fill in the blanks using suitable prepositions.

(i) Rita heard ……… her success.
(a) about (b) between
(c) in (d) aside

(ii) She came ……… time.
(a) by (b) on (c) at (d) up

(iii) He had no money ……… give you.
(a) for (b) of (c) from (d) to

(iv) Walk carefully ……… avoid falling.
(a) for (b) of (c) from (d) to

(v) The author ……… 'Saket' was very religious minded.
(a) for (b) from (c) of (d) to

(vi) I go ……… bed at night.
(a) for (b) of (c) to (d) from

(vii) The thief climbed ……… the roof.
(a) upon (b) up
(c) above (d) over

(viii) He is dedicated ……… his work.
(a) for (b) of
(c) from (d) to

4. Fill in the blanks using suitable prepositions.

(i) Does this book belong ……… you?
(a) by (b) for (c) to (d) at

(ii) I saw him felling a big tree ……… an axe.
(a) by (b) on (c) with (d) from

(iii) These people are always quarrelling ……… themselves.
(a) among (b) aside (c) between (d) besides

(iv) Himani borrowed a pen ……… use.
(a) at (b) to (c) for (d) from

(v) I met him ……… Alipur.
(a) on (b) at
(c) upon (d) up

(vi) I have been waiting here ……… 6 o'clock.
(a) for (b) by
(c) with (d) since

(vii) ……… the last ten years, he had done all the good.
(a) in (b) at
(c) on (d) up

(viii) The situation has grown ……… a big menace.
(a) into (b) inside
(c) in (d) All of these

5. Fill in the blanks using suitable prepositions.

(i) Nobody cares .... a weak, old man.
(a) of (b) for
(c) from (d) None of these

(ii) Shobha burst .... tears.
(a) in (b) inside
(c) into (d) None of these

(iii) Mohan was charged .... the murder of Rajan.
(a) by (b) from
(c) with (d) Both (a) and (c)

(iv) The boys are confident .... a huge victory.
(a) for (b) by (c) from (d) of

(v) I saw the monkey charge .... the house.
(a) in (b) beside
(c) on (d) into

(vi) Let us divide the money .... ourselves.
(a) among (b) aside
(c) between (d) besides

(vii) I am worried .... her.
(a) about (b) since (c) from (d) of

(viii) She is busy .... her work.
(a) by (b) for
(c) with (d) from

6. Fill in the blanks using suitable prepositions.

(i) She is pursuing a degree course .... a university.
(a) at (b) from (c) for (d) of

(ii) His trousers were washed .... the washing machine.
(a) on (b) in (c) at (d) by

(iii) We had to climb slowly .... the hill.
(a) upon (b) by
(c) on (d) up

(iv) His house looks .... a temple.
(a) alike (b) since
(c) like (d) also

(v) How many .... your group will join the trip?
(a) for (b) of
(c) from (d) All of these

(vi) Don't lean the ladder .... the wall.
(a) for (b) since
(c) against (d) None of these

(vii) He stood .... me firmly.
(a) among (b) before (c) aside (d) by

(viii) She yelled .... me.
(a) on (b) at
(c) up (d) in

7. Fill in the blanks using suitable prepositions.

(i) Don't clap .... I finish talking.
(a) until (b) after (c) before (d) since

(ii) Children always quarrel .... toys.
(a) over (b) below
(c) above (d) among

(iii) She has applied .... a job.
(a) of (b) from (c) by (d) for

(iv) She came .... a week.
(a) of (b) for (c) from (d) by

(v) I was invited .... dinner.
(a) since (b) with
(c) for (d) by

(vi) I am satisfied .... your work.
(a) by (b) for (c) with (d) from

(vii) He resorted .... thievery.
(a) at (b) in (c) on (d) to

(viii) Sarla has been called .... an interview.
(a) by (b) for (c) at (d) of

8. Fill in the blanks with appropriate words. ***[2014 Modified]***

(i) The teacher spoke .... for Raju when he was wrongly accused of stealing money.
(a) up (b) in
(c) down (d) upon

(ii) We can visit her in the hotel .... 3 pm and 5 pm on Saturday.
(a) between (b) amongst
(c) among (d) None of these

(iii) The Suhas have lived in New Delhi .... 1943.
(a) by (b) with (c) for (d) since

(iv) Little children are often afraid .... the dark.
(a) for (b) from
(c) of (d) All of these

(v) Sneha has applied .... a scholarship.
(a) of (b) from
(c) for (d) None of these

(vi) It took Ahmed many months to get .... the loss of his friends.
(a) among (b) over
(c) above (d) beside

(vii) She turned ...... the generous offer made by the manager.
(a) with (b) for (c) by (d) down

(viii) We were asked to take .... our footwear as we were entering a place of worship.
(a) for (b) of (c) from (d) off

Subjective Type Questions

1. Fill in the blanks with appropriate words. *(2023)*
   (i) A bird .... hand is worth two in the bush.
   (ii) The boy is crazy .... football.
   (iii) She was tired .... fighting and struggling all the time.
   (iv) He opted .... of the race.
   (v) We borrowed the bikes .... our uncle.
   (vi) The police station is .... the right.
   (vii) I looked at the stars .... the telescope.
   (viii) There was an accident .... the crossroads.

2. Fill in each blank with an appropriate word. *[2020]*
   (i) It has been raining .... two hours.
   (ii) He just scrapped .... his examination.
   (iii) Mrs Kapoor was bent ...... attending the meeting.
   (iv) She is proud and looks .... on her colleagues.
   (v) Rahul plays football .... his grandfather.
   (vi) The mother was sitting ..... the sick child all night.
   (vii) Monica is leaning the .... wall.
   (viii) Rosie is very good .... art and craft.

3. Fill in the blanks with appropriate words. *[2019]*
   (i) The puppy was hiding .... the sofa.
   (ii) Stop worrying .... your future.
   (iii) When I stepped .... the lift, I found it had stopped working.
   (iv) We had to use a bridge to go .... to river.
   (v) I have lived in this town .... ten years.
   (vi) Please switch .... all lights and fans when you leaves the room.
   (vii) Ronnie is married .... my cousin.
   (viii) The gift came .... a birthday card.

4. Fill in the blanks with appropriate words. *[2018]*
   (i) The poet's mother was stung .... a scorpion.
   (ii) "Please write......... what I tell you otherwise you will forget", the teacher said..
   (iii) The dog was hiding .... the bed, barking at the stranger.
   (iv) Sheila's grandmother found it difficult to climb .... the steep staircase.
   (v) The soldier fought bravely .... his country.
   (vi) There is no use crying .... split milk.
   (vii) I don't know what they were arguing .... but I could hear angry voices.
   (viii) The school playground is out .... bounds for the pupils of the primary school.

5. Fill in each blank with an appropriate word. *[2017]*
   (i) She shouted angrily .... the disobedient boy.
   (ii) I asked them to provide us......... a guide.
   (iii) The tree grew at a dangerous slant and had to be cut ....
   (iv) My daughter believes .... fairies.
   (v) He drew a beautiful diagram .... the board.
   (vi) She battled her way .... the crowd.
   (vii) We were asked to gather .... the teacher.
   (viii) They had to climb .... the steep pathway to reach the top.

6. Fill in the blanks with appropriate words. *[2016]*
   (i) There was a steep rise .... onion prices.
   (ii) Air pollution is responsible for the spread .... bronchitis.
   (iii) He was .... pressure to complete the work.
   (iv) John jumped .... the river to rescue the child.
   (v) His teacher is very pleased .... him.
   (vi) Ali took .... his cap and wiped his face.
   (vii) The old woman could not get away ..... the shock.
   (viii) He should not get away .... such rudeness.

7. Fill in the blanks with appropriate words. *[2013]*
   (i) She takes a lot of trouble .... her work.
   (ii) Our English friends have taken .... Indian food quite quickly.
   (iii) He secured grade 'A' .... the Mathematics test.
   (iv) He jumped .... the river to save his friend from drowning.
   (v) Always be prepared .... a surprise test.
   (vi) She hid ...... the cupboard and gave everyone a fright.
   (vii) She is fond .... pets.
   (viii) The brothers quarelled .... themselves for their father's property.

8. Fill in the blanks with appropriate words. *[2012]*
   (i) He was touched ...... pity when he heard the tale.
   (ii) There is always a demand .... good tailors.
   (iii) The mother prevented her child .... going out in the farm.
   (iv) The baby crawled .... the table and hid there.
   (v) Once upon a time, the great king ruled .... all these villages and towns.
   (vi) She is the smarter .... the two.
   (vii) Shila insists .... wearing that dress, although her mother thinks it is too short for her.

(viii) The teacher complained .... him when she met his father in the market.

9. Fill in the blanks with appropriate words. *[2011]*

(i) He congratulated me .... my great achievement.
(ii) The poor man is afflicted .... arthoritis.
(iii) She is blind .... the faults of her husband.
(iv) The boss had many complaints .... Shyam.
(v) You must prepare .... the examinations.
(vi) She is not aware .... the danger.
(vii) Ravi was accurate .... his calculations.
(viii) They hid the money .... the carpet.

10. Fill in the blanks with appropriate words. *[2010]*

(i) I refrained .... telling Reeta the truth.
(ii) The leader counted .... the cooperation of his colleagues.
(iii) The public was cautioned .... pickpockets.
(iv) Janaki escorted her daughter to the cinema theatre as she was anxious .... her safety.
(v) The path was beset .... difficulties yet they succeeded.
(vi) The mouse crept stealthily .... the cheese.
(vii) It was good .... you to invite Sheila for the picnic.
(viii) Smoking .... public places is banned now.

11. Fill in the blanks with appropriate words. *[2009]*

(i) I prevailed .... him to join the gymnasium.
(ii) The curious child eagerly begged .... an answer to the riddle.
(iii) He was bent .... coming first in the examination.
(iv) The theory exam was followed .... a group discussion.
(v) I ran .... my teacher at the show last night.
(vi) She is extremely anxious .... the interview next week.
(vii) What a contrast .... the two siblings!
(viii) The brothers fought .... their father's property.

12. Fill in the blanks with appropriate words. *[2008]*

(i) The elderly man prepared himself for a life .... retirement.
(ii) Do you take his word .... mine?
(iii) Rohini is very concerned .... her father's health.
(iv) Altaf had many books and papers scattered all .... the room.
(v) The phoenix is a legendry bird that rises ...... its ashes.
(vi) The police pulled the briefcase from ...... the table.
(vii) The mob rushed onto the pavement, everyone seemed angry .... everyone else.
(viii) The old woman looked .... the cupboard, searching for the photograph.

13. Fill in the blanks with appropriate words.

(i) Truth always prevails .... the long-run.
(ii) Sujata stood ..... the river and saw the ship pass by.
(iii) She took some money .... her father to buy a video game.
(iv) Shilpa gave me a rare gift .... my birthday.
(v) Deepak was very upset .... me.
(vi) Michelle is longing .... meet me.
(vii) It has been a long time .... I met my sister.
(viii) The worker asked .... his wages.

14. Fill in the blanks with appropriate words.

(i) He refused to put .... with their interference in his affairs.
(ii) She has been going .... the script for days.
(iii) It is our duty to protest .... injustice.
(iv) He soon became accustomed .... the harsh weather.
(v) Dilip went out .... his way to help the poor.
(vi) He was able to put .... his ideas so cleverly that he impressed everyone.
(vii) He persists .... teasing the other children in the class.
(viii) I have been waiting for you .... four o'clock.

15. Fill in the blanks with appropriate words.

(i) The safari parks of South Africa abound .... wild animals.
(ii) The young man excels ...... both music and dance.
(iii) She is a diligent student, worthy .... praise.
(iv) I saw .... his plan and realised that he was going to cheat us.
(v) I was .... the impression that the meeting had been cancelled.
(vi) Always be true .... yourself.
(vii) The villagers lodged a complaint .... the corrupt officials.
(viii) I can rely .... my sister for help.

Answers

Multiple Choice Questions (MCQs)

1. (i) (a) on (ii) (c) on
(iii) (b) for (iv) (b) beside
(v) (d) at (vi) (c) on
(vii) (c) since (viii) (b) in
2. (i) (a) with (ii) (d) to
(iii) (d) of (iv) (c) to
(v) (c) for (vi) (b) of
(vii) (b) in (viii) (a) from
3. (i) (a) about (ii) (b) on
(iii) (d) to (iv) (d) to
(v) (c) of (vi) (c) to
(vii) (a) upon (viii) (d) to
4. (i) (c) to (ii) (c) with
(iii) (a) among (iv) (b) to
(v) (b) at (vi) (d) since
(vii) (a) in (viii) (a) into
5. (i) (b) for (ii) (c) into
(iii) (c) with (iv) (d) of
(v) (d) into (vi) (a) among
(vii) (a) about (viii) (c) with
6. (i) (b) from (ii) (b) in
(iii) (d) up (iv) (c) like
(v) (b) of (vi) (c) against
(vii) (b) before (viii) (b) at
7. (i) (a) until (ii) (a) over
(iii) (d) for (iv) (b) for
(v) (c) for (vi) (c) with
(vii) (d) to (viii) (b) for
8. (i) (a) up (ii) (a) between
(iii) (d) since (iv) (c) of
(v) (c) for (vi) (b) over
(vii) (d) down (viii) (d) off

Subjective Questions

1. (i) in (ii) about
(iii) of (iv) out
(v) from (vi) on
(vii) through (viii) at
2. (i) for (ii) up
(iii) upon (iv) down
(v) with (vi) beside
(vii) against (viii) at
3. (i) beneath (ii) about
(iii) into (iv) across
(v) for (vi) off
(vii) to (viii) with
4. (i) by (ii) down
(iii) under (iv) up
(v) for (vi) over
(vii) about (viii) of
5. (i) at (ii) with
(iii) down (iv) in
(v) on (vi) through
(vii) near (viii) up
6. (i) in (ii) of
(iii) under (iv) into
(v) with (vi) off
(vii) with (viii) with
7. (i) for (ii) to
(iii) in (iv) into
(v) for (vi) inside
(vii) of (viii) among
8. (i) with (ii) for
(iii) from (iv) under
(v) over (vi) of
(vii) on (viii) against
9. (i) on (ii) with
(iii) to (iv) against
(v) for (vi) of
(vii) with (viii) under
10. (i) from (ii) on
(iii) against (iv) about
(v) with (vi) towards
(vii) of (viii) in
11. (i) upon (ii) for
(iii) on/upon (iv) by
(v) into (vi) about
(vii) between (viii) over/for
12. (i) after (ii) over
(iii) about (iv) over
(v) from (vi) under
(vii) with (viii) inside/into
13. (i) in (ii) beside
(iii) from (iv) for
(v) with (vi) to
(vii) since (viii) for
14. (i) up (ii) through
(iii) against (iv) to
(v) of (vi) up
(vii) on (viii) since
15. (i) with (ii) in
(iii) of (iv) through
(v) under (vi) to
(vii) against (viii) on

CHAPTER 5

Conjunctions

Conjunctions

Conjunctions are the connectors that help in joining two words, phrases or clauses together.

Conjunctions can be divided into four categories. They are

Coordinating Conjunctions

Coordinating conjunctions join two words, clauses or sentences of equal ranks. There are seven coordinating conjunctions, which are and, but, for, or, yet, so and nor.

e.g. (a) She must weep or she must die. (b) He is very rich, yet he is not contented.
(c) Take this and give that. (d) I like you but not her.

Subordinating Conjunctions

A subordinating conjunction joins a subordinate clause to a principal clause.

The common subordinating conjunctions are though, although, since, after, as, because, before, lest, than, till, until, if, while, when, whether, etc.

Subordinating conjunctions show the following

(a) **Time**

e.g. The patient had died before the doctor came.
I will complete my work before it is five.
You have grown weak since I last saw you.

(b) **Cause or Reason**

e.g. I will give it to you since you demand it.
He failed because he did not work hard.
As he was not there, I spoke to his father.

(c) **Effect**

e.g. He is so poor that he cannot pay his fee.
He is so weak that he cannot walk.

(d) **Place**

e.g. I want to live where you live.
Stay where you are.

(e) **Purpose**

e.g. I ran away lest I should be killed.
I eat so that I may live.

(f) **Condition**

e.g. I shall pass if you teach me.
You will fail unless you study.

(g) **Comparison**

e.g. I am happier than you.
She is taller than her sister.

(h) **Extent or Manner**

e.g. He is a good person as far as I know.
He talks as if he were a minister.

(i) **Concession or Contrast**

e.g. Though she was poor, she was happy.
Although they performed their best, they failed.

Correlative Conjunctions
(Conjunctions Used in Pairs)

Some conjunctions are used in pairs. They are called Correlative Conjunctions.

The following are some correlative conjunctions

(a) **Either .... or**

e.g. Either Rana or his sister will attend the wedding.

(b) **Neither .... nor**

e.g. My friend can neither sing nor dance.

(c) **Both .... and**

e.g. We offered them both food and drinks.

(d) **Not only .... but also**

e.g. He not only studies but also teaches in a school.

(e) **Whether .... or**

e.g. I do not know whether she will meet me today or not.

(f) **So .... that**

e.g. He is so weak that he cannot run.

(g) **Hardly/Scarcely .... when**

e.g. Amit was hardly 7 years old when his father died.

(h) **No sooner .... than**

e.g. No sooner did she reach the school than the bell rang.

Compound Conjunction

There are some compound conjunctions, which include conjunctions containing two or more words together.

(a) **In order that**

e.g. The notice was published in order that all might know the facts.

(b) **Even if**

e.g. Such an act would not be kind even if it were just.

(c) **As though**

e.g. He walks as though he were slightly lame.

(d) **As well as**

e.g. The principal as well as the teachers attended the Independence Day function.

(e) **As soon As**

e.g. He took out his umbrella as soon as it started raining.

Transformation of Sentences Using Different Conjunctions

If/Unless

'If' and 'Unless' are used for conditional sentences. Both of them join a subordinate clause with a principal clause. However 'Unless' means '
If not'. Hence, the affirmative sentence (principal clause) is converted into negative and *vice-versa* while changing the sentence containing 'If ...' into those containing 'Unless ... '.

But, if both subordinate and principal clause are negative, then while using 'unless' no changes are made.

Consider the following sentences

"If you keep patience, you will win."
"Unless you keep patience, you will not win."

If we reverse the order of clauses in both of the above sentences, the conjunction will be joining the two clauses thereby eliminating the need for 'comma' as,

You will win if you keep patience.

Or You will not win unless you keep patience.

e.g.

(a) **If** the weather is fine, the flight will take off.
The flight will not take off **unless** the weather is fine.

(b) **If** Mayank is not confident, he will not succeed.
Unless Mayank is confident, he will not succeed.

As soon as/Hardly/Scarcely ..... when /No sooner ..... than

'As soon as' is used for both present and future actions whereas 'Hardly/scarcely ..... when', 'No sooner ..... than' are used only for past actions.

All of them are used to denote actions that happen one after another. e.g.

(a) As soon as he heard the bang, he hid himself behind the door.
- No sooner did he hear the bang than he hid himself behind the door.
- Hardly had he heard the bang when he hid himself behind the door.

With 'No sooner......than', both Past Perfect Tense and Simple Past Tense can be used in the subordinate clause, while the main clause is in Simple Past Tense.

e.g.(b) No sooner did she hear the news than she started weeping aloud.

- Hardly had she heard the news when she started weeping aloud.
- As soon as she heard the news, she started weeping aloud.

(c) Ayesha joined the gym as soon as she put on a little weight.

- Hardly had Ayesha put on a little weight when she joined the gym.
- No sooner had Ayesha put on a little weight than she joined the gym.

Too ..... to/So ..... that

The adverb 'too' has a negative sense and means 'that much which is not desirable'.

Therefore,

"He is too weak to walk further." means "He is so weak that he cannot walk further".

Hence, when we use 'so' in place of 'too', the other clause is made negative and *vice-versa*.

e.g. (a) I am **too** tired **to** sit.
I am **so** tired **that** I can not sit.

(b) The chapter is **too** boring for her **to** read.
The chapter is **so** boring **that** she cannot read it.

(c) The mobile was **so** costly **that** he could not buy it.
The mobile was **too** costly for him **to** buy.

(d) He was **so** cruel **that** he never took pity on anybody.
He was **too** cruel **to** ever take pity on anybody.

EXAM PRACTICE

Multiple Choice Questions (MCQs)

1. Join the following sentences to make one complete sentence without using *and, but* or *so.* Choose the correct option. ***(2023)***

(i) He jumped up. He ran away.
 (a) He jumped up before he ran away.
 (b) Jumping up, he ran away.
 (c) He ran away after jumping.
 (d) He ran away because he jumped up.

(ii) He has failed many times. Still, he hopes to succeed.
 (a) He succeeds after he failed many times.
 (b) Despite of failing, he hopes to succeed.
 (c) In spite of many failures, he hopes to succeed.
 (d) He failed many times even though he hopes to succeed.

(iii) Do not be a jeweller. Do not be a goldsmith.
 (a) Be neither a jeweller nor a goldsmith.
 (b) Be both a jeweller and a goldsmith.
 (c) Either be a jeweller or a goldsmith.
 (d) Be a jeweller as well as a goldsmith.

(iv) A cottager and his wife had a hen. The hen laid an egg every day.
 (a) Everyday, a hen laid an egg for a cottager and his wife.
 (b) A cottager and his wife had a hen who laid an egg every day.
 (c) The cottager and his wife had an egg every day because they had a hen.
 (d) A cottager and his wife had a hen which laid an egg every day.

2. Join the following sentences to make one complete sentence without using *and, but* or *so.* Choose the correct option. ***[2018]***

(i) They have to go to bed early every night. They are allowed to stay up late on Saturdays.
 (a) They have to go to bed every night except on Saturdays.
 (b) On Saturday, they are allowed to stay up late or otherwise they have to go to bed every night.
 (c) They have to go to bed early every night except Saturdays, when they are allowed to stay up late.
 (d) None of the above

(ii) The children were delighted. The exams had been cancelled.
 (a) The children were delighted why the exams had been cancelled.
 (b) The exams had been cancelled because the children were delighted.
 (c) The children were delighted that the exams had been cancelled.
 (d) The exams had been cancelled as if the children were delighted

(iii) We are not allowed to play in the Sun. We are not allowed to play in the rain.
 (a) We are not allowed to play in the Sun or the rain.
 (b) We are not allowed to play in the Sun because of the rain.
 (c) And in the rain, we are not allowed to play or in the Sun.
 (d) In the rain and in the Sun, we are allowed to play.

(iv) This is the place. The dog was rescued from its cruel owner.
 (a) This is the place when the dog was rescued from its cruel owner.
 (b) This is the place where the dog was rescued from its cruel owner.
 (c) The dog was rescued from this place from its cruel owner.
 (d) All of the above

3. Rewrite the following sentences according to the instructions given after each sentence. Make other changes that may be necessary, but do not change the meaning of the given sentence. Choose the correct option.

(i) The book was so interesting that I could not put it down. ***[2016]***
(Begin : The book was too ....)
 (a) The book was too interesting that I could not put it down.
 (b) The book was too interesting, I could not put it down.
 (c) The book was too interesting to be put down.
 (d) The book was too much of interest to put down.

(ii) If Marry catches the first bus, she will be on time for school. *[2016]*
(Begin : Unless ....)
(a) Unless Marry catches the first bus, she will be on time for school.
(b) Unless Marry catches the first bus, she will not be on time for school.
(c) Both (a) and (b)
(d) None of the above

(iii) Hardly had the teacher left the room when all the children started making a noise.
(Begin : No sooner.........)
(a) No sooner had the teacher left the room than the children started making a noise.
(b) No sooner did the teacher left the room than the children started making a noise.
(c) No sooner the teacher leave the room than the children started making a noise.
(d) No sooner had the teacher leave the room than the children started making a noise.

(iv) If the boys do not reach the school on time, they will be punished.
(Begin : Unless ………)
(a) Unless the boys reach the school on time, they will not be punished.
(b) Unless the boys are punished, they will not reach the school on time.
(c) Unless the school punished the boys, they will not reach on time.
(d) Unless the boys reach the school on time, they will be punished.

(v) As soon as he reaches home, his friends call him.
(Begin : Hardly …………)
(a) Hardly does he reach home when his friends call him.
(b) Hardly had he reached home than his friends called him.
(c) Hardly, he reaches home, his friends call him.
(d) Hardly when he reaches home than his friends call him.

4. Join the following sentences to make one complete sentence without using *and*, *but* or *so*. Choose the correct option. *[2014]*

(i) He is good at gymnastics. His handwriting is beautiful.
(a) Not only is he good at gymnastics but his handwriting is also beautiful.
(b) Not only is he good at gymnastics but his handwriting is beautiful.
(c) Both (a) and (b)
(d) None of the above

(ii) Her grandfather gifted her a paint box. He knew she was good at art.
(a) He knew she was good at art because her grandfather gifted her a paint box.
(b) Her grandfather gifted her a paint box because he knew she was good at art.
(c) Though her grandfather gifted her a paint box, he knew she was good at art.
(d) Though he knew she was good at art, her grandfather gifted her a paint box.

(iii) Ravi fractured his arm. He insisted on playing the match.
(a) Even though he fractured his arm, Ravi insisted on playing the match.
(b) Ravi insisted on playing the match despite having his arm fractured.
(c) Both (a) and (b)
(d) None of the above

(iv) Mona has been ill for a month. She stood first in the examination.
(a) Mona has been ill for a month because she stood first in the examination.
(b) Mona stood first in the examination despite having been ill for a month.
(c) Mona stood first in the examination despite of having been ill for a month.
(d) Mona stood first in the examination inspite being ill for a month.

5. Join the following sentences to make one complete sentence without using *and*, *but* or *so*. Choose the correct option. *[2013]*

(i) We had better got ready now. We may not have time to reach the airport.
(a) We had better get ready now; otherwise, we might not have time to reach the airport.
(b) We had better get ready now and we might not have time to reach the airport.
(c) We might not have time to reach the airport because we had better get ready.
(d) None of the above

(ii) Mr. Liew has been sick. He has been so since he came back from Japan.
(a) Mr. Liew has been sick since he came back from Japan.
(b) Mr. Liew has been sick when he came back from Japan.
(c) Mr. Liew has been sick and he has been so since he came back from Japan.
(d) Mr. Liew has been sick because he came back from Japan.

(iii) The debating teams were very happy. Both were declared joint-champions.
 (a) Both the debating team were very happy and they were declared joint-champions.
 (b) Both the debating team were very happy; however, they were declared joint-champions.
 (c) Both the debating team were very happy after they were declared joint-champions.
 (d) Both the debating team were very happy as they were declared joint-champions.

(iv) He escaped from the prison. He looked for a place where he could hide.
 (a) While he escaped from the prison, he looked for a place where he could hide.
 (b) He escaped from the prison because he looked for a place where he could hide.
 (c) As he escaped from the prison, he looked for a place where he could hide.
 (d) Therefore, he escaped from the prison, he looked for a place where he could hide.

6. Join the following sentences to make one complete sentence without using *and*, *but* or *so*. Choose the correct option. ***[2012]***

(i) He lived in the city for many years. He could not find his way out.
 (a) Although he lived in the city for many years, yet he could not find his way out.
 (b) Although he lived in the city for many years, but he could not find his way out.
 (c) Although he lived in the city for many years, he could not find his way out.
 (d) None of the above

(ii) She complained that her brother did not know anything. Her brother claimed he knew everything.
 (a) She complained that her brother did not know anything before her brother claimed he knew everything.
 (b) She complained that her brother did not know anything whereas her brother claimed he knew everything.
 (c) She complained that her brother did not know anything when her brother claimed he knew everything.
 (d) She complained that her brother did not know anything after her brother claimed he knew everything.

(iii) The coffee isn't strong. It won't keep us awake.
 (a) The coffee isn't strong enough to keep us awake.
 (b) The coffee isn't strong for keeping us awake.
 (c) The coffee isn't strong because it will keep us awake.
 (d) The coffee isn't strong and it won't keep us awake.

(iv) I finished my homework. I switched on the TV.
 (a) I switched on the TV as I finished my homework.
 (b) I switched on the TV while I finished my homework.
 (c) I switched on the TV as soon as I finished my homework.
 (d) I switched on the TV while I was finishing my homework.

7. Join the following sentences to make one complete sentence without using *and*, *but* or *so*. Choose the correct option. ***[2012]***

(i) The minister was wise. The king did not trust him.
 (a) Although the minister was wise, yet the king did not trust him.
 (b) Although the minister was wise, but the king did not trust him.
 (c) Although the minister was wise, the king did not trust him.
 (d) All of the above

(ii) We reached the port. The storm came on.
 (a) As we reached the port, the storm came on.
 (b) Since we reached the port, the storm came on.
 (c) While we reached the port, the storm came on.
 (d) As soon as we reached the port, the storm came on.

(iii) One should not borrow money. One should not lend money.
 (a) One should neither borrow or lend money.
 (b) One should either borrow nor lend money.
 (c) One should neither borrow and lend money.
 (d) One should neither borrow nor lend money.

(iv) She will win the prize. She deserves it.
 (a) She deserves to win the prize and she will.
 (b) She will win the prize because she deserves it.
 (c) She will win the prize but she doesn't deserve it.
 (d) None of the above

8. Join the following sentences to make one complete sentence without using *and*, *but* or *so*. Choose the correct option. ***[2010]***

(i) You will surely be late. Hurry up!
 (a) Unless you hurry up, you will be late.
 (b) Unless you hurry up, you will not be late.
 (c) Unless you hurry up, you will barely be late.
 (d) Unless you hurry up, you will surely not be late.

(ii) The trekkers got lost due to the heavy fog. They had misplaced their map as well.
(a) Not only did the trekkers get lost due to the heavy fog but they also misplaced their map.
(b) Not only did the trekkers get lost due to the heavy fog but they misplaced their map.
(c) Both the trekkers get lost due to the heavy fog and they also misplaced their map.
(d) Both the trekkers got lost due to the heavy fog and they misplaced their map.

(iii) She has to apologise. He will not meet her again if she does not do so.
(a) He will meet her again unless she apologises.
(b) He will not meet her again if she apologises.
(c) He will not meet her again unless she apologises.
(d) He will meet her again if she does not apologise.

(iv) I wear this expensive outfit very sparingly. I bought it last month.
(a) I wear this expensive outfit very sparingly while I bought last month.
(b) I wear this expensive outfit very sparingly which I bought last month.
(c) I wear this expensive outfit very sparingly where I bought last month.
(d) I wear this expensive outfit very sparingly when I bought last month.

9. Join the following sentences to make one complete sentence without using *and*, *but* or *so*. Choose the correct option. ***[2009]***

(i) Swarna asked me a question. I was unable to answer it.
(a) I was unable to answer the question which Swarna asked me.
(b) I was unable to answer the question that Swarna asked me.
(c) Swarna asked me a question which I was unable to answer.
(d) All of the above

(ii) You helped Tania. She will always be grateful.
(a) Tania will always be grateful for your help.
(b) You helped Tania because she was grateful.
(c) Tani will always be grateful because you helped her.
(d) Both (a) and (c)

(iii) I heard you won a prize. I am extremely delighted.
(a) I am extremely delighted to hear that you won a prize.
(b) I am extremely delighted to hear which you won a prize.
(c) I am extremely delighted to hear when you won a prize.
(d) I am extremely delighted to hear and you won a prize.

(iv) There was heavy traffic. We reached the stadium on time.
(a) Though there was heavy traffic, but we reached the stadium on time.
(b) Though there was heavy traffic, yet we reached the stadium on time.
(c) Though there was heavy traffic, we reached the stadium on time.
(d) All of the above

Subjective Questions

1. Join the following sentences to make one complete sentence without using *and*, *but* or *so*.
(i) The heart attack was mild. Mr Bose stayed in bed for three weeks.
(ii) The men went out to see if anyone was missing. The women stayed behind to care for the injured.
(iii) Her mother warned her not to talk to strangers. She told her not to accept gifts from people she did not know.
(iv) Everyone was drenched by now. The rain had come down harder.

2. Join the following sentences to make one complete sentence without using *and*, *but* or *so*.
(i) John gave me the novel. John wanted me to review it.
(ii) Debjani received my note. She sent her reply within a week.
(iii) Raja is a great footballer. He is also popular.
(iv) Jenifer saw that I was confused. She came to my rescue.

3. Join the following sentences to make one complete sentence without using *and*, *but* or *so*.
(i) Sahil composed a wonderful song. It became a hit.
(ii) Rani reached the spot. We were to meet there.
(iii) Dick met me. I gave him the document.
(iv) Shenaz was very upset. I wanted to help her out.

4. Join the following sentences to make one complete sentence without using *and*, *but* or *so*.
(i) The young generation has learnt modern technologies. It has forgotten old culture and values.
(ii) There are many athletes in India. They were champions of one time. Nobody remembers them now.

(iii) I have read that book. The language of that book is very difficult.

(iv) Veeru likes to play cricket. He likes to watch movies too.

5. Re-write the following sentences according to the instructions given after each. Make other changes that may be necessary but do not change the meaning of each sentence.

(i) As soon as we lit the candle, the power supply was restored.
(Begin : No sooner ....) *[2014]*

(ii) The old woman was too slow to catch the bus.
(Begin : The old woman was so ....) *[2014]*

(iii) My mother said I could go with you only if I returned home by 5 o'clock.
(Use : as long as) *[2013]*

(iv) As soon as the Chief Guest had seated himself the play began.
(Begin : No sooner ....) *[2012]*

(v) The children will sit out in the garden if the weather is cool.
(Begin : The children won't ....) *[2011]*

(vi) The thief ran so fast that the police could not catch him. (Re-write using : too ....) *[2011]*

(vii) The child disappeared as soon as the bus stopped.
(Begin : Hardly ....) *[2011]*

(viii) Study hard now or you will regret it.
(Begin : Unless ....) *[2009]*

(ix) Megha is too tall to crawl under the table.
(Begin : Megha is so ....) *[2009]*

(x) As soon as the curtain came down the applause rang out.
(Begin : No sooner ....) *[2009]*

(xi) I suddenly realised that the room was too small for the three of us to share.
(Begin : I suddenly realised that the room was so..........)

(xii) As soon as the bell rang, the children rushed out of class. (Begin : No sooner ....)

6. Re-write the following sentences according to the instructions given after each. Make other changes that may be necessary but do not change the meaning of each sentence.

(i) Sachin stood first in class and he also excelled at debate. (Use : not only ....)

(ii) No sooner had Ram narrated the story than he was praised. (Begin : Hardly ....)

(iii) As soon as the chief guest arrived, the band started playing. (Begin : No sooner ....)

(iv) He was so tired that he could not stand.
(Use : too ....) *[2017]*

7. Join the following sentences to make one complete sentence without using *and*, *but* or *so*

(i) Sarah and Tyra are twins. They look exactly alike.

(ii) Rohan does not like to play cricket. He does not like to play hockey either.

(iii) Sania pushed as hard as she could. The door would not open.

(iv) The school bus drove through the gate. The clock was striking eight at that moment. *[2020]*

8. Join the following sentences to make one complete sentence without using *and*, *but* or *so*

(i) He was very ill. He did not take any medicine.

(ii) You come back from your holiday. We will discuss the problem.

(iii) He remained absent on Friday. It was foolish of him.

(iv) Rahul ran all the way to the bus stop. He missed the bus. *[2019]*

9. Rewrite the following sentences according to the instructions given after each sentence. Make other changes that may be necessary, but do not change the meaning of the given sentence. *[2020]*

(i) As soon as the teacher enters, she is greeted by her students.
(Begin: No sooner.................................)

(ii) Sheela will be selected for the competition only if she goes for the auditions.
(Begin: Unless.......................................)

10. Rewrite the following sentences according to the instructions given after each sentence. Make other changes that may be necessary, but do not change the meaning of the given sentence. *[2019]*

(i) As soon as the Sun rose over the hills, the fog disappeared.
(Begin: No sooner................................)

(ii) If your friends get here before 7 o'clock, we can take them out for dinner.
(Rewrite: Using 'unless'....................)

Answers

Multiple Choice Questions

1. (i) (c) He ran away after jumping.
(ii) (c) In spite of many failures, he hopes to succeed.
(iii) (a) Be neither a jeweller nor a goldsmith.
(iv) (d) A cottager and his wife had a hen which laid an egg every day.

2. (i) (c) They have to go to bed early every night except Saturdays, when they are allowed to stay up late.
(ii) (c) The children were delighted that the exams had been cancelled.
(iii) (a) We are not allowed to play in the Sun or the rain.
(iv) (b) This is the place where the dog was rescued from its cruel owner.

3. (i) (c) The book was too interesting to be put down.
(ii) (b) Unless Marry catches the first bus, she will not be on time for school.
(iii) (a) No sooner had the teacher left the room than the children started making a noise.
(iv) (d) Unless the boys reach the school on time, they will be punished.
(v) (a) Hardly does he reach home when his friends call him.

4. (i) (a) Not only is he good at gymnastics but his handwriting is also beautiful.
(ii) (b) Her grandfather gifted her a paint box because he knew she was good at art.
(iii) (c) Both (a) and (b)
(iv) (b) Mona stood first in the examination despite having been ill for a month.

5. (i) (a) We had better get ready now; otherwise, we might not have time to reach the airport.
(ii) (a) Mr. Liew has been sick since he came back from Japan.
(iii) (d) Both the debating teams were very happy as they were declared joint-champions.
(iv) (c) As he escaped from the prison, he looked for a place where he could hide.

6. (i) (c) Although he lived in the city for many years, he could not find his way out.
(ii) (b) She complained that her brother did not know anything whereas her brother claimed he knew everything.
(iii) (a) The coffee isn't strong enough to keep us awake.
(iv) (c) I switched on the TV as soon as I finished my homework.

7. (i) (c) Although the minister was wise, the king did not trust him.
(ii) (d) As soon as we reached the port, the storm came on.
(iii) (d) One should neither borrow nor lend money.
(iv) (b) She will win the prize because deserves it.

8. (i) (a) Unless you hurry up, you will be late.
(ii) (a) Not only did the trekkers get lost due to the heavy fog but they also misplaced their map.
(iii) (c) He will not meet her again unless she apologises.
(iv) (b) I wear this expensive outfit very sparingly which I bought last month.

9. (i) (d) All of the above
(ii) (d) Both (a) and (c)
(iii) (a) I am extremely delighted to hear that you won a prize.
(iv) (c) Though there was heavy traffic, we reached the stadium on time.

Subjective Questions

1. (i) Mr Bose stayed in bed for three weeks after a mild heart attack.
(ii) While the men went out to see if anyone was missing, the women stayed behind to care for the injured.
(iii) Her mother warned her neither to talk to strangers nor to accept gifts from them.
(iv) Everyone was drenched by now because the rain had come down harder.

2. (i) John gave me the novel to review.
(ii) Debjani replied to my note within a week of receiving it.
(iii) Raja is not only a great footballer but he is also popular.
(iv) When Jenifer saw that I was confused, she came to my rescue.
Or Jenifer came to my rescue on seeing that I was confused.

3. (i) Sahil composed a wonderful hit song.
Or Sahil composed a wonderful song which became a hit.
(ii) Rani reached the spot where we were supposed to meet.
(iii) I gave the document to Dick.
Or I gave the document to Dick when he met me.
(iv) Shenaz was very upset therefore I wanted to help her out.

Or I wanted to help Shenaz out because she was very upset.

Or Shenaz being upset, I wanted to help her out.

4. (i) Though the young generation has learnt modern technologies, it has forgotten old culture and values.
(ii) Nobody remembers many athletes who were the champions of one time, in India.
(iii) I have read that book the language of which is very difficult.
(iv) Veeru likes not only to play cricket but also to watch movies.

5. (i) No sooner did we light the candle than the power supply was restored.
(ii) The old woman was so slow that she could not catch the bus.
(iii) My mother said I could go with you as long as I returned home by 5 o'clock.
(iv) No sooner had the Chief Guest seated himself than the play began.
(v) The children won't sit out in the garden if the weather is hot.
(vi) The thief ran too fast for the police to catch him.
(vii) Hardly had the bus stopped when the child disappeared.
(viii) Unless you study hard, you will regret it.
(ix) Megha is so tall that she cannot crawl under the table.
(x) No sooner did the curtain come down than the applause rang out.
(xi) I suddenly realised that the room was so small that it could not be shared by the three of us.
(xii) No sooner did the bell ring than the children rushed out of class.

6. (i) Sachin not only stood first in the class but also excelled at debate.
(ii) Hardly had Ram narrated the story when he was praised.
(iii) No sooner did the chief guest arrive than the band started playing.
Or No sonner had the chief guest arrived than the band started playing.
(iv) He was too tired to stand.

7. (i) Because they are twins, Saran and Tyra look exactly alike.
(ii) Rohan neither likes to play cricket nor hockey.
(iii) The door would not open despite Sania pushing it was hard as she could.
(iv) When the school bus drove through the gate, the clock was striking eight.

8. (i) Although he was very ill, he did not take any medicine.
(ii) We will discuss the problem when you come back from your holiday.
(iii) It was foolish of him to remain absent on Firday.
(iv) Although Rahul ran all the way to the bus stop, he missed the bus.

9. (i) No sooner did the teacher enter than she was greeted by her students.
(ii) Unless she goes for auditions, Sheela will not be selected for the competition.

10. (i) No sooner did the Sun rose over the hills than the fog disappeared.
(ii) Unless your friends get here before 7 o'clock, we cannot take them out for dinner.

CHAPTER

6

Degree of Comparison

Degree of comparison is a tool of estimating, praising, comparing the qualities (like colour, size, shape and other virtues) of two or more people, places, ideas or things.

There are three degrees of comparison

1. Positive degree 2. Comparative degree 3. Superlative degree

Positive Degree

It is the adjective in its simplest form. It is used to denote the existence of a quality but can also be used to indicate comparison to an equal degree.

Positive degree is formed by using 'as ...... as' with adjective in positive (affirmative) sense and 'not as .... as' or 'not so .... as' in negative sense. e.g.

(i) Gunjan is **as smart as** Pritam.

(ii) Mumbai is **as busy as** Delhi.

(iii) My pen is **as expensive as** yours.

(iv) Vipin is **not as clever as** (or so clever as) his brother.

Consider the following sentences

(i) Rudra is a **kind** man. (ii) This baby is **gorgeous.**

Here, the qualities of 'Rudra' and 'baby' have been simply stated and not been compared with those of anybody else.

This is also **positive degree.**

Comparative Degree

It is generally used when two entities being compared possess an unequal degree of a certain quality.

In most cases of comparative degree, the suffix 'er' is added to the adjective and 'than' is used after the adjective. e.g.

(i) Shamli is **taller than** Sonali. (ii) Anurag is **braver than** Prayas.

(iii) Iron is **harder than** wood. (iv) Rutuja is **fairer than** Swapnil.

Some adjectives with more than one syllable do not take 'er' as a suffix. In such cases, 'more' is used before them as follows

(i) Ayan is **more intelligent than** Rehan.

(ii) Tokyo is **more expensive than** Delhi.

(iii) This room is **more spacious than** that.

(iv) He found Sherlock Holmes **more interesting than** Donald Duck.

Important Points about Comparative Degree

Adjectives ending in 'or' such as superior, inferior, prior, junior, senior, etc. are comparative in nature. They take 'to' in place of 'than'.

(i) Mr Sharma is **junior to** (not 'than') Mr Mishra.

(ii) This jewellery is **superior to** that one.

We use 'to' with the verb 'prefer'. Neither 'er' nor 'than' is used with 'prefer' as the verb itself means 'to like more'. e.g.

(i) I prefer tea to coffee.

(ii) Madhurima prefers eating fruits to drinking juices.

Superlative Degree

Superlative degree is used for the comparison of three or more things of unequal degree of a certain quality. It is the highest degree of quality and is used to express that one person or thing possesses the most superior quality among the things being talked about.

In most cases of superlative degree, the suffix 'est' is added to the adjective which is preceded by article 'the'. e.g.

(i) Resham is **the wisest girl** among them all.

Or Resham *is* **the wisest** of all girls.

(ii) This is **the funniest** of all books that I have read so far.

(iii) Rishi is **the strongest** boy in our class.

(iv) You are **the best friend** of mine.

Some adjectives with more than two syllables, that take 'more' in comparative degree, take 'most' in superlative degree. e.g.

(i) The snake is **the most dangerous** animal.

(ii) The Taj Mahal is **the most famous** epitome of love.

(iii) Chiraag is **the most handsome** boy in his family.

(iv) Room no. 15 in the hotel was **the most convenient** one for the businessmen.

Forming Comparatives and Superlatives

When you compare two items, you are using a comparative, so you use 'more' before the adjective or the suffix-'er' at its end. When you compare three or more items, you're using a superlative, so you use 'most' or the suffix-'est'.

The following rules should be remembered while forming comparatives and superlatives.

1. Most adjectives of one syllable form the comparative by adding 'er' and the superlative by adding 'est' to the positive degree.

Positive Degree	Comparative Degree	Superlative Degree
white	whiter	whitest
short	shorter	shortest
tall	taller	tallest

Note If the positive degree ends in 'e', only 'r' or 'st' is added.

2. When the positive degree ends in 'y', preceded by a consonant, the 'y' is changed into 'i' before adding 'er' and 'est'.

Positive Degree	Comparative Degree	Superlative Degree
wealthy	wealthier	wealthiest
merry	merrier	merriest
happy	happier	happiest

3. When the positive degree consists of a word of one syllable and ends in a single consonant preceded by a vowel, this consonant is doubled before adding 'er' and 'est'.

Positive Degree	Comparative Degree	Superlative Degree
thin	thinner	thinnest
fat	fatter	fattest
big	bigger	biggest

4. In case of adjectives of more than two syllables, the comparative and superlative degree are formed by putting 'more' and 'most', respectfully before the positive degree.

Positive Degree	Comparative Degree	Superlative Degree
beautiful	more beautiful	most beautiful
courageous	more courageous	most courageous
intelligent	more intelligent	most intelligent

5. Adjectives with two syllables ending in 'ful' (e.g. resentful), 'less' (e.g. senseless), 'ing' (e.g. boring) and 'ed' (e.g. surprised) and many others (e.g. polite, foolish, famous, certain, recent, modern) take 'more' and 'most'.

Positive Degree	Comparative Degree	Superlative Degree
polite	more polite	most polite
cruel	more cruel	most cruel
stupid	more stupid	most stupid

6. Two fold comparisons

Positive Degree	Comparative Degree	Superlative Degree
Near	nearer	nearest
Deep	deeper	deepest
Close	closer	closest

7. Irregular comparisons

Positive Degree	Comparative Degree	Superlative Degree
Good	better	best
Bad	worse	worst
Much	more	most

Note: older' and 'oldest' refer to age of persons or things, 'elder' and 'eldest' refer to order of birth within a family.

Change of Degree

Change of degree means transformation of one degree of adjective into another while retaining the same meaning of the sentence.

Let us try to understand the rules of transforming one form of degree of comparison into another.

Superlative Degree to Positive and Comparative

When we use superlative degree to estimate the quality of an object, we mean to say that it has the highest degree of that particular quality among all the objects being compared.

This means 'no other' object has that quality to the same degree.

Therefore, in positive degree, we use 'No other' and in comparative 'all other' or 'any other'. e.g.

(i) **Superlative Degree** Hardik is **the strongest** player of our team.

Positive Degree **No other player** of our team ↑ (Singular noun with 'no other') **is as strong as** Hardik.

Comparative Degree Hardik is **stronger than any other player** of our team.
↑ (Singular noun with 'any other') ↑ (The sentence begins with the same entity as

Or

Hardik is stronger than **all other players** of our team.
↑ (Plural noun with 'all other')

(ii) **Superlative Degree** Swara is **the cleverest** of all **girls** in my class.

Or

Swara is **the cleverest** girl in my class.

Positive Degree No other girl in my class is **as clever as** Swara.

Comparative Degree Swara is **cleverer than** any other girl (or all other girls) in my class.

(iii) **Superlative Degree** Mumbai is **the most expensive** place to live in Maharashtra.

Positive Degree No other place in Maharashtra is as expensive to live in as Mumbai.

Comparative Degree Mumbai is **more expensive than** any other place to live in Maharashtra.

(iv) **Superlative Degree** Suraj is **the most intelligent** of all boys.

Positive Degree No other boy is **as intelligent as** Suraj.

Comparative Degree Suraj is **more intelligent than** all other boys.

Positive Degree to Comparative Degree

Consider the following sentence

"Ram is as tall as Shyam."

This means both have equal heights. Its comparative degree will be

"Shyam is not taller than Ram."

When the positive and the comparative degree are used to compare only two things or persons (like the above sentences), they cannot be transformed into superlative degree.

Some More Examples

(i) **Positive Degree** A glass of juice is as good as a glass of water.

Comparative Degree A glass of water is not better than a glass of juice.

(ii) **Positive Degree** Question A is as simple as question B.

Comparative Degree Question B is not simpler than question A.

(iii) **Positive Degree** President Rule is not as good as democracy.

Comparative Degree Democracy is better than President rule.

(iv) **Positive Degree** Rose is as beautiful as tulip.

Comparative Degree Tulip is not more beautiful than rose.

Comparative Degree to Positive Degree

Consider the following example

"Metals are harder than non-metals."

This means non-metals are not equal in degree of hardness as metals. Therefore, its positive degree will be "Non-metals are not as hard as metals."

Some More Examples

(i) **Comparative Degree** Chocolates are tastier than cookies.

Positive Degree Cookies are not as tasty as chocolates.

(ii) **Comparative Degree** Arushi's house is bigger than her office.

Positive Degree Arushi's office is not as big as her house.

(iii) **Comparative Degree** Mobile phones are more convenient than tablets.

Positive Degree Tablets are not as convenient as mobile phones.

(iv) **Comparitive Degree** Drinking is not more dangerous than smoking.

Positive Degree Smoking is as dangerous as drinking.

In Case of Conversion from Positive Degree to Comparative Degree and Comparative Degree to Positive Degree

The sentence begins with the second entity (person, place, etc.) being compared.

An affirmative sentence is changed into negative and *vice-versa*.

EXAM PRACTICE

Multiple Choice Questions (MCQs)

1. Rewrite the following sentences according to the instructions given after each. Make other changes that may be necessary but do not change the meaning of each sentence. Choose the correct option. ***[2018 Modified]***

(i) India is the largest democracy.
(Use : larger)
(a) India is larger than no other democracy.
(b) India is larger to any other democracy.
(c) India is larger than any other democracy.
(d) India is larger than most other democracy.

(ii) The Pyramids of Egypt are the greatest architecture.
(Rewrite using positive degree of adjective)
(a) No other architecture is great as the Pyramids of Egypt.
(b) No other architecture is as great as the Pyramids of Egypt.
(c) None other architecture is as great as the Pyramids of Egypt.
(d) Any other architecture is great as the Pyramids of Egypt.

(iii) Mr. Sinha is the most successful businessman of his town.
(Rewrite using positive degree of adjective)
(a) No other businessman of his town is successful as Mr. Sinha.
(b) No other businessman of his town is as successful as Mr. Sinha.
(c) None other businessman of his town is as successful as Mr. Sinha.
(d) Any other businessman of his town is successful as Mr. Sinha.

(iv) Manoshi is my best friend.
(Use : better)
(a) Manoshi is better than no other friend of mine.
(b) Manoshi is better than most other friends of mine.
(c) Manoshi is better than any other friend of mine.
(d) Manoshi is better than some other friends of mine.

(v) Varun was as weak as Ravish.
(Use : weaker)
(a) Ravish was weaker than Varun.
(b) Ravish was not weaker than Varun.
(c) Varun was weaker than Ravish.
(d) All of the above

(vi) I have never worn a more ill-fitting suit.
(End : .... worn)
(a) This is the more ill-fitted suit I have ever worn.
(b) This is the ill-fitted suit I have never worn.
(c) This is the most ill-fitted suit I have ever worn.
(d) This is the most ill-fitted suit I have never worn.

(vii) Anil is too fast a runner not to come first in the race.
(Begin : Anil is so ....)
(a) Anil is so faster a runner, he came first in the race.
(b) Anil is so faster a runner that he came first in the race.
(c) Anil is so fast a runner that he came first in the race.
(d) Anil is so fastest a runner that he came first in the race.

(viii) Mobile phones are better than pagers.
(Use : good)
(a) Pagers are not as good as mobile phones.
(b) Pagers are as good as mobile phones.
(c) Pagers are not good as mobile phones.
(d) Pagers are good as mobile phones.

2. Rewrite the following sentences according to the instructions given after each sentence. Make other changes that may be necessary, but do not alter the meaning of each sentence. Choose the correct option.

(i) Grapes are as lovely as Jumblums.
(Begin : Jumblums ......)
(a) Jumblums are not lovelier than grapes.
(b) Jumblums are lovelier than grapes.
(c) Jumblums are lovely than grapes.
(d) Jumblums are not lovely than grapes.

(ii) Ganesha is the wisest among all Gods.
(Begin : No other ....)
(a) No other God is wise as Ganesha.
(b) No other God is as wise as Ganesha.
(c) No other Ganesha is as wise as God.
(d) No other Ganesha is wise as God.

(iii) Miheer is not weaker than this friend.
(Begin : His friend ....)
(a) His friend is as weak as him.
(b) His friend is weak as Miheer.
(c) His friend is weak as him
(d) His friend is as weak as Miheer.

(iv) English is as tough as French.
(Use : tougher)
(a) French is tougher than English.
(b) French is not tougher than English.
(c) English is tougher than French.
(d) French is not tough.

(v) Akhilesh Yadav is the youngest Chief Minister in India. (Use : younger)
(a) Akhilesh Yadav is younger than most other Chief Ministers in India.
(b) Akhilesh Yadav is younger than any other Chief Ministers in India.
(c) Akhilesh Yadav is younger than all other Chief Ministers in India.
(d) None of the above

(vi) Diamond is the costliest non-metal.
(Use : costly)
(a) No other non-metal is as costly as diamond.
(b) Other non-metals are costly than diamond.
(c) No other non-metal is costly as diamond.
(d) Other non-metals are not costly as diamond.

(vii) Iodine is the most lustrous non-metal.
(Use : as lustrous as)
(a) No other non-metal is as lustrous as iodine.
(b) No other metal is as lustrous as iodine.
(c) Some other non-metals are as lustrous as iodine.
(d) Other metals are as lustrous as iodine.

(viii) Groundnuts are good as cashewnuts.
(Use : better)
(a) Groundnuts are better as cashewnuts.
(b) Cashewnuts are not better than groundnuts.
(c) Cashewnuts are better than groundnuts.
(d) All of the above

3. Rewrite the following sentences according to the instructions given after each. Make other changes that may be necessary but do not change the meaning of each sentence. Choose the correct option.

(i) Tansen was the best singer in Akbar's court.
(Use : better) *[2006]*
(a) Some other singers in Akbar's court were better than Tansen.
(b) Tansen was better than any other singer in Akbar's court.
(c) Any other singers in Akbar's court were better than Tansen.
(d) Many other singers in Akbar's court were better than Tansen.

(ii) Very few doctors in the hospital are as dedicated as he is. *[2004]*
(Begin : He is ....)
(a) He is the most dedicated doctor in the hospital.
(b) He is one of the most dedicated doctors in the hospital.
(c) He is one of the few dedicated doctors in the hospital.
(d) He is not one of the few dedicated doctors in the hospital.

(iii) I have never seen a film as bad as this. *[2017]*
(Begin : This is ....)
(a) This is a bad film I have ever seen.
(b) This is the worse film I have ever seen.
(c) This is the worst film I have ever seen.
(d) All of the above

(iv) Nobody in our city can run as fast as Usha.
(Begin : Usha ....) *[2005]*
(a) Usha runs faster than anyone in our city.
(b) Usha runs fastest in our city.
(c) Usha runs the fastest in our city.
(d) Both (a) and (c)

(v) This is the funniest movie I have ever seen.
(Begin : Never ....) *[2016]*
(a) Never I have seen such a funny movie.
(b) Never have I seen such a funnier movie.
(c) Never have I seen such a funny movie.
(d) Never I have seen such a funnier movie.

(vi) No other substance is as soft as butter.
(Use : softest)
(a) Butter is the softest substance.
(b) Butter is not the softest substance.
(c) No other substance is the softest than butter.
(d) Butter is one of the softest substances.

(vii) Newspapers are the best media for a variety of news.
(Begin : No other ....)
(a) No other medium is good as the newspaper for a variety of news.
(b) Any other medium is as good than the newspaper for a variety of news.
(c) Some other medium is good as the newspaper for a variety of news.
(d) No other medium is as good as the newspaper for a variety of news.

(viii) He is as wise as Solomon.
(Use : 'wiser' ....) **2023**
(a) Solomon was wiser than he is.
(b) He and Solomon are wiser.
(c) Solomon was the wisest.
(d) Solomon was not wiser than he is.

Subjective Questions

1. Rewrite the following sentences according to the instructions given after each. Make other necessary changes but do not change the meaning of the sentences.

(i) Shakespeare is the most famous of all writers in English.
(Begin : No ....)

(ii) Iron is more useful than any other metal.
(Begin : Iron ....)

(iii) I earn as much money as Ram.
(Begin : Ram ....)

(iv) China is larger than India.
(Use : large)

(v) Air is lighter than water
(Use : as .... as)

(vi) I am taller than my brother.
(Begin : My brother ....)

(vii) Shyam is the strongest boy in the class.
(Use : stronger ....)

(viii) Supriya is the smartest girl in the class.
(Begin : Supriya is ....)

2. Rewrite the following sentences according to the instructions given after each. Make other changes that may be necessary but do not change the meaning of each sentence.

(i) Kochi is the best port in Kerala.
(Use : better instead of 'best')

(ii) Mount Everest is higher than any other peak in the world.
(Use : 'highest' instead of 'higher')

(iii) Mount Everest is the highest peak in the world.
(Use : 'high' instead of 'highest')

(iv) The Nile is longer than the Amazon.
(Use : 'long' instead of 'longer')

(v) Greenland is the largest island.
(Use : 'large' instead of 'largest')

(vi) Oranges are cheaper than apples.
(Use : 'cheap' instead of 'cheaper')

(vii) James is not as intelligent as Mark.
(Use : 'more' intelligent instead of 'intelligent')

(viii) I don't eat as much chocolate as you do.
(Use : 'more' instead of 'much')

3. Rewrite the following sentences according to the instructions given after each sentence. Make other changes that may be necessary, but do not change the meaning of the given sentence.

(i) Greenland is the largest island in the world.
(Rewrite : Using 'larger'..................) **[2019]**

(ii) The rabbit is as soft as cotton.
(Begin: Cotton.....................)

(iii) Blood is thicker than water.
(Use : thick)

(iv) Saree is the most graceful dress.
(Begin: No other dress.....................)

(v) Ayushmati is the fastest runner in our school.
(Use : faster)

(vi) She is the richest woman in the country.
(Use : rich)

(vii) Africa is hotter than any other continent in the world.
(Use : hottest)

(viii) Wordsworth is the greatest of all English poets.
(Use : greater)

Answers

Multiple Choice Questions

1. (i) (c) India is larger than any other democracy.
(ii) (b) No other architecture is as great as the Pyramids of Egypt.
(iii) (b) No other businessman of his town is as successful as Mr. Sinha.
(iv) (c) Manoshi is better than any other friend of mine.
(v) (b) Ravish was not weaker than Varun.
(vi) (c) This is the most ill-fitted suit that I have ever worn.
(vii) (c) Anil is so fast a runner that he came first in the race.
(viii) (a) Pagers are not as good as mobile phones.

2. (i) (a) Jumblums are not lovelier than grapes.
(ii) (b) No other God is as wise as Ganesha.
(iii) (d) His friend is as weak as Miheer.
(iv) (b) French is not tougher than English.
(v) (c) Akhilesh Yadav is younger than all other Chief Ministers in India.
(vi) (a) No other non-metal is as costly as diamond.
(vii) (a) No other non-metal is as lustrous as iodine.
(viii) (b) Cashewnuts are not better than groundnuts.

3. (i) (b) Tansen was better than any other singer in Akbar's court.
(ii) (b) He is one of the most dedicated doctors in the hospital.
(iii) (c) This is the worst film I have ever seen.
(iv) (d) Both (a) and (c)
(v) (c) Never have I seen such a funny movie.
(vi) (a) Butter is the softest substance.
(vii) (d) No other medium as good as the newspaper for a variety of news.
(viii) (d) Solomon was not wiser than he is.

Subjective Type Questions

1. (i) No other writer in English is as famous as Shakespeare.
(ii) Iron is the most useful of all metals.
(iii) Ram does not earn more money than I do.
(iv) India is not as large as China.
(v) Water is not as light as air.
(vi) My brother is not as tall as I am.
(vii) Shyam is stronger than any other boy in the class.
(viii) Supriya is smarter than any other girl in the class.

2. (i) Kochi is better than any other port in Kerala.
(ii) Mount Everest is the highest peak in the world.
(iii) No other peak in the world is as high as Mount Everest.
(iv) The Amazon is not as long as the Nile.
(v) No other island is as large as Greenland.
(vi) Apples are not as cheap as oranges.
(vii) Mark is more intelligent than James.
(viii) You eat more chocolate than I do.

3. (i) There is no island larger than Greenland in the world.
(ii) Cotton is not softer than the rabbit.
(iii) Water is not as thick as blood.
(iv) No other dress is as graceful as saree.
(v) No other runner is faster than Ayushmati in our school.
(vi) No other woman in the country is as rich as her.
(vii) Africa is the hottest continent in the world.
(viii) Wordsworth is greater than any other English poet.

CHAPTER

7

Transformation and Synthesis of Sentences

A feeling can be expressed in a number of ways. These number of ways may include the usage of different words of similar meanings, or using the words figuratively or using different syntaxes of sentences. Transformation means changing one form of a sentence into another without altering its meaning or sense. Different styles of sentences may help you in developing good writing skills. There are different ways of transforming a sentence form into another.

Types of Sentences

There are four types of sentences.

Assertive or Declarative Sentence

These are the sentences that make statements.

They are of two types

e.g. **Affirmative**

(i) (a) He is my brother. (b) We shall overcome.

Negative

(ii) (a) He is not my brother. (b) We shall not overcome.

Interrogative Sentence

These are the sentences that ask a question.

e.g. (i) Where does he want to go?

(ii) Did they find it very strange?

Imperative Sentence

These are the sentences that make commands, orders, requests etc.

e.g. (i) Stand in a queue.

(ii) Please, be silent.

Exclamatory Sentence

These are the sentences that express strong feelings.

e.g. (i) What a nice puppy it is!

(ii) How beautiful the night is!

The transformation of one form of a sentence into another does not mean the alteration of its meaning, as we have studied earlier. Let us see the interchange of sentences one-by-one.

Affirmative ⇌ Negative

In order to change affirmative sentences into negative and *vice-versa*, we need to know the antonyms of some regularly used words. Therefore, a little brush up of antonyms and synonyms will be of great help in this particular exercise. Some sentences can also be changed into affirmative or negative by changing the degree of the adjective qualifying the noun or by changing the adverbs or conjunction used in the sentence. Such sentences will be dealt with in the respective chapters.

Interchange of Sentences

You are often asked to interchange the type of sentences in the following ways

Affirmative ⇌ Negative (By using antonym)

e.g.

(i) Apurva is an industrious girl. → Apurva is not a lazy girl.

(ii) I don't understand why this happens. → I fail to understand why this happens.

Assertive ⇌ Interrogative

e.g. (i) You can wait for a minute.
Can't you wait for a minute?

(ii) Who doesn't know Hindi in India?
Everybody knows Hindi in India.

Assertive ⇌ Exclamatory

e.g. (i) This is a very beautiful sight.
What a beautiful sight this is!

(ii) How wonderfully she has done it!
She has done it wonderfully.

Interchange of Simple/ Complex/ Compound Sentences

Simple ⇌ Compound

e.g. (i) In spite of several attempts, he could not get the visa for Australia. *(Simple)*

He attempted several times but he couldn't get the visa for Australia. *(Compound)*

(ii) I will have lunch and come with you. *(Compound)*

After having lunch, I will come with you. *(Simple)*

Simple ⇌ Complex

e.g. (i) In spite of several attempts, he couldn't get the visa for Australia. *(Simple)*

Though he attempted several times, he couldn't get the visa for Australia. *(Complex)*

(ii) He carried an umbrella because he did not want to get drenched in the rain. *(Complex)*

He carried an umbrella for not getting drenched in the rain. *(Simple)*

(iii) Manpreet is too humble to disobey her mother.
Manpreet is so humble that she can not disobey her mother.

Complex ⇌ Compound

(i) He carried an umbrella that he might not get drenched in the rain. *(Complex)*

He did not want to get drenched in the rain, so he carried an umbrella. *(Compound)*

(ii) He promised to return my notes but he didn't. *(Compound)*

Although he had promised to return my notes, he didn't. *(Complex)*

Practice Exercises

1. Transform the following Affirmative sentences into Negative sentences.

(i) Pranay is a kind person.
Ans. Pranay is not a cruel person.

(ii) He will say the truth to you.
Ans. He will not lie to you.

(iii) This surface is very hard.
Ans. This surface is not soft at all.
('very' changes to 'at all')

(iv) We will always remember you.
Ans. We will never forget you.

Antonyms of both **'verb'** and **'adverb'** are used.

(v) Everybody will accept his involvement in the crime.
Ans. Nobody will deny his involvement in the crime.

(vi) All men are wise.
Ans. No men are fools.

(vii) Everybody is a little imperfect.
Ans. Nobody is absolutely perfect.

(ix) Mandira is very impatient.
Ans. Mandira is not patient at all.
(x) It is unlikely to happen.
Ans. It is not likely to happen.

2. Transform the following Negative sentences into Affirmative sentences.
(i) She will not go at all if you don't want her to go.
Ans. She will go only if you want her to go.
(ii) Darpan did not recollect Abhi's name.
Ans. Darpan failed to recollect Abhi's name.
(iii) No smoke exists without fire.
Ans. Smoke exists only if there is fire.
(iv) There's no mother who does not love her children.
Ans. Every mother loves her children.
(v) The fuel in the aircraft was not sufficient to keep it soaring in the sky.
Ans. The fuel in the aircraft was insufficient to keep it soaring in the sky.
(vi) Manav does not agree with this.
Ans. Manav disagrees with this.
(vii) He did not look cheerful on that day.
Ans. He looked gloomy on that day.
(viii) There is nobody who does not like music.
Ans. Everybody likes music.
(ix) They could not understand its significance.
Ans. They were unable to understand its significance.
(x) This place is no longer a peaceful place.
Ans. This place has become a noisy place now.

Assertive ⇌ Interrogative

There are no set rules on how to change an assertive sentence into interrogative and *vice-versa*.

It depends upon the meaning and sense of the sentence which has to be retained when framing the sentence in a different syntax.

Practice Exercise

3. Transform the following Assertive sentences into Interrogative sentences.
(i) We cannot live without water.
Ans. Can we live without water?
(ii) These shoes do not match with this dress.
Ans. Do these shoes match with this dress?
(iii) Money can't buy love and happiness.
Ans. Can money buy love and happiness?
(iv) Pushkar is not a trustworthy boy.
Ans. Is Pushkar a trustworthy boy?
(v) That she was lying is not acceptable.
Ans. Is it acceptable that she was lying?
(vi) The sun never revolves around other stars.
Ans. Does the sun ever revolve around other stars?
(vii) A horse cannot make friendship with grass.
Ans. Can a horse make friendship with grass?
(viii) He could have asked for somebody's favour.
Ans. Could he not have asked for somebody's favour?
(ix) Radheshyam could not escape the allure of mountain climbing when he went to Nepal.
Could Radheshyam escape the allure of mountain climbing when he went to Nepal?
(x) He is a stupid fellow.
Ans. Isn't he a stupid fellow?

Note We can infer from the above questions that positive-declarative (assertive) sentences are transformed into negative-interrogative questions whereas negative-declarative sentences are transformed into positive-interrogative sentences.

Assertive ⇌ Exclamatory

'What' is used for the sentences in which the adjective is followed by a noun.

e.g. This is a very beautiful picture.
What a beautiful picture (this is)!

'How' is used for the sentences in which the adjective is generally not followed by a noun.

e.g. This is very beautiful.
How beautiful this is!

Practice Exercises

4. Transform the following Assertive sentences into Exclamatory sentences.
(i) This has been planned wonderfully.
Ans. How wonderfully this has been planned!
(ii) The saree is very gorgeous.
Ans. How gorgeous the saree is!
(iii) She is a very dull girl.
Ans. What a dull girl she is!
(iv) The sun is shining very brightly today.
Ans. How brightly the sun is shining today!
(v) This is a wonderful morning.
Ans. What a wonderful morning this is!

5. Transform the following Exclamatory Sentences into Assertive sentences.
(i) What a shameful story!
Ans. This is a very shameful story.

(i) What a shameful story!
Ans. This is a very shameful story.
(ii) How disgusting!
Ans. This is very disgusting.
(iii) What a lovely shot it was!
Ans. It was a very lovely shot.
(iv) How amazing the designs are!
Ans. The designs are very amazing.
(v) What a peaceful place Nainital is!
Ans. Nainital is a very peaceful place.

Synthesis of Sentences

Definition

Synthesis means the combination of a number of sentences into one new sentence.

The following are the chief ways of combining two or more simple sentences into one long sentence.

By Using a Participle

- He sprang up to his feet. He ran away.
  Springing up to his feet, he ran away.
- She was tired of trying. She decided to quit.
  Tired of trying, she decided to quit.

By Using a Noun or a Phrase in Opposition

- This is my mother. Her name is Susie.
  This is my mother, Susie.

By Using a Preposition with a Noun or Gerund

- Her husband died. She heard the news. She fainted.
  On hearing the news of her husband's death, she fainted.
- He has failed many times. He still hopes to succeed.
  In spite of many failures, he still hopes to succeed.

By Using the Absolute Construction

- The watch was expensive. He could not buy it.
  The watch being expensive, he could not buy it.
- The cot was too small. He could not sleep on it.
  The cot being too small, he could not sleep on it.

By Using an Infinitive

- He wanted to pass the examination. He studied hard.
  He studied hard to pass the examination.
- I have some duties. I must perform them.
  I have some duties to perform.

By Using an Adverb or Adverbial Clause

- The sun set. The travellers had not reached their destination.
- The travellers had not reached their destination before sunset.

EXAM PRACTICE

Multiple Choice Questions (MCQs)

1. Rewrite the following sentences according to the instructions given after each. Make other changes that may be necessary but do not change the meaning of each sentence. Choose the correct option.

(i) She is weak, but she is courageous.
(Begin : Despite ....) ***(2023)***
(a) Despite of being weak she is courageous.
(b) Despite being weak, she is courageous.
(c) Despite being courageous, she is not weak.
(d) Despite weak, she is courageous.

(ii) Jaswant's grandfather is too old to take up this job.
(Use : ...... so ...... that ......) ***(2023)***
(a) Jaswant's grandfather is so old that he could not take up this job.
(b) Jaswant's grandfather is so old that he cannot take up this job.
(c) Jaswant's grandfather is so old that he could take up this job.
(d) Jaswant's grandfather is so old that he can take up this job.

(iii) Can the cat ever sing?
(Begin : The cat ....)
(a) The cat can ever sing. (b) The cat can sing.
(c) The cat can never sing. (d) None of these

(iv) He could not parachute down in the Taj Mahal.
(Begin : Could ....)
(a) Could he ever parachute down in the Taj Mahal?
(b) Could he never parachute down in the Taj Mahal?
(c) Could he not parachute down in the Taj Mahal?
(d) Could he parachute down in the Taj Mahal?

(v) How irritating his voice was!
(Use : very)
(a) His voice is very irritating.
(b) His voice was irritating.
(c) His voice was very irritating.
(d) His voice very is irritating.

2. Rewrite the following sentences according to the instructions given after each. Make other changes that may be necessary but do not change the meaning of each sentence. Choose the correct option.

(i) How could anybody cool down the sun?
(Use : nobody)
(a) Nobody can cool down the Sun.
(b) Nobody but could cool down the Sun.
(c) Nobody could cool down the Sun.
(d) Nobody but can cool down the Sun.

(ii) These pieces of furniture are not of superior quality.
(Use : inferior)
(a) These pieces of furniture are of inferior quality.
(b) These pieces of furniture is of inferior quality.
(c) These pieces of furniture are inferior.
(d) These pieces of furniture is inferior.

(iii) All these instruments were not known to us earlier.
(Use : unknown)
(a) All these instruments are unknown to us earlier.
(b) All these instruments are not unknown to us earlier.
(c) All these instruments were unknown to us earlier.
(d) All these instruments were not unknown to us earlier.

(iv) No one could infer what his last lines meant.
(Begin : It ....)
(a) It is difficult for anyone to infer the meaning of his last lines.
(b) It was difficult for no one to infer the meaning of his last lines.
(c) It was difficult for anyone to infer the meaning of his last lines.
(d) It is difficult for no one to infer the meaning of his last lines.

(v) Everybody will admit that he did his best.
(Use : deny)
(a) No one will not deny that he did his best.
(b) No one will deny that he did his best.
(c) Everyone will deny that he did his best.
(d) Everyone will not deny that he did his best.

3. Rewrite the following sentences according to the instructions given after each. Make other changes that may be necessary but do not change the meaning of each sentence. Choose the correct option.

(i) There have been people who have already written about this earlier.
(Begin : You are not the ....)
(a) You are not the only person to write about this.
(b) You are not the last person to write about this.
(c) You are not the former person to write about this.
(d) You are not the first person to write about this.

(ii) I am listening to such a miraculous and enchanting music for the first time.
(Begin : I have not ....)
(a) I have not listened to such a miraculous and enchanting music before.
(b) I have not listen to such a miraculous and enchanting music before.
(c) I have not been listening to such a miraculous and enchanting music before.
(d) All of the above

(iii) Can you imagine how the people at places having $-24°C$ temperature survive?
(Begin : You .....)
(a) You can imagine how people at places having -24 °C temperature survive.
(b) You can imagine how people at places not having -24 °C temperature survive.
(c) You cannot imagine how people at places having -24 °C temperature survive.
(d) None of the above

(iv) He never expected to receive such a nice gift from his friends.
(Begin : It was ....)
(a) It was beyond him to receive such a nice gift from his friends.
(b) It was beyond his expectation to receive such a nice gift from his friends.
(c) It was beside his expected to receive such a nice gift from his friends.
(d) It was beside his expectation to receive such a nice gift from his friends.

(v) Radhika is unable to accept this shocking news.
(Use : cannot)
(a) Radhika cannot accept this shocking news.
(b) Radhika cannot deny this shocking news.
(c) Radhika cannot reject this shocking news.
(d) Radhika cannot criticise this shocking news.

4. Rewrite the following sentences according to the instructions given after each. Make other changes that may be necessary but do not change the meaning of each sentence. Choose the correct option.

(i) Only a foolish person would be taken in by this trick. (Begin : None ....) *[2012]*
(a) None but than a foolish person would be taken in by this trick.
(b) None but a foolish person will be taken in by this trick.
(c) None other than a foolish person will be taken in by this trick.
(d) None other than a foolish person would be taken in by this trick.

(ii) The children will sit out in the garden, if the weather is cool. *[2011]*
(Begin : The children won't ....)
(a) The children won't sit out in the garden, unless the weather is cool.
(b) The children won't sit out in the garden, if the weather is hot.
(c) The children won't sit out in the garden, if the weather is cool.
(d) All of the above

(iii) I've never seen so many people in this building before.
(Begin : This is ....) *[2013]*
(a) This is last time when I see so many people in this building.
(b) This is the first time when I have seen so many people in this building.
(c) This is the last time that I have seen so many people in this building.
(d) This is first time that I see so many people in this building.

(iv) There is no success without effort.
(Begin : You will ....) *[2011]*
(a) You will get success unless you make an effort.
(b) You will get success if you make an effort.
(c) You will not get success unless you make an effort.
(d) Both (b) and (c)

(v) If you are not a member, you cannot borrow books.
(Begin : Only ....)
(a) Only members could borrow books.
(b) Only members can borrow books.
(c) Only members cannot borrow books.
(d) Only members could not borrow books.

5. Rewrite the following sentences according to the instructions given after each. Make other changes that may be necessary but do not change the meaning of each sentence. Choose the correct option.

(i) He arrived in school on time even though he stopped for a bit on the way.
(Remove : even though)
(a) In spite stopping for a bit on the way, he arrived in school on time.
(b) In spite of stopping for a bit on the way, he arrived in school on time.
(c) Despite of stopping for a bit on the way, he arrived in school on time.
(d) All of the above

(ii) Anil was wrong to lose his temper.
(Begin : Anil ought)
(a) Anil ought not to lose his temper.
(b) Anil ought to lose his temper.
(c) Anil ought to not lose his temper.
(d) Both (a) and (c)

(iii) The old woman was too slow to catch the bus.
(Begin: The old woman was so ....)
(a) The old woman was so slow that she could not catch the bus.
(b) The old woman was so fast that she could not catch the bus.
(c) The old woman was so slow that she could catch the bus.
(d) The old woman was so fast that she could not catch the bus.

(iv) He will issue the cheque only when he hears from the head office. (Begin : On)
(a) On hearing from the head office only he issue the cheque.
(b) On hearing from the head office only he will issue the cheque.
(c) On hearing from the head office only will he issue the cheque.
(d) On hearing from the head office he will only issue the cheque.

(v) I prefer reading a book to watching a movie.
(Begin : I would rather ....)
(a) I would rather watch a movie than read a book.
(b) I would rather read a book than watch a movie.
(c) I would rather read a book than watching a movie.
(d) I would rather watch a movie than reading a book.

6. Rewrite the following sentences without changing their meanings. Choose the correct option.

(i) The train was wrecked. No one was hurt.
(Use : although)
(a) No one was hurt although the train was wrecked.
(b) Although the train was wrecked, yet not one was hurt.
(c) The train was wrecked but no one was hurt.
(d) None of the above

(ii) Ram is ill. He still attends school.
(Remove : still)
(a) Ram attends school despite of being ill.
(b) Ram attends school despite being ill.
(c) Ram attends school in spite being ill.
(d) All of the above

(iii) I shall not oppose your plan. I cannot approve of it either.
(Begin : I shall)
(a) I shall oppose your plan; however, I cannot approve of it.
(b) I shall not oppose your plan and I cannot approve of it.
(c) I shall oppose your plan; however, I can approve of it.
(d) I shall not oppose your plan; however, I cannot approve of it.

(iv) He is a rich man. He does not earn his wealth.
(Use : but)
(a) He is a rich man but he earns his wealth.
(b) He is a rich man but he does earn his wealth.
(c) He is a rich man but he does not earn his wealth.
(d) He is not a rich man but he does not earn his wealth.

(v) The storm abated. The sun shone.
(Begin : The storm)
(a) The storm abated and the sun shone.
(b) The storm abated; however, the sun shone.
(c) The storm having abated, the sun shone.
(d) The storm having abated but the sun shone.

7. Rewrite the sentences without changing their meanings. Choose the correct option.

(i) He is poor. He is honest.
(End with : ....is honest)
(a) Despite of being poor, he is honest.
(b) In spite being poor, he is honest.
(c) In spite of being poor, he is honest.
(d) None of the above

(ii) Her father died. She heard the news. She fainted.
(Use : hearing)
(a) As soon as hearing the news of her father's death, she fainted.
(b) As she was hearing the news of her father's death, fainted.
(c) On hearing the news of her father's death, she fainted.
(d) On hearing the news of her father's death, but she fainted.

(iii) Marco Polo made many discoveries. The discoveries were wonderful.
(End with : ....wonderful discoveries)
(a) Marco Polo made many wonderful discoveries.
(b) Marco Polo has made many wonderful discoveries.
(c) Marco Polo makes many wonderful discoveries.
(d) Marco Polo have made many wonderful discoveries.

(iv) I have some duties. I must perform them.
(End with : ....by me)
(a) Some duties that should be performed by me.
(b) I have none duties that must be performed by me.
(c) Some duties that should be performed by me.
(d) I have some duties that must be performed by me.

(v) The police arrived. The crowd disappeared.
(Begin : The police)
(a) The police having arrived, but the crowd did not disappear.
(b) The police having arrived, the crowd disappeared.
(c) The police having arrived, but the crowd disappeared.
(d) The police having arrived and the crowd did not disappear.

8. Rewrite the sentences without changing their meanings. Choose the correct option.

(i) It must be done. The cost does not count.
(End with : ....cost)
(a) It must be done at without no cost.
(b) It must be done without any cost.
(c) It must be done at any cost.
(d) It must be done at no cost.

(ii) I have read Bacon. It profited me greatly.
(Begin : Reading)
(a) Reading Bacon has profited me greatly.
(b) Reading with Bacon has profited me greatly.
(c) Reading Bacon had profited me greatly.
(d) Reading Bacon profited me greatly.

(iii) He is a bad boy. It is certain.
(Use : that)
(a) It is certain that he is a bad boy.
(b) That is certain that he is a bad boy.
(c) It is not certain that he is a bad boy.
(d) That is certain that he is not a bad boy.

(iv) He kicked the goal keeper. It was his intention to do so.
(Use : intentionally)
(a) He did not kick the goalkeeper intentionally.
(b) He kicked the goalkeeper intentionally.
(c) He did kick the goalkeeper intentionally.
(d) He did not kicked the goalkeeper intentionally.

(v) He was not at the meeting. His absence was unavoidable.
(Begin : His absence)
(a) His absence at the meeting was avoidable.
(b) His absence at the meeting was not unavoidable.
(c) His absence at the meeting was not avoidable.
(d) His absence at the meeting was unavoidable.

Subjective Type Questions

1. (i) In spite of having high fever, the girl came to school. (Begin : Despite ....) *[2016]*

(ii) I prefer going out with friends to staying alone at home. (Begin : I would rather ....)

2. Rewrite the following sentences according to the instructions given after each. Make other changes that may be necessary but do not change the meaning of each sentence.

(i) Not many people read for pleasure these days.
(Begin : Few..............) *[2017]*

(ii) Since her childhood, Meera has been good in Mathematics. (End : ....childhood.)

(iii) It is dangerous as well as illegal to drive a motorcycle without a helmet.
(Begin : It is not ....)

(iv) Every one of them was an experienced mountaineer.
(Begin : There was no ....)

3. Rewrite the sentences, keeping in mind the three types of sentences, without changing the meanings of them.

(i) He hurt his foot. He stopped.
(End with : he stopped)

(ii) I was walking along the street one day. I saw a dead snake.
(End with: .... dead snake)

(iii) The magician took pity on the mouse. He turned it into a cat.
(Begin : Taking ....)

(iv) He was weary of failure. He emigrated to Africa.
(Begin : Being ....)

(v) I was returning home. I saw a man. He was lying by the roadside.
(Begin : While ....)

4. Rewrite the sentences, keeping in mind the three types of sentences without changing the meanings of them.

(i) Jawaharlal Nehru died in 1964. He was the first Prime Minister of India.
(Begin : Jawaharlal Nehru ....)

(ii) The word of command will be given. You will fire.
(Begin : You will ....)

(iii) The judge gave his decision. The court listened to it silently.
(Use: silently)

(iv) He amused us very much. He sang a funny song.
(Use : By)

(v) It was a very hot day. I could not do any work properly.
(Use : being)

5. Rewrite the sentences without changing their meanings.

(i) He does well. He is nervous at the start.
(Begin : Despite ....)

(ii) It is raining heavily. I will take an umbrella with me.
(Use : so)

(iii) I am in the right. You are in the wrong.
(Begin : I am ....)

(iv) Sheena is a good student. Sheena is a good singer.
(Use : but)

(v) He was fined. He was sent to prison.
(Begin : He was ....)

6. Rewrite the following sentences according to the instructions given after each. Make other changes that may be necessary but do not change the meaning of each sentence. *[2013]*

(i) My mother said I could go with you only if I returned home by five o'clock.
(Use : as long as)

(ii) Heavy rains have caused the cancellation of the outdoor garden party.
(Begin : Due to ....)

(iii) If we light the fire, the rescuers will see us.
(Begin : We will be ....)

(iv) Only a few books were remaining on the shelf when we left.
(Begin : Most ....)

7. Rewrite the following sentences according to the instructions given after each. Make other changes that may be necessary but do not change the meaning of each sentenc…e. *[2012]*

(i) My mother left a month ago.
(Begin : It has ....)

(ii) As soon as the chief guest had seated himself, the play began.
(Begin : No sooner ....)

(iii) Everybody has heard of Gandhiji.
(Begin : Who ....?)

8. Rewrite the following sentences according to the instructions given after each. Make other changes that may be necessary but do not change the meaning of each sentence. *[2011]*

(i) This horse is better trained than yours.
(Begin : Your ....)

(ii) The thief ran so fast that the police could not catch him. (Use : too)

(iii) The child disappeared as soon as the bus stopped.
(Begin : Hardly ....)

9. Rewrite the following sentences according to the instructions given after each sentence. Make other changes that may be necessary, but do not change the meaning of the given sentence. *[2020]*

(i) No one will deny that the children have worked very hard this year.
(Begin: Everyone ....)

(ii) She is so busy that she finds no time to entertain her friends.
(Rewrite using 'too')

(iii) In spite of the very hot weather, Kevin stepped out to buy.
(Begin: Despite ....)

(iv) I would rather eat fruit than a lot of unhealthy junk food.
(Begin: I prefer ....)

(v) The tree was cut down ruthlessly.
(Begin: They ....)

10. Rewrite the following sentences according to the instructions given after each sentence. Make other changes that may be necessary, but do not change the meaning of the given sentence. *[2019]*

(i) It rained so heavily that they could not go for the picnic.
(Rewrite : Using 'too .... to')

(ii) How cruel Shylock was to demand his pound of flesh!
(Begin : It was cruel ....)

Answers

Multiple Choice Questions

1. (i) (b) Despite being weak, she is courageous.
   (ii) (b) Jaswant's grandfather is so old that he cannot take up this job.
   (iii) (c) The cat can never sing.
   (iv) (d) Could he parachute down in the Taj Mahal?
   (v) (c) His voice was very irritating.
2. (i) (c) Nobody could cool down the sun.
   (ii) (a) These pieces of furniture are of inferior quality.
   (iii) (c) All these instruments were unknown to us earlier.
   (iv) (c) It was difficult for anyone to infer the meaning of his last lines.
   (v) (b) No one will deny that he did his best.
3. (i) (d) You are not the first person to write about this.
   (ii) (a) I have not listened to such a miraculous and enchanting music before.
   (iii) (c) You cannot imagine how people at places having −24°C temperature survive.
   (iv) (b) It was beyond his expectation to receive such a nice gift from his friends.
   (v) (a) Radhika cannot accept this shocking news.
4. (i) (d) None other than a foolish person would be taken in by this trick.
   (ii) (b) The children won't sit out in the garden, if the weather is hot.
   (iii) (b) This is the first time when I have seen so many people in this building.
   (iv) (d) Both (b) and (c)
   (v) (b) Only members can borrow books.
5. (i) (b) In spite of stopping for a bit on the way, he arrived in school on time.
   (ii) (a) Anil ought not to lose his temper.
   (iii) (a) The old woman was so slow that she could not catch the bus.
   (iv) (c) On hearing from the head office only will he issue the cheque.
   (v) (b) I would rather read a book than watch a movie.
6. (i) (a) No one was hurt although the train was wrecked.
   (ii) (b) Ram attends school despite being ill.
   (iii) (d) I shall not oppose your plan; however, I cannot approve of it.
   (iv) (c) He is a rich man but he does not earn his wealth.
   (v) (c) The storm having abated, the sun shone.
7. (i) (c) In spite of being poor, he is honest.
   (ii) (c) On hearing the news of her father's death, she fainted.
   (iii) (a) Marco Polo made many wonderful discoveries.
   (iv) (d) I have some duties that must be performed by me.
   (v) (b) The police having arrived, the crowd disappeared.
8. (i) (c) It must be done at any cost.
   (ii) (a) Reading Bacon has profited me greatly.
   (iii) (a) It is certain that he is a bad boy.
   (iv) (b) He kicked the goalkeeper intentionally.
   (v) (d) His absence at the meeting was unavoidable.

Subjective Types Questions

1. (i) Despite having high fever, the girl came to school.
   (ii) I would rather go out with friends than stay alone at home.
2. (i) Few people read for pleasure these days.
   (ii) Meera has been good in Mathematics since her childhood.
   (iii) It is not safe and legal to drive a motorcycle without a helmet.
   (iv) There was no inexperienced mountaineer among them.
3. (i) Having hurt his foot, he stopped.
   Or He hurt his foot; therefore, he stopped.
   Or He stopped because he hurt his foot.
   (ii) While walking along the street one day, I saw a dead snake.
   Or I was walking along the street one day and I saw the dead snake.
   (iii) Taking pity on the mouse, the magician turned it into a cat.
   (iv) Being weary of failure, he emigrated to Africa.
   (v) While returning home, I saw a man lying by the roadside.
   Or While I was returning home, I saw a man who was lying by the roadside.
4. (i) Jawaharlal Nehru, the first Prime Minister of India, died in 1964.
   Or Jawaharlal Nehru, who was the first Prime Minister of India, died in 1964.
   (ii) You will fire as the word of command will be given.
   (iii) The court listened silently to the decision given by the judge.

Or The judge gave the decision which the court listened to silently.

Or The court silently listened to the Judge's decision.

(iv) He amused us very much by singing a funny song.

(v) It being a very hot day, I could not do any work properly.

5. (i) Despite being nervous at the start, he does well.

(ii) It is raining heavily so I will take an umbrella with me.

(iii) I am in the right while you are in the wrong.

(iv) Sheena is not only a good student but also a good singer.

Or In addition to being a good student, Sheena is a good singer.

(v) He was fined and sent to prison.

Or He was not only fined but also sent to prison.

6. (i) My mother said I could go with you as long as I returned home by five o'clock.

(ii) Due to heavy rains, the outdoor garden party has been cancelled.

(iii) We will be seen by the rescuers if we light the fire.

(iv) Most of the books had been removed from the shelf before we left.

7. (i) It has been a month since my mother left.

(ii) No sooner had the chief guest seated himself than the play began.

(iii) Who has not heard of Gandhiji?

8. (i) Your horse is not as well trained as this.

(ii) The thief ran too fast for the police to catch him.

(iii) Hardly had the bus stopped when the child disappeared.

9. (i) Everyone will admit that the children have worked very hard this year.

(ii) She is too busy to find time to entertain her friends.

(iii) Despite the very hot weather, Kevin stepped out to buy.

(iv) I prefer eating fruit to a lot of unhealthy junk food.

(v) They cut down the tree ruthlessly.

10. (i) It rained too heavily for them to go to the picnic.

(ii) It was cruel of Shylock to demand his pound of flesh.

CHAPTER 8

Nominalisation

Nominalisation is a type of word formation in which a verb or an adjective or a common noun is used as or transformed into a noun generally, abstract noun.

e.g. guide (Verb) → guidance (Abstract noun)

smart (Adjective) → smartness (Abstract noun)

child (Common noun) → childhood (Abstract noun)

Formation of Nouns from Verbs

Nouns are usually formed by adding a **suffix** to the verb. Given below are the examples of the nouns that are formed by adding a suffix to the verb.

1. ication

Verb	Noun	Verb	Noun
Amplify	Amplification	Imply	Implication
Justify	Justification	Verify	Verification
Apply	Application	Multiply	Multiplication
Certify	Certification	Modify	Modification
Glorify	Glorification	Quantify	Quantification

2. ation

Verb	Noun	Verb	Noun
Activate	Activation	Combine	Combination
Adapt	Adaptation	Confirm	Confirmation
Admire	Admiration	Devastate	Devastation
Agitate	Agitation	Exam	Examination
Alienate	Alienation	Intimate	Intimation
Animate	Animation	Oblige	Obligation
Authenticate	Authentication	Prepare	Preparation
Cancel	Cancellation	Perturb	Perturbation
Civilise	Civilisation	Resign	Resignation

3. ment

Verb	Noun
Abandon	Abandonment
Align	Alignment
Amaze	Amazement
Appoint	Appointment
Deport	Deportment
Employ	Employment
Enact	Enactment
Improve	Improvement
Nourish	Nourishment
Procure	Procurement
Settle	Settlement

4. ure

Verb	Noun
Close	Closure
Context	Contexture
Enclose	Enclosure
Expose	Exposure
Fail	Failure
Please	Pleasure

5. ance

Verb	Noun
Absorb	Absorbance
Accept	Acceptance
Allow	Allowance
Avoid	Avoidance
Clear	Clearance
Comply	Compliance
Disturb	Disturbance
Govern	Governance
Hinder	Hindrance
Insure	Insurance
Perform	Performance
Tolerate	Tolerance

6. ion

Verb	Noun
Abort	Abortion
Act	Action
Attract	Attraction
Calculate	Calculation
Celebrate	Celebration
Collect	Collection
Contradict	Contradiction
Demote	Demotion
Disperse	Dispersion
Duplicate	Duplication
Generate	Generation
Incubate	Incubation

7. ence

Verb	Noun
Absent	Absence
Emerge	Emergence
Exist	Existence
Excel	Excellence
Insist	Insistence
Occur	Occurrence
Prefer	Preference
Reside	Residence

8. age

Verb	Noun
Assemble	Assemblage
Block	Blockage
Carry	Carriage
Cover	Coverage
Drain	Drainage
Link	Linkage
Marry	Marriage
Pack	Package
Pass	Passage
Post	Postage

9. al

Verb	Noun
Betray	Betrayal
Disapprove	Disapproval
Dismiss	Dismissal
Propose	Proposal
Survive	Survival
Try	Trial

10. sion

Verb	Noun
Admit	Admission
Concede	Concession
Convert	Conversion
Divert	Diversion
Emit	Emission
Omit	Omission
Permit	Permission
Submit	Submission

Formation of Nouns from Adjectives

1. ness

Adjective	Noun
Fit	Fitness
Happy	Happiness
Hard	Hardness
Rough	Roughness
Rude	Rudeness
Sharp	Sharpness
Smart	Smartness
Soft	Softness
Sweet	Sweetness
Tough	Toughness

2. ry

Adjective	Noun
Brave	Bravery
Gallant	Gallantry

3. th

Adjective	Noun
Deep	Depth
Long	Length
True	Truth
Warm	Warmth
Wide	Width

4. ity

Adjective	Noun
Able	Ability
Active	Activity
Brief	Brevity
Brutal	Brutality
Capable	Capability
Equal	Equality
Clear	Clarity
Curious	Curiosity
Extreme	Extremity
Generous	Generosity
Humble	Humility
Secure	Security

5. ty

Adjective	Noun
Cruel	Cruelty
Frail	Frailty
Poor	Poverty
Sovereign	Soverignty

6. 'nt' changes to 'nce'

Adjective	Noun
Brilliant	Brilliance
Congruent	Congruence
Confident	Confidence
Dependent	Dependence
Excellent	Excellence
Intelligent	Intelligence
Prudent	Prudence
Significant	Significance

Formation of Nouns from Common Nouns

1. by adding 'hood'

Common Noun	Abstract Noun
Baby	Babyhood
Brother	Brotherhood
Child	Childhood
Father	Fatherhood
Mother	Motherhood
Parent	Parenthood

2. by adding 'ship'

Common Noun	Abstract Noun
Apprentice	Apprenticeship
Citizen	Citizenship
Friend	Friendship
Lecturer	Lectureship

3. by adding 'ry'

Common Noun	Abstract Noun
Ballad	Balladry
Dentist	Dentistry
Herald	Heraldry
Legend	Legendry
Poet	Poetry
Tenant	Tenantry

Transforming a Verb in a Sentence into its Noun Form

A noun can be a subject or an object in a sentence. Therefore, when we are changing the 'verb' in a sentence into its 'noun' form, we need to provide another verb that may suit the context of the sentence and that may not harm its syntax or its meaning.

Let us consider following examples to learn this:

- You need to justify your answer.
  If we have been asked to use the noun form of the verb 'justify', i.e. 'justification', then the sentence will be :
- You need to give justification for your answer.

Or

- Your answer needs justification.

You can understand that both the sentences have the same meaning as the original sentence. But the syntax of both is different.

Therefore, if you comprehend the sentence with the context with which the words are used, you will be able to change their construction using different parts of speech.

Some More Examples

- The bright and intelligent youth of the country can **glorify** her.
  The bright and intelligent youth of the country can lead her to **glorification.**

  Or

  The bright and intelligent youth of the country can bring **glorification** to her.
- This plan needs to be **modified.**
  This plan needs **modification.**
- The company **agreed** to provide one-time food.
  The company made an **agreement** to provide one-time food.
- Venu went to cancel the tickets.
  Venu went for the **cancellation** of tickets. (Preposition 'to' changed to 'for' in order to suit 'noun')
- The gardener **examined** the plants carefully.
  The gardener made a careful **examination** of the plants. (the 'adverb' also changed to 'adjective' in order to define 'noun')
- Sanyukta has **prepared** everything nicely.
  Sanyukta has done a nice **preparation** of everything (you also need to supply a suitable article for noun).
- Vitamins and minerals **nourish** our body.
  Vitamins and minerals provide **nourishment** to our body.

Transforming an Adjective in a Sentence into its Noun Form

Consider the following example :

- The little boy gave a **brave** performance.
  We know that an adjective qualifies a noun. So, when we change adjective into abstract noun, the noun which is being qualified by it must either change its position or be provided with a suitable preposition to receive its effect.
  Sometimes, another suitable 'verb' also needs to be supplied in order to complete the sense of the sentence.

The above sentence can be rewritten as :

- The little boy exhibited **bravery** in his performance.

  Or

  The little boy's performance exhibited **bravery.**

Some More Examples

- They led a **happy** life.
  They led their life with **happiness.**
- The nurse devoted a **warm** care to the patients.
  The nurse devoted a care with **warmth** to the patients.
- How **wide** is the path?
  What is the **width** of the path?
- Granny was always **generous** to her grandchildren.
  Granny always showed **generosity** for her grandchildren.
- Alok's words are not **clear.**
  There's no **clarity** in Alok's words.
- They are menaced by being **poor.**
  They are menaced by **poverty.**
- Nobody can tolerate such a **brutal** act.
  Nobody can tolerate an act of **brutality.**

EXAM PRACTICE

Multiple Choice Questions

1. Rewrite the following sentences according to the instructions given after each. Make other changes that may be necessary but do not change the meaning of each sentence. Choose the correct option.

(i) We will never forget what we saw.
(Begin : Never ....) ***2023***
(a) Never forget what we see.
(b) Never will we forget what we had seen.
(c) Never will we see what we forget.
(d) Never will we forget what we saw.

(ii) We have an obligation to do our best.
(Rewrite using 'oblige')
(a) We are oblige to do our best.
(b) We are oblige doing our best.
(c) We are obliged to do our best.
(d) None of the above

(iii) Latest intimation on the capture of the suspect was given to media.
(Rewrite using 'intimate' in your sentence)
(a) The media was intimate about the latest news on the capture of the suspect.
(b) The media was intimated about the latest news on the capture of the suspect.
(c) The media were intimate about the latest news on the capture of the suspect.
(d) The media were intimated about the latest news on the capture of the suspect.

(iv) His resignation was not accepted by the Governor.
(Rewrite using 'resign')
(a) When he resigned, it was not accepted by the Governor.
(b) When he resign, it was not accepted by the Governor.
(c) When he resign, it is not accepted by the Governor.
(d) When he resigned, it is not accepted by the Governor.

(v) Closure time of the market has been shortened by one hour. (Rewrite using word 'close')
(a) The market will be close one hour earlier from the scheduled time.
(b) The market is close one hour earlier from the scheduled time.
(c) The market is closed one hour earlier from the scheduled time.
(d) The market will be closed one hour earlier from the scheduled time.

(vi) The animals were kept in the enclosure to keep them safe from outside disturbances.
(Rewrite using the word 'enclose')
(a) The animals were enclose to save them from outside disturbances.
(b) The animals were enclosing to save them from outside disturbances.
(c) The animals were enclosed to save them from outside disturbances.
(d) The animals were being enclose to save them from outside disturbances.

(vii) The fraud by the company was exposed by the police.
(Use the word 'exposure' in a sentence)
(a) The exposure of the fraud by the company was done by the police.
(b) The exposured of the fraud by the company is done by the police.
(c) The exposure of the fraud by the company is done by the police.
(d) All of the above

(viii) The failure to file IT Returns may lead to fine and punishment.
(Rewrite using the word 'fail')
(a) If you fail to filing IT Returns, you may be fined or punished.
(b) If you fail to file IT Returns, you may be fined or punished.
(c) If you fail in file IT Returns, I may be fined or punished.
(d) If you fail in filing IT Returns, I may be fined or punished.

(ix) The pleasures of reading are not felt by todays' young generation.
(Rewrite using 'please')
(a) Today's young generation is not please by reading a book or novel.
(b) Today's young generation is not pleased by reading a book or novel.

(c) Today's young generation was not please by reading a book or novel.

(d) Today's young generation was not pleased by reading a book or novel.

(x) Rohan was watching the circus show in amazement.
(Rewrite using the word 'amaze')

(a) Rohan was amaze to watch the circus show.

(b) Rohan was amazed to watching the circus show.

(c) Rohan was amazed to watch the circus show.

(d) None of the above

2. Rewrite the following sentences according to the instructions given after each. Make other changes that may be necessary but do not change the meaning of each sentence. Choose the correct option.

(i) The property dispute could not be settled amicably.
(Rewrite using the word 'settlement')

(a) The amicably settlement of the property dispute cannot be done.

(b) The amicable settlement of the property dispute could not be done.

(c) The amicable settlement of the property dispute cannot be done.

(d) The amicably settlement of the property dispute could not be done.

(ii) The governors are appointed by the President of India.
(Rewrite using the word 'appointment')

(a) The appointment of governors was done by the President of India.

(b) The appointment of governors is done by the President of India.

(c) The appointment of governors are done by the President of India.

(d) The appointment of governors were done by the President of India.

(iii) The procurement of wheat is not required at present.
(Use the word 'procure')

(a) We do not need in procure wheat at present.

(b) We do not need to procured wheat at present.

(c) We do not need in procured wheat at present.

(d) We do not need to procure wheat at present.

(iv) This enactment of the new law required a referendum in the entire state.
(Rewrite using the word 'enact')

(a) A referendum in the entire state was required to enacted the new law.

(b) A referendum in the entire state was required in enact the new law.

(c) A referendum in the entire state was required to enact the new law.

(d) None of the above

(v) The trade fair attracts thousands of visitors from all over India.
(Rewrite using the word 'attraction')

(a) The attraction of trade fair results in thousands of visitors coming to the fair from all over India.

(b) The trade fair attraction thousands of visitors from all over India.

(c) The trade fair causes attraction of thousands of visitors from all over India.

(d) Both (a) and (c)

(vi) The collections of the party fund was going at a low speed.
(Rewrite using the word 'collect')

(a) The collect of the party fund was going at a low speed.

(b) Party fund was being collect at a very low speed.

(c) Party fund was being collected at a very low speed.

(d) All of the above

(vii) Nobody appreciated the honest officer's demotion.
(Rewrite using the word 'demote')

(a) To demoted an honest officer was a matter of no one's appreciation.

(b) To demote an honest officer was a matter of no one's appreciation.

(c) In demote an honest officer was a matter of no one's appreciation.

(d) In demoted an honest officer was a matter of no one's appreciation.

(viii) His actions are a matter of serious concern.
(Rewrite using the word 'act')

(a) How he act is a matter of serious concern.

(b) How he acts is a matter of serious concern.

(c) How he acted is a matter of serious concern.

(d) None of the above

(ix) Seeds get dispersed with the help of wind and birds.
(Rewrite using the word 'dispersion')
(a) Wind and seeds help in the dispersion of birds.
(b) Wind and birds help in the dispersion of seeds.
(c) Seeds and birds help in the dispersion of wind.
(d) None of the above

(x) Our existence on this Earth is very limited.
(Rewrite using the word 'exist')
(a) We exist in this Earth for a very limited time.
(b) We existed on this Earth for a very limited time.
(c) We exist on this Earth for a very limited time.
(d) None of the above

Subjective Type Questions

1. Rewrite the following sentences according to the instructions given after each. Make other changes that may be necessary but do not change the meaning of each sentence.

(i) The minister dismissed the complaint suggesting it was done to damage his reputation.
(Rewrite using the word 'dismissal')

(ii) Our survival depends on our skills.
(Rewrite using the word 'survive')

(iii) The convict was asked to appear before the court for his trial in robbery case.
(Rewrite using the word 'try')

(iv) The public and the media proposed to continue the discussion.
(Rewrite using the word 'proposal')

(v) The student was not permitted to sit for examination due to very low attendance.
(Rewrite using 'permission')

(vi) Omission of a few passages from the text was brought to the editor's notice.
(Rewrite using the word 'omit')

(vii) Delhi University has made the admission procedure very cumbersome for new students.
(Rewrite using the word 'admit')

(viii) The demand for concessions was rejected by the committee.
(Rewrite using the word 'concede')

(ix) Submission of bail papers was not done in time so he had to stay in lock up for a day.
(Use 'submit' instead and frame a sentence)

(x) Her attitude often annoys me.
(Rewrite using 'annoyance') ***[2011]***

2. Rewrite the following sentences according to the instructions given after each. Make other changes that may be necessary but do not change the meaning of each sentence.

(i) His arrogance was the cause of his losing the election.
(Rewrite the sentence using the word 'arrogant') ***[2010]***

(ii) She was the only person capable of being house captain. (Use : capability) ***[2008]***

(iii) He does not intend to leave the company.
(Use : intention) ***[2006]***

(iv) It doesn't matter which chemical you put into the mixture first, the results will be the same.
(Use : difference) ***[2013]***

(v) The teacher forgave the student who had misbehaved with her and it was welcomed by all.
(Rewrite using 'forgiveness')

(vi) She could never accept the fact of being betrayed by him. (Rewrite using 'betrayal')

(vii) Swara hesitated to tell her that she irritated her by stupid questions.
(Use 'irritation')

(viii) Sandhya always wanted to go for lectureship.
(Rewrite using 'lecturer')

(ix) Our lives were devoid of any difficulties when we were children. (Use 'childhood')

(x) Arun was asked by his mother to explain the missing buttons on his shirt.
(Rewrite using 'explanation') ***[2019]***

Answers

Multiple Choice Questions

1. (i) (b) Never will we forget what we had seen.
(ii) (c) We are obliged to do our best.
(iii) (b) The media was intimated about the latest news on the capture of the suspect.
(iv) (a) When he resigned, it was not accepted by the Governor.
(v) (d) The market will be closed one hour earlier from the scheduled time.
(vi) (c) The animals were enclosed to save them from outside disturbances.
(vii) (a) The exposure of the fraud by the company was done by the police.
(viii) (b) If you fail to file IT Returns, you may be fined or punished.
(ix) (b) Today's young generation is not pleased by reading a book or novel.
(x) (c) Rohan was amazed to watch the circus show.

2. (i) (b) The amicable settlement of the property dispute could not be done.
(ii) (b) The appointment of governors is done by the President of India.
(iii) (d) We do not need to procure wheat at present.
(iv) (c) A referendum in the entire state was required to enact the new law.
(v) (d) Both (a) and (c)
(vi) (c) Party fund was being collected at a very low speed.
(vii) (b) To demote an honest officer was a matter of no one's appreciation.
(viii) (b) How he acts is a matter of serious concern.
(ix) (b) Wind and birds help in the dispersion of seeds.
(x) (c) We exist on this Earth for a very limited time.

Subjective Type Questions

1. (i) The minister expressed dismissal of the complaint saying that it was done to damage his reputation.
(ii) Skills are required to survive.
(iii) The court wanted to try the convict in the robbery case.
(iv) The proposal by media and the public was to continue the discussion.
(v) The permission to sit for examination was not given to the student because of very low attendance.
(vi) The editor was informed that a few passages were omitted from the text.
(vii) Delhi University has made the procedure to admit new students very cumbersome.
(viii) The committee did not concede to any demands.
(ix) He had to stay in the lock up for a day as the bail papers could not be submitted on time.
(x) Her attitude often causes annoyance for me.

2. (i) He lost the election because he was arrogant.
(ii) She was the only person who had the capability of being house captain.
(iii) He has no intention of leaving the company.
(iv) It doesn't make a difference which chemical you put into the mixture first, the results will be the same.
(v) The teacher's forgiveness to the student who had misbehaved with her was welcomed by all.
(vi) She could never accept the fact of betrayal by him.
(vii) Swara hesitated to tell her that her stupid questions caused her irritation.
(viii) Sandhya always wanted to become a lecturer.
(ix) In our childhood, our lives were devoid of any difficulties.

Or

Our childhood was devoid of any difficulties.
(x) Arun's mother asked him to give her an explanation about the missing buttons on his shirt.

Sample Question Papers (1-3)

ICSE
SAMPLE PAPER 1

Fully Solved

English Language-X (Paper-1)

Time : 2 hrs | Max Marks : 80

General Instructions

1. Answers to this paper must be written on the paper provided separately.
2. You will **not** be allowed to write during the first **15** minutes. This time is to be spent in reading the question paper.
3. The time given at the head of this paper is the time allowed for writing the answers.
4. Attempt **all five** questions.
5. The intended marks for questions or parts of questions are given in brackets [ ].
6. You are advised to spend not more than **30** minutes in answering **Question 1** and **20** minutes in answering **Question 2**.

(Do not spend more than 30 minutes on this question.)

1. Write a composition (300 - 350 words) on *any one* of the following: **[20]**

(a) Write a short story beginning with the line: 'I just wish I had ....'.

(b) You had to attend an important event which you could not miss. You had to use public transport but there was a sudden transport strike. Narrate your experience in detail.

(c) Your class visited a Biodiversity Park. Describe in the detail what you saw there.

(d) *'Examinations are not a way of assessing a person's ability.'*

Express your views either for or against this statement.

(e) Study the picture given below. Write a story or a description or an account of what the picture suggests to you. Your composition may be about the subject of the picture or you may take suggestions to from it; but there must be a clear connection between the picture and your composition.

(Do not spend more than 20 minutes on this question.)

2. Select *one* of the following. **[10]**

(a) Your sister is always on her cellphone or on her computer. Write a letter to her drawing attention to the harm of such a sedentary life as well as highlighting the importance of regular physical exercise for a healthy body and a robust mind.

(b) As Head Boy of your school, write a letter to the Manager of a factory in your city requesting permission for your students to visit the factory. Give details such as the probable date, number of students and so on.

3. (a) You are the Secretary of the Cultural Club of your school. The club has decided to organise an overnight tour to visit places of historical importance in and around Jaipur. Write a notice in about 50 words informing students about the tour. Give the relevant details. **[5]**

(b) As the Secretary of the Cultural Club, write an e-mail to the Proprietor of M/s Reliable Tours, a travel agency, for arranging the bus, staying arrangement and catering for the overnight tour to Jaipur. Invent the necessary details. **[5]**

4. Read the following story carefully and answer the questions that follow.

From the edge of a steep ridge, I **peered** down into the Red Stone Valley. Like many summer days in North-West Alaska, the morning had begun bright and wind-swept, but now a dark cloud was drifting in from the East. I decided to move on. Camp was still three kilometres down the hill.

As I slung my pack on to my shoulders, a big Arctic mosquito thudded against my cheek. There had been a few of them through the day, but it was early in the season, the ice had melted just two weeks before and I'd scarcely noticed the mosquitoes. But now, as I wound down the ridge, the last breeze faded and they were on me. Rising in clouds from the **soggy** Tundra, they pelted against my face. I looked for the repellent in my pack, but in vain.

I was flailing away, nailing five or six at a whack, but there were thousands mobbing me now. They were diving in nose-first, piercing me right through my clothes, dozens at a time. Years of Alaskan experience had taught me what to do in a situation like this. I turned up my collar, cinched my pack straps tight and sprinted.

When I saw my tent, I was still going strong, but so were the mosquitoes. Each time I slowed down, the attack resumed. Pausing just long enough to unzip the screen door, I dived through to safety. It took me fifteen minutes to hunt down the hundred or so that entered the tent with me. After I'd cornered the last one, I took stock and tried to relax. My hands and neck were smeared with blood, and every centimetre of the exposed skin was punctured. Outside, the insistent wail was nearly deafening.

Not until later that night, when a cold rain swept in and scattered the mob, did I stick my own itching nose outside again. Bloodthirsty though they are, the big Arctic mosquitoes are frail creatures. These infamous insects, averaging a little over half a centimetre in length, can't even withstand a substantial breeze. They'd wither under bright Sunlight. Too hot or too cold, too much or too little rain, and they run for cover.

They spend most of their brief lives hiding under leaves, waiting for the right feeding conditions. A still, humid, cloudy evening is perfect. The upper Kobuk Eskimos know how to handle mosquitoes. As soon as the river is clear of ice, many Ambler people load up their boats and head for the chilly, wind-swept coast to spend the summer. Of course, they also fish and hunt seals, but it's no coincidence that this annual migration sidesteps the worst of the mosquito season.

(a) For each word given below choose the correct meaning (as used in the passage) from the options provided. **[2]**

(i) peered (para 1)

(a) looked at with great anger
(b) looked with concentration or difficulty
(c) looked with happiness and love
(d) None of these

(ii) soggy (para 2)

(a) completely strong (b) completely dry

(c) completely wet (d) completely weak

(b) Which word in the passage means the opposite of the word 'hidden'?

(a) Punctured (b) Stock

(c) Exposed (d) Insistent

(c) Answer the following questions briefly in your own words.

(i) Why did the author feel that he should move on? [2]

(ii) For whom is a 'still humid, cloudy evening perfect' and why? [2]

(iii) Why did the author consider the Arctic mosquitoes 'frail creatures'? [2]

(iv) According to the author, in which season was the mosquito menace at its peak? [1]

(v) Why did the Ambler people head for the chilly wind-swept coast? [2]

(d) In not more than 50 words of your own, describe how the mosquitoes came upon the author and how he managed to escape from them. [8]

5. (a) In the following passage, fill in each of the numbered blanks with the correct form of the word given in brackets. Do not copy the passage but write in correct serial order the word or phrase appropriate to the blank space. [4]

Example

The car .... (0) (slow) down at the curve.

Answer: (0) slowed.

When a child learns to stand up and tries to walk, he .... **(i)** (be) found to fall down again and again. And by nature, and instinct, he gets up, and again tries .... **(ii)** (step) forward, although again he falls down. But ultimately, he succeeds in walking. The same thing .... **(iii)** (happen) with each one of us, when we were children.

Similarly, in spite of his .... **(iv)** (repeat) failures, a man having perseverance does not admit his defeat. He .... **(v)** (try) again and again, and finally attains success. A resolute person .... **(vi)** (be) one who has great self-confidence, strong determination, and a natural urge towards hard labour, and untiring energy .... **(vii)** (continue) till the last, without.......... **(viii)** (grumble) or expressing dissatisfaction.

(b) Fill in the blanks with appropriate words. [4]

(i) The girl mistook Anil ...... a celebrated artist.

(ii) He was irritated ..... the situation.

(iii) I drove .... the bridge.

(iv) We located the key .... the door.

(v) The train went .... the tunnel.

(vi) The scream came from .... the room.

(vii) She ran .... the track with me.

(viii) An awful gale raged .... the foothills.

(c) Join the following sentences to make one complete sentence without using *and*, *but* or *so*. [4]

(i) The car dashed against a wall. It was going at over 150 kmph.

(a) The car dashed against a wall as it was going at over 150 kmph.

(b) The car dashed against a wall and it was going at over 150 kmph.

(c) The car dashed against a wall before it was going at over 150 kmph.

(d) The car dashed against a wall whenever it was going at over 150 kmph.

(ii) Jyoti met a man at the party. He is a famous football player.

(a) Jyoti met a famous football player at the party.

(b) Jyoti met a famous football man at the party.

(c) Jyoti meets a famous football player at the party.

(d) Jyoti is meeting a famous man at the party.

(iii) My uncle gave her a watch. She did not thank him.
(a) Although my uncle gave her a watch, yet she did not thank him.
(b) Although my uncle gave her a watch, but she did not thank him.
(c) Although my uncle gave her a watch, so she did not thank him.
(d) Although my uncle gave her a watch, she did not thank him.

(iv) Here are the letters. They arrived this morning.
(a) Here are the letters when arrived this morning.
(b) Here are the letters while arrived this morning.
(c) Here are the letters that arrived this morning.
(d) None of the above

(d) Rewrite the following sentences according to the instructions given after each of them. Make other changes necessary, but do not change the meaning of the sentence. **[8]**

(i) If they do not leave now, they will not catch the train.
[Begin: Unless...]
(a) Unless they leave now, they will catch the train.
(b) Unless they leave now, they will not catch the train.
(c) Unless they leave now, if they will not catch the train.
(d) All of the above

(ii) He played like a well-trained player.
[Use: as if]
(a) He as played if he was a well-trained player.
(b) He played as if he was a well-trained player.
(c) As he played as if he was a well-trained player.
(d) If he played as he was a well-trained player.

(iii) Keep the papers in a file. You may misplace them.
[Use: lest]
(a) Keep lest the papers in a file you misplaced them.
(b) Lest keep the papers in a file you misplaced them.
(c) Lest keep the papers in a file lest you misplaced them.
(d) Keep the papers in a file lest you misplace them.

(iv) The tourists said, "We did not enter the memorial without permission."
[Use: denied]
(a) The tourists denied that they had not entered the memorial without permission.
(b) The tourists denied that they had not entered the memorial with or without permission.
(c) The tourists denied that they had entered the memorial without permission.
(d) All of the above

(v) Amelia is one of the most studious girls in the class.
[Begin: Very few....]
(a) Very few girls in the class are studious as Amelia.
(b) Very few girls in the class are as studious as Amelia.
(c) Very few girls in the class are as studious Amelia.
(d) Very few girl in the class is as studious as Amelia.

(vi) We should show sympathy for the poor.
[Begin: The poor....]
(a) The poor should be show sympathy by us. (b) The poor should show sympathy by us.
(c) The poor should be shown sympathy by us. (d) Both (a) and (c)

(vii) I saw the suspect at the theatre yesterday. Immediately I informed the police.
[Begin: No sooner....]
(a) No sooner had I see the suspect at the theatre yesterday than I informed the police
(b) No sooner did I see the suspect at the theatre yesterday than I informed the police
(c) No sooner did I saw the suspect at the theatre yesterday than I informed the police.
(d) None of the above

(viii) The girl was so excited that she could not contain herself.
[Use: too...to]
(a) The girl was too excited to contain herself. (b) The girl was too excite to contain herself.
(c) The girl is too excited to contain herself. (d) None of these

Answers

1. (a) I just wish I had told my father about stealing the sugar from the jar at home. The temptation was irresistible as my sweet smelling fingers clawed in and out of the jar. If only I could rewind time and tell the truth this time. That way a large rat would not be running in my room foraging for the tiny grains of sugar I had accidentally dropped in my hurry. I lay cuddled up in the corner of my room crying, clinging tightly to my video game. All the while, the rat ran around the room.

I had to confess the truth regardless of the consequences that lay ahead. I silently crept towards my room's open door, tiptoeing to the entrance. I had just reached the door of my foul smelling bedroom when a strong gush of wind slammed it shut. Luck really wasn't on my side.

I turned to see the rat fall from the curtains right on top of my head. Its vicious fangs suddenly bit into my skin, drawing blood. Its claws scraped vigorously at my face. It was agonising and I had never experienced such excruciating pain in all my life, but only one thought went through my head. I wished I had been brave and told the complete truth to my father.

I screamed as it bit me again and suddenly the door to my room opened. My father came rushing in, looking scared. He took three long struides towards me and chased off the rat. He then took me out to the living room. He sat me down and brought the first aid box to treat me. His care made me feel more guilty and I apologised immediately. He laughed after hearing what had happened and said in a relaxed voice that when he had heard me screaming, he assumed the worst.

(b) The proverb "Opportunity seldom knocks twice" is really true in my case. I could have landed a wonderful job which promised to end my financial difficulties, but I messed it up by being careless and overconfident.

I am a qualified software developer working in a small company designing websites. The salary is not enough to manage my expenses as I am working far away from home. That is why I have to keep on asking my father to send me money every month, although he has retired and is only getting pension.

Last week, I got a test and interview call from a multinational company. Some of my former classmates were working there. So I knew that they would offer double the salary I was currently getting. So, I confirmed that I would attend the interview. I then planned out my journey because the place where I had to go was more than 15 kilometres away. I would have to go by public transport as I did not have either a bike or scooter.

On the morning of the day when the test and interview were to be held, the newspaper reported that all the local buses, auto rickshaws and other public transports would be on strike due to some festering issue with the government. I hurriedly got ready and went out to find some means of transport. Even after trying for almost an hour, I failed to find any. Then, just when I had given up, a kind motorist gave me a lift for half the distance. From there, I got another lift and finally walked the last kilometre to reach the company two hours late.

I found that the written test had been long over and the shortlisted candidates were being interviewed. I was told to apply again when there would be vacancies.

That is how I lost a golden chance.

(c) **Visit to a Biodiversity Park**

A field trip was organised for our school students to the Yamuna Biodiversity Park in Delhi. It is a landmark project of ecological restoration in an urban setting on the banks of the River Yamuna. It is located in North Delhi and has attempted to recreate the original ecosystem that River Yamuna had in Delhi before it became a huge metropolis.

The field trip began with introductory remarks about biodiversity conservation and the efforts being made at the Yamuna Biodiversity Park by the park authorities. The Park Director met us and explained the purpose of the park as well as species of animals and birds residing in it. He also explained the measures taken to make these species feel comfortable in living in the park.

This was followed by a visit to the Nature Interpretation Centre (NIC) which has been made near the entry point to the Park. The NIC provided the students with a basic understanding of the various stages through which the Park has gone, from being a barren piece of land and a fruit orchard supporting thorny trees to a fully functional and self-sustaining river ecosystem that it is today.

This was followed by a visit to various zones of the park including the two wetlands located inside it. Wetlands are land areas that are saturated with water, either permanently or seasonally, such that they take on the characteristics of distinct ecosystems. Then, the students were shown several species of herbs and trees that were once found in plenty in Delhi's urban ecosystem, but have become considerably reduced in number in the city. The two wetlands served as sites for spotting waterfowl, including some migratory species of birds as well.

A healthy discussion about the migration of birds and ability of the Park to provide a habitat for them was a good learning experience for the students, as was the overall trip experience.

(d) (i) **For the Motion**

Respected Principal,honourable teachers and my worthy opponents. Today,I am here to express my views in favour of the motion 'Examinations' are not a way of assessing a person's ability'.

Exams are a problem for the majority of students for different reasons. One type of student feels that the duration of the exam is too limited to write down the necessary points . This happens in the case of a slow writer. Other students can sometimes lose their ability to memorise when they get stressed. They may even fall ill due to stress. Further, there are students who can't focus in intense silence with the invigilator staring down at them. Thus, most of the conditions prevalent in the exams are completely unrealistic and cannot be expected to represent a student's knowledge and skills as a whole.

In addition to all this, as examinations only test certain aspects of a student's abilities, students who just happen to not have that particular ability would not be able to do well in that exam/test.

There are a large number of students who are very good in their homework but fail exams and tests. Schools just use tests to weed out all the not-so-smart children to really focus on the really smart ones. All students are aware that the smart students always sit up front in the classrooms and the teachers always answer their questions first. Anyone who doesn't live up to the school's standards is simply forgotten. Therefore, the students who really need help with the material don't get any and fail the tests and exams.

Therefore, it is true that tests and examinations are not the correct way of assessing a person's ability.

Against the Motion

Respected Principal, honourable teachers and my worthy opponents. Today, I am here to express my views against the motion 'Examinations are not a way of assessing a person's ability'.

Evaluating a student's ability through examinations is very well established. It is true that different students have different abilities and methods of thinking. Some can be very good at certain aspects but they may be lacking in other aspects. For instance, although a student may be good at managing his/her time or at collecting necessary information, he/she may be poor in teamwork or controlling his/her temper because he/she always wants everything to occur according to his/her expectation.

If a student expects to get the best result, he/she has to coordinate all his/her skills such as managing time, planning, teamwork and collecting information. Therefore, examinations are fair indicators to show how well a student can manage all his/her abilities.

Further, we need to understand the difference between ability levels and the amount of experience and knowledge students actually possess. If this is not done, students will work in an environment unsuitable for them and will not be able to learn properly. There is no way to assess them properly other than by testing them in a fair and impartial manner. Exams are good because they are not vague-they have clear and measurable guidelines.

Exams also allow students to independently work out answers on their own, unlike at home, where they can simply take out their books and see the answers.

Exams are also the only objective way to measure progress. If teachers could simply gave a grade based on what they think, making sure the teacher likes you would be more important than actually knowing the material.

Thus, evaluating students' abilities based on examinations is correct and should be followed universally.

(e) **Educate the Girl Child**

The global community and the organisations like the United Nations have periodically underlined the need to focus on urgent national and international steps to be taken to ensure education for the girl child. Hundreds of millions of young children, mostly girls, throughout the world are often deprived of education along with other essential needs like adequate food, clothing and healthcare. Going by these yardsticks, the development of a nation is truly measured by many indicators. Among these, literacy levels, especially those of women and girl children, are vital to judge the nation's progress.

A literacy drive among girl children would work as a catalyst for social uplift and thereby ensure progress on a nationwide scale. Keeping this as the target, eradication of illiteracy and bringing the girl child into the realm of education has been a major national concern for many decades.

It is relevant to mention the publication by the Directorate of Adult Education a few years ago called 'Literacy in India', which carried a cover page showing a young village girl holding the slate inscribed with the words "*ab mein likh sakti hoon* (Now I can write)". The picture-story only rightly emphasises the importance of education for the girl child and how gender inequality in the literacy drive continues to remain a serious challenge.

In 1988, the Government of India undertook the National Literacy Mission. With a new sense of urgency, it brought upon itself and the nation the seriousness of this challenging task in adult education, with a fixed goal, clear time frame and a well-defined target group. Today, over 98 per cent of the districts in India have been covered under literacy campaigns and lifelong learning opportunities are being made available in more than 200 districts.

The National Literacy Mission had endeavoured to ensure functional literacy for all adult non-literates in the country. By the turn of 2001, there was an indication that overall literacy rate had shot up substantially, particularly those of women. So, education of the girl child has become a reality.

2. (a) Room 365, Malviya Hostel,
National Institute of Technology,
Patna - 800004
10th January, 20XX

Dear Sanjana,

How are you? I hope you are healthy and hearty.How are your preparations for the Board exams going on? I wish I could be at home to guide you, but I am in my second semester here and the rules of our institution do not allow us to commute from home.

When I was home for the week-long break between semesters last week, I observed that every day you were busy either on your laptop or your mobile phone. You did not even go out in the evening to play any game, although you had been practising playing basketball and volleyball regularly earlier. In fact, I was very proud to tell my friends that my sister represents her school girls' team in both basketball and volleyball.

Wise people say, "A healthy mind lives in a healthy body." This implies that if we do not take care of our physical health, our mental health will automatically suffer. Taking regular physical exercise, even during exam days, is necessary to keep your brain fresh so that you can do better in your upcoming Board exams. So I suggest that you should go out in the evening for about an hour for playing any game or exercising. This will keep you active and fit.

I will be coming home for three or four days during Holi, when we have a mid-semester break. I expect to see you active and fit by then.

Yours affectionately,
Arvind

(b) Brahma Public School,
Sector 73,
NOIDA - 201305

17th October, 20XX

The Manager,
Solartron Paels Ltd,

Alpha Sector,
Greater NOIDA - 210303

Dear Sir

This is to inform you that our school conducts tours for the senior students to manufacturing plants in the area to acquaint them with current technology. We have identified your plant as one which manufactures solar panels for various applications using the latest technology. A group of about 40 students from Classes XII of our school wants to visit your plant to understand the process used and any other relevant information.

Kindly inform us about a convenient date and time next week when the group can visit. We would prefer to visit the plant during the morning hours.

Thanking you,

Yours sincerely,
Dilip Vashishth
(Head Boy)

3. (a)

LEARN ON THE GO!

Overnight Educational Trip to Jaipur

Date–24th January, 20XX to 26th January, 20XX

Expenses-5500/- per person

Highlights

- 5 star hotel stay
- Visit to historical places. How a Mahal among many
- Food and travel covered
- Shapping in local markets

For further details contact Mrs. Swara.
(Secretary, Cultural Club)

(b) **To** kkgupta@reliabletoursindia.com

Subject Overnight Tour to Jaipur for 50 School children

Dear Sir/Madam,

We have come to know from your website that your company organises group package tours to tourist sites in Rajasthan. Our school's Cultural Club wants its members to visit tourist sites in Jaipur area with a qualified tourist guide. The details are as follows:

Dates of tour 24th to 26th January, 20XX.

Departure from Delhi on morning of 24th January.

We will stay 2 nights in Jaipur and return on the evening of 26th January.

Number of persons 50 students from Classes IX to XII. (About 20 students will be girls.)

Arrangements to be made by you

1. Transport by luxury bus
2. Overnight stay arrangement at a 5 star hotel (2 persons to a room)
3. Complete catering for the entire trip
4. Availability of a qualified tourist guide at Jaipur
5. Entrance tickets at all sites visited

Separate accommodation in the hotel should be provided for girl students.
Kindly inform us about the total expense which will be incurred by us along with any other details.

Thank you,
With Regards,
Sanjeev Lal
(Secretary, Cultural Club)
Bal Bharti Public School
Mobile no 98106XXXXX

4. (a) (i) (b) looked with concentration or difficulty (ii) (c) completely wet
(b) (c) exposed
(c) (i) The author felt that he should move on because a dark cloud was drifting in from the East which may bring rain and camp was still three kilometres down the hill.
(ii) A still, humid, cloudy evening is perfect for the Arctic mosquitoes because they can neither withstand a substantial breeze nor bright sunlight or rain.
(iii) The author considered the Arctic mosquitoes 'frail creatures' because they cannot survive in adverse weather conditions like bright sunlight, rain or a substantial breeze.
(iv) According to the author, summer is the season when the mosquito menace is at its peak.
(v) The Ambler people headed for the chilly wind-swept coast in summer to avoid the worst of the mosquito season as well as for fishing and hunting seals.
(d) When the breeze stopped blowing, the Arctic mosquitoes came out in huge numbers to attack him and suck his blood. So, he raised up his collar to cover his neck, tightened his pack straps and started running towards his tent. He escaped from them by entering his tent, entering the mosquito screen and zipping it closed.

5. (a) (i) is (ii) stepping
(iii) happened (iv) repeated
(v) tries (vi) is
(vii) to continue (viii) grumbling
(b) (i) for (ii) by/ at
(iii) over (iv) near/by
(v) through (vi) within/ inside
(vii) along (viii) across
(c) (i) (a) The car dashed against a wall as it was going at over 150 kmph.
(ii) (a) Jyoti met a famous football player at the party.
(iii) (d) Although my uncle gave her a watch, she did not thank him.
(iv) (c) Here are the letters that arrived this morning.
(d) (i) (b) Unless they leave now, they will not catch the train.
(ii) (b) He played as if he was a well-trained player.
(iii) (d) Keep the papers in a file lest you misplace them.
(iv) (c) The tourists denied that they had entered the memorial without permission.
(v) (b) Very few girls in the class are as studious as Amelia.
(vi) (c) The poor should be shown sympathy by us.
(vii) (c) No sooner did I see the suspect at the theatre yesterday than I informed the police.
(viii) (a) The girl was too excited to contain herself.

ICSE SAMPLE PAPER 2

Unsolved

English Language-X (Paper-1)

Time : 2 hrs | Max Marks : 80

General Instructions

1. Answers to this paper must be written on the paper provided separately.
2. You will **not** be allowed to write during the first **15** minutes. This time is to be spent in reading the question paper.
3. The time given at the head of this paper is the time allowed for writing the answers.
4. Attempt **all five** questions.
5. The intended marks for questions or parts of questions are given in brackets [ ].
6. You are advised to spend not more than **30** minutes in answering **Question 1** and **20** minutes in answering **Question 2**.

(Do not spend more than 30 minutes on this question.)

1. Write a composition (300 - 350 words) on *any one* of the following: **[20]**

(a) Write a short story which illustrates the truth of the statement 'Self-help is the best help.'

(b) You have lived in your ancestral home since birth. The house is to be sold so that flats may be built in its place. Narrate the circumstances that led to this decision and describe your feelings about moving out of this house.

(c) Write about two deeds you have done, one of which gave you immense joy and satisfaction, while the other was a cause of deep regret.

(d) *'Teenagers today are more worldly-wise than their parents.'*

Express your views either for or against this statement.

(e) Study the picture given below. Write a story or a description or an account of what the picture suggests to you. Your composition may be about the subject of the picture or you may take suggestions from it, but there must be a clear connection between the picture and your composition.

(Do not spend more than 20 minutes on this question.)

2. Select *one* of the following. **[10]**

(a) Your mother has won the National Award for Meritorious Teachers. Write a letter to a friend giving details of the award, the award ceremony and the celebrations that followed.

(b) Your school had contributed a large sum of money to the Prime Minister's Relief Fund to help the victims of the floods in Assam. You visited the state recently and were shocked to see the poor living conditions in the camps made for the victims of the flood. Write a letter to the Officer Incharge of the Prime Minister's Relief Fund, drawing his attention to the plight of the people in the affected area.

3. (a) You are the Literary Secretary of Sardar Patel School, Secunderabad. You have been asked to inform students of Classes IX to XII about an Interschool Dramatics Competition to be held at Ravindra Bharati Auditorium in Saifabad, Hyderabad. Draft a notice in not more than 50 words for the school Notice Board with all necessary details. **[5]**

(b) As the Literary Secretary of your school, write an e-mail to the Manager, Ravindra Bharati Auditorium, asking for reservation of 80 seats in the auditorium for staff and students from your school during the duration of the Interschool Dramatics Competition. Invent the necessary details. **[5]**

4. Read the following story carefully and answer the questions that follow.

Although Harrods has over a hundred thousand customers a week, the quietest period is always between ten and eleven on a Monday morning. Kenny knew every detail about the great store, in the way a football **fan** knows all the statistics of his favourite team.

He knew where all the CCTV cameras were placed, and could recognise any of the security guards at thirty paces. He even knew the name of the assistant who would be serving him that morning, although Mr Parker had no idea that he had been selected as a tiny **cog** in Kenny's well-oiled machine.

"Good morning, Sir" said Mr Parker, turning to face his first customer of the day. "How can I help you?"

"I was looking for a pair of cufflinks", Kenny said, in the **clipped** tones he hoped made him sound like a Guards officer.

"Yes, of course Sir", said Mr Parker.

It amused Kenny to see the deferential treatment he received as a result of the Guards tie, which he had been able to purchase in the men's department the previous day for an outlay of £ 23.

"Any particular style?", asked the sales assistant.

"I'd prefer silver."

"Of course, Sir", said Mr Parker, who proceeded to place on the counter several boxes of silver cufflinks.

Kenny already knew the pair he wanted, as he had picked them out the previous Saturday afternoon. "What about those?" he asked, pointing to the top shelf. As the sales assistant turned away, Kenny checked the TV surveillance camera and took a pace to his right, to be sure that they could see him more clearly. While Mr Parker reached up to remove the cufflinks, Kenny slid the chosen pair off the counter and slipped them into his jacket pocket before the assistant turned around.

Out of the corner of his eye, Kenny saw a security guard moving swiftly towards him, while at the same time speaking into his walkie-talkie.

"Excuse me, Sir", said the guard, touching his elbow. "I wonder if you would be kind enough to accompany me."

"What's this all about?" demanded Kenny, trying to sound annoyed, as a second security guard appeared on his other side.

"Perhaps it might be wise if you were to accompany us, so that we can discuss the matter privately", suggested the second guard, holding onto his arm a little more firmly.

"I've never been so insulted in my life", said Kenny, now speaking at the top of his voice. He took the cufflinks out of his pocket, replaced them on the counter and added, "I had every intention of paying for them."

Kenny knew that on an average day, forty-two people were arrested for shoplifting at Harrods, and over 90 per cent of them were prosecuted.

(a) For each word given below choose the correct meaning (as used in the passage) from the options provided. [3]

(i) fan (para 1)

(a) admirer (b) hater

(c) flatterer (d) critic

(ii) cog (para 2)

(a) whole (b) part

(c) entity (d) None of these

(b) Which word in the passage means the same as 'quickly'?

(a) Counter (b) Swiftly

(c) Accompany (d) Privately

(c) Answer the following questions briefly in your own words.

(i) How do we know that Kenny prepared the act of shoplifting well in advance? [2]

(ii) How can we tell that Kenny wanted his crime to be detected immediately? [2]

(iii) How can we understand that shop assistants at Harrods do not often serve customers wearing a Guards tie? [2]

(iv) What did Kenny know about the prosecution of shoplifters at Harrods? [1]

(v) Why did the second security guard want to "discuss the matter privately" with Kenny? [2]

(d) In about 50 words of your own, describe how Kenny stole the cufflinks. [8]

5. (a) In the following passage, fill in each of the numbered blanks with the correct form of the word given in brackets. Do not copy the passage but write in correct serial order the word or phrase appropriate to the blank space. [4]

Example

(0) am convinced

I **(0)** ...... (convince) that my father **(i)** ...... (remember) by all those who value integrity. He **(ii)** ...... (be) a man of learning and also saw to it that he **(iii)** ...... (teach) his pupils with passion and patience. He, at times **(iv)** ...... (use) to lose his temper, but that was because he always **(v)** ...... (want) his pupils to learn and learn well. As a person, he was honest and simple. His greatness **(vi)** ...... (lie) in the fact that he **(vii)** ...... (have) a pure heart, devoid of malice. Such a man is always valued and **(viii)** ...... (be) very rare to find.

(b) Fill in the blanks with appropriate words. [4]

(i) Truth always prevails ...... the long run.

(ii) Sujata stood ..... the river and saw the ships pass by.

(iii) She took some money .... her father to buy a video game.

(iv) Shilpa gave me a rare gift .... my birthday.

(v) Deepak was very upset .... me.

(vi) Malvika is longing .... meet me.

(vii) It has been a long time .... I met my brother.

(viii) The worker asked .... his wages.

(c) Join the following sentences to make one complete sentence without using *and*, *but* or *so*. [4]

(i) Ravi gave me the novel. Ravi wanted me to review it.

(a) Ravi gave me the novel because he wanted me to review it.

(b) Ravi gave me the novel while he wanted me to review it.

(c) Ravi gave me the novel although he wanted me to review it.

(d) Ravi gave me the novel even if he wanted me to review it.

(ii) Jyoti saw that I was confused. She came to my rescue.

(a) For Jyoti saw that I was confused, she came to my rescue.

(b) When Jyoti saw that I was confused, she came to my rescue.

(c) Jyoti saw that I was confused; however, she came to my rescue.

(d) Though Jyoti saw that I was confused; therefore, she came to my rescue.

(iii) Raja is a great cricketer. He is also popular.

(a) Not only was Raja a great cricketer but he is very popular.

(b) Not only is Raja a great cricketer but he is also very popular.

(c) Not only is Raja a great cricketer but he was very popular.

(d) Not only was Raja a great cricketer but he was also very popular.

(iv) Debjani received my letter. She sent her reply within a week.

(a) Before Debjani received my letter, she sent her reply within a week.

(b) After Debjani received my letter, she sent her reply within a week.

(c) While Debjani received my letter, she sent her reply within a week.

(d) None of the above

(d) Rewrite the following sentences according to the instructions given after each of them. Make other changes necessary, but do not change the meaning of the sentence. [8]

(i) Tanuja is a very friendly girl and is always cheerful.
[Begin: Besides ....]

(a) Besides being very friendly, Tanuja is also always cheerful.

(b) Besides being friendly, Tanuja is also cheerful.

(c) Besides being very unfriendly, Tanuja was also cheerful.

(d) Besides being unfriendly, Tanuja was also always cheerful.

(ii) The business talks failed because neither side was willing to compromise.
[Begin: Since ....]

(a) When neither side was willing to compromise, the business talks failed.

(b) While neither side was willing to compromise, the business talks failed.

(c) Since neither side was willing to compromise, the business talks failed.

(d) None of the above

(iii) They were very afraid and so they could not speak.
[Begin: Being ....]

(a) Being very afraid, they cannot speak.

(b) Being little afraid, they cannot speak.

(c) Being very afraid, they could not speak.

(d) Being a little afraid, they could not speak.

(iv) No sooner had Ram narrated the story than he was praised.
[Begin: Hardly ....]

(a) Hardly had Ram narrate the story when he was praised.
(b) Hardly had Ram narrated the story when he was praised.
(c) Hardly did Ram narrate the story when he was praise.
(d) Hardly did Ram narrated the story when he was praised.

(v) They had to put off the garden party because of the heavy rain.
[Begin: The heavy ....]
(a) The heavy rain cause the garden party to be put off.
(b) The heavy rain caused the garden party to be put off.
(c) The heavy rain causing the garden party to be put off.
(d) All of the above

(vi) Margaret said to me, "Please do not forget to meet me tomorrow."
[Begin: I was ....]
(a) I was requested by Margaret to not forget to meet her the next day.
(b) I was requesting by Margaret to not forget to meet her the next day.
(c) I was requested by Margaret to not to forget to meet her the next day.
(d) I was requesting by Margaret to not to forget to meet her the next day.

(vii) In spite of my warning Dev, he ignored me.
[Begin: Though ....]
(a) Though I warned Dev, he ignored me.
(b) Though I warned Dev, but he ignored me.
(c) Though I warned Dev, yet he ignored me.
(d) All of the above

(viii) Arpita paid a heavy price for her recklessness.
[Begin: It ....]
(a) It was a heavy price while Arpita paid for her recklessness.
(b) It was a heavy price that Arpita paid for her recklessness.
(c) It was a heavy price since Arpita paid for her recklessness.
(d) It was a heavy price when Arpita paid for her recklessness.

ICSE

SAMPLE PAPER 3

Unsolved

English Language-X (Paper-1)

Time : 2 hrs Max Marks : 80

General Instructions

1. Answers to this paper must be written on the paper provided separately.
2. You will **not** be allowed to write during the first **15** minutes. This time is to be spent in reading the question paper.
3. The time given at the head of this paper is the time allowed for writing the answers.
4. Attempt **all five** questions.
5. The intended marks for questions or parts of questions are given in brackets [ ].
6. You are advised to spend not more than **30** minutes in answering **Question 1** and **20** minutes in answering **Question 2**.

(Do not spend more than 30 minutes on this question.)

1. Write a composition (300 - 350 words) on *any one* of the following. **[20]**

(a) Write a short story which illustrates the truth of the statement 'Advice not taken results in disaster'.

(b) Siblings often grow up side by side in families, yet they have very different life experiences. Imagine that you have one or more siblings and feel that your lives have differed significantly. Explain the reasons and the effects of such differences.

(c) Describe a remarkable event of social importance in your city or locality. Give a little of its background, the event as it occurred and its impact on the lives of people.

(d) *'Bollywood cinema both entertains and educates the masses.'*
Express your views either **for** or **against** this statement.

(e) Study the picture given below. Write a story or a description or an account of what the picture suggests to you. Your composition may be about the subject of the picture or you may take suggestions from it, but there must be a clear connection between the picture and your composition.

(Do not spend more than 20 minutes on this question.)

2. Select *one* of the following. **[10]**

(a) Your grandmother has just celebrated her 80th birthday. Write a letter congratulating her on her birthday, expressing gratitude, praise and admiration for the way she has lived her life.

(b) A company has been marketing spurious medicines while claiming that its product is effective in preventing bird flu and other forms of influenza. Write a letter to the Drug Controller General of India, Ministry of Health and Family Welfare, Government of India, for examining the claim of the company and explaining the harm these kind of claims can cause.

3. (a) You are the President of the Students Council of St Peter Secondary School, Agra. You have invited a Russian Ballet Troupe to conduct a ballet performance in your school auditorium. Draft a notice informing students about this event in not more than 50 words for the school Notice Board with all necessary details. **[5]**

(b) As the President of the Students Council of your school, write an e-mail to the Coordinator of the Russian Ballet Troupe, explaining the directions to reach your school from the airport and the facilities available in the school auditorium. **[5]**

4. Read the following story carefully and answer the questions that follow.

At last he felt ready to **startle** the town. He pulled himself to his feet, and, keeping tight hold of the weather-vane, managed to stand on top of the ball. It was well that he had a cool head and iron nerves.

Someone must have cast a casual glance up at the vane and, seeing his little figure, cried out. In a minute or two, Michael was delighted to see the market-place full of people who had rushed out of their shops and houses to gaze at the dizzy sight. It was splendid to have all those eyes and hearts glued upon him.

But Michael did not intend to stay there until he was fetched down, to be handed over to his father and **cuffed** by him before the crowd. After a while he prepared to descend of his own free will.

He leaned over the ball. The ladder had gone. The workmen had taken it away! A sudden feeling of sickness and giddiness came over Michael. He mastered it. To wait for rescue was a humiliating end to his escapade. He would come down alone, even if it cost him his life.

The church spire at the base of the ball was only half slated, and Michael saw some hope of gaining a foothold on the old part. He clasped his arms round the top of the ball and let his body swing down; he was just able to feel the first slate with his toes. Those toes were shod with iron toe-caps, for Michael was hard on his shoes. Michael kicked with his armoured toes till the slate crashed and fell in; then he got a foothold on the wooden strips beneath.

He rested for a minute, with aching arms and a stiff body. He must change his grip on the ball, which was too big to slide his arms down; he must get clear of it, and somehow grasp the spire beneath. One false move and he would be hurled to death on the cobbles below.

Slowly, he began to slide his hands together at the top of the ball, and then downward over its bulging face. Every inch was packed with peril; every inch pushed him backward towards death. It seemed to him that he would be too weak to hold on when the time came for him to grasp the spire.

But at last the steady, deadly creeping of his fingers brought him to a point where he could bend forward. With a sudden snatch he caught the base of the ball. The next moment he was kicking out a stairway in the old tiles and swarming swiftly down. He reached the foot of the spire, lifted the trapdoor of the tower, ran down the steps, and was caught by his father, who was waiting for him in the loft.

(a) For each word given below choose the correct meaning (as used in the passage) from the options provided. [3]

(i) startle (para 1)

(a) anger (b) surprise

(c) disturbed (d) annoy

(ii) cuffed (para 3)

(a) set free (b) punished

(c) secured with handcuffs (d) None of these

(b) Which word in the passage means the opposite of the word 'praising'?

(a) Humiliating (b) Giddiness

(c) State (d) Rushed

(c) Answer the following questions briefly in your own words.

(i) How did Michael display 'a cool head and iron nerves'? [2]

(ii) Which sight filled Michael's heart with delight and why? [2]

(iii) What discovery made Michael sick and giddy? Why? [2]

(iv) Why did Michael not wait for rescue? [1]

(v) How did his armoured toes help Michael in his descent? [2]

(d) In not more than 50 words of your own, trace Michael's descent from the top of the ball to the foot of the spire. [8]

5. (a) In the following passage, fill in each of the numbered blanks with the correct form of the word given in brackets. Do not copy the passage but write in correct serial order the word or phrase appropriate to the blank space. [4]

In the olden days, when merchant ships usually **(i)** .... (employ) teenage boys as part of the crew, a lad applied for one of these jobs. The owner of the **(ii)** .... (ship) company asked him what he **(iii)**...... (can) do.

"I can do my best", the boy answered, "to do what you are kind enough **(iv)** .... (let) me try."

"What have you done?" asked the owner.

"I **(v)** .... (saw) and split wood for my mother for nearly two years", replied the boy.

"What have you not done?" asked the employer.

After some **(vi)** .... (think) the boy said, "I have not gossiped in school for over a year."

"That is enough", said the merchant, "I **(vii)** .... (take) you aboard on my vessel and I hope some day **(viii)** .... (see) you as its captain. A boy who can master a wood-pile and control his tongue must have good stuff in him."

(b) Fill in the blanks with appropriate words. [4]

(i) A cow feeds ...... grass.

(ii) I am indebted ..... my teacher for helping me.

(iii) The sister was deprived .... her property.

(iv) The army rounded .... the insurgents last night.

(v) The old man hankered .... money.

(vi) The aeroplane flew .... the clouds.

(vii) Who will take ..... when the Mayor retires?

(viii) I do not have any complaint .... her.

(c) Join the following sentences to make one complete sentence without using *and, but* or *so.* **[4]**

(i) He finished his work. He went out to play.

(a) After he finished his work, he went out to play.

(b) Before he finished his work, he went out to play.

(c) While he finished his work, he went out to play.

(d) All of the above

(ii) The mangoes were very sour. He couldn't eat them.

(a) He couldn't eat the mangoes while they were very sour.

(b) He couldn't eat the mangoes; however, they were very sour.

(c) He couldn't eat the mangoes due they were very sour.

(d) He couldn't eat the mangoes because they were very sour.

(iii) He is a good tennis player. There is no doubt about it.

(a) There is no doubt which he is a good tennis player.

(b) There is no doubt when he is a good tennis player.

(c) There is no doubt why he is a good tennis player.

(d) There is no doubt that he is a good tennis player.

(iv) Come back soon. We will wait for you till then.

(a) We will wait for you till you come back.

(b) We will wait for you if you come back.

(c) We will wait for you uptill you come back.

(d) None of the above

(d) Rewrite the following sentences according to the instructions given after each of them. Make other changes necessary, but do not change the meaning of the sentence. **[8]**

(i) He received my message and immediately came to see me.

[Begin: As soon ....]

(a) As soon he received my message, he came to see me.

(b) As soon as he received my message, he came to see me.

(c) As soon than he received my message, he came to see me.

(d) None of the above

(ii) He never admitted that he had cheated me.

[Begin: At no time ....]

(a) At no time had he admit that he had cheated me.

(b) At no time did he admit that he had cheated me.

(c) At no time does he admit that he had cheated me.

(d) At no time do he admit that he had cheated me.

(iii) He inquired of us whether we were going home.

[Begin: He said to us,. "........]

(a) He said to us, "Is you going home?"

(b) He said to us, "Were you going home?"

(c) He said to us, "Are you going home?"

(d) He said to us, "Have you been going home?"

(iv) "Would that I could swim like a fish!" said Anil.
[Begin: Anil wished ....]
(a) Anil wished that he could swim like a fish.
(b) Anil wished that he could not swim like a fish.
(c) Anil wished that if he could swim like a fish.
(d) Anil wished that he would if he could swim like a fish.

(v) It is most probable that it will rain today.
[Use: probability]
(a) It is a strong probability that it will rain today.
(b) It is not a probability that it will rain today.
(c) It is a possible probability that it will rain today.
(d) It is a weak probability that it will rain today.

(vi) He is the cleverest man I have ever met.
[Use: clever]
(a) I have never met a man as clever as me.
(b) He has never met a man as clever as him.
(c) I have never met a man as clever as him.
(d) None of the above

(vii) None but a fool would believe you.
[Begin: Only ....]
(a) Only a fool would believe you.
(b) Only but a fool would believe you.
(c) Only a fool would not believe you.
(d) All of the above

(viii) If you wear thin clothes you will feel cold.
[Use: unless]
(a) Unless you wear thick clothes, you will feel cold.
(b) Unless you wear thick clothes, you will feel cold.
(c) Unless you wear thin clothes, you will feel hot.
(d) None of the above

ICSE SOLVED PAPER 2024

Fully Solved

English Language-X (Paper-1)

Time : 2 hrs | Max Marks : 80

General Instructions

1. Answers to this paper must be written on the paper provided separately.
2. You will **not** be allowed to write during the first **15** minutes. This time is to be spent in reading the question paper.
3. The time given at the head of this paper is the time allowed for writing the answers.
4. Attempt **all five** questions.
5. The intended marks for questions or parts of questions are given in brackets [ ].
6. You are advised to spend not more than 30 minutes in answering **Question 1** and **20** minutes in answering **Question 2**.

1. Write a composition (300-350) words on **any one** of the following. **[20]**

(i) Write an original short story entitled 'A Strange Visitor'.

(ii) Narrate an incident from your experience in which your parents had entrusted you with a difficult task. Give details of the task, how you carried it out and your feelings at the end.

(iii) Describe how you speed your time on a holiday afternoon. Why do you think it is necessary to have these times of quietness and solitude?

(iv) Express your views either for or against the statement 'Junk food should be banned'.

(v) Study the picture given below. Wirte a story or a description or an account of what it suggest to you. Your composition may be about the subject of the picture, or you may take suggestions form it; however, there must be a clear connection between the picture and your composition.

2. Select **any one** of the following. **[10]**

(Do not spend more than 20 minutes on this question.)

(i) Your friend was absent from school on a day when an unfortunate incident took place for which you were blamed. Write a letter to your friend giving details about the incident, your role in it and how the matter was finally resolved.

(ii) You wish to stage a play to create awareness about the importance of saving electricity. Write a letter to the Manager of a nearby shopping mall / supermarket requesting permission to use the space in front of the shopping mall/supermarket to stage the play. Give him / her details about your requirements and state why the play will be beneficial to the shoppers.

3. (i) Your school is hosting an Inter School Dance Competition. Write a notice to be put up on your school notice board informing the students about the event. **[5]**

(ii) Write an e-mail to the Principal of a neighbouring school to request him / her to send their dance teacher to act as a judge for the competition. **[5]**

4. Read the following passage carefully and answer the questions that follow.

Ashamanja Babu lived in a small flat in Bhowanipore. A Clerk in the registry department of Lajpat Rai Post office, Ashamanja Babu was fortunate as he could walk to his office in seven minutes flat without having to fight his way into the buses and trains of Calcutta. He lived a rather carefree life as he was not the kind of person to sit and brood about what might have been had Fate been kinder to him. On the whole, he was quite content with his lot. Two Hindi films and fish twice a week-these were enough to keep him happy. The only thing that **perturbed** him at times was his lack of companionship. A bachelor with few friends and relatives, he often wished he had a dog to keep him company. It need not be a huge Alsation like the one owned by the Talukdars, who lived two houses down the lane; it could be any ordinary little dog which would follow him around morning and evening. Wag its tail when he came home from work and obey his orders faithfully. Ashamanja Babu's secret desires were that he would speak to his dog in English, 'Stand up', 'Sit down', 'Shake hands' - How nice it would be if his dog obeyed such commands! That would make him really happy.

On a cloudy day marked by a steady drizzle, Ashamanja Babu went to the market in Hashimara to buy some oranges. At one end of the market, beside a **stunted Kul** tree, sat a man. As their eyes met, the man smiled. Was he a beggar? His clothes made him look like one. Ashamanja Babu noticed at least five sewning-on patches on his trousers and jacket. But the man didn't have a begging bowl. Instead, by his side was a shoe - box with a little pup sticking its head out of it.

'Good morning!' said the man in English. Ashamanja Babu was obliged to return the greeting. 'Buy dog? Dog buy? Very good dog.' The man had taken the pup out of the box and had put it down on the ground. Very cheap. Very good. Happy dog?

The pup shook the raindrops off its coat, looked at Ashamanja Babu and wagged its minuscule two inch tail. Ashamanja Babu moved closer to the pup.

Crouched on the ground and stretched out his hand. The pup gave his ring finger a lick with its pink tongue. Nice, Friendly dog.

'How much? What price?

'Ten rupees'

A little haggling and the price came down to seven rupees. Ashamanja Babu paid the money, put the pup back in the shoe box, closed the lid to save it form the drizzle, and turned homewards, forgetting all about the oranges.

–Ashamanja Babu's Dog by Satyajit Ray

(i) For each word given below choose the correct meaning (as used in the passage) from the options provided. **[2]**

1. perturbed *(line 7)*

(a) frightened (b) unsettled

(c) confused (d) mocked

2. stunted (line 15)

(a) prevented form growing (b) prepared for tricks

(c) prevented form taking action (d) allowed to do stunts

(ii) Which word in the passage means the opposite of the word 'expensive'? **[1]**

(a) Carefree (b) Ordinary

(c) Cheap (d) Haggling

(iii) Answer the following questions briefly in your own words.

(a) What kept Ashamanja Babu happy? **[2]**

(b) What does this tell you about him? **[2]**

(c) What is that one other thing he needed to complete his hapiness? **[1]**

(d) Why did Ashamanja Babu think the man was a beggar? **[2]**

(e) Why did Ashamanja Babu forget about his oranges? **[2]**

(iv) In not more than 50 words, narrate the series of events form the time the puppy was taken out of the box till it was paid for. **[8]**

5. (i) Fill in each of the numbered blanks with the correct form of the word given in brackets. Do not copy the passage but write in correct serial order the word or phrase appropriate to the blank space. **[4]**

Example:

Next day my uncle (0) .... (speed) a lot of time.

Answer: (0) Spent

He (1) .... (select) clothes for me, and my aunt (2) .... (give) my face a scrub and (3) .... (groom) me. My uncle (4) .... (follow) me about (5) .... (utter) several pieces of advice before (6) .... (let) me out, 'You must never scowl even if the Sun (7) .... (hit) you in the eyes. You must try (8) .... (look) pleasant. **[4]**

(ii) Fill in the blanks with appropriate words.

(a) There's a black cat sitting .... the wall.

(b) The horse jumped .... the hedge.

(c) Mother goes .... the market every day.

(d) Several people have climbed Mount Everest .... recent years.

(e) I often go to school .... my friend.

(f) I have left my keys .... home.

Instead of talking , prove your worth .... doing something.

(h) I have not slept .... yesterday.

(iii) Choose the correct option to make one complete sentence **without using and but or so**. **[4]**

1. The magician took pity on the mouse. He turned it into a cat.

(a) Showing pity on the mouse he turned it into a cat.

(b) Taking pity on the mouse he turned it into a cat.

(c) The magician turned the mouse into a cat by taking pity .

(d) Taking pity on the mouse the magician turned it into a cat.

2. This work must be completed. There is a deadline.
   (a) Since this work must be completed, there is a deadline.
   (b) This work must be completed because there is a deadline.
   (c) This work must be completed though there is a deadline.
   (d) This work must be completed when there is a deadline.
3. He fled somewhere. His pursuers could not follow him.
   (a) He fled where his pursuers could not follow him,
   (b) He pursued somewhere his followers could be flee.
   (c) He fled somewhere when his pursuers could not follow him.
   (d) He fled where his pursuers cannot follow him.
4. He began late. He finished first.
   (a) He finished first and began late
   (b) He began first but finished late.
   (c) Though he finished late, he began first.
   (d) Though he began late, he finished first.

(iv) Choose the correct option and rewrite the sentence according to the instruction given after each. **[8]**

Arun and Nikhil had climbed the mountain.
(Add a question tag)
   (a) Arun and Nikhil had climbed the mountain, didn't they ?
   (b) Arun and Nikhil had climbed the mountain, had they ?
   (c) Arun and Nikhil had climbed the mountain, hadn't they ?
   (d) Arun and Nikhil had climbed the mountain, did they ?
2. The children have broken the window pane.
   (Begin The window pane ....)
   (a) The window pane had been broken by the children.
   (b) The window pane has been broken by the children.
   (c) The window pane has not been broken by the children.
   (d) The window pane had not been broken by the children.
3. The apples are so cheap that they cannot be good.
   (Use : 'too')
   (a) The apples are too cheap and good.
   (b) The apples are to cheap as well as good.
   (c) The apples are too good to be cheap.
   (d) The apples are two cheap to be good.
4. She is very clever and beautiful
   (Use : 'not only')
   (a) Not only is she very clever but also beautiful.
   (b) Not only was she beautiful and she was also clever.
   (c) Not only is she clever she was also very beautiful.
   (d) Not only was she very beautiful but is also clever.
5. I prefer a simple vanilla ice cream to fancy desserts.
   (Begin : I would rather ....)
   (a) I would rather have a simple vanilla ice cream to fancy desserts.
   (b) I would rather have a simple vanilla ice cream than fancy desserts.
   (c) I would rather prefer a simple vanilla ice cream than fancy desserts.
   (d) I would rather have a vanilla ice cream than a fancy dessert.

6. He asked, "When do you intend to make the payment ?"
   (Begin : He asked ....)
   (a) He asked when he did intend to make the payment.
   (b) He asked when she is intending to make the payment.
   (c) He asked when I intended to make the payment.
   (d) He asked when they are intending to make the payment.
7. If the rain does not stop, Mariam will not be able to do the laundry.
   (Begin : Unless ....)
   (a) Unless the rain does not stop, Mariam will not be able to do the laundry.
   (b) Unless Mariam does the laundry, the rain will not stop.
   (c) Unless the rain stop, Mariam will not be able to do the laundry.
   (d) Unless the rain stops, Mariam will not be able to do the laundry.
8. This is the best move I have ever seen.
   (Begin : Never ....)
   (a) Never had I seen a good movie than this.
   (b) Never I have seen a better movie than this.
   (c) Never have I seen a better movie than this.
   (d) I have never seen a good movie as this.

Answers

1. (i)

A Strange Visitor

It was a bleak and a sad day for I was knee deep in debt and no resource to pay for it. Unfortunately, I had unconsciously become a part of a fraud scheme and had given up all my savings in it. Due to my job, I had been unable to look into the scheme and was satisfied that I was getting huge returns. Consequently, I had lived a modest but a fulfilling life. My happiness was snatched a few months back when the reality came out and I found that the organisers of the scheme had racked up many debts in my name. Further, only I could pay for it as the scammers were nowhere to be found.

Much like other days, that day also, my mind was filled with these thoughts and my mistakes. With sadness, anger and many other emotions, I went outside to look around. It was a cold frosty morning. The fields were white and scenic but cold. I lived in rural Ireland which was very quiet. By the side of my house, there is a large stone and that's nothing unusual as Ireland is full of large stones. Some stones are said to be Fairy Stones which is believed to take living form to help those in need.

However, that day someone was sitting on the stone. As I went near the person, I saw that it was a very charismatic looking man. He was not anyone I knew and he did not look like he was of this time as he wore funny clothes. He looked to be freezing, so I asked him if he was ok but he didn't reply. I asked him if he was hungry, no response. I asked him into the house to warm himself by the fire. I went in before him and left the door open behind me.

After a few moments he came in, stood at the door, looked around and sat on the stool near the open fire. I made him a cup of hot tea and offered him some baked bread and a few biscuits. He sat there and seemed to enjoy his tea but he did not speak a word to me.

After he had finished his tea, I took his cup from him and asked if there was anything else he would like. Just as he smiled, there was a knock at the front door. As I opened it, there was no one there so I turned around to try to get the man to speak again. However, he was gone. I was baffled. Where had he gone? There was only one way out, that was past me by the front door. As I was wondering, I saw a pouch on the stool. Much to my surprise, it contained 20 gold coins. I think the man forgot it, so I kept the coins for him. My situation has improved since then but the man did not come back.

(ii) I remember one incident where my parents gave me a difficult task to do which I was nervous about. It was about driving a car. I had been taking driving lessons at that time for a few weeks and was fairly good at it. I used to go for my lessons thrice a week and was getting a hang of it. During one of those lessons, my father accompanied me and sat at the backseat while I was practising my skills. I felt somewhat nervous and intimidated but I ended up doing quite well in that lesson and my father also gave me a reassuring smile when we headed back home after the lesson.

The next day was Sunday and my parents had decided to go for a small outing to the City Mall for some lunch and shopping. I was excited and started getting dressed up for the outing. After I was dressed, I went downstairs to the living room to take out the keys to lock the house. As I was looking for the house keys in the drawer, my father asked me to take out the car keys as well. I took both the keys and gave the car keys to him. To my surprise, my father told me that he didn't need the car keys as it would be me who would be driving today. I felt a little anxious as it would be my first time driving my parents in a car. But I took the keys from him and said that I would love to drive, without giving any hint that I was nervous about it. We left the house and I started driving slowly but attentively. I gained a fair speed after a few minutes and got a little confident. The rest of the drive went smoothly and we reached the mall in 15 minutes. I felt relieved that I did well without facing any obstacles. My parents gave me a proud and reassuring smile as they got out of the car and patted my back for the drive.

(iii) In this highly busy and competitive world, no one has free time. I also do not have much time to relax. However, when I get a chance I tend to utilise it to take a breather and spent some time relaxing. The concept of relaxing on a holiday afternoon means different things for different people. For me, it means a variety of things depending upon my mood. Generally, these things range from painting to watching a movie.

There are days when I am inspired by the attractive doodles and paintings on pinterest. With much enthusiasm, one day, I decided to do mandala art of Goddess Saraswati. For the same, I gathered my art supplies that I needed and sat to work. It was a tiring process which took me 3 whole holiday afternoons to complete but that art piece now resides in my grandparents house as a framed photo.

Sometimes, you would find me watching latest movies on my home projector. I would sit on my couch, arrange for my food and randomly pick a movie which is generally either a comedy or a horror movie.

Spending my time doing nothing but giving my mind a break is essential for me. And I think it should a necessity for everyone. These times of quietness and solitude help us reenergize for the coming days. If we do not take a break and do what makes us happy, our lives can take us on the path of burn-out or a situation wherein we are physically and mentally exhausted. In such situations, we do not wish to do anything and suffer from many lifestyle diseases.

Thus, a break from the hustle and bustle of life is required by our mind and body. In this break, we need to do what we want to do without anyone ordering us around or nagging us. This is our moment of peace, relaxation and joy away from the stress of life. Giving yourself the gift of 'me time' is important for your well-being all year, but especially if you're feeling particularly stressed out.

(iv)

Junk Food Should be Banned

For the Motion

Good morning to esteemed judges and respected opponents. I stand here today to advocate for the banning of junk food in our society.

Wise people, including our parents, have often been quoted to say that health is wealth. It is only the foolish who choose not to listen.

Before we consider the merits of banning something particular, we must investigate its long-term effects on the human body. Junk food is an umbrella term that refers to highly processed and calorie- dense foods that are low in nutritional value. These foods often contain high levels of unhealthy ingredients such as sugar, salt, unhealthy fats, and artificial additives. These food items affect the human body in a number of ways. The short term effects include energy spikes and crashes, bloating, constipation, and dehydration. Various scientific studies and researches have associated junk food with many other lifelong illnesses including obesity, diabetes, heart disease, hypertension, tooth decay and cavities, and even nutritional deficiencies.

Respected audience, I would like you to consider the following question: Why do we eat food?

Is it to make our life functions slower? To ensure that we live shorter, diseased lives full of pain and medicines? If so, then I invite all of you to continue eating the poison that is called junk food, because that is the only path that it will lead you on. Eating junk food is similar to giving an open invitation to all the diseases in the world.

If, on the other hand, you are reasonable individuals, then you will be aware of the fact that all living beings eat food to gain energy and to cultivate a strong body which can fight off diseases and ensure a painless existence.

Unfortunately, youngsters cannot be trusted to make the right decisions for themselves. Hence, it is essential that the decision to stop partaking in this particular form of poison be taken for them. Considering the significant risk to the health and wellbeing of humans as individuals and as a society, I support the complete ban of all non-nutritious junk foods in a vision to create a healthier society.

Thank you.

Against the Motion

Good morning to one and all. Ladies and gentlemen, esteemed judges, and respected opponents, I stand here today to advocate against the banning of junk food in our society.

I agree with my opponent in the fact that junk food is often harmful to health and that it has practically nothing to say for its lack of nutritional value. I would also agree that it is in fact a slow poison! However, while it may not be nutritious and conducive to a healthy lifestyle, for many people it is the only choice. The rushed lifestyle of the modern world does not allow people the time to carefully choose ingredients according to their nutritional value and cook it. Many people only have the time to cook two minute noodles before rushing off to work. Would you stand in front of them and proclaim that just because they are not eating anything healthy, they cannot eat anything at all?

Junk food does serve a purpose after all. It may not be nutritious but it does fill the stomach. For the people with limited time and limited choices, junk food stands for comfort.

Although it is imperative that we cultivate good eating habits, unfortunately the ability to have a nutritious meal is not a necessity; it is a luxury. As the residents of a country whose 7% population is below poverty line, it would be a grave injustice to pass laws in favour of those who can afford luxuries.

Therefore, I call upon your humanity and condemn the complete ban of junk foods.

Thank you

(v) A few weeks back I paid a visit to my Grandma's village which is located on the outskirts of a city. I was mesmerised by seeing the straw and clay houses and the swings on the trees where children were playing and having fun. The whole atmosphere was very lively and energetic and surprisingly calm at the same time. I felt relaxed to be away from the noisy city and being around nature.

After having some delicious lunch that my Grandma had prepared especially for me, I went out for a quick stroll around the village. The cool breeze under the shade of the trees felt really pleasant and comforting. As I was walking, I came across a bunch of small children sitting under a huge banyan tree. I walked towards them and saw that they were all sitting in a circle around a Carrom board which was placed on the ground near the tree's trunk. The children saw me approaching, looked at me and smiled. They asked me if I wanted to play to which I politely said no. I asked them about the Carrom board and to whom it belonged. The children rejoiced and said that they bought the Carrom board at the village fair with the money that my Grandma had given them. It was their first time playing with it. I felt such joy after hearing that my generous Grandma had given these kids money so that they could buy themselves this game to play together. The children then started to arrange all of the pucks together in a circle in the middle of the board. They also played rock, papers, scissors to decide who would play the first shot. The excitement of the children made me appreciate the little things in life and to enjoy every moment as it comes.

2. (i)

XYZ Apartments
Delhi
8th February, 20XX

Dear Vayu,

I hope you are fine now. I missed you a lot during the exhausting day. I know you must be very curious to know about why I called the day exhausting. Well, something happened and I was wrongly blamed. While going to the playground in a queue during recess, Ravi fell down the stairs which resulted in many serious injuries. When we all were asked about how it happened, Stuti blamed me saying that I was just behind him and must have pushed him as a revenge for the humiliating prank he did on me. I was shocked by such a blame. I agree I was angry but we had resolved the issue way before which many of our classmates pointed out.

Now, without further questioning, the school decided to call my parents. When they arrived, my parents were informed about the situation and my punishment- they were rusticating me. Calmly, my father reminded them of the CCTV cameras, which had recently been installed. He asked to show him the footage so that he can see for himself if I really did this.

The school authorities were shocked that they had not thought of this. They hurriedly got the footage which clearly showed that I, in fact, was not immediately behind Ravi and that he had slipped on a banana peel. Looking at the truth, everyone was apologetic towards me. However, I was and still am hurt at the blame. The issue, though resolved, has shown me who are my true friends.

I just hope you were there today to see how bad it was. Get well soon so that we can visit Ravi.

Yours friendly
PQR

(ii) 16, ABC Apartments
Nashik
1st June, 20XX
The Manager,
XYZ Shopping Mall
Nashik
Dear Sir/Ma'am,

It is with great pleasure that I have written this letter to inform you on behalf of 'Live Happy Youth Club' that we are organising a small play to create awareness about the importance of saving electricity. For the same, I would request you to permit us to use the space in front of the shopping mall.

The play, though appears to be social, will increase footfall in your mall. While shopping is the main concern, event like ours will also include the entertainment aspect encouraging more and more people to visit the mall. Further, it will boost your overall sales.

I hope that you would consider our request and permit us to stage our play in your premises. Hoping for a positive response.

Thanking you,
Yours faithfully,
PQR
(Secretary, Live Happy Youth Club)

3. (i)

DAZZLING DANCERS
Inter-School Dance Competition
Date 31st January, 20XX
Time : 11:00 a.m. onwards
Venue : Auditorium, XYZ School
Come, participate, cheer and witness the dancing extravaganza.

(ii) **To :** principalpqr@gmail.com
Subject : Invitation to judge the Inter School Dance Competition
Sir/Ma'am

With great pleasure, I would like to inform you that XYZ School, Delhi is going to organise an Inter-School Dance Competition on 31st January, 20XX from 11:00 a.m. onwards in the school auditorium. For the same, we would love to have the dance teacher of your school as a judge the competition.

Kindly accept our invitation and increase the glory of the competition. Hoping for a positive response.

Thanking You,
Yours obediently,
ABC
(Principal)
XYZ School

4. (i) 1. (b) unsettled

2. (a) prevented from growing

(ii) (c) cheap

(iii) (a) Watching two Hindi films and having fish twice a week kept Ashamanja Babu happy.

(b) This tells us that he was a simple man who was content with his life.

(c) Since he was a bachelor, he longed for companionship to complete his happiness. He wished that he had a dog.

(d) Ashmanja Babu thought that the man was a beggar because his clothes had patches sewn on them.

(e) Ashmanja Babu forgot about his oranges because he came across a puppy for sale which he eventually ended up buying.

(iv) The man took the pup out of the box and kept it on the ground. The pup looked at Ashmanja Babu and wagged his tiny tail. Ashmanja Babu bent down and stretched out his hand when the dog licked his ring finger with its pink tongue. He then asked for the price when the man said "ten rupees". After some haggling the price came down to seven rupees.

5. (i)

1. selected	2. gave	3. groomed	4. followed
5. uttering	6. letting	7. hits	8. looking

(ii)

(a) on	(b) over	(c) to	(d) in
(e) with	(f) at	(g) by	(h) since

(iii) 1. (d) Taking pity on the mouse the magician turned it into a cat

2. (b) This work must be completed because there is a deadline.

3. (a) He fled where his pursuers could not follow him.

4. (d) Though he began late, he finished first.

(iv) 1. c) Arun and Nikhil had climbed the mountain, hadn't they?

2. (b) The window pane has been broken by the children.

3. (d) The apples are too cheap to be good.

4. (a) Not only is she very clever but also beautiful.

5. (b) I would rather have a simple vanilla ice cream than fancy desserts

6. (c) He asked when I intended to make the payment.

7. (d) Unless the rain stops, Mariam will not be able to do the laundry.

8. (c) Never have I seen a better movie than this.

ICSE SOLVED PAPER 2025

Fully Solved

English Language-X (Paper-1)

Time : 2 hrs **Max Marks : 80**

General Instructions

1. Answers to this paper must be written on the paper provided separately.
2. You will **not** be allowed to write during the first **15** minutes.
3. This time is to be spent in reading the question paper.
4. The time given at the head of this paper is the time allowed for writing the answers.
5. Attempt **all five** questions.
6. The intended marks for questions or parts of questions are given in brackets [].
7. You are advised to spend not more than 30 minutes in answering **Question 1** and 20 minutes in answering **Question 2**.

1. Write a composition (300–350 words) on **any one** of the following. **[20]**
(Do not spend more than 30 minutes on this question.)

(i) Write an original short story in which a poor tailor wins an award which changes his/her life.

(ii) Your friends once played a harmless prank on you. Give an account of what happened, your response to the prank and what you learnt from the experience.

(iii) Describe what you see and hear as you move about the corridors and compound during your school break time. How does the scene change after the bell rings?

(iv) 'More collaboration, less competition is the need of the hour'. Express your views either **for** or **against** this statement.

(v) Study the picture given below. Write a story or a description or an account of what it suggests to you. Your composition may be about the subject of the picture, or you may take suggestions from it; however, there must be a clear connection between the picture and your composition.

2. Select **any one** of the following. **[10]**

(Do not spend more than 20 minutes on this question.)

(i) Your grandmother has taught you a special skill. Write a letter thanking her. Explain how you will use that skill and why it is important to you.

(ii) There is no bus stop in your locality. Write a letter to the Municipal Commissioner of your town/city complaining about the problem. Offer possible solutions.

3. (i) Your school is hosting an Inter School Story Writing Competition. Write a notice informing the students about the event. **[5]**

(ii) Write an email to a famous person inviting him/her to be the Judge on the occasion. **[5]**

4. Read the following passage carefully and answer the questions that follow.

A little later, when he went to the pump to wash, he saw the school children pouring by with their **satchels** across their shoulders. They all wore the same clothes - grey shorts or skirts and light blue shirts or blouses - faded and mended, and they all had their hair oiled and combed down very flat. Some went by in laughing, racing groups, others had to be led by their mothers or grandparents to the school building. This reminded him of his sisters in the village.

The boys in the kitchen now looked at him with less hostility. Jagu seemed pleased with Hari too, and sometimes handed him a glass of tea in the middle of the day. When he had a few moments to **spare**, Jagu sat down at one of the long wooden tables, drummed loudly on it and sang a song in a dialect Hari did not know. When he caught Hari listening and smiling, he smiled back. Then Hari knew that he too had a village somewhere that he called home. It was just that he was a silent, hardworking, worried man and had no time and no gift for speech.

It was the watch mender, Mr. Panwallah, who was truly a benefactor, the kindest and most helpful of all. One afternoon, during those hot, still hours when there were no customers for a change, Hari was standing in front of the eating house, idly watching the traffic because he was too tired to do anything else, and Mr. Panwallah called to him to come and sit beside him on the bench behind the counter in his shop.

"Want to help?" he asked. "Want to learn how to make a clock tick? I'm just going to open this big grandfather clock sent to me for repair - you'll be able to see the workings plain. Don't often get a piece like this anymore - wall clocks, yes, and electronic gadgets - but you don't often come upon a grandfather clock like this. It's a real piece of luck, being able to show you one of this size." Look, he said, swinging open the door at the back and revealing the machinery to a fascinated Hari who felt as if the door had opened into a new and strange house. Mr. Panwallah showed Hari what was wrong with it, what had made it stop. "Interesting, isn't it? How would you like to learn? Tell you what - I'll take you on as an apprentice. You don't have much to do between two and four, do you? Of course you will have to ask Jagu first. I can pay you a little, not much, and you can help me for two hours a day. Perhaps I can make a watch mender of you."

– *Village by the Sea, Anita Desai*

(i) For each word given below choose the correct meaning (as used in the passage) from the options provided. **[2]**

1. satchels *(line 2)*

   (a) snatching (b) scarves (c) school bags (d) sweaters

2. spare *(line 9)*

   (a) share (b) offer (c) thin (d) extra

(ii) Which word in the passage is the opposite of 'closed'? **[1]**

(a) Behind (b) Fascinated (c) Opened (d) Revealing

(iii) Answer the following questions briefly in your own words.

(a) How were the school children dressed? **[2]**

(b) In what way was Jagu kind to Hari? **[2]**

(c) What did the song tell Hari about Jagu? **[2]**

(d) Which sentence in the passage tells us that Jagu was not a talkative man? **[2]**

(e) Why were there no customers at that time of the day? **[1]**

(iv) In not more than 50 words describe how Mr. Panwallah introduced Hari to watch mending. **[8]**

5. (i) Fill in each of the numbered blanks with the correct form of the word given in brackets. Do not copy the passage but write in correct serial order the word or phrase appropriate to the blank space. **[4]**

Example :

One day we (0) _______ (lift) the box up.

Answer : (0) lifted

We (1) _______ (find) a dead mouse (2) _______ (lie) among our treasures. It (3) _______ (be) an exciting discovery. A boy took it up by its tail and (4) _______ (wave) it in front of our faces. "What shall we do with it?" he (5) _______ (cry). "It stinks!" someone (6) _______ (shout). "Throw it out of the window quick!"

He (7) _______ (hesitate). They all (8) _______ (look) at me.

(ii) Fill in the blanks with an appropriate words. **[4]**

(a) My best friend, John is named _______ his grandfather.

(b) A grey mist hung _______ the fields.

(c) The little girl spoke _______ against the bully.

(d) They accused him _______ theft.

(e) The police got the fire _______ control.

(f) There is a bridge _______ the river.

(g) The driver jumped _______ the car.

(h) I have not seen my uncle _______ last summer.

(iii) Choose the correct option to make one complete sentence **without using** ***and***, ***but*** or ***so***. **[4]**

1. These are fresh mangoes. I bought them yesterday.

(a) These are fresh mangoes which I bought yesterday.

(b) These mangoes were fresher when I bought them yesterday.

(c) These are fresh mangoes which were bought yesterday.

(d) These are fresh mangoes brought by me yesterday.

2. The debating teams were very happy. They were declared joint champions.

(a) The debating teams were very happy as they have been declared joint champions.

(b) The debating teams are very happy as they are declared joint champions.

(c) The debating teams were very happy as they had been declared joint champions.

(d) The debating teams will be very happy as they will be declared joint champions.

3. The rain came down. All the people ran away.

(a) When the rain came down, all the people ran away.

(b) When it rained, the people ran away.

(c) The rain had come down all the people ran away.

(d) The The rain having come, all the people ran away.

4. The disciple was wise. The teacher did not trust him.

(a) Although the disciple was wise yet the teacher trusted him.

(b) Although the disciple was not wise the teacher trusted him.

(c) Although the disciple is wise, the teacher trusted him.

(d) Although the disciple was wise, the teacher did not trust him.

(iv) Choose the correct option and rewrite the sentence according to the instruction given after each. **[8]**

1. The teacher said, "Come early tomorrow, the examination begins at eight o'clock."

(Begin: The teacher told us to.........)

(a) The teacher told us to come early the next day as the examination would begin at eight o'clock.

(b) The teacher told us to come early tomorrow as the examination begins at eight o'clock.

(c) The teacher told us the examination will begin at eight o'clock so come early tomorrow.

(d) The teacher told us to come by eight o'clock as the examination will begin early the next day.

2. Rahul not only plays the guitar but also the drums.

(Use: 'as well as')

(a) Rahul plays the guitar as well as the drums.

(b) Rahul plays the guitar as well the drums.

(c) Rahul plays the guitar as well as he does the drums.

(d) Rahul play's the guitar and the drums as well.

3. She said she would not be available.

(Add a question tag)

(a) Didn't she say that she would not be available?

(b) She said she would not be available, did she?

(c) She said she would not be available, didn't she?

(d) She said she would not be available, wouldn't she?

4. This is the most beautiful painting in the exhibition.

(Begin: No other......)

(a) No other painting is as beautiful as this exhibition.

(b) No other painting in this exhibition is beautiful.

(c) No other painting is beautiful as this painting in the exhibition.

(d) No other painting in the exhibition is as beautiful as this one.

5. I prefer aerobics to yoga.

(Use: 'rather')

(a) I would rather do aerobics to yoga.

(b) I would rather do aerobics than yoga.

(c) I would rather prefer aerobics than yoga.

(d) I would rather do yoga than aerobics.

6. The coach taught the children' the rules of the game.

(Begin: The rules.........)

(a) The rules have being taught by the coach to the children.

(b) The rules of the game have been taught by the children to the coach.

(c) The rules of the game is taught by the coach to the children.

(d) The rules of the game were taught by the coach to the children.

7. No sooner did the film star arrive than the crowd cheered.

(Begin: As soon as.........)

(a) As soon as the film star arrived then the crowd cheered.

(b) As soon as the film star arrives the crowd starts cheering.

(c) As soon as the crowd cheers the film star arrives.

(d) As soon as the film star arrived the crowd cheered.

8. School bags are often too heavy for students to carry.
(Use: 'so')
(a) School bags are so heavy students cannot carry them.
(b) School bags are often so heavy that students cannot carry them.
(c) School bags are often so heavy for students to carry.
(d) School bags are heavy so students cannot carry them.

Answers

1. (i) Ravi was a poor tailor who lived in a small town. He had a tiny shop where he stitched clothes for the people in his neighbourhood. He worked hard every day, but he barely earned enough to buy food for his family. Even though life was tough, Ravi never complained. He loved his work and always tried to make beautiful clothes. His dream was to become a famous tailor one day, but he did not know how to achieve it.

One day, a big announcement was made in the town. A famous fashion company was holding a competition for tailors. The winner would get a big cash prize and a job in the city. Ravi's friends told him to participate, but he was unsure. "I am just a simple tailor. How can I win such a big contest?" he said.

His wife, Meena, smiled and said, "You must try. You are talented, and this is your chance." Encouraged by her words, Ravi decided to take part. He worked day and night on a special dress. He carefully stitched every piece of fabric, adding beautiful patterns by hand. When he finished, he felt proud of his work. His children also admired the dress and told him he would surely win.

On the day of the competition, Ravi saw many talented tailors with fancy designs. He felt nervous but stayed hopeful. When the judges saw his dress, they were amazed. "This is wonderful! Such fine stitching and unique design," one of them said. After much discussion, Ravi was declared the winner!

Tears filled Ravi's eyes as he accepted the award. The prize money helped him expand his shop, and soon, he got many new customers. A few months later, the fashion company offered him a big job in the city. His life changed forever.

Ravi had once doubted himself, but now he knew–hard work, belief, and the courage to try could make dreams come true.

(ii) One evening, my friends and I were sitting in the park, talking and laughing. It was a normal day, and I had no idea that they were planning to play a prank on me.

Suddenly, my friend Rahul pointed towards a tree and said, "Look! There's a snake!" I froze in fear. I have always been scared of snakes. My heart started beating fast, and I quickly moved away. My other friends also pretended to be scared. They ran in different directions, making me even more frightened.

Rahul then shouted, "It's coming towards you!" That was enough for me–I turned around and ran as fast as I could. I didn't stop until I reached the park gate. My friends burst into laughter. Confused, I turned back and saw them holding a rubber snake in their hands. That's when I realised they had tricked me!

At first, I felt embarrassed. But soon, I started laughing too. I had to admit, they got me really well. It was just a harmless joke, and they didn't mean to hurt me. Later, we all sat together, and they promised not to scare me like that again. We talked about other funny pranks we had seen or experienced before.

This experience taught me an important lesson. Sometimes, we take things too seriously, but it's okay to laugh at ourselves. I also understood that friends may play pranks, but they do it for fun, not to make us feel bad. However, I also learned that we should be careful while playing pranks so that no one gets truly hurt or scared.

That day, I realised that friendship is about fun, laughter, and understanding. Even though I was scared at first, in the end, it became a funny memory that we still talk about and laugh about today. It showed me that the best friendships are filled with joy, trust and unforgettable moments.

(iii) As soon as the bell rings for break time, the quiet classrooms suddenly come alive. Students rush out into the corridors, their footsteps echoing on the tiled floor. Some are laughing and chatting, while others hurry towards the canteen. The air is filled with the mixed sounds of voices, laughter, and the clatter of shoes on the ground. Excitement is visible on every face as they enjoy their short break from studies.

In the school compound, small groups of students gather under trees or sit on benches. Some enjoy their lunch, while others share jokes and stories. A few students run across the playground, playing tag or football. Others prefer to relax and watch their friends play. The canteen is the busiest place, with students lining up to buy snacks. The smell of samosas and noodles fills the air, making everyone feel hungry. Some students quickly finish their food to have more time to play.

Teachers walk around, keeping an eye on the students. Some remind the students to keep the place clean, while others chat with their colleagues. Near the water taps, a group of students splash water on each other and laugh loudly. The whole school is full of energy and excitement. Even those who were tired during class now seem refreshed.

Then, the warning bell rings, and everything changes. Students quickly gather their things and start walking towards their classrooms. The noise begins to fade as friends say goodbye and hurry inside. Some students finish the last bites of their food, while others rush to the washroom before class. The playground, once full of movement, becomes empty.

When the final bell rings, silence takes over. The corridors are now quiet, with only a few latecomers running to their rooms. Teachers stand at the doors, waiting for students to settle down. Within minutes, the school returns to its usual calm, and the sound of lessons begins again.

(iv) **For the motion**

In today's world, people focus too much on competition. Everyone wants to be the best, but this often leads to stress and unhealthy rivalry. Instead of competing, we should work together and support each other. More collaboration and less competition can create a better society.

First, collaboration helps in learning and growth. When people work together, they share ideas and knowledge. This leads to better solutions and faster progress. In workplaces, teams achieve more when they cooperate instead of competing. In schools, students can understand concepts better when they help each other.

Second, competition creates pressure and stress. Many students and employees feel anxious because they always have to prove themselves. This can harm their mental health. Instead of focusing on beating others, people should focus on improving their skills through teamwork.

Moreover, collaboration leads to a peaceful and friendly environment. When people work together, they build strong relationships. It reduces jealousy and promotes kindness. Society benefits when people help each other instead of trying to win all the time.

In the modern world, innovation happens through teamwork. Scientists, doctors, and engineers work together to solve big problems. If they only competed, they would not make such great discoveries. Even in business, companies succeed when they form partnerships and share ideas.

Some people believe that competition pushes people to do better. However, too much competition can create selfishness and dishonesty. People may focus only on winning instead of learning and growing together. A balance is needed, but in today's world, collaboration should be encouraged more.

In conclusion, working together is better than competing. Collaboration leads to learning, reduces stress, and creates a friendly environment. To build a better future, we must support and uplift each other instead of always trying to be better than others.

Against the motion

Competition is an important part of life. It motivates people to work harder, improve their skills, and achieve success. While collaboration is useful, focusing only on teamwork and reducing competition may not always be the best approach.

First, competition encourages progress. When people compete, they try to do better than others. This leads to new inventions, better services, and higher-quality products. For example, in business, companies compete to provide the best products, which benefits customers. Without competition, progress may slow down.

Second, competition builds confidence and resilience. In schools, students work hard to score well in exams because they compete with their classmates. This makes them disciplined, focused, and goal-oriented. If competition is reduced, many may lose interest in improving themselves.

Moreover, competition prepares people for real-life challenges. In the professional world, people compete for jobs, promotions, and recognition. Those who work hard and prove their skills succeed. If there is no competition, people may not feel the need to develop their talents.

Some argue that collaboration is better because it promotes teamwork and reduces stress. While this is true, collaboration works best when people have already developed their skills through competition. Without competition, collaboration alone may lead to laziness and a lack of innovation.

In conclusion, while collaboration is important, competition should not be reduced. A balance between the two is needed. Healthy competition pushes people to do their best, while collaboration helps in sharing knowledge and working towards a common goal. Instead of removing competition, we should encourage fair and positive competition that benefits everyone.

(v) In a small village, a mother and her children worked in their vegetable garden. Every morning, they stepped into their green fields, caring for their plants with love. Their hard work made the crops grow fresh and healthy. It was not just about growing food; it was about connecting with nature and learning patience.

One bright morning, the family was harvesting brinjals. The mother, dressed in a pink saree, smiled as she handed the vegetables to her children. The boy, wearing a vest, held a basket filled with colorful brinjals. His younger sister, in a blue dress, stood nearby, watching happily. Their faces glowed with joy and satisfaction. They knew that their efforts had borne fruit, and their happiness was pure.

For them, farming was not just work-it was a way of life. They enjoyed growing their own food and felt proud of their efforts. The mother had taught her children that nature rewards those who care for it. With patience and dedication, their small garden provided enough vegetables for their daily meals. Sometimes, they even shared extra produce with neighbours. This created a strong bond among the villagers.

The village believed in working together. People helped each other during planting and harvesting seasons. They knew that unity made life easier and happier. Unlike cities, where people bought everything from markets, villagers valued the food they grew with their own hands. It was fresh, healthy and free from chemicals. Their connection with the land was deep and meaningful.

As they gathered the last batch of brinjals, the children laughed and played. The mother looked at them with love, knowing she was teaching them valuable lessons-hard work, teamwork and gratitude for nature.

The picture of this happy family in their green fields shows the beauty of simple living. It reminds us that joy comes not from wealth but from the satisfaction of honest effort, the love of family, and the strength of a close-knit community.

2. (i) Nilima
Mamura, Sector - 66
Noida - 201301

4th March, 20XX

Dear Grandma,

I hope you are doing well. I am writing this letter to thank you for teaching me gardening. I really enjoyed learning how to plant seeds, water them, and take care of the plants.

This skill is very special to me because it connects me to nature and reminds me of you. I will use it to grow my own flowers and vegetables. It will help me keep the environment green and beautiful. Gardening also teaches me patience and hard work.

I will always remember the time we spent together in the garden. Thank you for your love and guidance. I feel lucky to have you as my grandmother.

Take care and stay healthy.

With love,
Nilima

(ii) Reshmi Saikia
H.No. 45, Greenwood Colony
Rajgarh Road, Guwahati - 781003

4th March, 20XX

The Municipal Commissioner
Guwahati Municipal Corporation
Guwahati - 781001

Subject Request for a Bus Stop in Our Locality

Respected Sir/Madam,

I am writing to bring to your attention the lack of a bus stop in our locality. Many people, including students, office workers, and senior citizens, face great difficulty because of this. We have to walk a long distance to catch a bus, which is very inconvenient, especially during bad weather.

I request you to kindly arrange a bus stop in our area. A suitable place for it would be near Lachit Nagar Point on Rajgarh Road. This will help many people and make travel easier for everyone.

I hope you will consider our request and take action soon. Thank you for your time and support.

Yours sincerely,
Reshmi Saikia

3. (i)

Inter-School Story Writing Competition On 4th March, 20XX Inter-School Story Writing Competition Our school is hosting an Inter School Story Writing Competition. Students from all classes can participate. The event will be held on 6th March, 20XX, in the school auditorium. Interested students must register by 5th March, 20XX. For details, contact your class teacher.

(ii) **To** XYZ@gmail.com

Dear Dr. Tharoor,

I hope you are doing well. We are organising an Inter School Public Speaking Competition on 28th March, 20XX at St. Xaviers College, Gurgaon. We would be honoured if you could be the judge for the event. Your presence and guidance would inspire our students.

Please let us know your availability.

Best regards,

Ravi Shashank

St. Xaviers College

4. (i) 1. (c) school bags

2. (d) extra

(ii) (c) Opened

(iii) (a) The school children wore grey shorts or skirts and light blue shirts or blouses. Their clothes were faded and mended, and their hair was oiled and combed flat.

(b) Jagu was kind to Hari by giving him a glass of tea during the day and smiling at him when he noticed Hari listening to his songs.

(c) The song made Hari realise that Jagu also had a village he called home.

(d) "It was just that he was a silent, hard-working, worried man and had no time and no gift for speech."

(e) There were no customers because it was a hot afternoon, a quiet time for business.

(iv) Mr. Panwallah called Hari to sit beside him and showed him the inside of a big grandfather clock. He explained what was wrong with it and how to fix it. He then offered to take Hari as an apprentice, paying him a little and training him for two hours daily.

5. (i) 1. found 2. lying 3. was 4. waved

5. cried 6. shouted 7. hesitated 8. looked

(ii) (a) after (b) over (c) out (d) of

(e) under (f) over (g) out of (h) since

(iii) 1. (a) These are fresh mangoes which I bought yesterday.

2. (c) The debating teams were very happy as they had been declared joint champions.

3. (a) When the rain came down, all the people ran away.

4. (d) Although the disciple was wise, the teacher did not truest him.

(iv) 1. (b) The teacher told us to come early tomorrow as the examination begins at eight o'clock.

2. (a) Rahul plays the guitar as well as the drums.

3. (c) She said she would not be available, wouldn't she?

4. (d) No other painting in the exhibition is as beautiful as this one.

5. (b) I would rather do aerobics than yoga.

6. (d) The rules of the game were taught by the coach to the children.

7. (d) As soon as the film star arrived the crowd cheered.

8. (b) School bags are often so heavy that students cannot carry them.

ICSE

Specimen Paper 2025

Fully Solved

English Language-X (Paper-1)

Time : 2 hrs

Max Marks : 80

General Instructions

1. Answers to this paper must be written on the paper provided separately.
2. You will **not** be allowed to write during the first **15** minutes.
3. This time is to be spent in reading the question paper.
4. The time given at the head of this paper is the time allowed for writing the answers.
5. Attempt **all five** questions.
6. The intended marks for questions or parts of questions are given in brackets [].
7. You are advised to spend not more than 30 minutes in answering **Question 1** and 20 minutes in answering **Question 2**.

1. Write a composition (300-350 words) on **any one** of the following. **[20]**

(Do not spend more than 30 minutes on this question.)

(i) Write an original short story in which a woman, her strange neighbour and a police officer form the main characters.

(ii) Your teacher has asked you to form a group and work on a particular project. Write an account of how you worked together and what each of you learned from the experience.

(iii) *'Peer pressure is a force for good.'*

Express your views either **for** or **against** this statement.

(iv) Describe the locality in which you live. Give details of the things you see and hear as you walk around your locality. What do you especially like about the place?

(v) Study the picture given below. Write a story or a description on an account of what it suggests to you. Your composition may be about the subject of the picture or you may take suggestions from it; however, there must be a clear connection between the picture and your composition.

2. Select **any one** of the following. **[10]**
(Do not spend more than 20 minutes on this question.)

(i) Your uncle was unable to attend your birthday celebration but has sent you one thousand rupees as a gift. Write a letter thanking him, tell him how you will spend the money and why you have made that particular choice.

(ii) The garbage bins in your locality have not been cleared regularly resulting in the overflow of garbage in the area. Write a letter to the Municipal Commissioner of your city/town complaining about the problem. Offer suggestions for the removal of the garbage and cleaning up of the place.

3. (i) Your school is hosting an Art and Craft exhibition. Write a notice informing the pupils at your school about the event. **[5]**

(ii) Write an e-mail to a local artist inviting him/her to inaugurate the exhibition and be the Chief Guest on the occasion. **[5]**

4. Read the following passage carefully and answer the questions that follow.

One day, I found the pond occupied by several buffaloes. Their keeper, a boy a little older than me, was swimming about in the middle. Instead of climbing out on the bank, he would pull himself up on the back of one of his buffaloes, stretch his naked brown body out on the animal's glistening ***hide***, and start singing to himself.

When he saw me staring at him from across the pond, he smiled, showing gleaming white teeth on a dark face. He invited me to join him in a swim. I told him I couldn't swim, and he offered to teach me.

His name was Ramu, and he promised to give me swimming lessons every afternoon, and so it was during the afternoons - especially summer afternoons when everyone was asleep-that we usually met. Before long, I was able to swim across the pond to sit with Ramu astride a ***contented*** buffalo.

Sometimes, I would slip into the water. Emerging in shades of green and khaki, I would sneak into the house through the bathroom and bathe under the tap before getting into my clothes.

One afternoon, Ramu and I found a small tortoise in the mud sitting over a hole in which it had laid several eggs. I presented the tortoise to Grandfather. He had a weakness for tortoises, and was pleased with this addition to his menagerie, giving it a large tub of water all to itself, with an island of rocks in the middle. If one of the dogs bothered it too much, it would draw its head and legs into its shell and defy all its attempts at rough play.

Ramu came from a family of bonded labourers and had received no schooling. But he was well-versed in folklore and knew a great deal about birds and animals.

'Many birds are sacred,' said Ramu, as we watched a blue jay swoop down from a peepul tree and carry off a grasshopper.

Both Ramu and Grandfather were of the opinion that we should be more gentle with birds and animals and should not kill so many of them.

"It is also important that we respect them", said Grandfather. "We must acknowledge their rights. Birds and animals are finding it more difficult to survive, because we are trying to destroy both them and their forests."

Ramu and I spent long summer afternoons at the pond. I still remember him with affection, though we never saw each other again after I left Dehra.

—*Rusty, the Boy from the Hills, Ruskin Bond*

(i) For each word given below, choose the correct meaning (as used in the passage) from the options provided. **[2]**

1. hide *(line 3)*

(a) blanket (b) fur (c) undisclosed (d) skin

2. contented *(line 9)*

(a) cheerful (b) lazy (c) satisfied (d) container

(ii) Which word in the passage is the opposite of 'easy'? **[1]**

(a) Sneak (b) Difficult (c) Labourer (d) Survive

(iii) Answer the following questions briefly in your own words.

(a) What did Ramu like to do once he had climbed on the back of a buffalo? **[2]**

(b) What offer did Ramu make to the narrator? **[2]**

(c) Why do you think the narrator would bathe before entering the house? **[2]**

(d) Who was the large tub of water for? **[1]**

(e) How would the tortoise protect itself from the dogs? **[2]**

(iv) Despite the lack of schooling, what did Ramu know? How, according to Ramu and Grandfather, should we treat birds and animals? Answer in not more than fifty words. **[8]**

5. (i) Fill in each of the numbered blanks with the correct form of the word given in brackets. Do not copy the passage but write in correct serial order the word or phrase appropriate to the blank space. **[4]**

Example:

(o) The Sun .... (shine) bright outside.

Answer: shone

It was hot in the railway compartment and the fan .... (1) (not work).

The elderly lady .... (2) (use) up all her water because she had cheerfully shared it with her fellow passengers. She knew that the train .... (3) (halt) at the station for only three minutes. Calling a shoeshine boy, she said, 'Will you help me? I .... (4) (need) a bottle of cold water and here is the money,' and she put a twenty rupee note in his hand. The boy snatched the money and ....
(5) (disappear) into the crowd on the platform. A fellow passenger .... (6) (cannot believe) what he had witnessed. 'What .... (7) (you do)?" He said, 'You .... (8) (never see) your money again. Just then, the whistle was heard and the train began to move. At that moment, the child appeared at the window with the water. 'Your water,' he gasped, out of breath. 'And the change.'

(ii) Fill in the blanks with appropriate words. **[4]**

(a) We can cut ...... this field instead of taking the main road.
(b) Passengers are advised ...... standing on the footboard of a moving bus.
(c) They have been working on the project ...... years now.
(d) Ever ...... the accident, he has been afraid of boarding buses.
(e) It is a hard climb ...... the hill.
(f) She turned ...... the offer because she did not like the terms and conditions.
(g) I will need to speak ...... my parents before I sign up for the school trip.
(h) The sports teacher was taken ...... when he heard how enthusiastic the team was.

(iii) Join the following sentences to make one complete sentence **without using *and, but*** or ***so***. Choose the correct option. **[4]**

1. Stay still. We cannot take your photograph otherwise.
   (a) Stay still, else we cannot take your photograph otherwise.
   (b) Stay still because we can take your photograph otherwise.
   (c) Unless you stay still, we cannot take your photograph.
   (d) If you stay still, we cannot take your photograph.
2. Roy's mother rang up the school office. She wanted to enquire about the swimming classes at the summer camp.
   (a) Roy's mother rang up the school office as she want to enquire about the swimming classes at the summer camp.
   (b) Roy's mother rang up the school office to enquire about the swimming classes at the summer camp.
   (c) Roy's mother has rung up the school office to enquire about the swimming classes at the summer camp.
   (d) Roy's mother rang up the school office wanting enquiry about the swimming classes at the summer camp.
3. I left my keys somewhere. Do you know where they are?
   (a) Do you know where I had left my keys?
   (b) Do you know where my keys were left behind?
   (c) Do you know where I left my keys?
   (d) Do you know where I would have left my keys?
4. The captain should not be blamed for the team's defeat. The players should not be blamed for the team's defeat.
   (a) The captain should neither be blamed nor the players should be blamed for the team's defeat.
   (b) Neither the captain nor the players should be blamed for the team's defeat.
   (c) The captain should not be blamed for the team's defeat as the players should not be blamed for the team's defeat.
   (d) The captain should not be blamed for the team's defeat but the players too should not be blamed for the team's defeat.

(iv) Choose the correct option to rewrite the following according to the instructions given after each sentence. **[8]**

1. The audience broke into loud applause as soon as he finished speaking. *(Begin with: No sooner...)*
   (a) No sooner he finished speaking that the audience broke into loud applause.
   (b) No sooner had he finish speaking when the audience broke into loud applause.
   (c) No sooner did he finish speaking than the audience broke into loud applause.
   (d) No sooner the audience broke into loud applause than he finished speaking.
2. The news surprised everyone in my family. *(Begin with: The news took ...)*
   (a) The news took everyone in my family by surprise.
   (b) The news took everyone in my family with surprise.
   (c) The news took with surprise everyone in my family.
   (d) The news took everyone in my family for a surprise.
3. Yesterday was so much fun. *(End with a question tag)*
   (a) Yesterday was so much fun, would you say?
   (b) Was yesterday much fun?
   (c) Yesterday was so much fun, isn't it?
   (d) Yesterday was so much fun, wasn't it?
4. I wouldn't eat that food if I was not really hungry. *(Use: 'unless')*
   (a) Unless I eat that food I will remain really hungry.
   (b) I wouldn't be really hungry unless I ate that food.
   (c) I wouldn't eat that food unless I was not really hungry.
   (d) I wouldn't eat that food unless I was really hungry.
5. It is so hot and humid that I cannot sleep. *(Use: too)*
   (a) It is hot and humid too sleep.
   (b) It is too hot and humid to sleep.
   (c) It is hot and humid too so I cannot sleep.
   (d) It is too hot and humid such that I cannot sleep.
6. I prefer going out with friends to staying alone at home. *(Begin with: I would rather...)*
   (a) I would rather go out with friends than stay alone at home.
   (b) I would rather prefer going out with friends than staying alone at home.
   (c) I would rather prefer to go out with friends than stay alone at home.
   (d) I would rather go out with friends to staying alone at home.
7. "Why were you absent yesterday?", the teacher asked me. *(Begin with: The teacher asked me why...)*
   (a) The teacher asked me why was I absent yesterday.
   (b) The teacher asked me why I had been absent yesterday.
   (c) The teacher asked me why I had been absent the day before.
   (d) The teacher asked me why was I absent the day before.
8. Very few dancers are as graceful as she is. *(Begin with: She is...)*
   (a) She is one of the most graceful dancers.
   (b) She is the most graceful dancer.
   (c) She is more graceful than all the other dancers.
   (d) She is more graceful than a few other dancers.

Answers

1. (i) In the small town of Willow Creek, Chaahat lived a solitary life after losing her family to flash floods. She had been living in the town for four years and had heard stories about many supernatural things happening in town. She never believed in them but, when she used to hear about them, she would get sacred. She believed that supernatural things were related to her neighbour, Mr. Henderson whom she always found to be a bit peculiar. The old man rarely left his house and, when he did, it was usually to tend to his chaotic garden and his hideous garden gnomes. Chaahat often watched him from her window, curious about his solitary life and his garden.

One chilly autumn evening, Chaahat found a small, intricately carved box on her doorstep. Assuming it was a misdelivered parcel, she decided to give it back to the post office the next morning. When she reached the post office, she was shocked that the address was hers. She did not have any idea what it was and whom it was from. So, she went to her neighbour suspecting it belonged to him. However, the moment Mr. Henderson saw the box, his face turned pale and he vehemently denied it was his. Perplexed but intrigued, Chaahat took the box home and set it on her mantelpiece.

Days passed and local rumours about a series of small thefts in the neighbourhood began to circulate. Items were mysteriously disappearing from homes, only to be found elsewhere in the town. The local police, led by Officer Arjun, were baffled having no leads or suspects.

One afternoon, Officer Arjun knocked on Chaahat's door inquiring if she had noticed any unusual activities around her home. Chaahat mentioned the strange box and her interaction with Mr. Henderson. Curious, Officer Arjun asked to examine the box. Upon inspection, he discovered a false bottom, revealing several stolen items including a vintage watch and a couple of old coins which had earlier been reported missing. Later, Officer Arjun and Chaahat visited Mr. Henderson with the box. Faced with the evidence, Mr. Henderson confessed but not to theft. He admitted that he had been finding these items in his garden, unearthed by his gnomes which seemed to move and rob people at night. Ashamed, he had tried to rid himself of the gnomes but they always seemed to come back.

Amused yet sympathetic, Officer Arjun decided to keep the matter quiet attributing the recovered items to their rightful owners. Chaahat, now viewing her neighbour with new understanding and a touch of fondness, offered to help him find what is happening with his gnomes. In this odd trio, a friendship blossomed, rooted in the peculiar mysteries of Willow Creek.

(ii) Working on a group project can be a rewarding experience, filled with challenges and opportunities for learning all the while strengthening your bonds with your friends and team mates. Recently, our teacher assigned a team-based project to our class on the various economics related topics that we have studied in our syllabi. The first task was to form teams which our teacher had already done. Then, we had to select our topic. Fortunately, my team had some of my childhood friends and after a lot of discussion we decided to take up migration as a topic. To complete the project, we had to submit a report and also make a presentation on our chosen topic.

For the project, my team decided to talk to different daily wage labourers that we can find around us. I took on the responsibility for the presentation part focusing on designing slides and preparing the speech. Other members, Jay and Mohak, conducted deep research compiling data and case studies while Mayank and Richa worked on writing the content and ensuring it flowed logically. Doing the project was easy as we were organised. Moreover, it not only enhanced our understanding of the Subject but also taught us valuable lessons in teamwork and individual responsibility.

Throughout the project, communication was our biggest asset. We set up weekly meetings to discuss our progress and address any issues. These meetings helped us stay aligned with our goals and maintain a cohesive approach. Through these interactions, I learned the importance of clear and consistent communication in keeping a team on track.

Each team member brought a unique perspective to the project which enriched our final output. For example, Jay and Mohak's detailed research introduced us to different reasons for migration starting from better livelihood to religious intolerance. Richa's writing skills helped articulate complex ideas in a way that was easy to understand and Mayank's keen eye for details ensured that our content was accurate and thorough.

Presenting our project to the class was a highlight. It was a moment of pride for all of us seeing our collective efforts come together seamlessly. The positive feedback from our teacher and peers was gratifying and reaffirmed the value of our hard work.

From this group project, I learned that successful collaboration requires patience, respect for others' ideas and an openness to learn from one another. Each member taught me something different whether it was a new fact about environmental conservation or a better way to communicate ideas. This project was not just about the environmental topics we explored but also about discovering each other's strengths and capabilities, making it a truly enriching experience.

(iii) **For the Motion**

The pressure to conform to do what others are doing can be powerful and hard to resist. A person might feel pressured to do something just because others are doing it. The pressure becomes even more powerful when it comes from one's peers or friends. Peer pressure is a phenomenon that can influence a person to do something because one's peers are doing it.

Peer pressure is often painted in a negative light evoking images of young individuals being coerced into harmful behaviours or adopting unhealthy habits. However, when channelled positively, peer pressure can be a powerful force for good. It can encourage individuals to strive for a better performance and adopt healthier lifestyles, thereby fostering personal growth and development.

One of the most significant benefits of positive peer pressure is its ability to motivate individuals towards excellence. In educational settings, the influence of peers who prioritise their studies can be contagious. For instance, students who see their friends dedicating time to homework and preparing diligently for exams are likely to feel motivated to mirror these productive behaviours. This form of peer pressure can create a supportive environment where students push each other to achieve their best, ultimately raising the academic standards of the entire group.

Moreover, peer pressure can promote healthy social behaviours and ethical standards. Young people learn a great deal about social interactions from their peers. When surrounded by friends who respect others, engage in community service and uphold integrity, individuals adopt these positive traits. This leads to a more compassionate and responsible community.

Additionally, peer pressure can be a pivotal force in discouraging negative habits. For example, a group of friends can influence a member to stop smoking or reduce alcohol consumption. The desire to fit in and be accepted can motivate individuals to make healthier lifestyle choices which might be difficult to undertake alone.

However, the positive outcomes of peer pressure depend significantly on the group dynamics and the prevailing attitudes within a peer group. It is crucial for individuals, especially young people, to choose their friends wisely. Being part of a group that values positive and constructive behaviours can transform peer pressure into a beneficial force that enhances one's life.

In conclusion, peer pressure undoubtedly has the potential to be a force for good. It encourages excellence, promotes ethical behaviour and supports healthy lifestyle choices. Like any tool, the impact of peer pressure depends on how it is used. If leveraged positively, it can lead to personal and communal improvement.

Against the Motion

We all share the need to connect with others, no matter our age. We want a sense of belonging at home and within the community. Being accepted by peers is an important part of adolescence. Teens yearn to fit in and to be seen in a favourable light. As a result, peers often have a strong influence on teen behaviours, choices and actions. More often than not, peer pressure takes a negative turn. Hence, I do not agree with the statement— 'Peer pressure is a force for good'.

The impact and scope of influence of peer pressure is so adverse that it has a negative impact on an individual. Friends or peers may encourage engaging in risky things such as doing drugs, reckless driving, alcoholic habit, bunking classes, etc. As a result, one could get distracted and go on a path that ruins one's future.

The impact of peers can be easily found in the age of social media wherein individuals participate in reckless acts to fit in with peers. They try to follow the standard and, in doing so, go against their values and belief systems. Often, children, enticed with what their friends have, become entitled and show immature behaviour. They even participate in illegal activities to fulfill their need to fit in.

If an individual does not fit in and give in to peer pressure, he/she is often bullied to the point that the person develops mental health problems and even causes self-harm. Now and then, the effect of peer tension on young teenagers is disrupting to the point that they can barely remain in their skin, are separated from loved ones and become discouraged and restless.

Thus, peer pressure is not a force for good.

(iv) Locality refers to the specific geographical area or neighbourhood in which a community of people live and work. It is a fundamental concept that helps define the character, culture and identity of a particular place. The term is often used to describe the unique features of a specific region as well as the social connections and shared experiences of its residents.

One of the most important aspects of locality is the sense of community that it fosters. Whether it is a small town, a large city neighbourhood or a rural area, a locality can create a strong sense of belonging and shared identity among its residents. This sense of community is often built around common interests, traditions and values which are strengthened by the interactions and relationships between people in the area.

I live in a great residential locality in Delhi. It is society with multiple complexes. There is a huge park nearby with lush greenery and many different kinds of birds. Multiple amenities are easily accessible in my locality. We have three malls which are 10 minutes ride away with many big brands and eateries. There are also many famous street food stalls which offer a diverse range of food options. From vegetarian delights to international cuisines, you'll find it all here. The nearby market is bustling with a variety of snacks, chaat, candies and cuisines. And, the best part? You can enjoy all this in one place from hotdogs and momos to hot and cold beverages like coffees, teas, milkshakes and juices.

Another gem is the local market. From 10:30 a.m. until 8:30 p.m., it's a bustling market with hundreds of retailers selling anything and everything. But, as evening descends, this place undergoes a magical transformation into a foodie's paradise. The aroma of Gulab jamun, Dahi vada, Samosa, Dosa, Pav bhaji, Pani puri, Chinese food and Soft beverages fills the air. You'll also find mobile food vendors here. This market focuses on traditional Indori food. Poha Jalebi merits special mention, as it is the city's king of street food. Poha is available at all times, 24 hours a day, 365 days a year.

Overall, it is a fantastic and well-known street market in my city where people enjoy shopping.

(v) He was the funniest boy I had ever met. He would make everyone laugh even in the most trying times. Blessed with a funny nature, Varun would make everyone forget his/her worries in his company. No amount of sadness could dampen his spirit.

I remember once three of us friends including Roshni and Varun and I had failed the chemistry exam badly. Our parents had been called and we were told that we would have to repeat a year. That was a very hard time but, even then, no look of worry could be spotted on Varun's face or in his behaviour. His cheer remained undiminished even when his father suffered a major financial loss in business. Even during that time, Varun was known to spread cheer around. He always pushed his worries to the backseat and dedicated himself towards making others happy.

However, the loss of Varun's pet Munch, a few months ago, immersed him in grief. That was the only time that robbed him of his smiling face. For days, he did not speak to anyone and shut himself up in his room. We could not see him like that so Roshni and I decided to do something to dispel his gloom.

One day, we all went to his place and rang the doorbell of his house. There, we kept a little box, slightly open from one side and hid ourselves so that he could not see us. When he opened the door, he was surprised to find no one. He picked up the box with a look of amazement on his face. He took the lid off and out came a puppy, quite like Munch. He held it in his hands and started to play with it. It brought his smile back. Then, we all came into the sight and shouted with excitement, 'Surprise!'

Indeed, that little effort from our end helped Varun come out of his sorrow. Later, we played with the puppy and, then, went to the park. We played till late in the evening and enjoyed as our friend was back again.

2. (i) XYZ Apartments
PQR City
14th July, 20XX

Dear Uncle,

I hope this letter finds you in the best of health and spirits. I am well and happy here. I have written to tell you that it upset me that you couldn't attend my birthday party. At the same time, I want to thank you for the money (1000 rupees) that you sent me as a birthday gift. I can't tell you how much I appreciate it. It really means a lot to me that you remembered my special day. I've already put your gift to good use. I have given it as fee for an educational tour that our school is organising to Amritsar. We will be going to the Wagah border, the Jallianwallah Bagh, the Golden temple and many other places.

I am grateful for your generosity and support. You've always been an amazing uncle to me and I feel truly blessed to have you in my life.

Thank you again for your kindness and thoughtfulness. I hope we can catch up soon and celebrate properly.

Yours loving,

XYZ

(ii) 202, M.G. Road,
Agra

27th July, 20XX

The Municipal Commissioner,
Municipal Corporation,
Agra

Subject Complaint regarding overflowing garbage and lack of cleanliness in locality

Dear Sir/Ma'am,

Through this letter, I would like to draw your attention to the overflowing garbage and lack of cleanliness in M.G. Road, Agra. It is a matter of great disappointment that in the times when the entire country is striving towards cleanliness and sanitation, our locality presents a picture of dirt. It is not the lack of garbage bins or cleaning staff, but the lack of action on the part of the staff that the bins are always overflowing. As a result, there is a bad odour in the locality and people are becoming prone to diseases.

Hence, I request you to solve this problem and ensure that the locality maintains its cleanliness. For the same, I suggest that garbage vans and staff should come regularly to clean the locality. Further, regular inspection can ensure that the system is effective in its implementation. With your aid, we would be able to move ahead in our path towards cleanliness.

Thanking you,

Yours faithfully,

ABC

3. (i) **Mix and Mould**
Inter School Art and Craft Competition

Date: Friday, 3rd August, 20XX

Time: 10:00 am -3:00 pm

Venue: The Assembly Area, ABC School

All the interested students should submit their names to their respective Class Teachers by 20th July, 20XX.

(ii) **E-mail-id** xyz@gmail.com

Subject Invite to inaugurate the Arts and Crafts exhibition as a Chief Guest

Respected Sir/Ma'am,
With great pleasure and pride, ABC School would like to inform in that it is organising an Arts and Crafts Exhibition on 3rd August, Friday from 10:00 a.m. to 3:00 p.m. in the Assembly Area, ABC School. For the same, we would be honoured if you could inaugurate and grace the exhibition as the Chief Guest.

With your valuable experience and knowledge, students would be motivated to participate in creative activities and take up art as a proper career. Hoping for a positive reply.

Anticipating a positive response,

Yours faithfully,

PQR

4. (i) 1. (d) skin

2. (c) satisfied

(ii) (b) Difficult

(iii) (a) Once he had climbed the back of the buffalo, Ramu liked to stretch his naked brown body out on the animal's glistening hide/back and start singing to himself.

(b) Ramu offered to teach the narrator to swim every afternoon.

(c) The narrator would bathe before entering the house to avoid being scolded for swimming in the village pond when everyone was asleep. He thought that his elders become angry so he would sneak into the house through the bathroom and bathe under the tap to get clean first.

(d) The large tub of water was for the tortoise presented by the narrator to his grandfather.

(e) To protect itself from the dogs, the tortoise would draw its head and legs into its shell and defy all the dogs' attempts at rough play.

(iv) Despite the lack of schooling, Ramu was well-versed in folklore and knew a great deal about birds and animals. He also knew that many birds were sacred and that we should not kill so many of them. According to Ramu and his grandfather, we should be gentler with birds and animals. We should respect and acknowledge their rights and not destroy their forests.

5. (i)
1. was not working
2. had used
3. halted/would halt
4. need
5. disappeared
6. could not believe
7. are you doing
8. will never see

(ii)
a. across
b. against
c. for
d. since
e. up
f. down
g. to
h. aback

(iii)
1. (c) Unless you stay still, we cannot take your photograph.
2. (b) Roy's mother rang up the school office to enquire about the swimming classes at the summer camp.
3. (c) Do you know where I left my keys?
4. (b) Neither the captain nor the players should be blamed for the team's defeat.

(iv)
1. (c) No sooner did he finish speaking than the audience broke into loud applause.
2. (a) The news took everyone in my family by surprise.
3. (d) Yesterday was so much fun, wasn't it?
4. (d) I wouldn't eat that food unless I was really hungry.
5. (b) It is too hot and humid to sleep.
6. (a) I would rather go out with friends than stay alone at home.
7. (c) The teacher asked me why I had been absent the day before.
8. (a) She is one of the most graceful dancers.